Love and Death i[n]

Love and Death in Kubrick

A Critical Study of the Films from Lolita *through* Eyes Wide Shut

PATRICK WEBSTER

McFarland & Company, Inc., Publishers
Jefferson, North Carolina, and London

LIBRARY OF CONGRESS CATALOGUING-IN-PUBLICATION DATA

Webster, Patrick, 1953–
    Love and death in Kubrick : a critical study of the films from
Lolita through Eyes wide shut / Patrick Webster.
        p.   cm.
    Includes bibliographical references and index.

    ISBN 978-0-7864-5916-2
    softcover : 50# alkaline paper ∞

    1. Kubrick, Stanley — Criticism and interpretation.   I. Title.
PN1998.3.K83W43   2011
791.4302'33092 — dc22   2010037767

BRITISH LIBRARY CATALOGUING DATA ARE AVAILABLE

On the cover: Nicole Kidman and Tom Cruise in the
1999 film *Eyes Wide Shut* (Warner Bros./Photofest)

Manufactured in the United States of America

McFarland & Company, Inc., Publishers
    Box 611, Jefferson, North Carolina 28640
    www.mcfarlandpub.com

To Mary Webster *née* Stott
July 17, 1915 – February 1, 2008

My mother would not let me see *Spartacus* at age seven,
but she took me to my first Kubrick film,
2001: A Space Odyssey, in 1968.

This book is dedicated to her memory;
none of this would have happened without her.

Acknowledgments

I am grateful to a large number of people who have, over the years, made this book possible. In terms of the development of this book I would first like to thank the many colleagues and students of the University of Leeds who contributed (albeit sometimes unknowingly) to this research — specifically: Terry Gifford, Linden Peach, Eileen Fauset, Steven Keane, John Gray, Jo Willoughby, Rebecca O'Rourke, Luke Spencer, Tony Ellis, Emma Storr, Catherine Bates, Jenny Todd, Melanie Greenall, Becci Thorpe, Lianne Beasely, Sue Coates, Lucy Mellor, James Whelan, Amy Goring, Julia Lawson, and many others too numerous to mention.

Also, in their reading of the final manuscript, I would offer thanks to the following: Larry Brownstein, David Thom, Paula Wilkins — again amongst sundry others. In addition, thanks must go to Linda Marsden, Barbara Varley, Susan Brown, Dorcas Vallely, Linda Robinson, Maurice Bouette, John Bauldie, John Stokes, Stephen Webster, Claire Webster, Elizabeth Williams, Ian Smith, John Brown, Mel Gamble, Roger Hargrave, Julie Reed and a further myriad of sundry others.

Finally, the last word must go to my wife, Julie, for her constant support and understanding, for her patience in allowing me to expend vast amounts of time on this book during the last six years.

Contents

Preface

This present book represents an aspiration to further develop a discussion of the work of Stanley Kubrick. In a moment of uncharacteristic bombast, Kubrick once claimed of his unmade film *Napoleon*, "I expect to make the best movie ever made." It is therefore tempting to offer the claim: "I expect to write the best book ever written about the work of Stanley Kubrick." This is not the case; however, it is a book that attempts to place Kubrick's work within a framework it deserves. In a specific sense the book aspires to position Kubrick's work, at least to a degree, within an arena of cultural theory. This is something that has seldom been attempted, at least not to the extent envisaged here. However, this is not to suggest the book is difficult or unapproachable; while it will consistently develop arguments around contemporary theory, it will also aspire to appeal to a diverse cross-section of readers, in its overall aim to represent itself as a work of mainstream scholarship.

The choice of Stanley Kubrick was not a difficult one. One might recall here a comment of Roger Caras, a mutual friend of Kubrick and Arthur C. Clarke. In 1964, during the early stages of developing the film that would become *2001: A Space Odyssey*, Kubrick had asked Caras which science fiction author he might think of working with. "Why waste your time?" Caras is said to have replied, in citing Arthur C. Clarke, "Why not start with the best?" So it is with Kubrick, to put it simply, "Why not start with the best?" The taking of such a point of view is subjective, however, the importance of Kubrick's work would seem to be self-evident. The magazine *Sight and Sound* has been running polls of the greatest films for each decade since 1952, and is generally considered to be one of the most reliable and respected monitors of cinematic achievement. In its most recent poll, of 2002, Kubrick was voted fifth and sixth in the all time list of greatest film directors—fifth by the critics, sixth by fellow directors. In addition, *Dr. Strangelove* was voted fifth best film by directors, while *2001: A Space Odyssey* was voted the sixth best film by the critics. Finally, all ten of Kubrick's final ten films were included in the "long list" of films voted for — a distinction few if any other directors have achieved.

A further significant factor in the choice of Kubrick is the issue of *auteur* theory. While having significant doubts about the underlying claims of *auteur* theory, it does at least offer the opportunity to develop an argument around an artist's body of work. Also, it would seem clear that if there has ever been a true *auteur*, in other words a filmmaker with an authentic signature on each of his films, it is Stanley Kubrick. In contrast to this, one should note that this book has little if any interest in Kubrick, the man. One beneficial gift cultural theory bestows upon the reader is that they need not be bothered by any degree of biographical reading, what is presented lays purely within the context of Kubrick's work.

Finally, it is said that a classic text (whether it be a novel or a film or any other textual body) is one that never stops saying what it wants to say. In this sense the majority of Kubrick's films (perhaps all of them) are classics. Hence the appeal of commenting upon, of offering theoretical approaches, of positioning interpretative readings, of placing such work into cultural contexts— all are endlessly appealing. These films will continue to grow and find new resonances, this book — in an albeit modest way — would hope to act as an attendant voice and an added elucidation towards the films of Stanley Kubrick.

Introduction

Stanley Kubrick was one of the most notable and preeminent exponents of American filmmaking in the 20th century — at least this will be the argument put forward in this book. If this is the case, and if cinema (with its unique combination of sound and vision) may arguably be described as *the* most significant art form of the 20th century, then one could perhaps do worse than consider Kubrick's cinematic output in some depth.[1]

To date many authors have done just this; somewhere in the region of 50 books have thus far been published in English with Kubrick as their sole subject.[2] It is probable that few other 20th century "Hollywood" filmmakers, with the possible exception of the likes of Alfred Hitchcock and Orson Welles, have gained such critical currency. However, it might be argued that few of these books have considered Kubrick's work within a framework they merit. The majority of the major publications on Kubrick, almost routinely un-theorized, have underestimated and undervalued his work.[3] One argument this book will propose will be that Kubrick's work has a complexity, an intellectual weight, a depth and resonance of discourse; all of which argue for a more profound and a more theoretically aware discussion.

For reasons of practicality, this book will consider a carefully defined range of Kubrick's work, the following films: *Lolita, Dr. Strangelove, 2001: A Space Odyssey, A Clockwork Orange, The Shining, Full Metal Jacket* and *Eyes Wide Shut* will be looked at in depth. Kubrick's other works will not, for reasons of economy and necessity, receive the same attention. For example, the films Kubrick made in the 1950s (*Fear and Desire, Killer's Kiss, The Killing* and *Paths of Glory*) will not be considered in significant detail. In addition, *Spartacus,* the one film over which Kubrick did not have overall artistic control, will, likewise, not be fully detailed. Also, the book will not deal, in detail, with *Barry Lyndon.* It might be argued that *Barry Lyndon* may yet prove to be Kubrick's most important film, his masterpiece, for want of a better word. As such, it is simply not possible to fully embrace the full significance of such a film within the boundaries of this present book. In such a light, one might conclude the film perhaps deserves a monograph of its own, in order to fully embrace its qualities.

The book will attempt to approach Kubrick's films from a theoretical perspective, something — as stated — not yet accomplished, at least not in a significantly expansive manner. Thus the primary aim will be to offer a theoretical response to most of the major films of Stanley Kubrick, to consider one of the most seminal figures of 20th century cinema within a theoretical discourse. Aside from the obvious clear and present reasons for such an undertaking, there are also coincidental issues at play within this arena. By happy circumstance, Kubrick's work, from *Fear and Desire* in 1953 to *Eyes Wide Shut* in 1999, might arguably be seen as mirroring the age of high Theory; from Roland Barthes's pioneering work on structuralism in the mid-1950s, to Terry Eagleton's argument pertaining to the end of Theory in the late 1990s.[4] In taking such approaches as Marxism, feminism, Freudian and Lacanian psychoanalytical schools of thought, elementary structuralism and semiotics, poststructuralism and deconstruction, a range of postmodern concepts, and, most particularly, a gender studies/queer theory approach, Kubrick's work will be evaluated from a diverse range of perspectives.

Theory is a complex and shifting area, perhaps more characterized by conflict than by consensus. For example, Theory upholds that politics is pervasive; that language is constitutive; that truth is provisional; that meaning is contingent and that human nature is a myth.[5] In this sense, Theory proposes that there is a danger in perceiving of a text as a puzzle, a mystery to be solved. Theory argues there is no magical key to turn in order to discover what a text is about, and it is reductive to believe this is so. Every reading of a text is just that — a reading. A text is merely an organization of signifiers that contain as many meanings as there are readers to read it. Within the scope of a theoretical perspective, the act of interpretation, as Roland Barthes famously suggested, thus becomes a highly contentious activity, rather than a process for establishing conformity. It is within this light that Kubrick's films will be approached.

It is well known that Kubrick had little time for what he once famously referred to as "the bull crit stuff."[6] However, this would appear to be either something of a misquotation, a simplification, or perhaps even an obscuration. One might claim this insomuch as Kubrick's work *was* "a cinema of ideas,"[7] one in which the ideological discourse seemed by no means unaware of current intellectual debate. In a sense, one might thus describe Kubrick as an un-theorized theorist, insomuch as his films engaged with contemporary concepts and ideological approaches to new ways of thinking about ourselves, without engaging with (or showing enthusiasm for) specific intellectual models.

In addition, interlinked with a theoretical approach, there is also the significance of the thematic patterns at play within Kubrick's canon of work. While all of Kubrick's films were different, and one notes here the way he was able to continually reinvent himself with each film, it is readily apparent that certain thematic patterns run consistently throughout his work.[8] Thus there is a cumulative body of work for study: a diverse range of thematic elements to discuss within a theoretical framework. As suggested above, these thematic patterns are open to as varied a range of interpretations as there are viewers of the films; but disregarding this, some of the most important examples this book will follow are expressed below.

One of the most significant patterns in Kubrick's work was an interest in human sexuality. Here there is a clear example of Kubrick's work echoing some of the current concerns in intellectual thought, especially in the humanities. Since the 1960s — with the then-current wave of feminist ideas, and with the demise of a Marxist ideology as a viable option — a consideration of gender and sexuality has been at the forefront of intellectual debate. Thus it might be seen with the films of Stanley Kubrick, his work demonstrates a consistent preoccupation with the issue of sexuality, either explicitly or implicitly. For example, in nearly all of Kubrick's films, one finds a marginalization of women and the promotion of intense homosocial structures among the predominantly male cast of characters. In a similar sense, the thematic patterning of masculine aggression in Kubrick's work is relevant here. If Kubrick's work was primarily concerned with anything, it was concerned with male on male violence, which arguably often depicted a repressive desire. All of Kubrick's films, with the exception of *Eyes Wide Shut* (and in many ways this film is an exception within Kubrick's canon), have one thing in common: the idea that they are all primarily concerned with the concept that men kill other men and gain a degree of satisfaction, if not pleasure, from such an activity. The fact that Kubrick was so interested in this idea alludes to recent concepts pointing to the performative aspects equated with gender; the most relevant critic here being Judith Butler and her persuasive argument that sex and gender are mere social and cultural constructions.

Within a similar discursive space, Kubrick's films consistently appeared to equate narrative form with the idea of a masculine journey, often a circular journey, often with an Oedipal juncture, and often concerned with a return to a feminine domain. The fact that such journeys often concerned a masculine couple, two male protagonists, brings to mind the work of the American literary critic, Leslie Fiedler.[9] Fiedler's groundbreaking work, in the 1960s, looked primarily at the American novel; however, the American film, at least in Kubrick's case, offers the same scope for discussion, the same homosocial context. All of this will be seen as pointing toward at least one potential answer to the puzzling sense of skewed sexual politics, so readily apparent in Kubrick's work.

In a similar light, one of the other ubiquitous thematic patterns of significance in Kubrick's work was the idea of public and private spaces, and the way Kubrick's camera consistently found ways to explore them. On the one hand, there was the concept of the "citadel," the great houses in numerous Kubrick films wherein power was often expressed and violence planned and carried out. On the other hand, there was what might be described as almost an obsession with private spaces, most commonly seen within the redolent *mise en scène* of the bathroom, present in all of Kubrick's films. This theme offering a range of revealing elements, not the least being the obvious Freudian repercussions within such discursive maneuvers.

A further thematic pattern in Kubrick's work, and one often commented upon, consisted of the continually repeated trope that might be summed up as "the failed plan." The way in which Kubrick's work often depicted carefully structured systems, supposedly foolproof mechanisms, purported paradigms of infallibility — all of which, nonetheless, eventually break down and fail, no matter how much effort is made for the plan to succeed. This being seen in a wide range of Kubrick's films, perhaps most specifically in the trilogy of films from the mid–1960s and early 1970s: *Dr. Strangelove, 2001: A Space Odyssey* and *A Clockwork Orange*.

Also of interest was the way in which Kubrick's work operated, or at least appeared to operate, within the framework of established cinematic genres. The sense in which Kubrick demonstrated an interest in exploring most of the major genres of American cinema, while, in reality, deliberately subverting such genres.[10] This will be seen and discussed in a number of films, perhaps most pertinently in *The Shining*.

On a wider scale, albeit on a more subtextual level, there was the sense in which Kubrick's work responded historically to his own era. In other words, the way in which Kubrick's work was attentive to the socio-cultural milieu of a post-war discourse. The so-called bleak and cynical attitude toward humanity in Kubrick's films, his "ineluctable pessimism,"[11] the cold, misanthropic attitude toward the world, can, in a sense, be explained via an understanding of the underlying influence of such post–World War II events as the dropping of the atom bombs and the Holocaust. One might argue that the work of Stanley Kubrick, the 13 films he made between 1953 and 1999, were consistently concerned with the aftermath and consequences of World War II. Kubrick learned to stop worrying and love the Bomb, but what he couldn't do was to stop worrying about the Holocaust. Indeed, it is hard to think how any of us can stop worrying about the Holocaust, insomuch as we can hardly disregard what happened at the very core of Western civilization, how the very core of European culture so enthusiastically adopted the attempted destruction of the European Jews.

Kubrick was never able to directly confront the Holocaust, primarily because he was never able to find a narrative that would, in any plausible sense, begin to encapsulate it. However, it could be argued that his films were, nonetheless, preoccupied with the effects the Holocaust has had upon the way in which we view ourselves. In recent times, critics such as Geoffrey Cocks[12] have argued that there is a concealed preoccupation within Kubrick's work that points to what, at times, appears to be an obsession with the Holocaust. While this is obviously a matter of interpretation, such an approach may seem ultimately to render a reductive assessment of Kubrick's work. On the other hand, it is difficult to deny that Kubrick's sense of the world was deeply influenced by the weight of history, specifically the way the Holocaust has had such an influence on the way in which we view ourselves.

Perhaps one of the most important concerns in Kubrick's work was his interest, one might even say his obsession, with narrative itself, in a more specific sense, the ways in which narratives operated within cinematic spaces. In other words, if Kubrick was interested in one thing it was the way in which he told his stories. In this sense, for a man obsessed with narrative, it is somewhat ironic that Kubrick was unable to create his own, almost all of his films were based upon prior narratives, usually upon novels. However, disregarding this, Kubrick's inventive strategies in deploying cinematic narratives are worthy of attention. There are parallels here, not altogether risible, to Shakespeare, another great user of narrative who was unable to "come up" with his own original stories. In this light, the book will discuss the idea that Kubrick's narratives were, in their truest sense, simply narratives about narrative.

Finally, a minor thematic pattern, albeit one of some interest, was that of the only child. It would seem that Kubrick was drawn to narratives concerning the only child (in both realized and unrealized projects) for a range of both conscious and unconscious reasons. Insomuch this theme, although hitherto relatively unexplored, will find an interpretative space for discussion here.

The book will thus be structured around a consideration of seven of Kubrick's later films. While there will be a diverse range of discussion pertaining to each film, a rich repository of discursive ideas, some sense of specific elements in each chapter might be of use. For example, in the discussion of *Lolita*, the notion of gender will be seen as a significant component; the key issue being the way biological viability might be contrasted against social and cultural concerns of nubility. Within the chapter on *Dr. Strangelove*, the often-noted idea that Kubrick's films appear to be interested in the ways man's most carefully planned strategies eventually let him down, will be considered; together with an evaluation of the implications herein —

the way this film (and others) portrays such a pessimistic outlook toward tales of human progress. In the chapter on *2001: A Space Odyssey*, the idea that a number of Kubrick's films are structured around stories of masculine travel will be considered; together with a discussion of the mythic components of the narrative portrayed in the film. In a discussion of *A Clockwork Orange* the significance of "the citadel" will be discussed, the ways in which it represents a conscious and perhaps an unconscious way of escaping violence — this finding a linkage with the obvious misogynistic aspects of the film. In terms of *The Shining*, one of the issues discussed will be the use and perhaps even misuse of genre; the chapter will approach this question from both a structuralist and poststructuralist perspective. The chapter on *Full Metal Jacket* will look, in depth, at the theme of masculine violence in Kubrick's work; while this is something of a universal trope, the chapter will look toward ideas of the performative nature of gender to further explore the exaggerated construct of masculinity in Kubrick's work as a whole. In a discussion of Kubrick's final film, *Eyes Wide Shut*, the concept of narrative itself will be one of the main concerns; it will be suggested that the film integrates the two obsessions of Kubrick's work, love and death, in a unique positioning within its narrative discourse.

It must, in a final summation, be admitted that Stanley Kubrick possessed a pessimistic view of the world and that the general demeanor of his work was a bleak one. There was "a dark, sometimes even malevolent skepticism about the effectualness of human aspirations in the face of an unknowable cosmos,"[13] a "disenchanted, sardonic and generally pessimistic view of humanity."[14] However, as suggested earlier, one might ask that, given the times in which he lived, what other point of view might Kubrick have had. The stories we hear in the films of Stanley Kubrick enable us to look back on the 20th century and at least attempt to make sense of those times that were, to use a pertinent cliché, both the best and the worst of times. Kubrick chose to offer a relatively small canon of work, just 13 films; however, behind each of these films lay the preoccupation of a complex mind, one which repeatedly succeeded in offering a unique view of the world. Kubrick had a photographer's eye that seldom wavered; he had a pessimistic Hobbesian perspective on human existence, an almost Swiftian satirical take on the world; he possessed almost inexhaustible patience, a dark sense of humor, a subtle business brain, an unerring ability to reinvent himself, as well as near infallible casting instincts, an impeccable ability in editing, in framing, in selecting musical soundtracks and so on; not least the gift of telling cinematic stories in succeedingly more and more inventive ways. It is within such an arena that this book will now at least attempt to live up to that cinematic legacy.

CHAPTER 1

Lolita

A Shadow of a Shadow

There is no aphrodisiac like innocence. — Jean Baudrillard

In many ways *Lolita* might be considered Kubrick's most conventional film, or to put it another way, one of the least "Kubrickian" of Kubrick's films. It might be considered thus, insomuch as Kubrick's film either did not attempt, or perhaps could not attempt, to equal or match the reputation of the source narrative it was adapting. As Robert Kolker argued:

> *Lolita* does not achieve an identity: part adaptation of a celebrated book, part event (both novel and film received much publicity due to their content), part character study, part attempt to make England look like America, it remains a curiosity piece.[1]

A "curiosity piece" was possibly too harsh a consideration, but what might be said is that *Lolita* was one of Kubrick's few films that did not succeed in subsuming its original narrative source.[2] This being the case, it would seem implausible to attempt to discuss the film in isolation; hence this chapter will consider Kubrick's film in its own right, but when appropriate will also envelop a discussion of Nabokov's novel.

Vladimir Nabokov's *Lolita,* has generally been seen as one of the most significant novels of the 20th century, being described, for example, as "the most allusive and linguistically playful novel in English since *Ulysses*."[3] In the sense of the complexity of its discourse, its textual playfulness, its allusive prose, its numerical and acrostic tricks, its deliberate sense of intertextuality, its unequivocal exuberance with language, one might tend to agree that *Lolita* was paradigmatically Joycean. Insomuch one might argue how this may, at least in part, have been one of the reasons why *Lolita* remains what might be described as Kubrick's most conventional film. In other words, the source material, to some extent at least, overpowered the adaptive process. It is in this sense a text Kubrick was not able to completely subsume within a cinematic discourse.[4] In an interview two decades after making the film, Kubrick would comment:

> As for *Lolita*, I'm aware that it doesn't manage to capture the magic of Nabokov's book, the magic that is in the style. *Lolita* is a major example of how there are great books that don't make great films.[5]

In contrast, *Lolita* appears to have been one of Kubrick's less trouble-some films to shoot. It was filmed in just 88 days, an unusually short period of time, at least in comparison to Kubrick's later films. In addition, the film was a financial success, being made at a cost of somewhere between $1.9 and $2.25 million, going onto gross an estimated $4.5 million upon its opening. However, the preparations for the film's production had taken somewhat longer. As early as 1958 (before the book had even been published in the USA) Kubrick and James Harris had expressed an interest and had begun negotiating for the film rights. Then, in July 1958, via agent Irving Lazar, Kubrick and Harris approached Nabokov with the offer that he should write the screenplay. Nabokov at first refused, but then relented, even though he had no experience of writing for the cinema. After a series of correspondences, the Nabokovs arrived in the USA on February 23, 1960, and journeyed overland (by train) to Los Angeles, meeting with Kubrick in Hollywood, for the first time on March 1, 1960. Several days later, on March 11, Kubrick sent Nabokov a rough outline of scenes discussed and Nabokov started work on the screenplay. In June 1960, Nabokov sent Kubrick a first draft; this was some 400 pages long, what has been estimated to have been a seven-hour film. After negotiations a second version — a shorter script — was delivered in September 1960. Kubrick and Harris then worked intensively on the screenplay, possibly with the unaccredited help of Calder Willingham.[6]

It seems clear that Nabokov's screenplay was un-filmable; it is evident that, although Nabokov was a highly regarded and consummate novelist, he was inexperienced as a screenwriter and hence had little sense of how to adapt his own novel.[7] Thus it would seem possible that all of this was a mere ploy, that Kubrick and Harris never had a genuine intention of producing a film from a "Nabokovian" screenplay; that their real intention was merely to preserve Nabokov's name on the credit titles. In other words, that Nabokov's authorial prestige was what was needed for the film. Unlike the majority of Kubrick's adaptations, Nabokov could not be overlooked as an author; to bring such a prestigious novel to the screen Kubrick needed Nabokov's authorial name to be imprinted on his cinematic adaptation.

The critic Richard Corliss has made the point that Nabokov's script could "only exist on the page."[8] In reading Nabokov's screenplay this becomes readily apparent; it was overwritten, albeit elegantly overwritten, and parts were simply implausible, if not un-filmable. In addition, some of the dialogue, often simplified from the novel, came across as stilted and false within the medium of a film script. In reading Nabokov's screenplay it becomes apparent that Kubrick and Harris had simply discarded large sections and written their own. That is: a comparison reading of Nabokov's published screenplay and the screenplay apparent on screen clearly demonstrates that very little of Nabokov's script was used.[9] Nabokov himself would appear not to deny this:

> I had discovered that Kubrick was a great director, that his *Lolita* was a first rate film with magnificent actors, and that only ragged odds and ends of my script had been used.[10]

James Harris:

> When it came to the preparation of *Lolita*, I was able to contribute much more to the film, to the development of the story line. On our arrival in London, we weren't satisfied with the lengthy screenplay that Nabokov had written. We shut ourselves in one room for a month and rewrote it scene by scene. Of course when shooting got under way, Stanley gave each scene a new dimension, as for example in a few improvised exchanges between Sellers and Mason. But I felt I had participated in the shaping of a movie.[11]

It is thus somewhat ironic that *Lolita* was Kubrick's only film (other than *Spartacus*) on which he received no screenwriting credit; whereas this was probably one of the films in which he had a significant degree of scriptwriting input.

It is clear that Kubrick was interested in making a film of *Lolita*, but, as usual, he was not interested in making a literal adaptation of the novel, no matter how significant a novel it may have been. This was one of the consistent factors in all of Kubrick's many adaptations, as, it may be argued, is the case in other successful cinematic adaptations. It is evident that Kubrick was attentive to a duty of authenticity when dealing with a core source, as this comment to Michel Ciment made clear:

> Your first responsibility in writing a screenplay is to pay the closest possible attention to the author's ideas and make sure you really understand *what* he has written and *why* he has written it.... The next thing is to make sure that the story survives the selection and compression which has to occur in order to tell it in a maximum of three hours, and preferably two.[12]

However, it is also clear that Kubrick was cognizant that it was seldom possible to faithfully render a written narrative within a cinematic form. This was possibly a point that Nabokov (and others, including Anthony Burgess, Stephen King, and so on) perhaps never fully appreciated.[13] Thus whether

Kubrick succeeded in fully rendering the intent of Nabokov's narrative to a cinematic context is perhaps a meaningless question, as this was not his intention in the first place. Although Kubrick's films have nearly all been based on literary source material, it is obvious that he seems to have been fully aware of just what a film can and cannot do.

In addition to the problems of adaptation, Kubrick's film also had to contend with a degree of censorship with which Nabokov's novel had not been burdened. Although Nabokov had initial difficulties in publishing his novel he eventually succeeded, the novel being less rigidly controlled than film. In contrast, Kubrick, working in a different medium and in a repressive time and place, had much greater problems, the new freedoms of American cinema being over a decade in the future. The publicity byline of the film was: "How did they ever make a movie out of *Lolita*?" Bosley Crowther, of the *New York Times*, was one of several critics to suggest the answer was simple: "They didn't."[14] Kubrick would later comment he would have made a different film had the climate of the day been different, stating, in an interview from 1968:

> I think that it should have had as much erotic weight as the novel. As it was, it had the psychology of the characters and the mood of the story. Nabokov liked it. But it certainly didn't have as much of the erotic as you could put into it now.[15]

Two years earlier, in conversation with Jeremy Bernstein, Kubrick had made a similar point:

> I think the total lack of eroticism in the story, in the film's presentation of it, spoils some of the pleasure. You know, you can imply all the eroticism you want, but there's nothing like delivering some to help to understand a little more the enslavement that Humbert Humbert was under.[16]

*   *   *

Richard Corliss was to argue that Kubrick's Lolita was "a nymphet emeritus,"[17] in other words, she was too old, she had retired from her role as a nymphet. In the novel, when Humbert first encounters Lolita, she is 12 years old, four feet ten inches tall, with a 27-23-29 figure, in other words and for all obvious intent, she resembled a child. To portray this on film would simply not have been possible. It would not have been possible when Kubrick filmed the novel in the early 1960s, it was not possible when Adrian Lyne refilmed the novel in the 1990s,[18] and it would not be possible today.

Sue Lyon was born in 1946; she was 14 years and four months when filming began and 14 years and nine months when filming finished; hence she was relatively close to the spread of ages of Lolita in the novel.[19] However, the significant issue is not how old Sue Lyon actually was in relation to Lolita, but how old she *appeared* to be. In the film Sue Lyon, whatever her chronological age, had the apparent look of a "young woman," she did not look like a child.[20] As Daniel DeVries noted, while Sue Lyon may have been 14 at the time of the filming of *Lolita*, she looked "a well developed seventeen.... Humbert's desire for her comes off as ordinary lust, quite unlike the elaborately conceived and described perversion which possesses Nabokov's Humbert."[21] DeVries notes that Kubrick's Lolita does not have the novel's "nymphetness" but instead possesses a "convincing sullen adolescent sexuality."[22] In other words, Humbert's affair with Lolita in the film was at least portrayed in a potentially acceptable manner.

In this light it is of interest to note that, in the novel, Nabokov deliberately evokes the differences between social and cultural attitudes toward the age of consent; compared, that is, with the issue of a biological component to sexual maturity. This might appear to be speculation; however, in a significant section of the novel (seemingly overlooked by most commentators) Nabokov explicitly points to a biological component that suggests sex is permitted as soon as a girl is sexually viable, albeit in a purely biological sense. At the beginning of Chapter 33, in Part One of his novel, just prior to the beginning of Humbert and Lolita's extensive travels across America, Nabokov recounts:

> In the gay town of Lepingville I bought her four books of comics, a box of candy, a box of sanitary pads, two cokes, a manicure set, a travel clock with a luminous dial, a ring with a real topaz.[23]

The point at play here resides in the sense that one of the items Humbert buys Lolita, to prepare for their journey, is a box of sanitary towels. Thus we learn that, in a biological sense at least, "child" Lolita is, in fact, "woman" Lolita — if she can menstruate she can procreate. Thus she could be seen, in a biologically specific way, as being sexually mature.[24]

However, no matter her biological age and breeding viability — in a social and cultural context Lolita remained a child; and, in terms of a cinematic narrative, the sense of being able to realistically release a major Hollywood film in 1962, showing a pedophiliac relationship in explicit detail, was not an option. Kubrick had to compromise, although one might argue that he succeeded in compromising on his own terms. As Richard Corliss put it: "Kubrick seemingly had the choice of making Lolita the censors' way, or not making it at all. He did something more devious: he made it their way his way."[25]

Note how, in the film, there was no intention of fetishizing Lyon, as, for example, by dressing her in pigtails, or in suggestive schoolgirl attire. Kubrick's camera merely depicted her in terms of how a typical teenager of the time might have appeared. It is clear that Kubrick, freed of all restraints, might have made a very different film. A sense of what this may have consisted of can be found in the overtly suggestive images stills photographer Bert Stern took of Sue Lyon as Lolita. The photographs were apparently designed for use in publicity materials, but the great majority of them were judged too risqué for publication.[26] It is probable that Kubrick would have gone further, had the moral climate of the early 1960s allowed. Thus, in this sense, it would appear that Kubrick made the film a decade too early. For example, if one considers the explicit nature of A Clockwork Orange, a decade on and made within a new liberal milieu, then it is not difficult to envisage what kind of adaptation Kubrick might have made within a 1972 version of Lolita.[27] In any case, circumstances prevailed to engender the making of the film at the beginning of the 1960s.

*   *   *

In terms of casting Lolita herself, at one of their final script meetings, on September 25, 1960, Kubrick showed Nabokov photographs of Sue Lyon, of whom Nabokov gave final approval, describing her as "a demure nymphet"[28] going on to suggest Kubrick would be able to make her "younger and [somewhat tellingly] grubbier" for the part.[29] James Mason, always Kubrick's probable first choice for the role of Humbert Humbert, was an actor with the ability to offer the full range of the character's make-up.[30] Humbert, within the narrative discourse of both novel and film, was not a repellent figure — never a mere evil pedophile. While it is clear that an adult man is having a sexual relationship with an underage girl, nonetheless, we have at least a degree of sympathy and even empathy for Humbert. Also, the fact that there is little explicit sexual activity displayed, in either film or novel, in some senses negates our actual awareness of the sordid reality of the abuse taking place. The erotic pedicure at the opening of Kubrick's film was arguably the most suggestively erotic imagery we were offered. However, even this scene was somewhat slanted, insomuch as it offered a sense in which Humbert was subservient and passive, while at the same time expressing a clear sense of his love for Lolita. The actual level of abuse in his relationship with Lolita was therefore circumvented via an air of black humor, and by the unambiguous fact that Humbert does have feelings for Lolita; no matter how depraved his love may be — we have to accept that Humbert does love Lolita.

One would be hard pressed to find a single "obscene" word in the entire film, as indeed one would be hard pressed to do so in the novel. We are, as viewers and readers, arguably much more troubled by Humbert's intelligence, by his sense of humor, by his use of language, by his vulnerability and by his sheer likeability. As viewers and readers, we do not perceive him as a monster and we cannot help but feel at least some kind of affinity. In this sense, it has been suggested that one way of approaching film and novel would be to see it as an account of Nabokov's love affair with the English language; to envisage Nabokov as more interested in the perverse nature of writing than in writing about a so-called sexual perversion.[31] The final sentence of Part 1, Chapter 8 of the novel reads: "Oh, my Lolita, I have only words to play with!"[32] To a significant extent this defines the novel, and, to a lesser extent, the film. One might argue this was a facet Kubrick's film could never quite succeed in embracing to the same extent. There is a sense here that the complexities of the novel were beyond Kubrick's adaptative abilities, hence his approach thereafter (and to some extent, before) to adapt less linguistically complex literary works; only Anthony Burgess's *A Clockwork Orange* in any way approaches the linguistic complexity of *Lolita*.

However, one aspect of the novel that Kubrick arguably succeeded in translating was the sense in which he rendered the narrative as a love story. Lionel Trilling famously claimed that *Lolita* was a book about love and not sex,[33] and, as previously intimated, it is clear, from a viewing of Kubrick's film, that Humbert loves as well as lusts after Lolita.[34] In a previously unpublished interview (by Terry Southern in July 1962) Kubrick had explained how his interest in the novel derived from the fact that it represented an "illicit" love story. Kubrick cited other great love stories: *Romeo and Juliet, Anna Karenina, Madame Bovary,* as having the same quality,[35] and, in this sense, one can perceive of how Kubrick was simply interested in telling a love story, albeit from a previously untold perspective. In fact, one might argue that a significant body of Kubrick's work, up to and including *Eyes Wide Shut,* attempted to do this, although from a range of differing perspectives. Hence, we may conclude that any great love story, including the examples by Shakespeare, Tolstoy and Flaubert to which Kubrick alludes must possess a device by which the lovers are never able to live happily ever after (such a story having little dramatic interest), there must be a narrative device for keeping them apart. In this sense the narrative of *Lolita* merely offered a somewhat singular and original method for accomplishing this: Humbert's attempt to turn a tawdry tale of abuse into a great romance.[36]

Hence the fact that Humbert loves Lolita is never in doubt: "You see, I loved her. It was love at first sight, at last sight, at ever and ever sight."[37] So Humbert tells us in the novel, and Kubrick at least makes an attempt to intimate this throughout the film. In the novel Humbert pauses to describe his intense love for Lolita — he describes four or five moments of epiphany — and then questions whether the human heart can survive more than two or three. This comment having the obvious intent of drawing attention to the fact that Humbert will die of a heart attack, the implication being that he literally dies of a broken heart. At the end of the novel Humbert offers a poignant admittance of what he has actually done; Humbert hears the "melody of children at play," the distant sounds of children playing in a school yard, he listens for awhile and then comes to the realization of what he has done to Lolita:

> I stood listening to that musical vibration from my lofty slope, to those flashes of separate cries with a kind of demure murmur for background, and then I knew that the hopelessly poignant thing was not Lolita's absence from my side, but the absence of her voice from that concord.[38]

In the film Kubrick did not possess the space to include such narrative information; nonetheless, the general discourse of the film alluded to this.

In this sense the power and destructive nature of love and obsession might be seen as one of the key ideas of both novel and film. One might argue that the reality beneath the surface of both texts was that Lolita — a 12-, 13- or 14-year-old girl — was continually raped, or at least subjected to unwanted and inappropriate sexual attention. A feminist reading of *Lolita* might thus suggest that Humbert's narration usurps Lolita's right to an individual existence — he "rapes" her totally: her body, her mind, her self and her voice. Humbert attempts to explain this via his account of hungering for that time and space when nymphets hold their magic, on the cusp of childhood and adulthood. In addition, Lionel Trilling may have argued that *Lolita* was a love story, but from a feminist perspective this was patently irrelevant. From a feminist point of view, *Lolita* was not a text about love; it was a text about incest and rape, what was, in reality, a betrayal of any reasonable representation of love. Thus the novel (and to a great extent, the film), albeit from such a specific perspective, might be said to completely underestimate and underplay the sexual abuse of children.

In this way it might seem fair to argue that the novel (and hence the film) possessed an inherent perversity, albeit a perversity of a complex and beguiling kind. One could contend Kubrick's film was ideologically aware of such issues, but whether Nabokov's novel was similarly ideologically aware is a more problematical issue. As Susan Bordo has argued:

> [The novel] forces us to confront aspects of human behavior that even today we'd prefer not to face.... The dirty secret of our culture is hardly childhood sexuality. Freud took care of exposing that one, I believe. It's the other secret, the one that he may have covered up, that we're still concealing. I'm speaking, of course, about the eroticization of children.[39]

This is perhaps the key issue, for while childhood, and the innocence it implies, has become almost venerated within the culture, this is contrasted with the way in which young girls have become more and more fetishized. The ideal of feminine beauty becoming that of clear skin, big eyes, a slim figure, the removal of body hair, the wearing of short skirts and other immature clothing. This being perceived via such current iconic cultural figures as Britney Spears, Calista Flockhart, Scarlett Johansson, Kirsten Dunst and so on, all of whom appear to pose, at times, as versions of Nabokov's ideal nymphet.

However, such a partisan position would arguably overlook the complexities of the narrative of *Lolita*. The story being told was much more than a love story, a love story that may have been, depending on one's point of view, either genuine or perverted. The narrative of *Lolita* has also been variously seen as: a fairy tale, a literary parody, a study on the destructive nature of sexual obsession, a detective story (with the reader/viewer as detective), an evocation of American life, a repudiation of Freudian ideas, a metaphor for Old Europe debauching Young America,[40] not to mention it being considered, by some, as a work of shocking pornography. However, in 1962, when he released his film, Kubrick was dealing not so much with the narrative complexities of Nabokov's novel (which have since become to be seen as more and more manifest) but rather what was then the contemporary cultural reputation the novel had garnered from the late 1950s and into the 1960s.

In such a sense Kubrick's film was a film of compromises, and in order to compensate for these compromises Kubrick was forced to embrace an erotic discourse via more subtle methods. In this context the film is perhaps best perceived as one charged with deliberate and intentional sexual innuendo. For example: Humbert's comment on feeling "as limp as a noodle"; Jean Farlow's "extremely broad-minded views"; John Farlow's comment to Humbert at the high school dance: "Mind if I dance with your girl? We could, um, sort of swap partners"; Charlotte's promise to Humbert of their being "meals and late snacks"; Humbert's comment to Lolita that "Your mother has created a magnificent spread," and so on. In addition, some viewers may have noted the erotic pointers in some of the names Kubrick concocted: Mona Farlow[41] being an obvious example.[42] However, in terms of actual eroticism, *Lolita* was simply not able to depict any explicit material, bounded, as it was, within the era of its making.

* * *

In addition to his "pederastic" tendencies, it is clear Humbert was also a deeply ingrained misogynist. In fact there is an ingrained misogynistic discourse throughout the novel, and, to some extent, throughout the film. One immediate way in which Kubrick's film encapsulated the misogyny of the novel can be seen in the detail of Humbert shooting bullet holes — into Quilty — through the face of the young woman in the Gainsborough-esque painting, at the start of the film.[43] In addition, one might consider Humbert's repugnance toward Charlotte; what Susan Bordo called "a disgust with mature womanliness ... Charlotte Haze [is] the monster of the story."[44] In this sense one might perceive of a feeling of female abjectness, a theme that prevails throughout Kubrick's work, especially in *The Shining*. Humbert's recoil here, from the adult female, the sense of the female as abject, is clearly apparent in the consistent sense of vaginal loathing in the narrative discourse, an issue that will be considered again, later in this chapter.

In terms of representations of the female, one might also consider the depiction of Lolita herself. In the film, as in the novel, Lolita is a passive figure, little more than a female mannequin, not so far removed from the mannequins of *Killer's Kiss,* the Korova Bar's eroticized mannequins in *A Clockwork Orange,* and the real (but still passive) mannequins from the orgy scene in *Eyes Wide Shut.* Lolita is a real girl (at least within the fictional discourse of film and novel), but if there is a real girl in the text of *Lolita* (in film and novel) one might ask why did it takes so long to find her? This might be seen as *the* archetypal feminist question to ask of *Lolita* — is there a girl in the text?[45] In the novel Lolita was arguably given only one line of any depth, one line in which she told us, the reader, what she feels from the interior of her character, the line being: "You know, what's so dreadful about dying is that you're completely on your own."[46] In the film Kubrick manages to imbue Lolita with a greater presence and arguably manages to offer a more rounded portrayal of her character. However, there is still the sense of Lolita as a plaything, as a "fille-fetale." Lolita's diminutive name, Dolly, perhaps being less innocent than it might seem, insomuch as it logically refers to Lolita as a doll, to an inanimate body with which to have animate and illicit sexual activity. Humbert's ability to block out Lolita's voice in the novel, via his more sophisticated intellect, is less marked in the film. However, as a corollary of this, one might argue that we (reader or viewer of novel or film) in our attempt to possess the text, run the risk of doing just the same — to strip *Lolita*/Lolita of all her secrets — and arguably to be as guilty as Humbert in trying to possess her.

There *is* a girl in the text (novel and film), but, as suggested, we rarely hear or see her directly. For example, the sex life Humbert shares with Lolita is always seen from his perspective, never from hers.[47] Lolita, as a fictional creation, was probably not an exceptional person, in stereotypical terms: an average teenager. However, she is, nonetheless, forever locked outside of her own story, her own discourse. As noted above, it would be possible, within a feminist theoretical arena, to posit the suggestion that, in a sense, the female in the text becomes the text itself, a text with which the universally male or "masculinized" reader has intercourse, as Humbert has intercourse of a differing kind with Lolita. A Lacanian reading in which language itself is profoundly masculine, forever penetrating and never penetrated, would be one obvious way of interpreting the complexities of the text. In terms of film this is especially relevant when linked to the idea of the masculine gaze of the camera, an issue which will be discussed later in this book, particularly in relation to *Eyes Wide Shut.*

In looking toward a Freudian reading, the fact that Nabokov appeared to have such a low opinion of Freud is of some legitimate interest. Nabokov's lifelong argument with Freud is well known and recorded; and here in the novel, via Humbert, Nabokov rarely misses an opportunity to undermine Freudian thinking; for example: "I was always a good little follower of the Viennese medicine man"[48] and "[the] standardized symbols of the psychoanalytical racket."[49] In addition to this, Nabokov consistently burlesques Freud; for example, in his use of classic Freudian symbols: as when Humbert believes the (impotent) bullets in his (phallic) gun are going to trickle out of the barrel[50]; or when he offers a satirical slant in Humbert talking of "a young lady's new white purse."[51] In a similar sense, one could read a classic Oedipal triangle in Humbert, Charlotte and Lolita: Humbert makes love to the mother while imagining it is the daughter with whom he is having sex, again a clear demonstration of Freudian thinking. In addition, there were other deliberately constructed Freudian pastiches; when the aptly named Miss Pratt, headmistress of Beardsley, tells Humbert that Lolita is "shuttling ... between the anal and genital zones of development."[52] And yet, for all of Nabokov's dislike of Freud, a Freudian reading is still readily apparent within both novel and film. A clear paradigm being the *coitus interruptus* between the young Humbert and Annabel within their enchanted island of childhood; within a Freudian reading this suggests Humbert as being forever entrapped in a Freudian world of childhood sexuality before adult sexuality could develop. In other words, because young Humbert was unable to consummate his first love affair (owing to the death of Annabel) one might suggest he was thus forever trapped within the spell of young "nymphets."

While somewhat tenuous, it is possible to perceive of Nabokov's dislike of Freud as a latent defense mechanism. Nabokov's decision to write a book about a pedophile was, in the first place, open to obvious Freudian speculation. One might ask the question: why did Nabokov decide to write such a book; what reasons, what grounds, what motivations did he have? There are obvious autobiographical overtones in the novel: Nabokov had emigrated to the USA in 1948 and accepted a teaching post at Cornell University in New York, which, to some extent, parallels Humbert's experience in the novel. It would be somewhat sophistic to make further parallels between Nabokov and Humbert, but we might note that Nabokov considered *Lolita* his "best work in English,"[53] and, of all his characters, he claimed he had most affection for Lolita. Which is, in itself, a significant comment, as Richard Corliss put it: "His [Nabokov's] prose is in a perpetual state of ecstasy for Lolita."[54] Thus one might fairly ask the obvious question: why was Nabokov's prose in such a perpetual state of ecstasy for a 12-year-old girl? Also, Nabokov's decision to position "Vladimir Nabokov" within the text as Vivian Darkbloom further personalizes the novelist and the novel. There has seemingly been little critical comment on this, as Krin Gabbard noted: "As far as I know there is no speculation in the critical literature about why Nabokov has identified himself with the grown-up female lover of a man who prefers little girls."[55]

However, this, together with the wider question of why Nabokov chose to write the novel, remains, perhaps deservedly, unresolved. In the same way, one might question why Kubrick was drawn to adapt the novel into a film; while Kubrick may have at least had the "excuse" of a beguiling narrative — ripe for cinematic adaptation, such a question still lingers.

One Freudian element that is worthy of study, and one clearly apparent in both novel and film, was the consistent equation of sex being coupled with death and disease. "Your mother is dead," Humbert tells Lolita in both texts; a line redolent of exaggerated Oedipal tension. In the novel Nabokov was able to depict other instances; for example, the scene in which Humbert covertly masturbates while Lolita sits on his knee, was redolent with imagery of sex and disease: "I cautiously increased the magic friction ... between the weight of two sunburnt legs, resting athwart my lap, and the hidden tumor of an unspeakable passion."[56] Humbert sees his hidden and aroused penis as a hidden tumor, portraying both a sense of disgust and a clear linkage between sex and death. In Kubrick's film such a scene, of necessity, could not be rendered in such an explicit way, but nonetheless the linkage between sex and death was apparent. For example, the way both texts, novel and film, appeared to fear the female presence might partially be explained by seeing sex as ultimately linked with death. It might be noted that almost all the primary female characters in the novel do not survive its narrative closure: Charlotte, Jean Farlow, Lolita, Lolita's stillborn daughter, Humbert's first love, Annabel,[57] all die. Vivian Darkbloom being the only major female presence to survive — living on to write a memoir of Quilty within the fictitious discourse that extends beyond the narrative's closure. In the film this sense of a linkage between the female and death was not so extreme; nonetheless, a linkage, between sex and death, was clearly apparent in the film, a Freudian Thanatos responding to a Freudian Eros.

A Freudian reading might also be seen as pointing toward the obvious scatological issues present in the novel, reinterpreted, at least in part, in Kubrick's film. In this context Kubrick would presumably have had little difficulty, as the bathroom, in his work, was routinely positioned as having a significant and satiric intent. In any case, a scatological reading of *Lolita* might begin by recalling Nabokov's comment to Kubrick, during the casting of the film, that he might be well advised to make Sue Lyon a bit "younger and grubbier" in order to enhance her portrayal of Lolita. This potentially revealing comment by Nabokov is enhanced in both novel and film, when we are famously told that what drives Humbert's desire for Lolita is a mixture of her "dreamy childishness" and "a kind of eerie vulgarity."[58] Kubrick uses this phrase as part of one of Humbert's voice-overs, and it is also a phrase worth emphasizing, insomuch as it represents a significant point of view, when compared to the general "dirtiness" and "grubbiness" surrounding Lolita. This is not something Humbert finds objectionable; at one point in the novel he comments: "Is she still brushing her teeth — the only sanitary act Lo performs with zest?"[59] Later in the novel Humbert reveals his desire for Lolita was "brown and pink, flushed and fouled."[60] Later he calls to Lolita: "Come here my brown flower."[61] He talks of Lolita's: "fundament jiggling."[62]

The implication here in the novel (once again Kubrick's film did not have the means of offering as much narrative detail) might appear to suggest the idea that sex with a nymphet is, in itself, dirty, in both a literal and a metaphorical sense. As Humbert's affair with Lolita progresses he begins to analyze her body in what, at times, appears to be an overtly scatological manner: "Lo, whose lovely prismatic entrails had already digested the sweetmeat."[63] The fact that Humbert's love for Lolita was often depicted within what might be described as a scatological discourse[64] could be interpreted as suggesting his actual desires lay elsewhere — an issue which will be discussed below. However, in quasi–Freudian terms, the issue also suggests the idea of Humbert being forced to describe Lolita's immature and childhood sexuality, almost as if it were pre-genital, as if Humbert was equating Lolita's immature sexuality to the anal stage of development. As suggested, in the film Kubrick had little opportunity to interpret and to develop this element of the novel. In the film Lolita was simply portrayed as an average American teenager; whether she was unwashed, grubby, vulgar (and hence pre-genital) was left open to the viewer's interpretation.

In the novel, Humbert asks if "it was still a nymphet's scent that in despair I tried to pick up, as I bayed through the undergrowth of the dark decaying forests."[65] Humbert was here referring to his attempt to find a sense of Lolita while making love to Charlotte. As described above there is a sense of a "vaginal loathing" in the narrative discourse of both novel and film. Humbert finds sex with an adult woman less appealing than sex with a young girl, and thus the feeling of self-disgust Humbert experiences is readily apparent. The novel offers other similar instances; for example, Humbert refers to his journey across America as leaving "a sinuous trail of slime," for slime we might easily read sperm, the seminal fluid Humbert leaves behind him, which again suggests a kind of disgust with the body and sexual activity. In this context Humbert's sexual desire might be interpreted in a different way, one could speculate that Humbert's predilection for young girls acts not so much as a retreat from his fear of adult female sexuality — but that his real desires may lay elsewhere. As previously intimated, Humbert constantly tells the reader of his liking for "boyish" nymphets,[66] and it may not be too tenuous to speculate whether Humbert is repressing a desire for a same-sex relationship. This is something he can never face up to, but nonetheless it could be construed as at least a potential reason for his pedophiliac tendencies. To put this bluntly, Humbert recoils from adult heterosexuality and escapes to a prepubescent heterosexual embrace to avoid his potential erotic desire — same-sex sexual contact.[67]

In the film Kubrick appeared to demonstrate an awareness of this potential discursive space, offering a clear linkage toward the homosocial subtext expressed obliquely in the novel. Kubrick's treatment of masculinity, his treatment of the intense homosocial discourses that, at times, pointed almost to the verge of the homoerotic, being the focus of interest here. While *Lolita* was a novel named after a teenage girl; with the first and last words being "Lolita," it is interesting to note that the first and last words of the film were "Quilty."[68] Thus on the one hand, Nabokov's text, enclosed by Lolita's name, enunciated a narrative of sexual infatuation with a young girl. On the other hand, Kubrick's film could be read as being more concerned with men and their relationships. Hence, the narrative of the film, or so it might be argued, was not so much concerned with the eponymous girl of the title, but with the two men and their relationship with each other: Humbert Humbert and Clare Quilty.

One could argue, drawing on ideas from Leslie A. Fiedler's *Love and Death in the American Novel,* that in this film (and, in fact, in the majority of Kubrick's work) men are primarily interested with each other, rather than with women. Fiedler argued that, in the American novel, men were routinely involved with themselves and with other men. Fiedler also argued that in the American novel (and one could also read into this the American film, as Fiedler refers to film as "the child of the novel"[69]) there was "an odd relationship," that there was "an unnatural triangle," in which "two men are bound to one another through the women they jointly possess."[70] Such a threesome is clearly apparent in the film, both in terms of Quilty, Humbert and Charlotte, and later, and perhaps more pertinently: Quilty, Humbert and Lolita. Fiedler does not explicitly delineate his thesis in too brutal a way, but he suggests men attach themselves to the same female love object to subvert their actual desire for each other.

Thus, we might note how Quilty has had sex with Charlotte and Lolita — as has Humbert — hence there is a linkage, in Fiedlerian terms, between the two men within a homosocial embrace; this idea being reinforced by Kubrick, perhaps knowingly, throughout the film. For example, the song Quilty makes up just before his death: "The moon is blue and so are you ... she's mine tonight ... she's yours tonight." Here, in this albeit small detail, we find another indication of two men sharing one woman. In addition, during their game of table tennis, replete with testicular ping-pong balls and Humbert's phallic gun, Quilty's remark: "I sort of like it up this end," resonates with ambiguity. It is a *double-entendre* almost worthy of a *Carry On* film, a perverse and barely opaque comment that an astute reader of the film might infer as a reference to passive anality. Thereafter, the two men ascend the stairs; as if parodying a distorted version of a couple going to bed. Humbert fires his gun, he shoots Quilty in the leg: "Ouch — that hurts," Quilty says as Humbert's first bullet penetrates his body, such a penetrative act cannot help but recall a less explosive and less violent act; Quilty is, in other words, metaphorically deflowered.

Later in the film, when Humbert and Quilty meet together at the Enchanted Hunters, they have a conversation loaded with further homosocial intent and innuendo. To begin with, it might be noted how Quilty assumes a passive posture — bending over the veranda rail, with his back to Humbert — as if inviting a metaphorical congress of pederastic possibility. In addition, Quilty's dialogue is loaded with innuendo; he begins by telling Humbert he believes men should rid themselves of excess energy via judo; going on to comment:

> Tell me something, I couldn't help noticing when you checked in tonight. It's part of my job. I notice human individuals, and I noticed your face. I said to myself, when I saw you, I said, "That's a guy with the most normal-looking face I ever saw in my life." It's great to see a normal face, because I'm a normal guy. It would be great for two normal guys like us to get together and talk about world events — you know, in a normal sort of way.[71]

Quilty's burlesque on normality here further adds to the sense of ambivalent gender relationships in the film.

In *Lolita*, Peter Sellers played three multiple roles (as he would do in *Dr. Strangelove*): Quilty himself, Quilty masquerading as the policeman at The Enchanted Hunters, and Quilty masquerading as Dr. Zemph. However, in the light of the present argument it is interesting to note that, instead of Dr. Zemph, Sellers was originally to have played a variation of the role in drag: as Miss Pratt, the headmistress of Beardsley.[72] For reasons that are not entirely clear this idea was abandoned; however, photographs of Sellers in the role[73] offer some sense of the burlesque of femininity that may have been portrayed.[74]

Of course Humbert and Quilty were not explicitly located with one another within a homoerotic discourse; they were merely presented to be as polymorphously perverse as society, culture and decorum allowed. What the narratives of both novel and film do suggest is that such a desire is offset by female figures such as Charlotte, Lolita herself, and by the enigmatic figure of Vivian Darkbloom — Quilty's obscure companion and accomplice. As will be seen (throughout this book) all of Kubrick's films are either explicitly or covertly homosocial, insomuch as they most often privilege male characters over female ones. This veers toward the extreme in such films as *Paths of Glory, Dr. Strangelove* and *Full Metal Jacket* where there are scarcely any female characters at all, to the general discourse of other films which all, almost without exception, tend to downplay a feminine presence. One has to look long and hard to find many significant female protagonists in Kubrick's work;

Charlotte Haze here in *Lolita*, Alice in *Eyes Wide Shut*, and Wendy in *The Shining* are rare examples—but for the most part women are positioned on the periphery of Kubrick's narrative discourses.

To proceed toward a more exaggerated stance and argue that Kubrick's film, as well as being homosocial, was also overtly homoerotic, would perhaps be too outspoken; however, it would appear reasonable to argue that all of Kubrick's work was, to some degree, imbued with what Leslie Fiedler called a "delicate homosexuality." Fiedler famously argued that *all* American novels are, to some extent, imbued with such a quality. While Kubrick was to some extent restricted because of censorship issues, nonetheless the relationship between Quilty and Humbert is clearly established as having a tangible, if remote, homoerotic component. Thus Kubrick's decision to give Quilty a more substantial presence in the film is given at least some degree of explanation.

This sense of a homosocial, and possibly a homoerotic subtext, is strengthened when placed within a wider context of Kubrick's other films. A brief account of the undoubted homoerotic subtextual signals within Kubrick's work, as a whole, delineates such a proposal. For example, there was clearly a "covert homosexual attachment"[75] between Johnny Clay (Sterling Hayden) and Marvin Unger (Jay C. Flippen) in *The Killing*. There was the well-known homoerotic subtext between Crassus (Laurence Olivier) and Antoninus (Tony Curtis) in *Spartacus*, especially in the infamous oysters and snails scene. Then there was Bat Guano's (Keenan Wynn) fear of "sexual perversion" in *Dr. Strangelove*; with the inherent repressed homosexual desire such a denial presumes. There was the issue of Hal as the so-called "gay" computer in *2001: A Space Odyssey*. There was the almost stereotypical portrayal of Mr. Deltoid as the sexual predator of Alex in *A Clockwork Orange*. In addition: the two soldiers bathing in the river in *Barry Lyndon*, Watson and Ullman (not to mention the two spectral partygoers engaging in oral sex) in *The Shining*, the constant reductive feminization of the recruits in *Full Metal Jacket*, and, finally, the questions about Bill Harford's sexuality in *Eyes Wide Shut*.[76]

In the 1980s literary critic Eve Kosofsky Sedgwick began to write influentially on the issue of homosociality, making the point that male desire in western society was legitimated on a homosocial basis—that male on male relationships must be carefully regulated—that male on male desire was almost universal—but had to be controlled. Sedgwick argued that the privilege granted to male and male relationships stood in a dangerous proximity to a homosexual desire, a desire a patriarchal, capitalist society was forced to condemn. Sedgwick made the point that male homosociality (including but not entirely consistent of repressed male homosexual desire) was essential for society to maintain its patriarchal control, but that it must be rigidly monitored. Nonetheless, the inherent tensions resulting from this continually resurfaced in barely concealed direct male on male desire. Hence, in Sedgwickian terms, one of the significant roles of the cultural critic was to have an awareness of such tensions as were portrayed in cultural discourses. Here in *Lolita* the relationship between Humbert and Quilty, the tensions between the two men were readily apparent. Sedgwick's ideas, building on the earlier work of Leslie A. Fiedler, were clearly delineated here in this film, and, it could be argued, throughout Kubrick's entire canon of films.

* * *

In a linkage to such an argument, Nabokov's choice of names for the two male characters, Humbert and Quilty, offer a number of revealing issues within such an arena of interpretation. In the case of Humbert Humbert, a reading revolves around the way we actually pronounce his name. The general usage from the novel and the pronunciation in both film adaptations is to utter the name in its anglicized form, in other words with an audible "H" and "T." However, Humbert Humbert, in the French, would be spoken as something approximating: *"Umber Umber"* — hence Nabokov's possible intent might then be perceived.[77] Thus Humbert becomes a doubled shadow, insomuch as the sound of the French accented version of his name is not dissimilar from *umbra*. Further to this, we might note that Lolita's surname, Haze,[78] suggests obscurity, in this sense adding weight to the idea of Humbert as a shadow, or the shadow of a shadow.[79]

Thus Humbert Humbert might be read as a shadow of a shadow, but a shadow of a shadow of whom? One might reasonably argue of Clare Quilty, his twin, his shadowy other self — in both novel and film. Quilty is Humbert's double, his nemesis, his partner in crime, his mirror image. As Roger Lewis put it: "Quilty is quicksilver, he's the mask behind the mask."[80] Also, one might note how, in the novel, Humbert describes Quilty as "a fellow of my age in tweeds,"[81] and later declares he is "free to destroy my brother."[82] Furthermore, before Humbert murders Quilty, he describes himself and Quilty thus: "He and I were two large dummies."[83] In addition, Humbert and Quilty are almost literally twins insomuch as they were born at almost the same time: Humbert born in Paris in 1910, Quilty in Ocean City in 1911.[84] Michel Ciment has pointed out that the double is "one of Kubrick's most deeply rooted obsessions."[85] Ciment notes how the boxer in *Day of the Fight* has a twin brother; he notes the "bizarre and ambiguous presence of another self" in *Fear and Desire;* he notes how, in *2001,* Bowman sees himself at various stages in the ageing process. In addition, one might note the doubling of Charles and Delbert Grady in *The Shining,* the deliberate ambiguity of the woman who redeems Bill Harford in *Eyes Wide Shut,* and so on.

In terms of Clare Quilty's name, in one sense he is "Clearly Guilty," as has often been commented upon. However, one might also look at the name Clare Quilty in a different light: is Clare Quilty also a Clear Text? The word: "Quilty," seen in semiotic terms, becomes the simple signifier: *quilt,* suggesting stitching and weaving, the joining together of layers of fabric; in other words, a signifier with connotations of the word textile — and hence text. Thus one might perceive of a sense in which Quilty can be read as representing the "clear text" of the narrative of both film and novel. Quilty's story is the one we never hear, the one we might wish we could hear. In this sense, one might speculate that Quilty's "clear text" is the reliable narrator from whom we never hear, contrasted against Humbert's unreliable narrative voice from whom we cannot avoid hearing. In addition to this, it is perhaps relevant to note that Quilty's first name, Clare, is ambivalently gendered — it can be either male or female.[86] This being pertinent when considering how Quilty is seemingly feminized in both novel and film. For example, he is referred to in the novel, at one point, as "Aunt Clare,"[87] Quilty is also portrayed as being covertly "camp," insomuch as the summer camp Lolita attends is referred to as Camp Q, it is difficult to perceive of this as anything but a not-so-subtle clue Nabokov invents and Kubrick restates.

In a generic way *Lolita* could thus be envisaged as representing an early version of the so-called "buddy movie." The film would appear to possess most of the main constituents of this genre: a journey with no authentic goal; a marginalization of women; the lack of a domestic life; a male love story (albeit repressed); the early death of one of the lead characters (Charlotte) and so on. In the relationship between Humbert and Quilty we find these main archetypal gestures; specifically the idea that, in everything but consummation, the buddy movie follows all the conventions of a love story: they come together; they fall apart; they come together again. However, perhaps the primary requirement of the "buddy movie" is that a woman will never succeed in splitting up the male couple; herein that role being served by Lolita.[88] Thus one might ask, because of the clear homosocial signals, whether a certain delicate and sublimated homoeroticism did not inhabit the narrative space of the texts (novel and film); be this because of a fear of the female, or possibly because of sheer narcissistic pleasure of male-on-male, buddy/buddy relationships.

In another generic expectation, Richard Corliss saw the film as "a road movie in embryo,"[89] noting how most of the book was set in 1947, the year after the release of Edgar G. Ulmer's film, *Detour,* arguably *the* archetypal road movie. Corliss commented how *Lolita* is "as curious about motel architecture and diner menus as it is about the mismatched man and girl who have sex in those beds and get sick on the food."[90] Vincent LoBrutto also thought of the film in terms of something approaching this genre, noting it had the resonance of "a Jack Kerouac novel, a Robert Frank photograph, and an Allen Ginsberg poem."[91] However, unlike Kerouac's *On the Road*— *Lolita* did not consist of a traveling masculine couple, Humbert traveled and was accompanied by Lolita—but with Quilty never far behind.

In addition to these generic leanings it was evident that both novel and film — at least in terms of their narrative structure — both privileged the fairy-tale motif. In the novel Nabokov reached for the fairly tale, for a greater part, via Edgar Allan Poe. Poe being alluded to more often in the novel than any other writer, including Joyce and Shakespeare, possibly because Nabokov connected Poe to Humbert in that they both took child brides.[92] In the film Kubrick alluded only to one poem: "Ulalume," but nonetheless a clear inference was made. In addition, Nabokov may have been interested in Poe inasmuch as Poe wrote one of *the* classic *doppelgänger* tales, "William Wilson." In this sense it is possible that Nabokov was referencing the aforementioned idea of Humbert and Quilty being shadows of each other. Finally, Nabokov referred consistently throughout the novel to three of Poe's most well-known poems: "Annabel Lee," "The Raven" and "Ulalume." It is interesting to note that all three of these works were concerned with the deaths of very young women — which may have given the resourceful reader a clue to the ultimate fate awaiting Lolita.[93]

As to Kubrick's interest in fairy tale—this is well known. For example, Alexander Walker has spoken of Kubrick's "early love of fables and fairy tales," of "his belief in the energizing power of myth to work on our unconscious."[94] The influence of the narrative appeal of fairy tale in this film, and throughout Kubrick's work, is self-evident, although it is universally presented in a much bleaker fashion than would be found in a classic fairy tale. As Walker again comments: "The film of *Lolita* reinforces the black fairy-tale element of the novel out of Kubrick's own admitted fascination with 'magic,' especially its darker sides."[95] There were numerous other examples in the texts of both novel and film; obviously there is the Beauty and Beast connotation, with Lolita as beauty and Humbert as beast. In the novel Nabokov specifically alludes to such a theme: "Beast and beauty — between my gagged, bursting beast and the beauty of her dimpled body in its innocent cotton frock."[96] The beginning of Kubrick's film, with Humbert's drive through the mist to Quilty's mansion, Pavor Manor, enhances this theme, adding weight to the idea of the narratives belonging to the genre of dark fairy tale. The novel informs more here, Quilty's house is located on "Grimm Road,"[97] and, furthermore, it is in the middle of a "dank, dark, dense forest,"[98] and finally, when Humbert pushes open the front door, it swings open "as in a medieval fairy tale."[99] Kubrick was not able to offer such narrative detail, but was nonetheless most probably aware of these narrative connotations, deliberately alluding to the underlying context of a fairy tale discourse.[100]

In terms of narrative itself, Kubrick's use of narrative voice in the film was, as in all of his work, of some significance. In the novel, one is forced to consistently question how reliable and how plausible Humbert is as a narrator. For example, we might be somewhat dismayed to be told, relatively early on in the narrative: "The reader will regret to learn that soon after my return to civilization I had another bout with insanity."[101] This is not what we, as readers, might wish to learn about the storyteller in whom we are putting our trust.[102] However, a film can never be as autodiegetic (a wholly first-person narrative) as a novel, and, as such, our perception of what happens "becomes slightly more detached and balanced."[103] Hence our relationship to Humbert is not as intimate in the film, as in the novel. In the film, Humbert's voice-over at first suggests he has greater knowledge of the narrative than anyone else; however, this proves to be a false premise. Humbert has more knowledge than anyone else (after all we presume it is he who is recounting our story from his prison cell), but he does not have total knowledge, he is not omnipresent in the narrative. For example, one might note Humbert's verifiable lack of authorial control at specific points in the novel; at the end of Chapter 26 of the first part of the novel, Humbert instructs the printer to fill the rest of the page with Lolita's name until the page is full. The printer does not obey. Insomuch Humbert is no Tristam Shandy; in Laurence Sterne's novel, Shandy does have authorial power over the printer, often leaving whole pages blank or else depicted in some abstracted fashion. Also, not only is Humbert an unreliable narrator — he is an unreliable reader — insomuch as he fails in reading Quilty. This being unlike most, if not all the actual readers of the text (either novel or film), most of whom will have succeeded in reading through Quilty's disguise long before Humbert. Quilty's narrative power in the novel, and to some extent in the film, might thus be assimilated as pointing toward the impotence of interpretation, as Luis M. Garcia-Mainar commented:

> Quilty is the artist, the man who can devise deception and can spot it. Humbert is only the scholar who studies the artist and who, ironically, cannot perceive artifice, which is what he is supposed to study.[104]

In this sense the film has a final trick to play. We might note that in terms of its overall narrative design, the film's story was recounted in one long analepsis, allowing Kubrick an obvious way of ending the film: returning, in a loop, to its beginning. Thus it is here, as the film seems about to repeat itself, that we get the final narrative twist, the following caption: "Humbert Humbert died of coronary thrombosis in prison awaiting trial for the murder of Clare Quilty."[105] Hence, while it has previously appeared as if Humbert might be the narrator of the film, there is a disparity, the fact that we now subsequently learn that Humbert has died in jail — before the narrative ends — at least suggests there is some other frame narrator in control. Humbert would not have been able to write his own epitaph; another narrator has drafted the end caption, the final imparting of narrative information.

In summation, although *Lolita* was described, at the start of this chapter, as Kubrick's least "Kubrickian" film, it was, nonetheless, the first Stanley Kubrick film to begin to depict a greater part of the main thematic concerns of his work. As has been discussed in this chapter, within *Lolita* we can perceive of: a clearly depicted homosocial discourse, an overt concern with the mechanics of narrative, the idea of the circular journey (both literal and metaphoric), the overt use of Freudian subtexts, the concept of the failed plan, the thematic notion of the citadel, a subtextual concern with anti–Semitism, the subversion of generic expectations, and an overtly slanted sexualized discourse. All of these thematic patterns, to a greater and lesser extent, were enveloped within *Lolita*. In Kubrick's succeeding films (a mere six films over the course of the next 37 years) such thematic patterns would continue to be explored — and will be explored in the succeeding chapters of this book.

CHAPTER 2

Dr. Strangelove, or: How I Learned to Stop Worrying and Love the Bomb

An Immodest Proposal

It's the End of the World as We Know It (And I Feel Fine) — R.E.M.

The Marxist critic, Theodor Adorno, once suggested that certain horrors should be avoided in art and literature, insomuch as there were some things not possible to place into an aesthetic form; that there was a "holy dread" about certain subject areas that we simply cannot face.[1] One obvious example in the 20th century would be the Holocaust; and indeed this would appear to have been the one subject to have haunted Stanley Kubrick, the one horror he could not approach directly. However, Kubrick did find a way of successfully approaching another kind of 20th century holocaust, the prospect of nuclear war and the ultimate end of human civilization. He did this via humor, via black humor, via very black humor; in Kubrick's own words, he learned to stop worrying and love the bomb.

Kubrick was concerned, as any intelligent individual in the immediate post–World War II period might have been, with the prospect of nuclear conflict.[2] Hence it seemed a wholly appropriate subject area to deal with as a film. As usual Kubrick researched the subject thoroughly, and by the time he was ready to make the film he had attempted to read almost everything of significance on the subject. In terms of a narrative framing device Kubrick decided upon Peter George's novel *Red Alert;* in this seemingly slight novel he had a source narrative around which to base his film.[3] While the novel lacked any specific literary depth or quality, it encapsulated its subject with an exacting narrative flair, it possessed a technical knowledge of its subject, it expressed a clear message as to the absurdity of nuclear deterrents, and it offered an obvious scope for adaptation to film.[4]

Peter George was an ex–RAF pilot and possessed an in-depth knowledge of both military procedure and (arguably) the military mind, something he used to great effect both in his novel and in his contribution to the screenplay of the film.[5] George's novel (which had sold in the region of 250,000 copies in the USA alone) was significantly changed in its adaptation, but still shared the same basic plot: a renegade American general launches an unauthorized nuclear attack on the Soviet Union. A number of the same characters can be seen in both novel and film: the president, General Turgidson, General Ripper, Major Kong, the Russian Ambassador and so on, although there were numerous amendments made (most significantly in the choice of names and characterization) to suit the film's satirical discourse. (In George's original novel he gave the protagonists names such as Clint Brown, Andrew Mackenzie, Franklin, Quinten, etc. Names that according to Randy Rasmussen "suggest a stereotypically American brand of integrity, sensibility and determination."[6] In the film, as is well known, the names were deliberately given a sardonically sexualized subtext. Perhaps the most inventive name was that of the president, Merkin Muffley. The *OED* suggests the word *merkin* is of early 17th century origin, a noun denoting "an artificial covering of hair for the pubic region," the word *muff* being "vulgar slang" for a "woman's genitals." It might be noted here that Kubrick may have originated the president's singular name from his reading of *Lolita*. In the novel, Nabokov recounted Humbert Humbert's attempts to replace his desire for "nymphets" with that of an adult woman, Valeria: "Although I told myself I was looking merely for a soothing presence, a glorified *pot-au-feu*, an animated merkin, what really attracted me to Valeria was the imitation she gave of a little girl."[7])

However, it is perhaps significant to consider how much of George's original novel actually informed the film. The original novel began with a foreword, which told of "a battle fought in the skies over the Arctic,"[8] a scene that approximately corresponds to the film's opening views over the Zhoklov Islands. The B52 (named *Alabama Angel* in the novel, as against the film's *Leper Colony*) is similarly being refueled in mid-air, prefiguring the film's opening: "A KC-135 Stratotanker had been waiting patiently for them, ready to slake the thirst of the eight great engines."[9] Often dialogue or narration from the film was drawn directly from the novel; for example, in a discussion of the flight of the B52's: "They had only one geographical fact in common. They were all approximately two hours flying time from a Russian target of primary importance."[10] The concept of the doodles on General Ripper's/General Quinten's notepad, as a clue to the recall code, derived from the novel;

the phrase "Peace on Earth" being repeated consistently in both novel and film. The novel provided the film's first line of dialogue: "You recognize my voice?"[11] There was the same plot device of a portable radio playing normal programming,[12] the same plot line of the base being "sealed tight."[13] Wing attack, plan R — survives into the film,[14] as does CRM 114.[15] The War Room is described in a similar way as in the film: "At one end of the huge, rectangular room, a dozen comfortable chairs were arranged in a semi-circle facing a wall ... on it were three maps, all of them of the world."[16] In addition, significant parts of other dialogue from the film, especially Ripper's/Quinten's, were derived from the novel.

However, George's novel had no inkling of the character of Dr. Strangelove, this seems to have been the creation of Kubrick and Terry Southern at a later stage in the script's development. There have been various candidates put forward as the basis for the character of Dr. Strangelove: Henry Kissinger,[17] Werner Von Braun,[18] Edward Teller, Herman Kahn and so on. Kissinger had the accent, Von Braun the Nazi background, Teller the enthusiasm for nuclear weapons[19] and Kahn worked at the Rand Corporation — parodied in the film as the Bland Corporation.[20] It is likely that all of these real-life personalities (and perhaps others) played some kind of a role in the character's creation.[21] In any case, the introduction of the character of Strangelove into the film signaled a change of direction. It is clear that Kubrick's original intent was to render a dramatic adaptation of George's novel, but it seems that he soon realized the prospect of two superpowers starting a nuclear conflict was, in itself, so absurd as to make any depiction other than comedy untenable. In taking a satirical approach Kubrick was characteristically in tune with the sign of the times, the 1960s as the era of protest and rebellion.[22] One could go further and argue that Kubrick was able to catch the mood (the *zeitgeist*, if you will) of what would come to be called the "Swinging Sixties"; Robert Brunstein has noted how the film was "the first American movie to speak truly for our generation."[23] While to Oliver Stone:

> It was one of the first films that I saw as a young man that pointed to the government as indifferent to the needs of the people, government as an enemy to the people. I suppose many of our fears of big government are rooted in that theme, in Kubrick's paranoia.[24]

One must recall that the film was made in the pre–Vietnam era and hence was arguably ahead of its time within an ideological discourse. This was so much the case that some elements of the media were able to criticize the film for its supposed contempt of America's military establishment.[25] An approach that now seems somewhat absurd, given the changing attitude toward the military since the experience of the Vietnam War. In this way the disclaimer at the film's beginning, from the U.S. Air Force, now almost appears as if it were merely another part of the film's satirical discourse.[26]

Insomuch as all of Kubrick's work has a satirical edge of a certain kind, it was not wholly surprising that he introduced a satirical note to the adaptation of George's novel. Terry Southern[27] was the writer Kubrick approached;[28] on November 2, 1962, Kubrick telegrammed Southern proposing they work together. According to Lee Hill, Southern's biographer:

> The initial George/Kubrick draft walked an uneasy line between the inexorable gloom of George's source novel and a broad, almost juvenile slapstick. Kubrick and George [had] devised a cumbersome meta-satirical structure using the plot of *Red Alert* as a film within a film produced by alien intelligence.[29]

Hill, as Southern's biographer, perhaps not unsurprisingly downplayed Peter George's role in the film, referring to him as "a hack with pretensions" who would have made "pulp novelist Jim Thompson ... look like a Nobel laureate."[30] Hill argues that it was only when Kubrick began to work with Southern that a real satirical discourse began to develop in the film. However, Hill did acknowledge George's military background and erudition, noting how this aspect of the film "anchored the satire in a kind of hyper-realism that made the absurdity and horror mesmerizing to watch."[31]

One obvious literary influence on Kubrick as a satirist, in his work as a whole and in this film specifically, was Jonathan Swift. Thus Southern, who was once described as "the closest thing America had to Jonathan Swift,"[32] was obviously a key issue within this aspect of the film. It would appear that Kubrick and Southern were fully conscious of this as the screenplay, at times, appeared to make deliberate intertextual indicators toward Swift. This can primarily be seen in the naming of one of *Leper Colony*'s targets as Laputa;[33] Laputa being a land in Part III of Swift's novel, *Gulliver's Travels*.[34] While the satirical points offered in the film were not quite as conspicuous and exaggerated as Swift's; nonetheless, Kubrick's film presented a depiction of human moral turpitude, via savage burlesque, with a clear Swiftian intent.

In the film Kubrick's method of introducing satire was primarily expressed via a burlesqued sexuality, again a Swiftian device. This was presented via the range of irrational fears and sexual hang-ups possessed by the various military figures, often in repressed and "deviant" forms. The habitual linkage of sex and death in Kubrick's work is portrayed here in a clearly delineated form; from the use of the word "strangelove" in the title on down. The reason such an approach was so convincing was possibly because such an explanation of sexual neuroses, as exhibited in the military mind and body, may not have been so far-fetched. Kubrick never denied such a subtextual reading; for example, in a reply to a personal letter from Le Grace G. Benson, dated March 20, 1964 (Benson, incidentally, seems to have been the first voice on record to have delineated this subtext in detail), Kubrick responded by thanking Benson on his "well thought out analysis" which, according to

Benson, had detailed "the sexual framework [of the film] from intromission to the last spasm."[35]

Since then a wide range of varied and diverse critics have commented upon the sexual metaphors at work in the film; from the overt symbolism over the opening credits, to the ludicrously sexually loaded names, to the ambiguous language and to other overt metaphors. However, it would seem fair to argue that the sexual imagery may have been misread, or at least there are alternate interpretative maneuvers to make. For example, one might argue that the sexual imagery more often pointed toward the masturbatory, rather than typifying metaphorical heterosexual sex, as has usually been perceived. Thus one might fairly suggest that the men in the film, whose sexual fears and neuroses are so vividly inscribed, invariably have deeply instilled immature attitudes toward sexuality, alongside what might be described as a homosocial panic.

It is General Ripper's paranoid and delusional fears that ultimately result in the apocalyptic consequences of the film's conclusion. Ripper begins a nuclear war because he feels a "loss of essence" which he concludes, within his paranoid delusion, is a result of a communist-inspired pollution of the water supply. This has been interpreted, by some critics, as a reference to Ripper suffering from impotence, yet it would seem possible to perceive of this as representing sexual anxieties of a different kind, a repressed homoerotic yearning expressed via masturbatory activity. Ripper avoids the sexual attention of women: "Women sense my power, and they seek the life essence. I do not avoid women, Mandrake, but I do deny them my essence." Ripper first becomes aware of his sexual problem during what he calls "the physical act of love," he feels a "profound sense of fatigue, a feeling of emptiness" and a "loss of essence." If Ripper doesn't ejaculate, he doesn't lose "his essence," he will stay potent and hence preserve his illusion of masculine power. However, one might argue that the physical act of love Ripper describes is, in fact, a solitary activity — it is onanistic. Ripper denies women "his essence," but is forced into masturbatory activity to relieve his actual desire, which could be read as a repressed homoerotic desire, a desire for what he euphemistically describes as "his boys."

Further masturbatory indicators can be perceived throughout the film. Major Kong, astride his bomb, riding toward his and the world's destruction, has obvious masturbatory overtones, especially when linked to his previous "ogling" of Miss Foreign Affairs in *Playboy*.[36] In a similar masturbatory discourse, Dr. Strangelove's wayward Nazi arm could be read as an obvious onanistic signifier, a wayward Nazi appendage attempting a masturbatory gesture that will correspond to the climatic and orgasmic explosions of the film's ending.[37] Thus one reading of the film could be seen as one in which Kubrick uses our fears of the bomb to explore sexual anxieties and inadequacies in the American male. In this way, the sexual imagery offered throughout the film —from its beginning, with the coupling imagery as the two planes refuel, to the orgasmic explosions of the nuclear bombs at the close —could be seen as subtly different to that commonly interpreted.[38] One way of understanding such a reading would be to argue that the film is masturbatory and repressively homoerotic insomuch as it represents a study of the sexual desires of men trapped within an infantilized stage of development.[39]

In this light the sexual metaphors in the film are perhaps better understood via a recourse to a psychoanalytical understanding. For example, we might note the childlike pencil line opening credits, carefully but clumsily scrawled,[40] almost as if it were a game of apocalyptic hopscotch. In this sense, and as previously alluded, the visual imagery of the opening scene, of the planes refueling, points less to copulation and more to maternal love and nourishment; in other words, toward Freud's concept of infantile oral sexuality. In a similar way the name of Ripper's command base, Burpelson, has obvious childlike connotations of a minor bodily malfunction. Additionally, General "Buck" Turgidson's ludicrously loaded Freudian name, with its connotations of phallic prowess,[41] at the same time also suggests infantilism. We see this in Turgidson's gum chewing, his infantile concern with the "Big Board," and in his general immature demeanor. Elsewhere in the film the men depicted are scarcely mature; Major "King" Kong is a pilot of a B52 and yet one senses an almost total lack of maturity into his understanding of the world; note, for example, Kong's approach to nuclear war: "Well, boys, I reckon this is it, nuclear combat, toe to toe with the Russkies."[42] One might also point to infantile sexuality within the anal/excremental subtext to Bat Guano's name, contrasted with the ultra-exaggeration of his "hard core" heterosexuality.[43] "What kind of suit is that?" Guano asks Mandrake, revealing a set of sexual anxieties all his own. Guano thinks Mandrake a *prevert*— seemingly because of his "suit,"[44] calling into question the role of costume, of uniform in the military, the quasi-transvestite qualities in the military's pleasure in dressing up in uniforms. Guano believes that Mandrake has been "organizing some kind of mutiny of *preverts*." In the light of the subtextual metaphors at work in the film, this may have been closer to the truth than might otherwise have been thought.

One might also point to Ripper's exaggerated concern with his aforementioned precious bodily fluids, an issue with a diverse range of potentially revealing discourses.[45] This would again seem suggestive that the military mind is trapped within a non-genital stage of sexual development, a sexuality that does not extend into maturity. Ripper's concern with his "fluids," his obsession with a "purity of essence," is suggestive of this. It is perhaps relevant to note that, as in all of Kubrick's films, there is an element of a scatological discourse in *Dr. Strangelove*; herein perhaps additionally inspired via the previously alluded influence of Jonathan Swift. Note, for example, that Turgidson is in the bathroom when he learns of Ripper's attack and that Ripper shoots himself in another bathroom; also there is Bat Guano's name, and other scatological references, if one wants to see them.[46] Finally, if the film had ended in the way Kubrick had originally planned, then the idea of infantile sexuality would have been further entrenched by the famous custard pie fight of the film's original closure.[47]

*   *   *

As to the War Room itself, in this context one might reasonably envisage it as having a womb-like connotation, the *mise-en-scène* representing a dark, safe, warm place for the men within it to survive the bleak reality of the outside world.[48] In addition, the set of the War Room, once described as "one of the most functional and imaginative sets ever designed for film,"[49] also operates within the theme of the Citadel in Kubrick's work. In fact, the War Room perhaps serves as one of the most prominent examples; Robert Kolker saw it as: "a dark version of the chateau in *Paths of Glory*,"[50] while Mark Crispin Miller saw its "imposing structure" as one of Kubrick's "gleaming monuments of death."[51]

However, the forbidding nature of the War Room might potentially be seen as pertaining to another metaphor at work in the film, that of another holocaust, that of *the* Holocaust itself. As is clearly evident (from numerous personal comments and from interpretations of his work), Kubrick was, to a significant extent, preoccupied with the subject.[52] Thus, as suggested at the start of this chapter, here in *Dr. Strangelove,* in dealing with a vision of a nuclear holocaust, Kubrick was at least able to allude to a different (H)olocaust. Of course, while it was possible to take a comedic approach (albeit a very dark one) to the issue of nuclear holocaust, such an approach would not seem to have been viable in terms of the Holocaust itself. In other words, no matter how funny the joke, was it possible to laugh at the Holocaust? Such an undertaking has, at times, been made; one might think of such contemporary (and Jewish) filmmakers as Mel Brooks and Woody Allen. Brooks in the "Springtime for Hitler" segments of *The Producers;* Allen in a range of Holocaust jokes in films such as *Annie Hall* and *Manhattan*,[53] but it would seem untenable to extend such a comedic discourse over an entire film.

In *Dr. Strangelove* the idea of presenting a comedic discourse about the Holocaust was offered in a more subtle and subtextual way. The most obvious inference being the character of Dr. Strangelove himself. While it was never explicitly stated, it was nonetheless clear Strangelove was an ex–Nazi, or perhaps a still practicing (if undercover) Nazi. In one of his more lucid moments General Turgidson becomes concerned about Strangelove's antecedents: "Strangelove, what kind of a name is that? That ain't no Kraut name, is it?" Turgidson is told that Strangelove changed his name when he became a citizen, and that it used to be Merkwürdigichliebe, a translation of which, after some expurgation, correlates to Strangelove. In addition, Strangelove's final words: "*Mein Führer*, I can walk," was obviously an explicit reference toward this reading of the film. In fact, at the end of the film Strangelove's vision of the future seems like nothing less than a resurrection of the Third Reich. As Randy Rasmussen notes: "The Doomsday idea is Strangelove's variation of Hitler's Final Solution."[54] One notes how Strangelove seems to take delight in the very idea of mega-deaths, we might note his ecstatic delivery of the word *slaughtered* in the line: "Animals could be bred and *slaughtered*." In Peter George's novelization this was made more explicit; at one point Strangelove talks about the possibility of part of the human race surviving in a mine shaft and comments: "After all, the conditions would be far superior to those of the *so-called* concentration camps, where there is ample evidence most of the wretched creatures clung desperately to life."[55] If at least a segment of Kubrick's work could be seen as a response to the influence of the Holocaust on Western culture, then *Dr. Strangelove* could be seen as a significant element of this.

Alexander Walker would write of Kubrick's "self-protection" and how we must learn "to shut out tragedy on this scale."[56] Walker was talking of the fear of nuclear war, but the same could be said of the Holocaust itself. In *Dr. Strangelove* Kubrick found a way to deal with the fears of nuclear war via a satirical approach; however, such a recourse (as discussed) was not possible in relation to the Holocaust, not even for a filmmaker as resourceful as Stanley Kubrick. Instead, through subtle indicators such as Ripper recalling Hitler locked in his bunker suiciding via a pistol shot, Strangelove's idea of selecting and building a master race and the other indicators mentioned, Kubrick subtextualized the theme and withdrew from dealing with it directly, fulfilling Adorno's concept of the "holy dread," that art is negated from dealing with certain taboo issues.

In relation to the Holocaust subtext, one can perceive of an exploration of a subtle racist discourse throughout the film, a theme not uncommon in Kubrick's work in general. For example, the crew of the B52 offered a sardonic reading of Hollywood war movie racial stereotypes: "a Negro bombardier, a Jewish radio operator, a Texas pilot."[57] Major Kong, in his speech at the start of the bombing mission, tells us that the whole crew would be in line for important promotions and personal citations "when this thing's over with, regardless of your race, your color or your creed." However, this promise of equality might be seen to be as spurious and unrealistic as the idea of there being any way of gaining promotions and citations in a post-nuclear apocalypse. In other words, Kubrick, not for the first or the last time, was drawing attention to the hypocrisy of racial equality in American society.

*   *   *

The concern of the film with the prospect of nuclear holocaust, together with subtextual pointers to the Holocaust itself, pointed clearly to a death wish, to what Freud called the death instinct or Thanatos.[58] In addition, it is clear that this was consistently linked with sexuality, with an almost exclusively aberrant sexuality. This being apparent throughout the film as, it might be argued, it is throughout Kubrick's work as a whole. A linkage between sex and death can be seen from the very beginning of the film, with the imagery of a nuclear bomber refueling to the ironic strains of "Try a Little Tenderness." This is continued all the way to the close of the film, with Major Kong riding the bomb to world destruction, as if it were the ultimate if wholly risible masturbatory phallus.[59] In addition, there were numerous examples at points between, for example, Turgidson's promise to Miss Scott: "I know how it is, baby. Tell you what you do. You just start your countdown, and old Bucky'll be back here before you can say — Blast Off!" The terminology of "Blast off!" would appear to refer to Miss Scott's sexual climax, but it also obviously linked literally to a rocket launch and the death and destruction that will ensue. In a similar sense, the code for the Wing Attack is Plan R, in phonetic code, R for Romeo, once again forging a linkage between sex and death. There was also the aforementioned fact that Major Kong is reading *Playboy*, "ogling" Miss Scott aka Miss Foreign Affairs, just before the B52 receives the Plan R code, again creating a linkage between sex and death.[60] Herein we can perhaps see Kubrick's real intent, in a linkage between love and death, he offers an ironic and arguably accurate depiction of the U.S. military as being both sexually repressed and almost psychotically delusional in their view of the world.

*   *   *

One other significant issue in the film concerned the use of language. As with all of Kubrick's work, the film possessed an interest in the way language operated, with the use and misuse of language.[61] Such an interest is apparent from the beginning of the film, from the first line of dialogue: "Do you recognize my voice?" General Ripper asks Mandrake. Mandrake, as we soon learn, has only been talking with Ripper a few moments before, thus the fact that Ripper asks the question and that Kubrick decides to open the film with it, has a degree of significance. One might therefore suggest that *Dr. Strangelove* was, in a sense, a film about the inability of people to communicate with one another. If one takes a more pertinent example: General Ripper's speech concerning his "precious bodily fluids." Ripper's speech is of interest insomuch as he begins his explanation for attempting to start a nuclear war in a relatively lucid way, but then goes onto overly extend his argument with the mistaken view that fluoridation of the water supply was, in some way, a communist conspiracy. This then descends into the farcical and ludicrous idea that the life essence of his seminal fluid was, in some way and for some unspecified reasons, being drained from his body. As Robert Kolker noted:

> Ripper's speech ends in bathos, in perfect nonsense.... His great speech is a concentrated collapse from the somewhat shared clichés of reactionary discourse into the crazed, subjective discourse of someone who is creating his own meanings.[62]

The point in question is that the "perfect nonsense" of Ripper's speech was only marginally more credible than the rest of the linguistic discourse on display in the film. One thinks of lines such as "Peace is our Profession," and the way, underlying this ridiculous euphemism, the facile nature of nuclear defense and retaliation is exposed. The inability to understand language, to grasp the meaning of words being used, perhaps culminating in the ludicrous cry of President Muffley: "Gentlemen, you can't fight in here. This is the War Room!"

Kolker also notes that: "*Dr. Strangelove* is about the lack of centre," and, "Ripper is the most radical example in *Dr. Strangelove* of the dislocation of word and meaning."[63] It is not necessary to extend a reading of the film much further in order to perceive of a poststructuralist interpretation. Kubrick was working at a time before such theoretical concerns about language had been fully developed, but nonetheless *Dr. Strangelove* might be envisaged as a clear paradigm of the way poststructuralist ideas might be put forward within the discourse of a cultural text. In poststructuralist thought, within its generally accepted terms, we enter a universe of uncertainty, a universe beyond linguistic accountability, a decentered universe in which, by definition, we cannot know where we are. All previous concepts which had a center, which includes just about all of Western thought, have thus been deconstructed and undermined. In effect we are no longer in control of the linguistic system.[64] This is not an entirely new way of thinking; for example, Nietzsche previously stated: "There are no facts, only interpretations." Insomuch, nothing is guaranteed, all is open to interpretation, nothing has a stamp of authority, and there is no central figure or framework that can validate our ideas. However, poststructuralism intensifies this still further, in that it regards any confidence in the "scientific" method as naïve, and even derives a certain masochistic intellectual pleasure from knowing for certain that we can never know anything for certain—fully conscious of the irony and paradox of this statement. Reality becomes textual; the verbal sign is seen as constantly floating free of the concept it is supposed to designate. In Jacques Derrida's famous phrase: "There is nothing outside the text."[65]

In this sense, poststructuralism distrusts the very notion of reason, the very notion of a human being *being* an independent entity; preferring instead the notion of a *dissolved* or *constructed* subject, wherein we think of the individual as merely a product of social and linguistic forces. Thus what is revealed is a fractured, contradictory essence, symptomatic of a cultural and linguistic malaise, cultural texts tending to emerge as angst-ridden, fissured enactments of linguistic indeterminacy.[66] These are wide-reaching ideas; however, Kubrick's film would appear to be at least suggesting that language, although it may seem to be within our control, is, in fact, far from this aspiration. Herein lies one crucial understanding of Kubrick's work; Kubrick's films from beginning to end were fully cognizant of the inadequacies of language. Hence, one could possibly argue, the consistent interrogation of language within Kubrick's work was, in some way at least, a response to what would later be seen as a poststructuralist approach to language.

In the context of *Dr. Strangelove*, a poststructuralist reading might offer, for example, an explanation for the name of Burpelson Base. As noted previously, it is a name with obvious childlike connotations of minor bodily malfunctions; however, in linking language to infantilization, the word "Burpelson" achieves a further connotation within a poststructuralist arena. In other words, poststructuralist concepts around the idea of words never reaching an ultimate meaning, is rendered here in the exaggerated sense of a mere "burp," rather than a formal, structured form of language.[67] Other poststructuralist dislocations in speech can be found elsewhere in the film; for example, in Major "Bat" Guano's risible malapropisms. Guano, whose name in itself raises infantile/scatological connotations, is a military man, a major in the U.S. Army, and yet he appears to have little control over language. In one of the film's most comedic scenes Guano tells Mandrake: "I think you're some kind of deviated prevert. And I think General Ripper found out about your perversion, and that you were organizing some kind of mutiny of preverts." Guano is not alone, the majority of the military men in the film appear to be unable to linguistically operate in a rational way; only the president (the ridiculously named Merkin Muffley) and Group Captain Lionel Mandrake, appear to be in control of their linguistic utterances. In contrast to this, all the other characters in the film appear to have little grasp of the situations they find themselves in and little grasp of the language they use.

In terms of narrative itself, the film was of particular interest in its use of space and location. Unlike the rest of Kubrick's work, the narrative of the film was confined to just three main settings, with each of these settings running within a parallel chronology to the others. In addition, the running time of the film appeared to be exactly that of the narrative being told. Thus the same clock was ticking in each of the three main spheres of action, adding to the sense of documentary realism the film possessed. In contrast to this, one element of the film's success lay in the absurdity of its characters, this being in direct opposition to the harsh and grotesque realism of the worlds they inhabited. As Lee Hill noted: "*Dr. Strangelove* may have sounded absurd, but it looked all too real."[68]

In this sense a significant part of the film's success might be seen to derive from the astute casting decisions made by Kubrick. It is perhaps worth noting this facet of Kubrick's filmmaking, how one key to an understanding of Kubrick's work was his (often) near-infallible choice in casting decisions.[69] Here, in *Dr. Strangelove*, it is difficult to envisage any role in the film being played to better effect than in the actors actually playing them. Of course, Kubrick had the significant advantage of Peter Sellers playing multiple roles in the film: the prissy R.A.F. group captain, the ex–Nazi megalomaniac and the ineffectual, U.S. president. (Kubrick's original intention, of having Sellers play the fourth role of Major Kong, meant Sellers would have been present in all three main spheres of action, and on screen for almost the whole of the film's running time. This may have afforded the advantage of adding a still further degree of distortion to the narrative, a further unsettling element in the *mise-en-scène* for the audience to deal with. In other words, the surreal effect of having the same actor — under differing disguise — in almost every frame and scene of the film. However, it is probable that Slim Pickens was ultimately better suited than Sellers for the role of Kong, specifically in the final image of Kong riding the bomb like a bronco— this suited Pickens's persona from the numerous westerns he had appeared in, not to mention his early experiences as a rodeo rider. See Appendix 3 for a further discussion of casting decisions in the film.)

The narrative tension the film achieved was derived, for the most part, via the sense of miscommunication between the three main spheres of action. The three specific settings: the War Room, Burpelson Air Base and Major Kong's B52, were all completely isolated from each other, with each having specific problems in communicating with one another. Of course, the theme of miscommunication was one that can be traced throughout Kubrick's work as a whole; but here in *Dr. Strangelove* it is enhance and exaggerated. In *Dr. Strangelove* communication is invariably foiled: epitomized by Mandrake having to appropriate money from the Coca-Cola machine in order to phone the president with the recall code. In a similar manner it is significant to note that most of the mechanical devices in the film turn against their makers; from the telephone Mandrake cannot get to work, to coffee spilt on the CRM 114, to the bomb doors failing to open, to the misapplication of the Doomsday Weapon. The lesson here would appear to be that if human plans can fail they will fail, perhaps *the* most ubiquitous theme in Kubrick's work.

Kubrick had filmed *Dr. Strangelove* relatively quickly, from January 28 to April 23, 1963, although he took a further painstaking eight months to edit it.[70] However, while Kubrick may have made the film within the presidency of John F. Kennedy, it was released in the wake of Kennedy's death. A special preview of the film, at Loew's Opheum in New York City, at 8:30 P.M. on the evening of November 22, 1963, had to be canceled because of the assassination.[71] The assassination also caused minor changes to be made in the film: a line by Major Kong had to be changed; after Kong had recited the long list of items in the Survival Kit he had originally said: "Gee, a fella could have a pretty good weekend in Dallas with all that stuff." In the light of Dallas's newly found gruesome connotations the line had to be changed to: "a pretty good weekend in Vegas." In a similar way Kubrick's decision to cut the custard pie scene at the film's conclusion may have been further influenced by Kennedy's death — such a burlesque, containing an albeit fictitious president, in such a farcical and risible scenario, may not have seemed entirely appropriate. However, in the sense of the "Camelot" effect of Kennedy's presidency, one might argue that Kubrick may not have had the confidence of setting a film about nuclear war within the genre of black comedy, had it not been grounded in the relatively optimistic and liberal mode of the Kennedy administration. In any case, history would prove such an optimism unfounded. Kubrick's work was never to find a way of engaging with the tragic events in Dallas, the closest approach was perhaps the 1968 setting of *Full Metal Jacket*, a war that, more than likely, would not have come to pass, had Kennedy escaped the assassin's bullets in Dallas.[72]

The film ended with a series of cataclysmic explosions, representing the detonation of the Doomsday Weapon and presumably the end of all human life on the surface of planet Earth. In a final satiric rejoinder, Kubrick chose to accompany these scenes with Vera Lynn singing "We'll Meet Again" on the soundtrack. As such, it was a way of offering a certain ironic and lyrical reference to the fate of the world. In its original context, as one of the most anthemic songs of World War II, the song had possessed a resilient optimism, redolent in such lines as: "When the blue skies drive the dark clouds away." However, within the context of an envisaged post–World War III setting, this seemed something of a forlorn hope. The ending of the film, with its multiple nuclear explosions, thus offered a final bitter satiric gesture; a metaphor of sexual release and climax (granting General Ripper's wish of an ultimate loss of essence) that was far from the optimistic tone of the song's original setting. There would be no blue skies to drive the dark clouds away, only the Doomsday Machine's lethal cloud of Cobalt-Thorium-G, to enshroud the world for the next 93 years.[73]

Kubrick's decision to conclude his film with such an anthemic song from World War II offers an apt way in which to begin to forge a final summation of *Dr. Strangelove*. It might reasonably be argued that this was a film fully redolent of Theodor Adorno's inscription, alluded to at the beginning of this chapter: that there was a "holy dread" preventing the artist from fully confronting certain facets of human behavior. In other words, Kubrick made a film about a potential nuclear holocaust because there was no way of confronting *the* Holocaust. It would appear fair to suggest that this was a consistent dichotomy Kubrick faced, and, furthermore, one he was never able to fully reconcile within his art. Instead, he forged and channeled other areas, one of which being the incisive satire of *Dr. Strangelove*; a film that has found its way into the *zeitgeist*.[74] A diverse range of ubiquitous themes, so redolent in Kubrick's work, were present in the film: the Citadel, intense male homosociality, the use and misuse of language, aberrant sexualities, the exploration of narrative itself — all were clearly apparent in the film. However, perhaps the most overarching theme of the way the memory of the Holocaust has haunted Kubrick's work that was, ultimately, most significant. This was clearly encapsulated in the last spoken words of the film: "*Mein Führer*, I can walk."[75] In Kubrick's next film, *2001: A Space Odyssey*, there would be a complete change of approach, in this film, arguably one of Kubrick's greatest masterpieces, a much more optimistic view of humanity would be put forward, as will be explored in the next chapter.

CHAPTER 3

2001: A Space Odyssey

To Infinity and Beyond

However vast the darkness, we must supply our own light— Stanley Kubrick

The actual year of 2001 was to be somewhat different to the year Stanley Kubrick and Arthur C. Clarke envisaged when they started work on the film, *2001: A Space Odyssey,* in April 1964. The iconic memory of the historical year of 2001 would become one in which hijacked planes, full of high-octane fuel, exploded as they hit the Twin Towers; far from iconic images of revolving space stations, the Hal 9000 computer, the Star Gate, the Star-Child and so on.[1] Thus in many ways *2001: A Space Odyssey* failed to achieve its vision of the future; for example, space travel has not developed to the extent depicted in the film, the conflict between the USA and the USSR did not prevail beyond the late 1980s, computer science has not developed as quickly and so on. However, it is perhaps important to note that prophecy was not the main concern, nor the main artistic legacy of the film.[2] Instead the film allowed Kubrick to explore some of his usual thematic concerns, albeit placed here in a more epic forum; ubiquitous themes consisting of: masculine violence, Freudian relationships, the Citadel, the only child, intimate and public spaces, the flawed plan, an exploration of narrative itself. In *2001* all of these themes can plainly be perceived.

Kubrick had apparently had the idea of making a science fiction film as early as the mid–1950s;[3] however, it would not be until he had completed *Dr. Strangelove,* in 1963, that Kubrick turned his attention to such a project. Kubrick's choice to collaborate with Arthur C. Clarke came about on the advice of Roger Caras, a mutual friend of both Kubrick and Clarke. "Why waste your time," Caras is quoted as saying, on hearing that Kubrick was looking for a science fiction author to work with. "Why not start with the best?"[4] Kubrick followed Caras's advice and wrote to Clarke on March 31, 1964, famously suggesting that they collaborate to make the "proverbial 'really good' science fiction movie." Clarke telegrammed back and the two men first met on April 22, 1964, at Trader Vic's in the Plaza Hotel, New York City.

Whether Clarke was aware, at this early stage, of just how ambitious were Kubrick's aims in making the "proverbially good science fiction movie," is uncertain. Kubrick was interested in working within the genre of science fiction; but, as usual, he was also interested in extending its boundaries. Thus, within the bounds of the generic science fiction film, he was intent on forging a contemporary "celluloid myth,"[5] attempting to portray nothing less than the full story of mankind's evolution, from beginning to end, from birth to death. It is possible that, at this early stage, Kubrick was contemplating the mythic scope of Clarke's 1954 novel, *Childhood's End,* indeed it might be argued that this novel by Clarke has always been the underlying inspiration for the film. *Childhood's End,* one of Clarke's most profound works (and arguably one of the most profound works of 20th century science fiction) has the same underlying plot as Clarke and Kubrick's resultant film; that of confronting the next stage of man's evolution, what in *Childhood's End* Clarke referred to as "the Overmind." The novel takes man from his beginning to his end, its *denouement* being the merging of mankind into a higher life form, comparable to the emotional force at the close of the film, with the appearance of the Star-Child.[6]

David Storey, a postmodernist theorist, has argued:

> The purpose of myth is to make the world explicable, to magically resolve its problems and contradictions ... myths are stories we tell ourselves as a culture in order to banish contradictions and make the world understandable and therefore habitable; they attempt to put us at peace with ourselves and our existence.[7]

From this perspective the ambition of Kubrick (and, to a certain extent, Clarke) becomes clear, an explicit intention of *2001: A Space Odyssey* was the desire to create a myth, a way of offering at least an explanation of some kind for the inexplicable aspects of human evolution.[8]

The mythic derivation for the film was clear and obvious, the title gestured toward Homer's *Odyssey,* albeit updated into the space age.[9] Thus *The Odyssey,* a seminal work within Western culture, was used in a modern context — to create a modern myth. There are a diverse range of inferences in the film that point toward a Homeric context, not the least being the issue of masculine travel and the desire for adventure; but one might, for example, also point toward the noise the monolith emits — in a sense it is a siren call, but it is also a Siren call; likewise, it is clear that David Bowman responds to

Homeric traditions in his warrior name,[10] the single red eye of Hal[11] could be seen as alluding to the one-eyed Cyclops of Homer,[12] even the rolling rocks of the Odyssey is gestured by the brief scene of meteorites hurtling past the Discovery.[13]

One of the other ways in which Kubrick sought to give the film a mythic resonance can be seen in his approach to narrative structure. It could be argued that *2001: A Space Odyssey* was one of Kubrick's most ambitious exercises in cinematic narrative, the film that possessed his most "radically unconventional narrative."[14] In a particular sense it represented Kubrick's most concerted attempt to subvert the conventional ways of telling stories within feature films, to create both a non-linear and a non-verbal cinematic experience.[15] In the light of Kubrick's well-known respect and appreciation of silent cinema, one might speculate as to whether he may have considered making a completely silent, or at least a completely non-verbal film.[16] The use of title cards, the lack of a voice-over narration, the use of montage (specifically during Floyd's trip to the moon on the Orion), the open textual ambiguities, the apparent lack of character motivation, the equivocal ending, together with the minimalist dialogue, might all be seen as an attempt to break free of the confines of "the three-act play,"[17] and, perhaps more significantly, all pointed to a move toward a silent cinematic discourse. As has often been noted, there is little dialogue in the film, less than half the film contains dialogue, and such dialogue is often deliberately insignificant and banal. On the one hand this might be seen as pointing to Kubrick's overall distrust of language in his work; however, there is also the point that Kubrick may have at least been attempting to move toward making what would probably have been the first silent film in a "post-talkie" world.[18]

Thus *2001* can be read as a radical break with cinematic narrative tradition, an attempt to remove itself from a conventional way of telling a cinematic story. It was a "new way of assimilating narrative," it was not "an articulated plot," but "a succession of vivid moments."[19] Kubrick's celebrated notion of narrative as a series of "non submersible units" is potentially of relevance here; Kubrick often spoke of approaching cinematic narrative in this way and, in the case of the narrative structure of *2001,* one might perceive of four such units. However, of significance to the originality of the film's narrative discourse, was the contrivance of having each of the four parts of the film bisected by a clear if allusive narrative ellipsis. The four sections of the film: "The Dawn of Man," an untitled second section, the third section, "Jupiter Mission — 18 Months Later," and finally, "Jupiter and Beyond the Infinite," were each separated by a narrative ellipsis. The most famous one occurring between the first and second parts, what has been called "the most audacious match cut in cinema history,"[20] the famous jump cut from stone-age bone to space-age orbiting satellite. Here, with a degree of narrative economy, Kubrick managed to compress four million years of human evolution into 1/24th of a second of film time; what Luis M. Garcia-Mainar called "the longest temporal ellipsis in the history of cinema."[21] In this precise way, and in the light of seeing ways of forging new narrative strategies, it is possible to perceive here of Kubrick attempting to push the boundaries of conventional storytelling still further; in other words, to instill the maximum amount of narrative information into the minimum amount of time and space.

In contrast to the rapidity of design within examples of narrative ellipsis, the film was accused of having an uncompromising slowness. In one sense this would seem to have been deliberate, a part of Kubrick's specific aim to work within a discourse pointing more to the silent film; together with a further move away from a conventional use of dialogue. In another sense it appears to have simply been a deliberate attempt to offer narrative detail at a slower rate. The most extreme example of such narrative slowness coming in the Star Gate sequence, as Luis M. Garcia-Mainar commented: "The Star Gate sequence is astonishingly long if compared to the amount of information it gives. For many viewers the sequence becomes unbearably distended to the point of causing boredom."[22]

The actual reasons why Kubrick chose such a technique remain obscure; however, the deliberate slowness of the film, the ambition to envelop it with mythic proportions and the innovative narrative structure appeared to perplex many of the film's immediate critics. To Andrew Sarris, Kubrick had an "inability to tell a story on the screen with coherence and a consistent point of view,"[23] such a comment being indicative of the degree of misunderstanding the film initially received, insomuch as narrative ambiguity was arguably just what Kubrick was attempting to achieve. A number of other mainstream critics formed a similar judgment: Pauline Kael called the film "a monumentally unimaginative movie," Stanley Kauffman spoke of "a major disappointment," to Renata Adler the film was, "incredibly boring," while to the aforementioned Andrew Sarris the film was, in a final summary "a disaster."[24] However, as Michel Ciment noted: "Who now remembers the firing squad directed at *2001: A Space Odyssey* by New York's 'establishment.'"[25] This immediate and predominantly negative critical response did not seem to damage the film, insomuch as the older critical response did not reflect the response of a predominantly younger audience. However, perhaps of greater lasting significance, was the response of Kubrick himself; as is well known he simply stopped taking such critics seriously after the debacle of the initial critical receptions of *2001*.[26]

One of the reasons the early critics may have found the film somewhere between "the hypnotic" and the "immensely boring," possibly lay in the fact that they experienced the earlier, and much rarer, 156-minute version of the film. It is a well-known fact that Kubrick re-edited the film, to 141 minutes, shortly after its initial screenings in New York, in early April 1968. Gene Phillips was one of those critics to have had the opportunity of seeing the initial longer version of the film and (obviously) the later edited version. Hence his comments are pertinent:

> Having seen both versions of the film, I fully agree with all of the director's minor revisions. It is a tribute to his skill as an editor that, while I was aware that the running time was shorter when I saw the film for a second time, I could not guess where the cuts had been made.[27]

In a similar sense, Michaela Williams spoke of: "thirty delicate excisions" in which the scars were "visible in the present 2 hour 21 minute version only, as they say in the cosmetic surgery business, if you know the operation was made."[28] (The details of those scenes omitted from the film fall into two categories: those cuts made before and post the premiere. The omitted scenes before the premiere included: Floyd calling Macy's from the space station to order a bush baby, scenes at Clavius showing domestic and social life, scenes on *Discovery* showing a piano, a table-tennis table, a shower, etc. The omitted scenes after the premiere included: shots from the Dawn of Man, footage of Poole jogging in the centrifuge, Bowman looking for antenna spare parts in a storage area, Hal running down Poole's radio before the murder and shots from Poole's space walk before his murder.)

Kubrick himself commented on the reasons for his decision to re-edit the film:

> I made all the cuts in *2001* at no one's request. I had not had an opportunity to see the film complete with music, sound effects etc., until about a week before it opened and it needs a few runnings to decide finally how long things should be.[29]

The fact that the version of the film most critics initially saw was the longer, 156-minute version is therefore relevant. It would seem fair to suggest that the original version of the film *was* too long and too slow. However, the failure of the critics to fully appreciate *2001* arguably had a further, more overarching reason. Joseph Gelmis:

> When a film of such extraordinary originality as Stanley Kubrick's *2001: A Space Odyssey* comes along it upsets the members of the critical establishment because it exists outside their framework of apprehending and describing movies.[30]

In other words, the average film critic of the time simply did not have the requisite time or space to fully embrace such a film. John Allen: "For one thing, *2001* is so full of such touches of cinematic artistry and sleight of hand as to require that a book, rather than an essay, be written."[31]

*   *   *

Thus one might observe how *2001* was intent on telling its story in another way, creating what was arguably Kubrick's most original and most challenging film. As Alexander Walker put it: "Kubrick took the risk of making the first mainstream film that required an act of continuous inference from those who went to see it."[32] In this sense, the film might be seen as an experiment in pure cinema, a film that attempted to speak the "pure language of cinema."[33] There was narrative interest, but it was not posed in a conventional way, rather it was generated by the sheer mythic breadth of the story Kubrick (and Clarke) created.

All of this is not to say, as suggested at the start of this chapter, that Kubrick's thematical interests were not present in the film. Such thematical elements were present, not least within an underlying sexual subtext. Human sexuality, always one of the primary subtexts in Kubrick's work, was fully apparent here in *2001*. Freud, always "relevant to Kubrick's *oeuvre*,"[34] is an apt place in which to start. One might note that all of Freud's three stages of human development were represented in the film: oral, anal and genital. For example, eating is an intended and deliberate concern in each of the four parts of the film.[35] The apes in the Dawn of Man sequence are shown devouring animal flesh; Heywood Floyd eats throughout his journey into space; Bowman and Poole are shown eating "space-food" on the *Discovery*; and finally, Bowman partakes of a "Last Supper" in the film's final sequence. Thus one could interpret a deliberate indication into Freudian notions relevant to the pleasures of eating and oral activity. In terms of the anal stage of development, one might argue that the film's one intentionally humorous scene, Heywood Floyd's reading of the instructions for the Zero Gravity Toilet, was a conscious pointer toward a Freudian element.[36] Note also, that Rachel, Squirt's babysitter, is "in the bathroom" when Floyd calls home, and lastly, that Bowman walks into a decidedly stylized bathroom at the film's conclusion."[37] (In terms of genital development, this was presented in an entirely different way, as is discussed below.)

Thus, within such an arena of Freudian discourse, we might note how the "men" of the space-age seem almost infantile; insomuch as they eat what appears to be baby food; they appear to require toilet training (at least in space); and, in addition, they are tied to a parental figure, in the shape of Hal. However, while the film seems enthusiastic to depict oral and anal stages of human development — eating and defecation — it seems more reluctant to portray the genital stage of sexuality. There is, for example, a decided lack of women in the film and conventional heterosexual relationships would appear to be purposefully avoided. As Arthur C. Clarke commented: "There will be no women among those who make the trip.... We weren't going to have any blonde stowaway in the airlock."[38] Also, it might be noted how few of the characters in the film appear to be sexually viable: Floyd wants to speak to his wife but she has "gone out shopping," and he ends up having an inane conversation with his daughter,[39] while Elena, the female Russian scientist on the space station, tells Floyd she does not see much of her husband, and finally — neither Bowman nor Poole appear to have any sexual ties— at least none that are ever alluded to.

The women we see in space appeared to be merely stewardesses, thus while the film attempted to look forward to the future, attempting to depict some of the changes in the way we saw ourselves and the world, in some significant ways it did not wholly succeed. In other words, in terms of a feminist approach, the film scarcely seemed to envisage the ways in which the complacencies of patriarchy might be challenged in the next 30 to 40 years. As Piers Bizony commented: "From the perspective of 1968 when 2001 was released, there is no hint that women might actually fly a spacecraft instead of serving food.[40] In Arthur C. Clarke's novel, an even more pronounced if benign sexist discourse prevailed; for example, Clarke, casually talking of the space pods: "They were usually christened with feminine names, perhaps in recognition of the fact that their personalities were sometimes slightly unpredictable."[41] Hence the novel and the film might be interpreted as being at some distance from a feminist viewpoint.

Shortly after the release of the film, Kubrick was questioned on the role of women in the film:

> Q. The role of women is not brought into *2001* much. Was there a specific reason why?
> A. No, it's just in telling the story women didn't seem to have a lot to do with it.
> Q. Well, the astronauts being so well equipped for their voyage into space, sex is the only thing that's missing.
> A. Well, you obviously aren't going to put a woman on the crew. It's a problem that they've never really gone into. What will deep-space missions be like, and how will the crew take care of their sex urges? It's very unlikely that they'll do it by providing a mixed crew.[42]

All of this adds weight to the idea that a great majority of the narrative spaces in Kubrick's work point, albeit obliquely, to a more homosocial (and even homoerotic) arena than a heterosexual one.[43] As previously intimated, none of the male characters in the film have any sense of a romantic attachment; thus while the film may claim to be an odyssey, there are no indications of a Penelope, a Molly Bloom or even an Alice Harford awaiting the return of the masculine adventurers.[44] To reiterate, in her book, *Between Men: English Literature and Male Homosocial Desire*, Eve Kosofsky Sedgwick (famously) argued that patriarchy requires intense male homosocial bonding, a bonding that is both rigidly homophobic and repressively homoerotic; patriarchy being compelled in bringing men together but disallowing overt mutual sexuality. A reading of the film in this light (along with the majority of Kubrick's other works) thus offers at least some degree of an explanation for the persistent absence of women and the persistent presence of masculine couples.

Leslie Fiedler's argument, in his book *Love and Death in the American Novel,* is perhaps again relevant here. Fiedler's idea of the masculine couple, bound together within a quest narrative, fearing women and desiring each other in a "pseudo-marriage of males."[45] To repeat: the pseudo-marriage of males being such pairings from literature and popular culture as: Huck Finn and Tom Sawyer, the Lone Ranger and Tonto, Don Quixote and Sancho Panza, Robinson Crusoe and Man Friday, Ishmael and Queequeg, Hawkeye and Chingachgook, Holmes and Watson, Dean Moriarty and Sal Paradise, even Captain Kirk and Mr. Spock. Fiedler's ideas can be seen repeatedly in Kubrick's work; here, in *2001,* David Bowman and Frank Poole are the homosocial couple[46] who go on a masculine journey together; elsewhere in Kubrick's canon this being seen in the pairings of: Joker and Rafterman, Humbert and Quilty, Barry and the Chevalier, Alex and his droogs, David and Teddy and so on.

In a certain sense, and in such a specific context, *2001* might thus be said to resemble a Western; as Barry Keith Grant, writing on the sexual politics of the film, put it:

> Outer space, like the frontier in the western genre, is a dangerous place that requires the fortitude of men to traverse it ... [thus depicting] the dread of femininity and homoerotic desire within stories of male adventure.[47]

Or, as Jane Tomkins, who has written extensively on the Western, argued:

> The hero [of the Western] frequently forms a bond with another man — sometimes his rival, more often his comrade — a bond that is more important than any relationship he has with a woman and is frequently tinged with homo-eroticism.[48]

Or, in turn, to return to Fiedler's argument:

> The typical male protagonist of our fiction has been a man on the run, harried into the forest and out to sea, down the river, or into combat — anywhere to avoid "civilization," which is to say, the confrontation of a man and woman which leads to sex, marriage and responsibility.[49]

This can be seen most typically in the hero of the Western film, the stereotype of a man walking away, into the sunset, into a "dying star." Here in Fiedler's argument there is a sense of a man escaping the world of women and domesticity and the compromise they pose; instead men can escape to the wilderness, with its promise of adventure among other men. In this sense the West might be seen as an invitation to experience a new Eden, or at least to experience a landscape unstained and unsullied, a new frontier, whether it be in the wilderness of the Western or here, in *2001*, in the wilderness of space.

In support of a homosocial reading of the film, one might point to the way in which conventional sexuality is deliberately and consistently undermined by the satiric metaphors of phallic and vaginal symbols present throughout the film. For example, one might look to Moon-watcher's phallic bone, to Heywood Floyd's pen, to the docking spaceships, to the shape of the *Discovery* and so on. Such symbols are sometimes grandly allegorical, but often humorously subversive. For example, Floyd's floating pen could be seen as speaking of sexual dysfunction; a metaphor of phallic insignificance, a metaphor for the impotence of masculinity in the film. One notes here the limp and decidedly detumescent arm of Floyd and his wayward pen, compared to Moon-watcher's decidedly virile arm and weapon; the "burst of inchoate triumph"[50] as Moon-watcher hurls the animal femur into the air, compared to Floyd's decidedly unheroic pen.[51]

In addition, one clear metaphor within the sexual imagery of the film was concerned with an allegory of conception, albeit again in a somewhat satiric setting. Michel Ciment has commented how Bowman's rebirth as a star child was prefigured in the "erotic and genital visions" portrayed throughout the voyage.[52] Ciment is probably referring here to the phallic imagery inherent in the design of the *Discovery*, as alluded to above. In addition, one might consider the spermatic imagery of the space pod leaving the bulbous head of the phallic-shaped *Discovery* to "enter" the vaginal Star Gate. Such an interpretation is enhanced if one considers that the journey of the space pod leads to a womblike environment in the final room, which will eventually produce the conception of the embryonic Star Child. One could go further: birth and conception symbolism can also be seen within the detail of Bowman forgetting his helmet when he attempts to rescue Poole; the fact that Bowman's head is uncovered, without his helmet, points to the idea of his phallic body, unsheathed, as if without a prophylactic covering, as he forcibly penetrates the *Discovery* in the explosive manner depicted in the film.[53] Thus Bowman's penetration of the mother ship becomes both phallic and potent.[54]

Carolyn Geduld extrapolated upon this interpretation by seeing sexual symbolism within the idea of sperm and ova on a much wider scale; according to Geduld: "The entire universe is made to seem an outsized uterus, a sanctuary for the fetal life-force that is still embryonic after billions of years of existence."[55] In a similar way Geoffrey Cocks argued that: "The journey through the Star Gate is clearly a scene of copulation and fertilization ... a masculine means to usurp female reproductive powers."[56] In this sense the Star Child appears to be that of a virgin birth, the Star Child has no mother, hence there is the sense of it being an asexual male birth. Thus, there is an almost risible subtext in the idea of two men, Bowman and Poole, traveling into space in a decidedly phallic spaceship, having a cumulative copulatory experience in the Star Gate, with the eventual resolution of the birth of a baby.[57] In this sense the caption of this section of the film: "Jupiter Mission — 18 Months Later," resonates with numerical symbolism, as if to suggest the 18 months represents two sets of a gestative nine months, one for each of the two astronauts on the Discovery.[58]

In the context of a homosocial reading of the film, one cannot fail but bring up the character of Hal. A so-called "gay" component to Hal's makeup has often been noted. For example, Charles Champlin, of *The Los Angeles Times*, referred to "a rather epicene talking computer named Hal,"[59] to Michaela Williams, of *The Chicago Daily News*, Douglas Rain was present as "the (gay?) voice of Hal the computer,"[60] while to Joseph Morgenstern, of *Newsweek*, Hal "carries on like an injured party in a homosexual spat."[61] In addition, a number of critics seem to have been influenced by Hal's voice; Jerome Agel informs that Kubrick was "looking for an unctuous, patronizing, neuter quality,"[62] an uncredited reviewer from *Time* thought Hal was "possessed of a wistful, androgynous voice,"[63] while Susan White claimed: "Hal's voice is equivocally gendered."[64]

In an interview with Joseph Gelmis, in 1970, Kubrick was questioned on this issue:

Gelmis: Some critics have detected in Hal's wheedling voice an undertone of homosexuality. Was that intended?
Kubrick: No, I think it's become something of a parlor game for some people to read that kind of thing into everything they encounter. Hal was a "straight" computer.[65]

However, even Kubrick's insistence of Hal being "a straight computer" would appear to imply Hal at least had a sexuality of some kind; and, in any case, authorial intent is not the significant issue here. Hence it is perfectly feasible to perceive of Hal as being "gay" insomuch as a close textual reading of both the film and the novel would at least appear to suggest this. In fact, in the novel, Arthur C. Clarke placed what seemed to be intentional clues, noting at one point, for example, that "[Hal] had been living a lie."[66] To be living a lie is a flexible phrase, but the reader may well note the potential meaning of a same-sex fixated computer's programs going awry via a sense of sexual jealousy.[67] In the film there are similar indicators, albeit of a more subtle kind; for example, during the television interview with the BBC, Hal comments that he has "a stimulating relationship with Dr. Poole," while Bowman later says of Hal: "I can't put my finger on it, but I sense something strange about him."[68]

Hence it would seem fair to suggest that there are subtle indicators that question Hal's sexuality. Of course, one might question whether a machine, a computer, a synthetic intelligence, could have a sexual identity, still less an ambiguous sexual identity. This is a difficult area to fully respond to, but within the narrative discourse of the film it would at least appear to be a reasonable one to explore. Hal is the one character in the film that expresses any kind of emotion, the one character that we, as an audience, emotionally identify with. Bowman and Poole are human beings, but they are so emotionless as to be machine-like, while Hal is a machine that assumes the emotional constituents of what it means to be a human being.

What we can be sure of is that Hal is a sentient being; this was plainly the intent of Kubrick and Clarke's script. It is clear that Hal had emotions, whether they may be programmed or actual emotions; as Bowman tells us in the film: "He acts like he has genuine emotions. Of course, he's programmed that way to make it easier for us to talk to him." However, emotions, whether they are programmed or not, tend to develop and evolve and to forge a life of their own. Thus Hal can be seen as exhibiting feelings of pride, envy, fear, and even love, all of which culminate in his homicidal attack on the crew, an action which is readily explained by the primary instinct of any sentient life-form: that of self-preservation. In what is arguably the film's most poignant scene, his own death, Hal says: "I'm afraid, Dave," and goes on: "I can feel it. My mind is going ... I can feel it ... I'm afraid." Hal feels, Hal fears, Hal has real emotions in a way no one else in the film admits to. Hence it is a culminative moment, potentially one of the most emotionally moving moments anywhere in Kubrick's work. Michael Herr: "Not even Bergman or Bresson showed more suffering in their films.... In *2001*, even the last words of a dying ... computer are pitiful."[69]

Kubrick and Clarke's decision to imbue emotion into a computer, such as Hal, is a significant element in the narrative. Obviously, there were dramatic implications, the need to inject climactic tension into the film. However, it is possible to infer that Clarke especially, and Kubrick as well, were inferring that synthetic intelligence with emotions was the most likely technological and evolutionary outcome, if not by the year 2001 itself, then in time to come. In any case, Hal represents the most "human" character in the film, a character full of ambiguities and neuroses and anxieties, to the extent that he eventually descends into mental instability, becoming both paranoid and homicidal. When Hal sings: "I'm half crazy, all for the love of you" in a certain sense he is telling us the literal truth. Thus one of the main concerns of the middle part of the film points to the question: why does Hal lose his mental stability? The obvious interpretation would be to assume it was the result of conflicting programming. The fact that Hal knows the mission's actual purpose (a response to the discovery of the monolith on the moon and hence knowledge that alien intelligence had once visited the solar system) and the fact that he has to keep this information secret could be seen as setting up an insecurity in his "mind." In other words, Hal is forced to perjure himself, to falsify, to dissemble; and this, we can presume, sets up a conflict of interests. Hal appears to be trying to work this out when he says to Bowman: "In view of some of the things that have happened I find them difficult to put out of my mind." Hal is referring to the rumors from the Moon — and yet if Hal knows the truth about the discovery of TMA1, but he cannot tell Bowman and Poole, then he is forced to begin weaving "a tangled web." "I never gave these stories much credence," says Hal, while being fully aware of the credence of the stories in question. Thus, Hal has been programmed to lie, and this renders him "half crazy." Hence the contrary programming generates complexes within Hal; he appears to become first neurotic, then paranoiac and finally, psychotic, which leads to his acts of murder and, ultimately, his own demise.

In addition to this, one presumes such a sense of interior contradiction has caused Hal, the infallible machine, to make a mistake and to predict the AE35 unit will fail. Out of hubris Hal is then locked into maintaining this prediction, his pride in being a perfect machine, an infallible computer, an entity incapable of making a mistake, becoming his "fatal flaw." Hal must cover up his error,[70] and when this is discovered and Bowman and Poole consider disconnecting him, then Hal has no choice but to make drastic plans, plans that lead him to start killing the crew. It is the only rational decision he can make if he is to survive. In Hal's rational perspective such violence differs little from the violence committed by Moon-Watcher at the waterhole; it is simply the "survival of the fittest."

By way of a final word on Hal, the derivation of his name is of interest and perhaps worthy of comment. The common suggestion that it was a play on "IBM," each letter being one letter back in the alphabet, would appear to be simple coincidence. IBM computers are in evidence in the film, but all one needs to do is note the practical difficulty Kubrick and Clarke would have had in finding the name, even if they had wanted to encode a hidden satiric wordplay at IBM's expense. The other alternative, Clarke's supposed acronym of *H*euristically programmed *A*lgorithmic Computer, appears somewhat contrived and unconvincing. However, a more convincing derivation (and one that to my knowledge has not been mentioned previously) is the sense in which Hal's name may have been a tribute to one of Clarke's mentors: the scientist: J.B.S. Haldane. John Burdon Sanderson Haldane was primarily a biologist who published a wide and diverse range of significant works on heredity and ethics. He appears consistently throughout Clarke's nonfiction writings, as a core influence and, at times, almost as a father figure. An apt example being the chapter "Haldane and Space," from Clarke's *Report on Planet Three and Other Speculations*,[71] herein Clarke states Haldane was "the finest intellect it has ever been my privilege to know."[72] Finally, one might note Haldane died in 1964, the same year Hal was "born."[73]

*   *   *

The general sense of paranoia, of Hal seeing conspiracies against him, raises the idea of a general sense of conspiracy in the film as a whole. In other words, the general sense in which a number of characters in the film (along with us, the audience) have not been fully informed of the whole story. "I am not at liberty to discuss this," says Floyd to the Soviet scientists early on in the film, and, in a sense, Kubrick chose not to be at liberty to offer a full disclosure of the film's narrative to his audience. Hal may sing: "Give me your answer, do," but the film consistently refuses to fulfill this interdiction. Hal's line may thus be seen as pointing, self-referentially, to the desire of the audience to understand the meaning of the film's mysteries, but these are mysteries that are continuously withheld. There are big questions, such as: what does the monolith represent, why does Hal become mentally unstable, what is the meaning of the room at the end; along with lesser, but nonetheless, thought-provoking questions; such as: why is Heywood Floyd alone on what appears to be an otherwise regularly scheduled flight?[74] It is as if Kubrick (and Clarke) deliberately chose to create underlying ambiguities, as if to purposefully disorientate their audience, creating an "otherness" that has perhaps given the film part of its lasting appeal.

However, in wider terms, disregarding the purposeful ambiguities of the plot, one might say that if the film was specifically "about" anything, it was about evolution. As Daniel De Vries put it, *2001* was "a scripture of the human race's evolution from ape to man to god."[75] Such an idea is inherent in the numerical aspect of the film's title, the idea of a new start, of the clock starting again at 001, and, as such, the theme of evolution was ubiquitous throughout the film. One might note how the film opens with a perfect conjunction of earth, sun and moon,[76] this image being suggestive of the film's main theme: evolution and order, as against chaos and entropy. In a sense the film has a certain evolutionary linearity, as it begins (somewhat portentously entitled) with "The Dawn of Man." The opening part of the film depicts man's ancestors, some three to four million years in the past; the significant issue being that it was human aggression, coupled with intelligence that was key in terms of human evolution. As previously alluded, in relation to Hal, Kubrick puts forward a specifically Darwinian universe: the survival of the fittest. Moon-Watcher and the fellow members of his tribe have the predicament of surviving in a ruthless world, and it is not so large a jump to Alex and his droogs, or Joker and his "grunts," these are men whose instincts are quintessentially those to hunt down and kill. Moon-Watcher (his Biblical name might have been Cain) is simply the first in a long line of killers.

This sense of an almost formalized violence is repeated throughout the film, beginning with the tribal battles over Moon-Watcher's water hole, continuing via the national rivalry between the USA and USSR, the martial arts contest on television, Poole's shadow boxing around the *Discovery*, the game of chess between Dave and Hal,[77] and finally, the dual to the death between Dave and Hal. As Michel Chion noted:

> The little pond is also the focus of a territorial rivalry between clans (our first fights are with our brothers, suggests Kubrick), which announces the centrality of war in future human history.[78]

In contrast to this, to cultural critic Camille Paglia, the moment of triumph when Moon-Watcher discovers the bone as weapon, implicates all human civilization, art and culture:

> It takes in all creation, the great themes of nature and art, and talks about the limits of the human mind. It has such a visionary vastness that to this day I am in awe of it.[79]

Paglia goes onto link "male testosterone" with a "homicidal impulse" to both "create and to kill"[80]; the notion of linking creativity with violence being a significant issue in the film. We might note the enjoyment and pleasure, the aforementioned "burst of inchoate triumph," the sheer exhilaration Moon-Watcher feels with his new found power; a power that, significantly, finds its ultimate expression in killing.[81] The scene also possesses a feeling of power and exhilaration for us, the audience, possibly because we are all aware how it depicts our beginnings as a species; we celebrate this, no matter the implications of violence that go along with it. In other words, we are ultimately a species of killers, yet we revel in it.

However, in one sense the film offered an optimistic point of view, in that it at least suggested man's propensity for Stone Age violence had lessened in the age of 2001. There is a sense in the film that man has risen above his violent past; this is certainly so within the benevolent gaze of the Star Child, who at least appears—in this elevated evolutionary stage—to be a creature of "good." The corollary being that the cosmos may be inhabited by more highly evolved, non-violent, benign beings.[82] Alternatively, we might note how the Russians on the space station, in a sense, merely represent another tribe at another water hole. We note that there is a veneer of politeness and good manners, but one wonders if the Americans and Russians are very different from Moon-watcher's tribe and the other rival tribe? We might note that Bowman attacks Hal's "brain" in much the same way as Moon-Watcher had battered the rival ape's head, three million years of evolution would not appear to have caused a major change in human aggression.[83] Once again Kubrick would appear to be following a Darwinian discourse: to survive we must fight, and, if necessary, we must kill our enemies.

*   *   *

As previously mentioned, one of the significant ambiguous elements to the film was the monolith. Clarke's novel makes it clear that the monolith was a learning device, a device that teaches Moon-Watcher (and with him the whole of his species) how to use the first tool, the first weapon, the first instrument of murder. The film is not so explicit, but nonetheless this is the clear inference, the monolith represents intelligence, the getting of wisdom. This is compounded by the fact that the monolith resembles the same shape and proportions as the elements of Hal's brain, and could thus be seen as representing, in its precise geometric design, a synthetic intelligence.

In symbolic terms the color of the monolith was of interest, insomuch as its inky blackness seemed resistant to the idea that black represents evil. In other words, the monolith is wholly black and dark, and yet seemingly wholly benign.[84] However, the color and shape of the monolith does bring with it ominous overtones; its appearance cannot help but link it to symbolic echoes of burial, as Clarke puts it in the novel: "It reminded Floyd, somewhat ominously of a giant tombstone."[85] In a similar spatial sense, in terms of the monolith's shape and proportions, Michel Chion commented how the shape of the monolith is reminiscent of a full-length mirror, but a mirror in which one sees nothing.[86] In a sense the monolith could thus be interpreted as a black mirror, the impenetrable black surface being envisaged as a metaphor for textual and cinematic ambiguity. In this sense one might note how the shape of the monolith also resembles the dimensions of a book, or, if turned on its side, a cinema screen.[87] Hence the monolith could be seen as resembling a closed book/screen in the sense it avoids making its meaning explicit, and metaphorically represents the ambivalence apparent throughout the film.

The monolith could be read in other ways; it obviously reverberates with ancient man's predilection for erecting standing stones; as Kubrick himself commented: "I suppose the idea had something to do with the strange sensation one has when the alignment of the sun takes place at Stonehenge."[88] The monolith might even be said to resemble the tablet on which Moses received the Ten Commandments, although here the commandments were decidedly unwritten.[89] In this regard, and also taking into account the way the monolith stands within the landscape of Moon-Watcher's tribe, incongruent and phallic, one might perhaps envisage a representation of Jacques Lacan's "Law of the Father."[90] This is not to say that either Kubrick or Clarke was consciously aware of Lacan's ideas, merely that such an interpretation can be made. Hence the blank face of the monolith, in this case interpreted within a Lacanian discourse, points to the issue of language itself in the film. While language must be envisaged as one of the most significant skills acquired by human beings, one notes that the film continually points to its apparent futility. As previously noted, in the context of Kubrick's desire to make a silent film, the film deliberately eschews the spoken word whenever it can.[91] The first spoken words: "Here you are, sir" are not uttered until about a third of the film's running time has elapsed, and spoken dialogue, as witnessed here and elsewhere, seldom seems to be of any great significance. When language is used it appears to be almost deliberately undermined; for example, we might note how Floyd is congratulated on his "brilliant speech" at Clavius Base, when in reality he has merely mouthed a collection of mostly meaningless clichés and platitudes.[92] In this sense the dialogue in the film is so routinely bland and vapid as to presume a deliberate satiric commentary upon the spoken word. "Hal can you read me?" Bowman says to Hal; with the subtextual point that few people in the film can read one another, and that we, the audience, often have difficulty "reading" what the characters on the screen are talking about. Hence there is a sense in which nearly everyone is detracting and dissembling from a veracious discourse throughout the film. Moon-Watcher hides the purpose of his new weapon from his rivals at the water hole, Floyd is markedly guarded with the Russian scientists in terms of the cover story at Clavius, Dave lies to Hal, Hal lies to Dave, the Monolith never says anything, and the Star Child is beyond any human understanding of language. "I don't think anyone can truthfully answer," says Bowman, discussing whether HAL has emotions, but it is also a line that operates within the discourse of the film as a whole.[93]

The sense in which language continually breaks down in Kubrick's work, not least in *2001*, ties in to another ubiquitous theme (as alluded in the previous chapter), that of the failed plan. The sense of the best laid plans going awry is patently a common thread in Kubrick's work, one of the key ways in which he presented an account of human fallibility. In *2001*, in the various stages of humanity offered, we see how all are prone to human frailty. For example, Moon-Watcher's bone, Floyd's pen, Bowman's glass in the final room, all generally malfunction in some way: the bone splinters, the pen floats free, the glass breaks. In this way such a theme might be said to represent Kubrick's inherent mistrust of technology and the men who use it, the sense that if something can fail it will fail.[94] Furthermore, it is of interest to note how many (if not all) of Kubrick's films have a primary concern with a fall from grace, with a fall from the perfect plan. At times this is a character, at times a system, at times a mechanism of some kind. In *2001* Hal is the obvious example, but the same theme can be found in *The Killing*, in which the perfect heist goes awry, or in *Lolita*, wherein Humbert's attempt to engender a love affair with his nymphet is ultimately doomed to failure, or *Dr. Strangelove*, wherein the fail-safe device of the nuclear deterrent in itself fails, or in *A Clockwork Orange* with the failure of the Ludovico Treatment, or Barry's fall from grace, from being a gentleman in *Barry Lyndon*, and likewise Jack Torrance's descent in *The Shining*, his fall from grace as caretaker, writer, husband, father. It would seem clear that Kubrick was a filmmaker who enjoyed telling stories in which carefully laid plans gradually unravel and fall apart, this being a significant element in *2001: A Space Odyssey*. In a specific sense this could be seen as offering one way of explaining Kubrick's allegedly misanthropic outlook on the world.

The issue of human fallibility might be seen as pointing to the film's intimations (however ambiguous) around the idea of infallibility of a supreme intelligence within the universe. Arthur C. Clarke:

> This is what makes *2001* so unique, I think. It poses metaphysical, philosophical and even religious questions. I don't pretend we have the answers. But the questions are certainly worth thinking about.[95]

Kubrick concurred: "On the deepest psychological level, the film's plot symbolizes the search for God, and it finally postulates what is little less than a scientific definition of God."[96] Thus, in an albeit simplistic interpretation, one could say the film was concerned with a godlike intelligence who leave monoliths to "uplift" less-advanced races it finds in the universe. In one of the key lines of the novel, talking about the evolution of the brain and intelligence, Clarke writes: "And if there was anything beyond that, its name could only be God."[97] Similarly, in 1970, Kubrick told Joseph Gelmis: "The God concept is at the heart of this film."[98] And in a long interview Kubrick gave to *Playboy* magazine in September 1968, he had further expanded on this theme, pointing toward a rational concept of God:

> I don't believe in any of Earth's monotheistic religions, but I do believe that one can construct an intriguing scientific definition of God, once you accept the fact that there are approximately 100 billion stars in our galaxy alone, that each star is a life giving sun and that there are approximately 100 billion galaxies *in the visible universe.*[99]

Kubrick went onto extrapolate on the nature and ultimate expanse of alien intelligence:

> These beings would be gods to the billions of less advanced races in the universe, just as man would appear as a god to an ant that somehow comprehended man's existence.... These entities might be in telepathic communication throughout the cosmos and thus be aware of everything that occurs, tapping every intelligent mind.... They might not be limited by the speed of light and their presence could penetrate to the furthest corners of the universe; they might possess complete mastery over matter and energy; and in their final evolutionary stage, they might develop into an integrated immortal consciousness. They would be incomprehensible to us except as gods.[100]

As far as can be ascertained, Kubrick did not specifically cite Pierre Teilhard de Chardin as an influence on the film; however, Teilhard de Chardin's ideas are clearly of importance within a discussion of the religious aspects apparent within the film.[101] In an earlier interview, from 1966, Kubrick had commented:

> It's generally thought that after a highly developed science gets you past the mortality stage, you become part-animal, part-machine, then all machine.

Eventually, perhaps, pure energy ... pure spirit may be the ultimate form that intelligence would seek.[102]

Such a position on the idea of spiritual evolution lies at the heart of Teil-hard de Chardin's thinking. This philosophical position might be pressed further; one might suggest the reason the Big Bang was an ultimately "per-fect" event (reductively the Bible's "Let there be light") was that the previ-ous universe had evolved into perfection. In other words, one might speculate that a universe, created in a Big Bang, gradually evolves into more and more complex forms. Life slowly emerges on a myriad of planets across the uni-verse and evolves into higher and higher stages, eventually merging into greater intelligences, much in the manner of the Overmind in *Childhood's End,* or the Star Child in *2001.*[103] Such life forms evolve to still higher and higher stages, eventually leaving behind biological or synthetic intelligence, moving toward intelligence aligned within pure spirit form; in Clarke's famous phrase from the novel: "Their thoughts [were contained] for eternity in frozen lattices of light."[104] Thus when such an intelligence is spread throughout the whole universe, and contains the whole universe, then there is no definition to contain it other than that of "God."[105] The universe is then perfected, and, having no reason to continue, it rapidly contracts, into a per-fect "Big Crunch" and the whole process begins again. Thus, or so one might argue, our purpose is perhaps not to revere "God," but to engender a universe within which such a "God" is created.[106]

Moon-Watcher's name is redolent here; Moon-Watcher looks up to the skies as if to associate God as dwelling in Heaven, in the same way as a num-ber of religions envisage God and Heaven as existing at some indeterminate position "out there" in the universe. In this light, an interpretation of the film presents a number of iconic religious images, often specifically Christian. For example, Bowman's last meal in the final room, at the end of the film, resem-bles a Last Supper.[107] Also, one might note how Poole, held in the arms of the space-pod, appears to deliberately resemble a Pietà—the dead Christ being cradled by his mother.[108] Finally, the most iconic religious imagery in the film can arguably be found at the closure, with the appearance of the Star Child.[109] Some critics have seen a specifically Christian iconography here; for exam-ple, Joseph Gelmis: "The evolution appears to be a biblical allusion about how one must be born again as a child before being allowed to enter the kingdom of heaven."[110] It is difficult not to see a sacred quality to the image of the Star Child, the iconic imagery of a holy infant, replete with the aura of a halo. Michael Herr commented:

> I think he made the single most inspired spiritual image in all of film, the Star Child watching with equanimity the timeless empty galaxies of existence-after-existence, waiting patiently again to be born.[111]

The final part of the film, "Jupiter and Beyond the Infinite,"[112] wherein Bowman journeys through the Star Gate to evolve into the Star Child, is perhaps best read as a metaphor. In narrative terms the nine-minute Star Gate sequence is of minimal significance. As previously alluded, many viewers of the film considered the sequence narratively insignificant and a purely visual experience. However, in metaphorical terms the Star Gate might be said to represent a journey toward both Man's origin and destination — back to the womb and forward toward a transcendental experience. As Luis M. Garcia-Mainar comments: "The Star Gate sequence presents us with a flight toward the centre of perspective, toward the vanishing point, in a metaphorical reference to the source of everything."[113] In addition, a psychedelic connotation is not without significance. After Louis Sweeney's famous comment, in the *Christian Science Monitor,* that *2001* was "the ultimate trip," such a connotation became difficult to dismiss. However, Kubrick's response was guarded:

> They [users of psychedelic drugs] seem to develop what I can only describe as an illusion of understanding and oneness with the universe. This is a phenomenon which they can't articulate in any logical way, but which they articulate emotionally. They seem very happy, very content and very pleased with the state of mind, but at the same time they seem totally unaware of the fact that it deprives them of any kind of self-criticism which is, of course, absolutely essential for an artist to have.[114]

The significant point at issue here would appear to rest within Kubrick's interest in constructing a "scientific definition of God," contrasted with his almost complete disavowal of spirituality obtained via hallucinogenic drugs.

If the Star Gate acted in a narratively metaphoric manner, then the closing sequence of the film, the final room, the so-called Louis XVI room,[115] certainly also operated on a metaphorical level, if not a "psychedelic" one. It is the most ambiguous part of the film, with a range of questions raised which the narrative is either unwilling or unable to answer on any literal level. For example, one might speculate how long Bowman inhabits the final room — is it the minutes of diegetic narrative time as shown in the film, or does Bowman inhabit the room for the remaining years and decades of his life? As to just what the room is meant to represent is an interesting question. (It has been seen as a human zoo, with Bowman as a human specimen; it has also been seen as a Jungian metaphor for the mind.) However, it would appear that the room might be more convincingly seen as representing a metaphoric womb, one in which Bowman gestates before emerging as the Star Child, before he changes into a highly evolved, if embryonic transcendent life form. In this sense the reappearance of the monolith offers another potential meaning in terms of its geometric shape; its dimensions now become reminiscent of those of a door — a way out, an opening, a metaphorical vaginal orifice through which the Star Child will be born.[116]

*   *   *

In terms of its enigmatic nature (especially at its closure), the date of the film's release was perhaps of potential significance — the year 1968 being a culminative period in intellectual thought, the year in which there was a shift from a structuralist to a poststructuralist way of thinking. Although it is unlikely that either Kubrick or Clarke were in any great sense aware of this at the time, nonetheless the film does offer (specifically in a narrative sense) a more fragmented means of responding to the world.[117] In other words, the film's deliberately fragmented narrative coincided (albeit in a coincidental way) with the beginnings of poststructuralist thought. One way in which the film at least appeared to respond to such changes in intellectual perspectives might be seen in the way the narrative was linked to the motif of the circular journey, to a motif of circularity.[118] For example, one perceives of the orbits of the various spacecraft, the orbits of the planets, the orbits of the moons around Jupiter, even the way Floyd creates a circle when walking to the lecture lantern at Clavius, and, perhaps most obviously, the scene of Poole shadow boxing several times around *Discovery*. All of these examples enhance the sense in which life, within the discourse of *2001* at least, points to the relentless, if ultimately pointless aspects of the gendered journey, gendered because it is almost always seen within a masculine referent. The sense in which poststructuralist thought denies a creator, disrupts the symbolic, promotes a lack of connection, celebrates the fragmentary nature of signification, could thus be read within Kubrick's ubiquitous thematic pattern of the circular journey.

"Daddy's traveling," Floyd tells his daughter, Squirt, as if to sum up the redolent issue of masculine travel. In the film men travel; however, suggestive of poststructuralist thought, they seldom appear to actually get anywhere. Thus, in a sense, Poole jogging and shadow boxing around the *Discovery* becomes the ultimate tracking shot — the ultimate circular journey — like a hamster on its wheel, there is a clear element of pointlessness to the exercise. In an opposing but relevant way the journey through the Star Gate appears to be straight and linear, it appears Bowman will ultimately reach an end point. However, whether he does is open to speculation, Bowman merely appears to return to his starting point: his own origins. All of this seems to offer a specific referent to the overall concept of poststructuralist thought: the lack of a center, the inability to fully define any discursive situation, to ever be able to grasp any kind of unified "truth" or "reality."

In terms of the film's circularity, Carolyn Geduld commented: "Lest we forget Homer's original thought that all 'odysseys' are really roundtrips."[119]

This comment is redolent of the issue of intertextuality, in itself one of the key concerns of poststructuralist thought. For example, Barthesian concepts that all texts are built from other texts, that all texts are a mosaic of other texts. As previously suggested, Homer's *Odyssey* is the obvious starting point, this is clear in the title of the film and in the basic narrative design. However, Herman Melville's novel *Moby Dick* is perhaps a more apposite comparison, insomuch as it portrays a masculine couple on an epic voyage, upon a circular journey toward a culminative event. Michel Ciment was one critic to observe similarities between the film and Melville's novel:

> *2001* thus takes on the aspect of a quest, reminiscent of that other great documentary voyage, that other interrogation into the meaning of life, *Moby Dick*, in which Melville proved no less well informed and accurate about whale-fishing than Kubrick on astronautics.[120]

Moby Dick also recalls Leslie Fiedler's aforementioned ideas of homoeroticism in American fiction. Fiedler:

> *Moby Dick* can be read then not only as an account of a whale hunt, but also a love story, perhaps the greatest love story in our fiction, cast in the peculiar American form of innocent homosexuality.[121]

As was seen in Chapter 1, in a discussion of the relationship between Humbert Humbert and Clare Quilty, a Fiedlerian discourse of "innocent homosexuality" can be perceived throughout Kubrick's other work.

In another sense the film was decidedly not intertextual, insomuch as it was one of Kubrick's few films not to be based on an existing novel.[122] As is well known, Kubrick developed the film simultaneous with Clarke writing the novel, the central idea deriving from Clarke's 1950 short story: "The Sentinel." The essential plot device being the idea of humanity, in the near future, finding an alien artifact on the moon; however, other than this the story contained few other narrative similarities.[123] Insomuch as *2001* remains one of Kubrick's few films created without recourse to a specific literary source, it is perhaps of interest to question whether Kubrick, at heart, saw any reason for publishing the finished novel. It is evident that there was a sense of disagreement between Clarke and Kubrick over the subsequent delay in publication; according to Clarke the novel was finished as early as April 1966. However, the novel would not be published until July 1968, some three months after the release of the film. Kubrick's reasoning would seem clear; the novel offered potential explanations for aspects of the film Kubrick may have preferred to remain ambiguous. Indeed, one could argue that the film may have been enhanced had the novel not been published and the narrative details of *2001* relied solely on the film. As Stephen Baxter, in the introduction to the 2001 edition of *2001*, argued: "Clarke's clear rationalism contrasts strongly with the obliquity of Kubrick's film."[124] In a similar sense, Michel Chion made the point that contemporary viewers of the film are no longer faced with its original perplexing elliptical quality, in other words Clarke's novel, together with the diverse critical response, "a whole tradition of exegesis,"[125] have offered a more reassuring understanding of the film's original ambiguities.[126] If the novel, with its explanatory detail, had either not been written or not been published, then it is possible to argue that the film may have achieved still greater critical and artistic acclaim.

The film concludes with the image of the Star Child, arguably one of the most ambivalent images in 20th century American cinema. On the one hand the expression of the Star Child is one of wonder, while on the other it appears to be almost one of dismay, as if it was aware of the three or four million years of bloody violence that had led to its creation. The image is so ambivalent, as if to imply an almost compulsory act of interpretation on behalf of the audience.[127] As Geoff King observed: "We spend most of the film situated outside the action, quite coldly withdrawn. Then, at the climax, we are overwhelmed by an intense identification."[128]

A large part of the appeal of the film's ending, into the stare of the Star Child, is this sense of ambivalence. In Nietzschean terms the Star Child could easily be envisaged as the new superman, beyond good and evil, a new step in man's evolution, with needs and desires to be fulfilled; however, what these needs and desires might entail seem uncertain. On the one hand, critics such as Piers Bizony offered an optimistic reading, describing the scene as "one of cinema's most extraordinary images of hope and wonder: the benevolent, wide-eyed Star-Child at the film's end, all wisdom and compassion."[129] In a similar sense, Steven Spielberg commented: "The Star Child ... is to me the greatest moment of optimism and hope for mankind that has ever been offered by a modern film-maker."[130] However, in contrast there was a sense (albeit derived mostly from the novel) in which the Star Child might be a destroyer. Clarke's novel ends with the Star Child detonating man's orbiting nuclear bombs:

> A thousand miles below, he became aware that a slumbering cargo of death had awoken ... the feeble energies it contained were no possible menace to him; but he preferred a cleaner sky. He put forth his will, and the circling megatons flowered in a silent detonation that brought a brief, false dawn to half the sleeping globe.[131]

As to whether we conceive of the Star Child as benign or destructive is open to question, the film had no motive for offering that information. In this sense one might observe how the greater part of the film had been mimetic rather than diegetic and here, at the ending, that mimesis was confirmed in a direct fashion. Once again, the film appeared to defer to what might be described as a poststructuralist discourse, one of its great strengths being in the way it offered a "perpetual generation of the imagination."[132] In other words, it was a film that understood the benefit of ambivalence, a film that understood it could not say the un-sayable or show the un-showable.

This was an issue that was perhaps best summed up in the final spoken words of the film, the final words of Heywood Floyd's message to Bowman on the *Discovery*: "Its origin and purpose, still a total mystery." A reading of this line, outside of its immediate context, can be seen to reveal a clear self-referential comment, one that points directly to the way in which we *must* approach the film itself. The line appends not merely to the discovery of the monolith on the moon, but to our understanding of the film in the light of the ultimate questions it raises about the mystery of the universe; and, in addition, perhaps also the mystery that awaits us all, as we contemplate the meaning (or lack of meaning) of our own existences.

As part of a final summation, Kubrick's film, arguably more than any other cultural production of the 20th century, offered a sense in which we can come to terms with the indifference of our place in the universe. The film offered a sense in which we might find a way of accepting the challenges of life, within the boundaries of our own mortality, while being cognizant of the immensity of the universe. In Kubrick's own words:

> The most terrifying fact about the universe is not that it is hostile but that it is indifferent; but if we can come to terms with this indifference and accept the challenges of life within the boundaries of death ... our existence as a species can have genuine meaning and fulfillment. However vast the darkness, we must supply our own light.[133]

In this sense *2001: A Space Odyssey* might ultimately be seen as a film that offered a means to provide some meaning to our universe and our place within it; to create a way of confronting its terrifying emptiness *without* recourse to the irrationality of a religious faith. Insomuch, *2001* might be considered as Kubrick's way of attempting to supply his own light, a light to illuminate an understanding of ourselves, both as a species and in terms of the cultures we have created.

CHAPTER 4

A Clockwork Orange

Strange Fruit

He who wants to live must fight, and he who does not want to fight in this world, where eternal struggle is the law of life, has no right to exist. — Adolf Hitler

It is thought that it was Terry Southern who first brought Anthony Burgess's novel to Kubrick's attention; this being sometime during the making of *2001: A Space Odyssey*. Kubrick did not have the opportunity to read the novel immediately; but then, sometime in 1969, with the prospect of making *Napoleon* becoming less and less likely, he turned to *A Clockwork Orange*. Kubrick reportedly read the book in one sitting; he read it again, and immediately realized its potential as a film. It would seem that Kubrick finished an initial draft of the screenplay on May 15, 1970,[1] shooting beginning in September 1970, lasting until March 1971, editing and post-production then took until the end of 1971, when the film was premiered in New York on December 20, 1971. All of this was as quick a turnaround as almost any Kubrick film, before or since. The film took little more than two years from inception to completion — a feat Kubrick would never manage to repeat again.

As to precisely why he chose the novel, a comment Kubrick made to Michel Ciment suggests it may have been due to his interest in archetypal narrative tropes:

Q. What attracted you to Burgess's novel?
A. Everything. The plot, the characters, the ideas. I was also interested in how close the story was to fairy tales and myths, particularly in its deliberately heavy use of coincidence and plot symmetry.[2]

Of interest here was a confirmation of Kubrick's interest in fairy tales as a

powerful narrative disseminator, something that will be found, most pertinently, in his next film, *The Shining*. In addition, there was also the fact that
the novel, in terms of its length alone, was particularly suitable for adaptation to film. Also, it would seem likely that Kubrick was drawn to the novel's
unique use of language; and also to its visual imagery — both of which would
be used to telling effect within the cinematic adaptation.

In a correlation with *auteur* theory, it is perhaps worth noting that,
while the script was wholly of Kubrick's authorship, there were two specific and pertinent points to bear in mind. Firstly, the fact that the script
Kubrick wrote was far from a final shooting script; in other words that numerous changes were made in collaboration with the actors during filming, as
Malcolm McDowell recalled: "There was a script and we followed it, but
when it didn't work he knew it, and we had to keep rehearsing endlessly until
we were bored with it."[3] One notes here the amount of time Kubrick spent
with his actors, his high take ratio, this perhaps pointing toward a collaborative and improvising method of working on his films within a textual arena.
The following description of filming during *Lolita* offers another example of
this:

> During rehearsals of each scene, Kubrick would start with the dialogue as
> written in the shooting script, and then encourage the cast to improvise new
> material as the rehearsal progressed, to replace lines that were not working.
> Then Kubrick would type the revisions into the screenplay, prior to shooting
> the scene.[4]

This is seen in the prologue, wherein most of Peter Sellers's lines reputedly
derived from Sellers, himself. Sellers:

> We'd sit round a table with a tape recorder and ad-lib on the lines of the pas-
> sages we'd chosen ... in that way, we'd get perfectly natural dialogue which
> could then be scripted and used.[5]

One might also think of other instances; for example, Kubrick typing
up the latest version of the day's shooting, as seen in *The Making of* The Shining; or Lee Ermey's improvised (and then transcribed) lines in *Full Metal
Jacket*. In this context it is perhaps interesting to note the similarities between
Kubrick's method of working with actors and that of fellow film-maker Mike
Leigh. Although Kubrick is not as famous for improvising with actors as Leigh,
there is, nonetheless, at least some degree of affinity. (In this light it is perhaps significant to note that Mike Leigh was one of the few fellow film directors invited to attend Kubrick's funeral.)

The second point to bear in mind, in relation to Kubrick's "authorship"
of the screenplay, is to note the consistent use of significant parts of the novel's
dialogue, often in an almost verbatim manner. For example, the opening
voice-over by Alex: "There was me, that is Alex" is taken, word for word, from

the novel. In the same way a considerable number of the film's iconic lines derive from the novel, for example:

> "...and I felt all the little malenky hairs on my plott standing endwise."
> "...a bird of like rarest spun heavenmetal...."
> "...and this is the real weepy and like tragic part of the story...."
> "...starry-eyed yahoodies tolchocking each other ... and bedding their wives' handmaidens...."

In addition, the dialogue in the police station was taken in an almost verbatim way from the novel, as was Alex's dialogue with the chaplain over the Ludovico Treatment, the scene wherein Alex's droogs challenge Alex in the foyer of his flat-block was again adapted almost word for word, likewise the dialogue in the scene with Deltoid was also used almost word for word, and so on.

However, while the film might have appeared derivative of the novel in terms of a reliance on dialogue, it was wholly original in terms of the visual images Kubrick created. One could argue that almost all of the iconic concepts we now associate with *A Clockwork Orange* derive, in fact, from the film. If one thinks, for example, of the bearing and demeanor of Alex and his droogs: the bowler hat, the eye make-up, the codpiece, the braces— all of these did not originate with the novel. In the same way the Korova Bar, with its sadomasochistic furniture, again this does not appear in the novel, neither does the Catlady's giant phallic sculpture, or the beating of Mr. Alexander to "Singin' in the Rain,"[6] the surgical lid locks[7] and so on through a diverse array of other examples. Thus it might be fair to argue that Kubrick's cinematic adaptation, to a significant extent, has subsumed the novel as a cultural artifact. In other words when we think of *A Clockwork Orange* it is arguably the film's array of iconic visual images that immediately come to mind — rather than the linguistic virtuosity of Burgess's prose.

The original motivation for Anthony Burgess writing *A Clockwork Orange* is of interest. Burgess was born in Manchester in 1917, into a Catholic family and of an Irish background; he was educated at the University of Manchester; he served in the Royal Army Medical Corps in World War II; and then worked as an education officer in the Colonial Service in Malaya. In 1959 Burgess was invalided out of his post with a suspected brain tumor that gave him only a year to live. In the light of this prognosis, during the course of the following year Burgess wrote five novels, with a view to provide for his prospective widow, one of the novels being *A Clockwork Orange*. However, in the event it proved Burgess did not have a brain tumor; he was to live for another 34 years, until 1993, when he died at the age of 76. Although he wrote over 30 novels and a similar number of non-fiction works, *A Clockwork Orange* (perhaps primarily due to Kubrick's film) remains his most famous work.

On his return to England, in the late 1950s, Burgess had witnessed the rise of the Teddy Boys, seeing them as a "personification of the *Zeitgeist*" that seemed to express a "brutal disappointment with Britain's post-war decline."[8] From this starting point Burgess began to think about a novel that would deal with youth subculture. At first Burgess considered setting the novel in the past, in the 1590s, in the late reign of Queen Elizabeth I, when young apprentices "used to riot" and were "dealt with in a summary way — sometimes hanged on the spot."[9] However, instead of this Burgess finally settled on setting the novel in the near future[10] — an astute move as it allowed the novel to take into its scope later youth subcultures of the 20th century: the mods and rockers of the 1960s, the punks of the 1970s and so on.[11] (A further reason in Burgess writing the novel may have been a more personal motive. It has been suggested that it was to exorcise the memory of the rape of his first wife, Lynn, who was attacked by four American deserters. In an attack similar to the one described in the novel, the four assailants broke into the family home one night in London during the Second World War. Burgess's wife was pregnant and lost the child because of the assault — this led to depression, a suicide attempt and, eventually, to her early death in 1968. Thus such a gratuitous act of violence could be seen as having a possible cathartic momentum in Burgess's writing of the novel.)

To emphasize the futuristic setting Burgess devised a new language; the novel, and hence the film, were to become famous for the use of Nadsat, the supposed teenage slang of the imagined future. This derived from a mixture of Anglicized Russian, baby talk, rhyming slang and Burgessian invention. Readers of the novel were thus either enchanted by the invention of a new language, and by the fact they painlessly learned rudimentary Russian — or else they were irritated by having to look up word after word in a glossary to find out what was actually being said.[12] In the film Kubrick made use of Nadsat, but in such a way as to ensure it did not establish a significant hindrance to an overall understanding of the dialogue. However, in each instance, in both novel and film, the use of Nadsat was unquestionably one of the key features in representing Alex and his droogs within a distinct subcultural discourse.[13]

*   *   *

The overall budget of the film was around $2 million, one of Kubrick's least expensive projects. He achieved this by shooting the film relatively quickly and also by shooting mainly on location (in various parts of London), thus avoiding the cost of building studio sets.[14] In addition, the film featured no star names, the cast being drawn, for the most part, from British actors of stage and television. However, the film would make an initial $15.4 million at the box office — eventually earning in excess of $40 million. In 1974

Burgess successfully sued executive producers Si Litvinoff and Max L. Raab, for a ten percent share of the profits.[15] Burgess would often claim that the film had only made him a few hundred dollars; however, the actual figure was different. Andrew Biswell: "According to a royalty statement, Warner Bros. had paid Burgess $713,081 by June 1985."[16] In addition, Burgess would have received royalties from the increased sales of his novel and, one presumes, an additional interest in his work as a whole. However, it is clear that Burgess still possessed a degree of resentment in the way Kubrick had hijacked authorship of his creation.

In the film Kubrick appeared to court controversy in much the same way as he had done so a decade earlier with *Lolita*, the polemic of underage sex being replaced with a discourse of sexual violence. As is well known, *A Clockwork Orange* was criticized for its supposed celebration of gratuitous violence and, even more so, the conjectural effects on violent behavior within wider society, outside of the cinema. However, a reading of the novel and a comparison with Kubrick's adaptation of it, in fact demonstrates a drastic *reduction* of the level of violence. In narrative detail after narrative detail one can see how Kubrick purposefully lessened the impact of the novel's violent discourse. For example, at the start of the film Alex and his droogs attack a tramp—in the novel it is a "doddery starry schoolmaster type veck" a scene described in much more graphic detail.[17] One might also note the girl Billyboy and his droogs are planning to rape, clearly a young woman in the film, is "a weepy young devotchka [of] not more than ten" in the novel.[18] In the same way the two girls Alex encounters (and has sex with) in the record store are prepubescent in the novel, while they are demonstrably older in the film.[19] In the novel the Catlady Alex murders is an elderly woman, not the age of Miriam Karlin's portrayal of the role in the film. Perhaps the most explicitly sadistic and squalid scene in the novel was Alex's murder of a fellow prisoner[20]; hence it was significant that Kubrick chose to omit the scene entirely from the film; this may have possibly been for reasons of pacing and length, but it may also have been excluded simply because of the level of graphic violence such a scene would have engendered.

It might be argued that Kubrick's film was disturbing, not so much for the level of violence it portrayed, but because it compelled its audience to reconsider its (arguably complacent) attitude toward the screen violence with which it was routinely presented. There was an honesty to the film in its treatment of violence. Alex is honest as to the motives for committing his many acts of violence; he does so simply because he enjoys it, as he put it in the novel: "But what I do I do because I like to do."[21] The inherent implication being the idea that we might all—to some extent at least—enjoy or become aroused by violence, much as we might wish to deny it. It appears that few people, or at least few people in a position of political and socio-cultural influence, could adequately deal with this.[22] The general response to the film was one that revolved around the ultimately facile suggestion that the supposed glamorization of violence made us, the viewers, more likely to commit violent acts ourselves. This appears, in retrospect, to be a wholly spurious argument, but it was one that was current at the time of the film's release and hence the film was blamed for a diverse range of copycat crimes.[23] What would seem more likely is that any individual who may have decided to commit a violent act after seeing the film (or any film) would have committed a violent act anyway. One is no more likely to beat and rape and murder after watching *A Clockwork Orange* than one is prone to blind someone after seeing Shakespeare's *King Lear,* or to dismember and cannibalize after seeing *Titus Andronicus.*

In this light it is interesting to note that Kubrick shows Alex reading the "big book" (in other words, the Bible) in prison. Alex then fantasizes around the violence and sex within; explaining how he was inspired by the stories of "starry yahoodies tolchocking each other." To take the view that Kubrick's film inspired violent activity would be to invite such a correlation from all cultural texts, up to and including the Bible. In this sense such a simplistic view would be to ignore the complexities of the way a cultural product operates within any given discourse, as Kubrick himself suggested, works of art do not affect us: "They merely illuminate something we already feel."[24]

Perhaps a key element to consider in this context is the subjective shot of Mr. Alexander, as Alex prepares to rape his wife. Thus far in the film the viewer has tended to identify with Alex, but when Alex utters the famous line: "Viddy well, little brother, viddy well" we, the audience, feel an ambivalence; for herein we are asked to experience the narrative events from the point of view, not of the perpetrator, but of the victim. In both the novel and film the story is told, for the greater part, from Alex's first-person narrative voice and hence we, the audience, experience an intimate, autodiegetic relationship with Alex. It is Alex's mocking but somehow appealing voice that leads us, complicitly, into a conspiracy with his way of life. We are complicit via his intelligence, his honesty, his command of language, his sheer *joi-de-vie* for life. Hence we become intimate with his attitude toward the world, but when we are positioned as a potential victim of his sadistic desires our attitudes undergo a significant change. This is perhaps one feasible explanation as to why the film has always possessed such a disturbing resonance as a cinematic text.

In an attempt to explain our identification with Alex, Kubrick, in several instances, compared him to Shakespeare's Richard III:

> The only character comparable to Alex is Richard III and I think they both work on your imagination in much the same way. They both take the audience into their confidence, they are both completely honest, witty, intelligent

and unhypocritical.... Alex has vitality, courage and intelligence, but you cannot fail to see that he is thoroughly evil. At the same time there is a strange kind of psychological identification with him, which gradually occurs however much you may be repelled by his behavior.[25]

The comparison was an apt one, but it was perhaps also resonant with the idea that both protagonists had a more overall command of language, how both seemed to be operating on a different linguistic level to the characters surrounding them. In this sense, the film (like Shakespeare's play) forced its audience to form at least some kind of sympathetic relationship with its main protagonist. Hence what was significant was the way in which the film allowed access into the interior mind of a wholly anti-social individual, one capable of committing acts of abhorrent violence, but one, nonetheless, who was not wholly a "monster." In this sense, what was perhaps most disturbing in the film was the way in which Kubrick offered a reality we would rather not accept. The film seemed to suggest that young males — given the right circumstance — do find enjoyment in violence and rape. "It's a glorious feeling to be happy again," Alex sings, as he beats Mr. Alexander and prepares to rape Mrs. Alexander. In this sense the film became an actual "horrorshow," in Tony Parsons' words, the film became:

A thesis on how good it feels to be bad.... And yet you can't help liking him ... one of cinema's most seductive heroes ... he rapes, murders and crushes testicles. And we want to be his friend.[26]

A large factor in Alex's appeal to us as a character lay in Malcolm McDowell's interpretation of the role, an intensely charismatic, almost demonically arrogant performance, a further testament to Kubrick's almost infallibly astute sense of casting. In McDowell's hands Alex is imbued with malice, but also with an intelligence that draws us to him.[27] It is Alex's mocking but appealing voice, "the magnificent wielder of club, penis and language"[28] that makes it impossible not to be complicit with his charm, his attractiveness, his intelligence, his honesty; culminating in a desire to become intimate with his demonic energy.

The character of Alex in the film, and the way we perceived of him, raised larger questions. Alex is not a mindless delinquent, he is a cultural being. Thus, we might, for example, ask: how did Alex's love of Beethoven's music equate with the violence he perpetrated? Alex is an amoral individual who commits acts of the "old ultra violence" for sheer pleasure, but he is also capable of being moved and uplifted by the music of Beethoven. In so doing the film (and the novel before it) appeared to deliberately undermine the Arnoldian belief that culture made one a good person.[29] In the novel Alex ridicules this idea:

Great Music ... and Great Poetry would like quieten Modern Youth down and make Modern Youth more Civilized. Civilized my syphilised yarbles. Music always sort of sharpened me up.[30]

In his 1975 novel, *The Clockwork Testament,* Burgess cogently reiterated the point:

> Well, there are some stupid bastards who can't understand how the comman-
> dant of a Nazi concentration camp could go home after torturing Jews all day
> and then weep tears of joy at a Schubert symphony.[31]

In his review of the film, the art critic Robert Hughes summarized the argument:

> At issue is the popular 19th century idea, still held today, that Art is Good for
> You, that the purpose of the fine arts is to provide moral uplift. Kubrick's
> message, amplified from Burgess's novel, is the opposite: art has no ethical
> purpose.... Without the slightest contradiction Nazis could weep over Wagner
> before stoking the crematoriums.[32]

It would appear that Kubrick was fully aware of such contradictions, the poster for the film claimed: "*A Clockwork Orange*: being the adventures of a young man whose principal interests are rape, ultra-violence and Beetho-ven."[33] In Kubrick's discourse there was no contradiction implied from this frame of reference, from these supposedly dichotomous perspectives. In other words, the love of rape and ultra violence and a love of the music of Beethoven were not incongruous. The idea that Kubrick was deliberately privileging in this thematic discourse is strengthened if one observes the way in which the film continually appeared to contrast culture with violence. For example, the ruined theatre-cum-casino was positioned as the backdrop to gang warfare, in Mr. Alexander's study Alex's overturning of the bookshelves (a literal over-turning of cultural constructs) was the precursor of assault and rape, and, in his fight with the Catlady, Alex wielded a giant phallus—she a bust of Bee-thoven. All of these examples appearing to offer the same dichotomous com-parison between culture and violence[34]; with the presentation of such ideas adding up to Kubrick's conclusion: "Culture seems to have no effect upon evil."[35]

The acts of violence presented in the film were perhaps ultimately as dis-turbing in terms of the violation of the home as that of the body. The viola-tion of the home being conceivably one of the greatest "middle-class" fears; and the fact that Kubrick refers to Mr. and Mrs. Alexander's house, simply as "Home" could be seen as a deliberate exaggeration of such fears. We might note the film was made only two years after the "Manson Family" attack on the home of Sharon Tate — and it is not wholly speculative to perceive of a metaphorical retelling of this attack, based on those inherent fears. Of course, it could have been far worse, Alex and his droogs attack a home of a husband and wife; had it been a home with children they would presumably have been attacked as well; hence such a scene would probably have been as un-filmable as it was unwatchable. Thomas Harris, in his novel *Red Dragon* (1981),[36] posits such an idea — a serial killer stalking and murdering entire families — but even Harris did not depict the murders, instead merely offering the aftermath of the crimes.

However, of greater polemical concern, at least in terms of immediate audience reception, was the *way* Kubrick's film depicted the violation of the body, specifically in the way it looked at the issue of rape. It is significant to note here that Kubrick made *A Clockwork Orange* at the cusp of the beginnings of the current feminist movement, and it is arguable if the same film could have been made in quite the same way at a later date. To take one notorious example, the depiction of Billy Boy's preparation of gang-rape of "a weepy young devotchka," here the film, unashamedly appeared to present the idea of a woman as victim, as a mere object, little more than a young, attractive body to be stripped in readiness for a sexual assault.

The feminist response to the film was warranted, if somewhat predictable; for example, in an early critique, Beverley Walker described it as being "an intellectual's pornographic film" having an attitude that was

> ugly, lewd and brutal toward the female human being: all of the women are portrayed as caricatures; the violence committed upon them is treated comically; the most startling aspect of the decor relates to the female form.[37]

More recently, Molly Haskell argued:

> Stanley Kubrick is a misanthropist and particularly a misogynist; but his hatred of women is not the visceral explosion of a deep Swiftian disgust but a fashionable and fastidious distaste.[38]

It was certainly correct that the film had an unashamedly appreciative disposition to the representation of the female form, this being most obviously found in the fetishistic furniture of the Korova Bar.[39] Here it was almost impossible not to perceive of an inherent misogyny in the female mannequins, here was a clear case of woman represented purely as a sexualized object.[40] While another obvious example, the bare-breasted young woman who tempts Alex on stage, could be seen as representative of the iconic nude woman often seen in Kubrick's work.[41] In Kubrick's defense, it might be noted that while (as previously discussed) he had deliberately underplayed the violence of the book, at the same time he may have deliberately overstated its erotic elements, perhaps for calculated shock value. One perceives this from the beginning of the film (with the aforementioned sadomasochistic imagery in the Korova Bar) to the end: with Alex's fantasy of having sex in front of an audience seemingly transported from an outtake of the Ascot scene in *My Fair Lady*. In other words Kubrick *was* being chauvinistic toward women, but he was fully aware of doing so for specific, if ambiguous, artistic reasoning.[42]

In 1975, four years after the release of *A Clockwork Orange*, Susan Brownmiller published her polemical tract: *Against Our Will: Men, Women and Rape*.

A book that probably remains one of the most influential feminist texts on the subject of rape, it contained this famous (or arguably infamous) definition of rape:

> It [rape] is nothing more or less than a conscious process of intimidation by which *all* men keep *all* women in a state of fear.[43]

The use of the word "all," in the definition, was the polemical issue; and, in what might be seen as an overtly radical stance, Brownmiller went on to claim that Kubrick was one of those artists who stand as "glorifiers of rape."[44] This is a somewhat problematical statement, a claim only making sense within Brownmiller's (arguably) extremist premise that *all* men are potential rapists, a premise many men (and perhaps many women) might take issue with. However, elsewhere in her book Brownmiller offered a convincing argument that put forward a precise and illuminating history of rape, together with our attitudes toward it. In the course of her discussion Brownmiller considered the depiction of rape in the then-recently released, *A Clockwork Orange.* In a chapter entitled: "The Myth of the Heroic Rapist," Brownmiller perceived of the representation of rape in *A Clockwork Orange* as "indicative of the male approach,"[45] going on to make the point that the rape in *A Clockwork Orange* was more concerned with male on male violence and that "within the myth of the heroic rapist women play a minor role."[46] Thus what Brownmiller appeared to argue was that the issue of real significance was not Alex's rape of Mrs. Alexander, but the dominance Alex achieved over Mr. Alexander in making him a witness to the savage and barbaric assault.

What Brownmiller appeared to be suggesting was the idea that rape often has a homosocial component. If one accepts the argument that the great extent of Kubrick's work demonstrates a decidedly homosocial leaning (as has been argued throughout this book), then such an approach would seem to offer a potential arena for discussion, here, in the context of this film. For example, one might first note Alex's ubiquitous address to his audience: "O my brothers," this purposefully gendered remark might be seen as a clear call toward a homosocial discourse. In other words, Alex was interested primarily in addressing other males, and, in this sense, it might be noted that Alex continually seeks male companionship, his droogs, and finds only sexual release via his contact with women. At times the homosocial context slips over into an ironically privileged (and so-called) "gay" context. It is particularly ironical in this film, insomuch as it is almost always purposefully exaggerated: "Are you now or have you ever been a homosexual?" the Chief Guard in Staja 84 asks, and thereafter carries out a somewhat theatrical anal examination of Alex. In the same arena, it is perhaps significant that, later in the film, Mr. Alexander (after the death of his wife) appears to have set up home with a decidedly "camp" companion, Julian.[47] In terms of the homosocial aspect of the relationship, which, significantly, is not found in the novel, one might argue that Kubrick was purposefully introducing a conscious (if ironic) homoerotic overture. In addition to this, one might consider such details as the homoerotic nature of the defaced mural in the lobby of Alex's block of apartments[48]; or the obviously prurient sexual advances toward Alex, both by Deltoid and (later in the film) by the prisoner who blows Alex a kiss during the chaplain's sermon. Finally, a homosocial context can also be clearly delineated in the film in the way each of Alex's and Billyboy's gang pair up to fight, offering an explicit definition of male homosociality using the twinned oppositions of sex and violence.

In this arena it is also significant to consider the deliberate feminization of the male body in the film. For example, Alex's false eyelash, here Alex wears a deliberate and obvious feminine attribute, a signal directly attributable to transvestism and drag; as Margaret DeRosia argued: "The film signals an ironic link between masquerade and masculinity."[49] In contrast to this, one might note how, in the film, Alex is often located in a deliberately overloaded phallic context. For example, one might consider Alex's mask with its long, erect nose; also, his cane, his codpiece,[50] and this is not to mention his actual penis, which we seem to be about to witness as Alex prepares to rape Mrs. Alexander. However, the most obvious phallic trope in the film perhaps derived from Alex's appropriation of the Catlady's sculpture. In one of the most "potently" iconic images in the film, the Catlady's giant phallic sculpture, we find significant and explicit homoerotic gestures. In fact it still remains a somewhat shocking image, for while the sculpture is obviously phallic, it is also clearly anal — as the erect phallus blends into a pair of provocative buttocks at its other end, thus suggesting both active and passive elements of male sexuality, the penetrator and the penetrated. This dual signification and the sculpture's suggestive rocking motion causes Alex to be slightly puzzled, slightly disconcerted, "Naughty, naughty, naughty," is all he can say to the sculpture. In this sense we can confidently note how the scene (and hence the film itself) succeeded in suggesting further ambiguities over masculine confusion in sexual role play. (In addition, there were other obvious homoerotic gestures in the film; for example, the way in which Alex straddles Dim in the lobby of the flat-block — Alex sits astride Dim, his codpiece pointing towards Dim's mouth in an obvious simulation of fellatio. One might also note the way Alex is attacked with a bottle of milk (a potential metaphor for semen), and the way in which it sprays over him in slow motion, a potential dominance metaphor — especially as Alex's phallic nose appears to lose its prowess during this attack.)

Thus one might speculate that the violence in the film, the various assaults on women, were not so much important in themselves, but were significant primarily in the way men define themselves as dominant over one another.[51] One might go on to argue that while the film did have an inherent misogyny — as arguably all of Kubrick's work possessed — but that this was at least partially explained via an interest in male on male relationships; thus women were routinely marginalized, but for coherent reasons. This is one way of accounting for the apparent misogyny in Kubrick's work, his films had a consistent and almost intense interest in men from a homosocial perspective; and in *A Clockwork Orange,* it simply reached one of its most extreme forms.

A psychoanalytical reading relating to these issues may, once again, be illuminating.[52] One might note how Alex could clearly be described as a creature of the id; in other words, his way of looking at the world is one that derived uniformly from his instinctive desires. Alex is an individual who appears to lack all sense of repression, with little if any sense of a socialized restraint over his baser instincts. This idea was enhanced by the suggestion of infantilism within Alex's personality; for example, in the film's opening scene, Alex is shown drinking milk, albeit laced with moloko-plus. Also, one notes how much of Alex's Nadsat was incorporated within the use of child-like language: "eggiwegs" and "guttiwuts," and so on. In addition, in the second "Home" sequence, Alex is shown being carried into the house by Mr. Alexander's companion, Julian — as Alex's voice-over put it: "Being held helpless like a babe in arms." Finally, in the hospital scene at the end of the film Alex is shown being literally spoon-fed by the Minister of the Interior.[53] However, in contrast to this, it is clear that Alex also possessed a fully adult sexuality; the film is redolent of sexual symbolism; notably of the breast and the testicles, together with the aforementioned phallus. The breast is apparent in the film from the beginning with the nude mannequins in the Korova Milk Bar, likewise it is evident in the fetishistic baring of Mrs. Alexander's nipples, and finally in the breasts of the model Alex is unable to touch after the Ludovico Treatment. The film is testicular in terms of the continuous use of the Nadsatian "yarbles"; likewise, in relation to the rubber balls Alex uses to gag his victims and, in a metaphorical context, via the way the film repeatedly draws attention to eyeballs. (In addition, one might also mention the spherical connotation of the title of the film itself, the imagery of the billiard balls, the curious absence of testicles on the Catlady's sculpture and the various other "testicular" gestures, literal and metaphorical, the film makes. Also, one might note how the metaphorical enactment of the eyeball/testicle metaphor was apparent from the opening of the film. This being evident in Alex's unwinking stare towards the camera; all the way to the ripped eyeballs ornamentation on Alex's shirt cuffs, and finally, the obvious imagery of Alex's lidlocked eyes during the Ludovico Treatment. Herein, the almost subliminal message of the vulnerability of the unprotected eyeballs was linked to the ever-present vulnerability of the testicles.)

In a Freudian context sex often does mirror infantile desires; as, for example, in the fetishizing of the female breast. In this sense Alex's location in both infantile and adult versions of sexuality, together with the clear perception of him as a creature of the id, at least goes some way of explaining, if not condoning, his behavior and actions. In terms of Freud's theories on the unconscious, Kubrick himself would comment:

> The psychiatrists tell us our unconscious has no conscience.... It may be that only as a result of morality, the law and sometimes our own innate character that we do not become like him [Alex]. Perhaps this makes some people uncomfortable and partly explains some of the controversy which has arisen over the film. Perhaps they are unable to accept this view of human nature.[54]

The alternative view, disregarding a psychoanalytical reading, would be to see Alex simply as a psychopath. A psychopath being defined here as an individual suffering from violent and asocial connotations, with an inability to demonstrate empathy toward other people. In addition, such an individual may sometimes appear, at least superficially, to have a charming and charismatic aspect to his character. This would appear to fit Alex in *A Clockwork Orange*: he has no conscience, no feelings for the victims of the crimes he perpetrates; yet at the same time he is charismatic, able to lead his droogs and has the ability to give his crimes an air of almost artistic performance. However, to read Alex simply as a psychopath would seem ultimately reductive; inasmuch as Alex is arguably one of *the* most significant and memorable characters within Kubrick's canon, to perceive of him as merely a mindless psychopath would reduce the narrative scope of the discourse. An alternative reading would be to suggest Alex is simply being true to himself, and that Kubrick's film is merely reflecting one authentic if unappealing aspect of humanity. Thus, while Alex may be an individual whose principal interests are "rape, ultra-violence and Beethoven," he is also one who had chosen to commit acts of violence because it is within his "natural" make-up to do so, the reality being that this is, in essence, arguably the way some young males perceive and interpret their environment.

In a wider discussion, what would appear to be at stake would seem to be the issue of free will; as Kubrick himself made clear:

> The essential moral idea of the book is clear. It is necessary for man to have choice to be good or evil, even if he chooses evil. To deprive him of this choice is to make him something less than human — a clockwork orange.[55]

What deprives Alex of choice, what makes him less than human is, of course, the Ludovico Treatment, the plot device through which novel and film turn Alex into the aforementioned "clockwork orange." In this respect it is of interest that B.F. Skinner's book, *Beyond Freedom and Dignity,* came out almost contemporaneously with Kubrick's film. This was a book arguing that it is possible to change an individual's way of behaving for the good of society; via so called Pavlovian techniques of behavior modification. It is doubtful whether either Kubrick or Burgess entirely believed in Skinner's theoretical concepts of human behavior; hence the Ludovico Treatment was perhaps meant to be read in a satirical way.[56] In this respect one might note a detail in Kubrick's film — careful observation reveals that there was a copy of another of Skinner's books, *Walden Two,* on the prison governor's desk in the scene in which Alex agrees to sign up for the Ludovico Treatment.[57] If the prison governor's reading habits include Skinner, then how much credence, one might ask, should we place in the value of Skinner's work?

* * *

It is clear that Kubrick's work, as a whole, had always possessed a strongly satirical slant, and here, in *A Clockwork Orange,* the Ludovico Treatment was perhaps best seen as a part of an overall satirical discourse. However, not everyone appeared to fully appreciate such a level of satire; on January 4, 1972, the *New York Times* published an interview with Kubrick: "Kubrick Tells What Makes Clockwork Orange Tick," by Bernard Weintraub. In the course of the interview Kubrick offered a characteristically bleak interpretation of the film's main character:

> Alex symbolizes man in his natural state, the way he would be if society did not impose its civilizing processes upon him. What we respond to is Alex's guiltless sense of freedom to kill and rape, and to be our savage natural selves, and it is in the glimpse of the true nature of man that the power of the story derives.[58]

Shortly thereafter, on January 30, 1972, Malcolm McDowell was also interviewed in the *New York Times:* "Malcolm McDowell: The Liberals, They Hate *Clockwork,*" and put forward a similar point of view:

> People are basically bad, corrupt, I always sensed that. Man has not progressed one inch, morally, since the Greeks. Liberals, they hate *Clockwork* because they're dreamers and it shows them realities, shows 'em not tomorrow but *now.* Cringe, don't they, when faced with the bloody truth.[59]

There was a follow-up response by what might be termed the liberal backlash. Craig McGregor, an Australian journalist who had won the Harkness Fellowship to the United States and who had published what was probably one of the most significant books ever written on Bob Dylan,[60] wrote a condescending and vaguely anti–Semitic piece: "Nice Boy from the Bronx?" in the *New York Times* on January 30, 1972. (McGregor's article began with the sentence: "So what's a nice Jewish boy from The Bronx like Stanley Kubrick doing making bizarre films like *A Clockwork Orange.*" The apparent racist slur, one assumes, pointing towards the idea that someone of Jewish descent should not make a fascist film.) In the article Kubrick was quoted, repeating his previous opinion of Alex, this time drawing on Rousseau's and Hobbesian ideas:

> Man isn't a noble savage, he's an ignoble savage ... he is irrational, brutal, weak ... unable to be objective about anything where his own interests are involved — that about sums it up. I'm interested in the brutal and violent nature of man because it's a true picture of him.[61]

In response to this, Fred M. Hechinger, in a piece entitled "A Liberal Fights Back," in the *New York Times* on February 13, 1972, added his case. Hechinger's main charge was that the film was fascist, he argued: "An alert liberal should recognize the voice of fascism." Although Hechinger seemed vague as to what his interpretation of fascism might be, at one point he went so far as to state: "The thesis that man is irretrievably bad and corrupt is the essence of fascism."[62] From any relevant perspective this would appear to be a somewhat eccentric definition, one might think it would seem more accurate to see fascism as an authoritarian and nationalistic right-wing system of government, one claiming racial supremacy and the worship of a demagogic leader. However, Hechinger made the charge the film was fascist, and, in a rare public response, Kubrick wrote an answering piece to the *New York Times*. This was published on February 27, 1972, in the piece Kubrick made the point that Hechinger hadn't analyzed the film itself, but had rested his case on the quote that man is not a noble savage.

> Mr. Hechinger is entitled to hold an optimistic view of the nature of man; but this does not give him the right to make ugly assertions of fascism against those who do not share his opinion.[63]

Kubrick went onto make the point that within a satire on fascism the artist need not be denounced as a fascist: "No more than any well balanced commentator who read *A Modest Proposal* would have accused Dean Swift of being a cannibal."[64] After having made this point, Kubrick seems to have resumed more significant work, presumably consideration of his next film.

The charge that *A Clockwork Orange* put forward a fascist voice now appears somewhat absurd[65]; however, questions around the bleak view of humanity Kubrick's films supposedly espoused still appears to be relevant. In his personal life Stanley Kubrick seems, from all appearances, to have been a man who loved his family: his wife and three daughters— not to mention numerous cats and dogs; yet his overall view of mankind was somewhat different. In his interview, McGregor had, perhaps somewhat patronizingly, asked Kubrick how he came to hold such a pessimistic view of humanity. "From observation," Kubrick responded, "knowing what has happened in the world, seeing the people around me.... I mean it's essentially Christian theology anyway, that view of man."[66] To which McGregor later commented:

"He's wrong. Kubrick's concept of man as essentially evil is straight Manichean, one of the most perverse yet persistent of Christian heresies.[67] However, it is clear that it was McGregor who was wrong, insomuch as Christianity
does contain (as Kubrick presumably inferred) the premise of original sin,
the fall of man, the need to be redeemed. (The key point is that, to some extent,
Burgess's novel — and hence Kubrick's film — still believed in original sin.
Burgess saw the story told in his novel as a "moral parable" and that to rid a
man of the capacity to choose between good and evil was a "sin against the
Holy Ghost."[68] Kubrick's rendition was less certain of this, it was more interested in the dangers of adopting a behaviorist model of the good and evil that
human beings do. However, it could be argued there was still an element of
the significance of original sin in Kubrick's film.) Manichaeism was hardly a
"perverse" and "persistent" heresy, it was arguably more of a parallel philosophy to Christianity, with the same dualism between good and evil.

It would appear that the film, along with Kubrick's work in general, was
concerned with representing a dark and (at least in Kubrick's argument) accurate portrayal of human behavior, whether it be classified as Manichean or
not. It would also appear that a significant number of critics, other than
McGregor and Hechinger, simply could not accept this position and hence
attacked the film on moral grounds. Pauline Kael was one such critic. Kael,
seldom a champion of Kubrick's in any case, in a particularly caustic and
vituperative response, took the view that the film was pornographic, posing
the question: "Is there anything sadder — and ultimately more repellent — than
a clean minded pornographer?"[69] Kael went onto claim that the film was "corrupt ... with an arctic spirit" and that it was "determined to be pornographic"
but had "no talent for it," that it was the stuff of "the purest exploitation."[70]
Kael claimed the girl being attacked by Billyboy's gang was "stripped for our
benefit [and that] at the movies, we are gradually being conditioned to accept
violence as a sensual pleasure."[71] Kael went on further: "I can't accept that
Kubrick is merely reflecting this post-assassinations, post–Manson mood; I
think he's catering to it. I think he wants to dig it."[72] Kael concluded her
piece with the charge that Kubrick was ultimately "sucking up to the thugs
in the audience."[73] However, there were other opinions, in a response written at around the same time, art critic Robert Hughes, evened up the balance:

> No movie in the last decade (perhaps in the history of film) has made such
> exquisitely chilling predictions about the future role of cultural artifacts—
> paintings, building, sculpture, music — in society, or extrapolated them from
> so undeceived a view in our present culture.[74]

In a similar light, the esteemed Spanish director, Luis Buñuel, would comment that *A Clockwork Orange* "is the only movie about what the modern
world really means."[75]

It would appear that it was the pessimism (one might almost say the relentless pessimism) expressed by the film that was *the* key problem for a number of critics. The film was, as Alex tells us, a "horrorshow," with the implicit corollary that the film thus spoke of the horror of the human condition itself. The fact that it was also a (horror)show that entertained while raising these fears appeared to cause further problematical issues for its audience. Alexander Walker once suggested that Kubrick's films tend to "plug in" to our fears, and thus it might be said that *A Clockwork Orange*, perhaps more than any other of Kubrick's films, plugged into some of our worst fears. In this sense, as Walker went on to say: "It is right that such a film should shock us."[76]

One recalls here Craig McGregor's question to Kubrick, as to how he came to hold such a pessimistic view of humanity, and Kubrick's response: "From observation [from] knowing what has happened in the world, seeing the people around me." It is arguable that Kubrick was referring here, at least in part, to the significant influence of the Holocaust on his life and, arguably, on all our lives. In other words "the "horrorshow" in the film was as much concerned with the horror of the Holocaust, as to the imagined horror of a dystopian future in which the violence of a youth culture threatened middle-class society. To support such a view one must first perceive of the film in the context of the thematic concerns of Kubrick's work as a whole, the argument that the Holocaust was always a significantly influential subtextual concern. Also, to then consider the ubiquitous range of nuanced references to the Holocaust in the film itself. On an obvious level one perceives of the Nazi regalia Billyboy's gang wears[77]; also, one perceives of the Nazi footage chosen for the Ludovico Treatment. In addition, one can perceive, in Kubrick's own comments, the way in which the government in *A Clockwork Orange* has comparisons to something close to Nazi Germany:

> The government eventually resorts to the employment of the cruelest and most violent members of the society to control everyone else ... not an altogether new or untried idea.[78]

The not altogether new or untried idea, to which Kubrick was alluding, operated as an allusion to totalitarian governments in general; however, one might argue Nazi Germany would appear to be one of the most likely of comparisons Kubrick was making.

These thematic resonances in Kubrick's work, arguably of a consistently homogenous nature, were compounded via the seemingly deliberately placed metafictional echoes present in the film. In other words, the idea of a narrative artifice constructed within the context of an already existent artifice. For example, the ruined theatre-cum-casino scene, here the idea that Billyboy's gang was planning to undertake a rape on a stage was not without significance—

it was literally a show, and arguably a deliberate metafictional gesture. This being apparent even to the extent of the girl escaping by running off the stage, hence making her exit in both an actual and a theatrical way. In the same sense, the location in which Alex underwent the Ludovico treatment, in what appeared to be a cinema, offered a notion of a metafictional discourse. The idea of Alex, strapped in his chair with his eyelids locked open, could not help but remind the viewers of the film that they themselves were being forced (albeit in a less than literal way) to view images they would perhaps rather not have witnessed. In Stuart Y. McDougal's words this scene thus becomes a "metafictional moment that forces us to reflect on our own activity as film viewers."[79]

This sense of a metafictional discourse was reinforced, in a more specific sense, via some of the more obvious intertextual gestures in the film. For example, there were a number of indicators toward Kubrick's previous film *2001: A Space Odyssey*. Michel Ciment has noted such allusions as the record sleeve in the boutique, the tramp's comment about men on the moon,[80] and the way "the fetus's eye at the end of *2001* prefigures the close up of Alex's 'mutant' eye at the start of *A Clockwork Orange*."[81] In addition the final line of the film, "I was cured all right," obviously echoed the final line of *Dr. Strangelove*: "Mein Führer, I can walk!" another psychopath at the end of another Kubrick film claiming a redemptive resurrection.[82]

Kubrick may have managed to incorporate metafictional ideas and intertextual themes into the film; however, at the same time, he also managed to stay relatively faithful to the narrative design of Burgess's novel. The narrative structure of the novel was depicted within three symmetrical parts: Alex before he goes to jail; Alex in jail; Alex after jail. The first and third parts being played out in an inverse but symmetrical way. Thus the narrative structure could therefore be seen as a mirror, the events that happen in the first part reoccurring again in the final part of the film; with Alex revisiting those he had previously assaulted, his victims now becoming his persecutors.[83] The original version of Burgess's novel had had a still more symmetrical design; the original British version having 21 chapters (three sections with seven chapters each) affording a numerological pattern adding up to 21— then being the traditional age of majority. The American version of the novel had deleted the last chapter — and significantly this was the version upon which Kubrick had initially based his screenplay. It was not until relatively late in the adaptation process that Kubrick became aware of the omitted chapter. When he discovered it Kubrick, nonetheless, decided not to include it in his adaptation. It has often been assumed that Kubrick was wholly oblivious of the extra 21st chapter; for example, publishing as late as 2005, Pat J. Gehrke was able to blithely claim, "Kubrick was completely unaware of the discrepancy between the two versions."[84] In reality Kubrick had been fully aware and carefully considered the option of whether or not to use the final chapter, as Anthony Biswell, one of Burgess's biographers, noted:

> An unpublished letter to Burgess from Deborah Rogers [Burgess's literary agent] which confirmed that Kubrick "confronted the problem of the novel's two possible endings in the course of preparing the script for his film adaptation."[85]

Biswell went further and quoted the letter, from February 27, 1970, a date significantly early in the process of the adaptation of the novel:

> I spoke to Stanley Kubrick the other day and he is most anxious to know what the correct [version] is from your point of view — whether the extra chapter in the original English edition was added at an editor's suggestion and dropped in America at your own wish — or what.... If you prefer the book without the final chapter (which Kubrick does), as in American editions, I will instantly make sure that the Penguin edition conforms with that — so please do solve the riddle for us. Mr. Kubrick is writing the script himself — and is hard at work.[86]

Biswell concluded: "Kubrick's decision to follow the Norton version, having first sought Burgess's permission to do so through his agent, therefore emerges as a carefully considered aesthetic choice."[87] The final chapter had begun in an almost identical way to the first; we learn that Alex had a new set of droogs, but that his heart is no longer in his old way of life. He has a conventional job, in the "National Gramodisc Archives," and his thoughts are beginning to turn away from the "old ultra violence," and "the old in out in out." Alex wanders into a cafe where he meets Pete — who is married, and Alex begins to think of settling down and having a wife and family himself. In a sense, the chapter could thus be read as a sentimental and optimistic change of heart by Burgess, but ultimately something of an unconvincing one.[88]

Therefore, the fact that Kubrick chose to end his film with the end of the American version of the novel, with the line "I was cured all right," enabled him to preserve a still further satirical quality to the film.[89] In this way the film was a dark comedy, as, in a sense, were all of Kubrick's films. In such a satirical sense, *A Clockwork Orange* was a very funny film, with what might be described as having, like *Dr. Strangelove,* a Swiftian overtone.[90] The epitome of irony within the film, being perhaps best seen in the prison chaplain's shout of "Damn you!" in the middle of his homily/sermon. Robert Kolker is relevant here, Kolker has suggested satire is "rare in American filmmaking," and that it has been replaced by parody or lampoon.[91] Kolker commented further on the sense of irony in the film: "Irony is not highly prized in commercial filmmaking ... [insomuch as] irony disallows redemption."[92] In this sense, irony, it might be argued, was always one of the most significant elements toward an understanding of Kubrick's work, and here, with this film, it was perhaps used to one of its most telling effects.

Finally, one matter to consider was Kubrick's decision (an almost unique one) to withdraw the film from exhibition in the U.K. in 1974. It was not until 2000, a year after Kubrick's death, that this ban was lifted, allowing the film to receive a successful 250-print re-release. When the film had originally been released, in the U.K. in January 1972, it was passed, uncut, by then-censor John Trevelyan, who said of the film:

> I think it is perhaps the most brilliant piece of cinematic art I have ever seen ... in an age when violence is on the increase Kubrick was challenging us to think about it and analyze it. He was trying to shock us out of our complacency and acceptance of violence; yet, although the violence in the film is horrifying, it is stylized, so it presents an intellectual argument rather than a sadistic spectacle.[93]

Nonetheless, Kubrick would later make the decision to personally withdraw the film. The actual and specific reasons for this have always been surrounded with uncertainty. Kubrick's wife, Christiane Kubrick, is on record as going so far as to state: "We received hate mail and death threats."[94] Kubrick's brother-in-law, Jan Harlan, confirmed this: stating that Kubrick "was singled out by various groups ... and received personal threats."[95] It has been suggested that there may have been still further and more sinister reasons, that Kubrick was the victim of potential blackmail or even the threat of kidnapping. In any case, it is clear Kubrick was persuaded/coerced into withdrawing the film in the U.K. for reasons that convinced him it was wise to do so. (The power of Kubrick's withdrawal of the film was so embracing as to even prevent the inclusion of the film in television news obituaries in the U.K. In addition, Kubrick was not averse in going to court if his ban was challenged; however, he cannot have taken much pleasure in witnessing Warner Bros. suing of the Scala cinema, in London, over its illegal showing of *A Clockwork Orange,* an action which would ultimately bring about the cinema's closure in 1993.)

*   *   *

By means of a summary: while *A Clockwork Orange* was perhaps one of Kubrick's least profound films (at least in a cerebral sense), it was certainly one of his most visceral and powerful — when considered from the perspective of an emotional response. It was clearly representative of Kubrick's work as a whole, following many of the same redolent themes found elsewhere in his work; for example: a subtextual wariness and caution toward history, an interest if not obsession with masculine violence, a barely disguised concern with homosocial/homoerotic leanings, a repeated consideration of technological failure, the continued theme of the citadel (here expressed specifically via concerns over the security of the domestic environment), the continued exploration of narrative space, and finally, even a passing glance at the circular journey.[96] From a wider perspective, what might be said to have been so disturbing about the film was both its believability and its beauty. The single-minded focus and the wholly cynical representation of a protagonist, such as Alex, carried a significant degree of narrative weight and power, perhaps one that went beyond even its maker's expectations and designs.[97] The film might be described, in generalized terms, as an attempt to dissect the inhumanity of man in the 20th century, but of course the same could be said of Kubrick's work as a whole. However, with its ideas of an increase in social violence, the use of sex as art, the general decline in culture, the increased use of drugs among the younger elements of society, the cynicism of governments and politicians, the corruption of the police, and other diverse subject areas—the film would appear to have been at least partially successful in portraying an accurate vision of the near future. Insomuch, it remains a deeply disturbing, if deeply thought-provoking film, one that continues to pose questions about ourselves, questions we would perhaps sometimes prefer not to confront.

CHAPTER 5

The Shining

The Misuses of Enchantment

Horror is essential to our literature ... our classic literature is a literature of horror for boys. — Leslie A. Fiedler

Stanley Kubrick's 11th feature film, *The Shining,* was arguably one of his most open and most thought-provoking cinematic texts. It also proved to be a much misunderstood film, although in this it was not alone, as the majority (if not all) of Kubrick's films were initially misunderstood upon their release. The misunderstanding in the case of *The Shining* would appear to have been founded in terms of the disruption of generic expectation. While on the one hand it is clear Kubrick intended to make a film within the horror genre; on the other hand it was perhaps not the horror genre a significant part of his audience was expecting. This, one might argue, is key to an understanding of the film, and hence one issue worthy of exploration in this chapter.

In addition, the film provided a rich repository of materials for critical and theoretical debate. Thus the film will be considered from a diverse range of perspectives: a critique of structuralist and formalist readings of the film as a dark fairy tale; poststructuralist theories of language within Jacques Lacan's concept of mirroring and doubling; Freudian readings of misogyny, the abject female and repressed sexuality; issues of masculinity related to responsibility and the family; fears of the environment linked with mental instability and human fallibility; Marxist issues; postmodern readings; and finally racist issues pertaining to African Americans, Native American culture, and, most polemically, a potential reading of the film as a metaphor for the Holocaust.

However, it would seem relevant to first consider the original source material on which Kubrick based his film. As intimated above, what seems to have attracted Kubrick to Stephen King's novel, of 1977, was the horror genre it was set in, along with King's impressive powers of storytelling. In other words, King's novel offered Kubrick an engaging narrative, coupled with the opportunity to explore another cinematic genre. The point has often been made that Kubrick's films never repeated themselves, and one way in which he achieved this was by exploring a succeeding variety of genres. As Daniel Richter, who played the character of Moon-Watcher in *2001: A Space Odyssey,* commented:

> A way to understand Stanley Kubrick's work is to see him as a genre director who always works in a new genre.... Stanley's way of working is to learn everything about everything. Such ravenous consumption of information needs a limiting factor to keep its bounds. Working within a genre seems to do that for him.[1]

Frederic Raphael would later make a slightly different point: "In a way what Stanley did was to deliberately make use of cinematic genres and change them, break them, subvert the codes you expect to find."[2] Hence one might conclude there was a sense here in which Kubrick deliberately "hijacked" conventional Hollywood genres in order to "interrogate their assumptions."[3] Thus it would seem fair to say that Kubrick consistently approached a cinematic genre with the intention of enclosing it within his own discourse, thereby reinventing it via his own vision. In using the "accumulated mass of inherited plot ideas and visual clichés"[4] from a given genre, Kubrick was able to gain a framework with which to forge his own narratives. In *The Shining,* to some extent, he thus reinvented the horror genre, just as he had previously reinvented the science fiction genre with *2001: A Space Odyssey.* In this sense *The Shining* was a horror film aware of the limitations of the genre it was set in; a genre Kubrick "systematically subverted" replacing it with a "genre all his own."[5] (On a more ideological level, the horror genre was a significant choice for Kubrick in two main senses. Firstly, there was the way in which the genre, at least in American film, tended to promote American values and the American Dream; for example: the idea that money and success are important, the primacy of heterosexual romance, the significance of marriage and family as the proper social forms, police and the legal system as legitimate sources of authority and, overall, that American values were basically benevolent and good. Secondly, there was the idea, as suggested by Leslie Fiedler — as in this chapter's epigraph — that the gothic was a pathological genre, a retreat into an immature, childish setting, with the idea of scaring oneself as ultimately a descent into a masochistic fantasy — fundamentally masturbatory in content.[6])

Thus it is possible to perceive, in the film, of Kubrick's disdain for the literalist and vulgar tastes of the horror genre and hence how he deliberately sidestepped the cheap thrills he could have employed. For example, although we were offered a cross-section of horror film archetypes: the ghosts, the haunted house, the "vampiric" attack to Danny's neck, the idea of selling one's soul to the devil: all these instances were, in some sense, subverted. In 1966 Kubrick had "confessed to a friend once that he would like to make the world's scariest movie, involving a series of episodes that would play upon the nightmare fears of the audience."[7] However, although Kubrick was cognizant of the horror genre's conventions, he had, nonetheless, other aims to this, other discursive levels to explore.[8]

It seems clear Kubrick was cognizant, at an early stage, that much of what happens in King's work was implausible unless it was set within the discursive environment of the horror genre novel. However, Diane Johnson, Kubrick's co-writer on the film's screenplay,[9] claims that from the beginning the film had at least a semblance of a belief in the existence of ghosts; with the inherent admission that the plot made no sense unless one accepted the existence of a supernatural element. In reality it seems there may have been a more subtle intention on Kubrick's part. As Kubrick himself later commented: "For the purposes of telling the story, my view is that the paranormal is genuine.... I hope the audience ... has believed the film while they were watching it."[10]

In other words, Kubrick asked his audience to suspend their sense of disbelief while they were watching the film, in order to experience the subtextual elements inherent in a generic narrative. In addition, one could look here to factors beyond those of artistic intent; insomuch as Kubrick was always a filmmaker as much alert to commercial as artistic considerations. That is, a version of The Shining that had not taken such a literalist account of the supernatural elements would not have made as much money. One must remember here that The Shining was one of the highest grossing films of 1980, one that went on to become one of the ten most commercially successful films ever made by Warner Bros. (In this context, the relative commercial failure of Kubrick's previous film, Barry Lyndon, may arguably be seen as a factor in Kubrick's decision to make The Shining.) Kubrick may possibly have preferred (at least artistically) to have left the narrative more ambivalent in relation to the supernatural elements, but, for wholly commercial considerations, he compromised and allowed the ghosts to remain "real."[11]

Hence one might perceive of a deliberately contrived artifice within The Shining. As intimated above, the film had an awareness, and an intelligence that purposely eschewed the emotional and visceral quality of an authentic horror film; and while Kubrick to some extent compromised in terms of generic expectations, he also consistently undermined the absurdities of the genre. As far as Stephen King was concerned the hotel was actually haunted, but to Kubrick there was much else in which to be interested. Thus, as we shall see, *The Shining* was not so much a horror film, but "a film about horror."[12]

Stephen King's novel, like much of his work as a whole, was determinedly and perhaps deliberately lacking in literary style. However, King's ability, as a storyteller, arguably has had few contemporary rivals, at least within the horror genre. Kubrick was clearly aware of this, he had no great interest in King as a literary figure; witness his rejection of King's screenplay reputedly unread,[13] but he was attracted to the story King had to tell. As Kubrick would later comment:

> The novel is by no means a serious literary work, but the plot is for the most part extremely well worked out, and for a film that is often all that really matters. With *The Shining*, the problem was to extract the essential plot and to re-invent the sections of the story that were weak. The characters needed to be developed a bit differently than they were in the novel. It is in the pruning down phase that the undoing of great novels usually occurs because so much of what is good about them has to do with the fineness of the writing, the insight of the author and often the density of the story. But *The Shining* was a different matter. Its virtues lay almost entirely in the plot, and it didn't prove to be very much of a problem to adapt it into screenplay form ... I had seen *Carrie*, the film, but I had never read any of his novels. I should say that King's greatest ingenuity lies in the construction of the story. He does not seem interested in writing itself. They say he wrote, read over, re-wrote maybe once and sent everything to the editor. What seems to interest him is invention and I think that is his forte.[14]

King described the origins of the novel in an essay entitled: "On Becoming a Brand Name"[15]; it was based on an unpublished short story King had written several years before, a story called "Darkshine"[16]; a story revolving around a plot in which the toys in a young boy's playroom came to life. Then, in the fall of 1974, on October 30, 1974 (the eve of Halloween), to be precise, King, and his wife, Tabitha, were traveling and stayed overnight at a hotel, high in the Rockies, near Boulder, Colorado. The Kings were given room 217, they had dinner in the hotel's Colorado Restaurant, and then, after dinner, unable to sleep, King went to the bar and was served by a bartender called Mr. Grady. A little later, heading back to his room, King got lost in a maze of corridors, but finally finding his way back, he went to the bathroom, and there, looking at the claw footed bath with a pink curtain drawn across it, he thought: "What if somebody died here?" At that moment, in King's words, "I knew I had the book."[17] (The name of the hotel the Kings stayed at, in one of those ironic twists of fate, wasn't the Overlook; it was called the Stanley Hotel.)

As with most of King's work *The Shining* was a long book, its narrative being framed within 447 pages, 58 chapters and five sections.[18] The five sections were titled:

PART ONE: Prefatory Matters
PART TWO: Closing Day
PART THREE: The Wasp's Nest
PART FOUR: Snowbound
PART FIVE: Matters of Life and Death

The 58 chapters were generally titled in a perfunctory way, seemingly reductive and literal; ostensibly more serving of the writer's own organization than being of any viable use to the reader. When Kubrick came to adapt the film he did not need to account for such structural devices, either the chapters or the book's sections. Kubrick's film, as we shall see, was divided into ten sections of its own, most of which were attentive to the compression of space and time.

The narrative voice of the novel was primarily *heterodiegetic*; in other words, it had a generally consistent, omniscient third person narrator. However, there were passages which were almost stream of consciousness in nature; herein the text became *autodiegetic*—first person narrator. This was primarily via Jack, but sometimes Danny and sometimes Wendy; all of whom, at times, recounted the story via their own internal thought processes. King's novel also employed a constant sense of analepsis and prolepsis; the main narrative being repeatedly interrupted with details from the past, mostly dark Oedipal tales of Jack and Wendy's childhood. These narrative techniques operated successfully in the novel, but in Kubrick's much pared down narrative such complex voicings and slippages in time were almost wholly excluded. In the film we were offered a much reduced narrative perspective, herein we were admitted to no one's confidence, and, although it was one of Kubrick's trademarks, the film had no outside narrator — unless, that is, one includes the film's ten title cards.

The viewer to the film was therefore offered a reduced narrative, one in which subtextual issues were arguably encouraged to come to the fore. In this sense the distant relationship between novel and film becomes more apparent; beyond the basic structure of the novel's narrative design, its main characters and a selection of verbatim dialogue, the film had relatively little in common with the novel. As the opening credits of the film stated, it was *"Based on the novel by Stephen King."* This was, on inspection an equitable statement; Kubrick, along with the help of co-adaptor Diana Johnson, took the main pivotal elements of the novel and then went on to forge a differing narrative, wholly of their own making.

This situation was one that was never to Stephen King's liking, King appears to have been under the persistent misapprehension that Kubrick wanted to make a faithful adaptation of his novel; King appears to have consistently failed to grasp that this was never Kubrick's intention. Of course King's novel is still there, on the shelf, exactly as he wrote it, but it was not a novel that interested Kubrick in terms of its adaptation in its own right. As Anthony Magistrale noted: "[Kubrick was] an *auteur* director who understood the absolute legitimacy of his art as a wholly separate entity from its original source."[19]

King famously described Kubrick as a man who "thinks too much and feels too little,"[20] and went on to claim:

> A skeptic such as Kubrick just couldn't grasp the sheer inhuman evil of the Overlook Hotel ... that was the basic flaw: because he couldn't believe, he couldn't make the film believable to others.[21]

However, as will later be argued, there is also the possibility that Kubrick was able to grasp an evil of a somewhat different kind; and that the "sheer inhuman evil of the Overlook Hotel" did not interest Kubrick because it did not, in any meaningful way, exist outside of King's somewhat naive discourse of the horror novel.

*   *   *

It is well known that, while writing the screenplay of the film, Kubrick and Johnson had read Bruno Bettelheim's book, *The Uses of Enchantment*. Diane Johnson:

> In an attempt to understand the essential seriousness of the genre, we discussed *Wuthering Heights, Jane Eyre*. How Poe ended his stories. We read Freud a lot. In his essay on the uncanny, Freud says specific things about why eyes are scary and why inanimate objects like puppets are scary in animate shapes. We talked about the role of memory ... and we read Bruno Bettelheim's book about fairy tales, *The Uses of Enchantment*.[22]

In the book Bettelheim argued, from a Freudian perspective, that fairy tales were far more than the simple stories they were generally thought to be. Bettelheim believed fairy tales revealed a number of ideological maneuvers that, when deconstructed, uncovered a number of significant facets about their own discourses. (For example, a young girl learns she is, by nature, a passive creature, she is the princess who waits patiently on top of the Glass Hill, or is asleep like Sleeping Beauty, or is incarcerated in a tower like Rapunzel — all the time waiting to be rescued by a handsome prince. She also learns she must make herself beautiful to men, because only beauty ranks as worthiness in the patriarchal society of the fairy tale. In addition, Bettelheim argued that fairy tales instructed young girls on the issue of virginity; for example, in *Cinderella* the slipper is made from glass, in Freudian terms shoes are obvious female symbols — small receptacles into which something can slip and fit tightly — the fact that Cinderella's slipper was made of glass reminds one of the hymen, something that can easily be broken and lost. From a male perspective, Bettelheim argued, fairy tales offered a different message; for example, the subtextual meaning of *Jack and the Beanstalk* [albeit drawn somewhat crudely] suggested the story was really about masturbation, it was a parable mitigating a boy's fear of punishment if he was caught with an erection — this being expressed via the metaphor of the beanstalk — while, at the same time, also offering the moral that after puberty a boy must find a constructive goal in society.) Thus fairy tales turn out to be more than mere entertaining fantasies, rather powerful disseminators of romantic myths; which, from a feminist perspective, encouraged the young girls who heard them to act in a way that was thought appropriate to their sexual role within a patriarchal society. In this sense a reading and a further understanding of *The Shining* is enhanced via recourse to some of Bettelheim's ideas; specifically, the film's consistent gestures toward a feminist discourse.[23]

In King's novel there were already a number of fairy tale references; however, it is possible to perceive of how Kubrick exaggerated the fairy tale theme in terms of his reading of Bettelheim, and, in so doing, presenting a diverse arena of provocative issues, both textual and subtextual. Hence, it might be argued, the film enhanced the idea of what might be called the "dark fairy tale" in a diverse number of ways. For example, one might think of Jack self-consciously becoming the big bad wolf to Danny; together with Wendy's portrayal of one of the three little pigs. One also notes the repeated use of the phrase "for ever and ever," in the film; a phrase redolent of fairy tales and a phrase both Jack and the Grady girls use on more than one occasion. Also, one might note the obvious *Hansel and Gretel* inference in Wendy's comment that she will have to leave a trail of breadcrumbs to find her way around the kitchen. One can also perceive of the way in which Jack is given the "three wishes" typical of fairy tale: Jack wishes for a drink and Lloyd appears; the nude young woman in Room 237 seems to fulfill Jack's sexual longing; and, finally, Mr. Grady unbolts the pantry door, allowing Jack to free himself from his prison.[24]

The film also contained references to the fairy tale genre that were, one assumes, deliberately satiric in nature. At one point Jack referred to Wendy as "Wendy-Darling" satirizing the derivation of her name from *Peter Pan*. In fact, one can perceive of King's resourcefulness here in naming the characters in the novel. Jack obviously reminds one of Jack the Giant Killer, while Wendy's name, as intimated, would seem to have originated from *Peter Pan*. In an interesting counterpoint Danny's name appeared to resonate from a differing source; in the Old Testament, Daniel being the only person able to see the writing on the wall; and, of course, in both novel and film Danny was the one who eventually decodes the words *Redrum*/Murder — written on the wall. (The structuralist theorist, Roland Barthes, might be considered here; Barthes often cited statement that the proper name in literary texts was "the prince of signifiers; whose connotations are rich, social and symbolic."[25] Other than

Jack, Wendy and Danny, there were other examples of King's proper names demonstrating rich, social and symbolic properties. Tony — so interested in showing Danny words in reverse — had his own reverse code, the rhetorical: Y NOT? The corporate Stuart Ullman's initials reversed likewise to U.S., while Watson's name was almost risibly Freudian. Al Shockley was the top man, an alpha male; hence Al resonated as an A.1 man. Mr. Grady's name deconstructed to Gray D., very much a gray daddy for the dead Grady girls. Finally, Kubrick added his own satiric gestures, Jack's middle name was Daniel — aptly so for an alcoholic — King seems to have overlooked this inherent joke, Kubrick did not and pertinently showed Jack drinking Jack Daniel's No. 7 bourbon.)

At an albeit more speculative level of interpretation, insomuch as there is no direct documentary evidence, it is possible to suggest that, through Bettelheim, Kubrick was also aware of the work of Vladimir Propp.[26] In 1928, using what would later be seen as structuralist techniques, Propp put forward an analytical design to the Russian folk tale, a design that could be extended to fairy tales in general, and, to a certain extent, to narratives in general. Within the folk tale Propp proposed there were seven spheres of action and 31 sequential narrative functions or situations.[27] The 31 key events within the narrative would take place in the order Propp designed; not all the key events would take place in any particular narrative, but they would take place in the order specified.

What was of interest, in the case of *The Shining*, was the exact way in which Kubrick's film appeared to follow both Propp's designated spheres of action and his narrative sequences. Propp's spheres of action, or character types, consisted of: a villain, a donor, a helper, a princess, a dispatcher, a hero and a false hero. In terms of Kubrick's film we can perceive of these as follows:

VILLAIN	The Overlook Hotel
DONOR	Tony
HELPER	Mr. Halloran
PRINCESS(ES)	The Grady Girls
DISPATCHER	Wendy
HERO	Danny
FALSE HERO	Jack

In terms of Propp's 31 narrative functions, the film directly followed numbers one to 23, and numbers 30 and 31.[28] This could be seen as mere coincidence, but it is possible to argue that Kubrick deliberately used such a Proppian narratological approach, in order to stress the importance of the fairy tale genre in which he chose to place his film. While in addition, as some of his other work shows, Kubrick may have been genuinely interested in structuralist theories of narrative as a whole. Hence, in this case the idea of *The*

Shining as a "dark fairy tale" was, to a greater extent, enhanced; King's novel had followed such an approach, but it would appear the film much more deliberately exaggerated such a property.

*   *   *

One of the most obvious theoretical approaches in which to begin to decode the film derives from a psychoanalytical reading, specifically in terms of Jacques Lacan's ideas surrounding the child's entry from the imaginary into the symbolic. Clare Hanson, in an essay of 1990, entitled: "Stephen King: Powers of Horror," offered one of the first and most perceptive ways in which to approach King's novel from a theoretical perspective; according to Hanson, King's work "betrays a fascination with those primary experiences which impel the construction of the self as a gendered social being."[29] The film did not have the narrative scope to render this theme as explicitly as the novel; but, nonetheless, an exploration of both texts in a Lacanian light arguably reveals a level of discourse worthy of study. Lacan, taking his lead from Freud, perceived of the human child as inhabiting two worlds: the imaginary and the symbolic. Lacan believed we leave the imaginary when we enter the world of language, when we learn how to speak, how to read and write. In addition, Lacan suggested this was exactly the same moment as we became gendered beings. In appropriating Freud's ideas on childhood; for example, the way the child first exists in a blissful state at the mother's breast, and is only removed via the intervention of the father; thus resulting in the incurring repression of Oedipal desires and the subsequent journey from oral to anal to genital stages; Lacan, however, then went further, suggesting the moment in which we leave that blissful state was the moment the unconscious was created. (Furthermore, the fact that we are severed from the mother's body — after the Oedipal crisis — means we spend the rest of our lives trying to rediscover it — sexual love being the obvious substitute. In other words sex promises a return to plenitude — to the blissful state we have lost — but it can never wholly satisfy those needs we have. Union with the mother is seen as perfect — what follows is fragmentation — outside of the satisfaction of the womb and the breast. As we grow up we continue to make such imaginary identifications — in Lacanian terms this offers an explanation for the creation of the ego — a narcissistic process whereby we generate a fictional sense of selfhood.)

In relation to King's novel, the text could be read as a narrative concerned with the child's entry into the symbolic. We note that Danny is desperately trying to accomplish just this throughout the novel. At various instances we are offered examples of how Danny is desperate to learn how to read:

I can't read yet at all.[30]

Mommy said you'd help me put it together as soon as I could read all of the first Dick and Jane.[31]

Danny was hunched over the first of the five battered primers Jack had dug up by culling mercilessly through Boulder's myriad second-hand bookshops.... He hunched over the little books ... as though his life depended on learning to read.[32]

In this sense it could be argued that the underlying strength of the book's narrative power derived from the Oedipal struggle between Jack and Danny. *The Shining* could thus be described as a narrative that follows a male journey through the Oedipal complex. What threatens Danny is Jack's insecure hold on the symbolic, thus Danny has to learn how to read, to decipher the meaning of *Redrum*. We could thus say that the novel plots Danny's journey from innocence to experience, from lack of language to knowledge of language: from the imaginary to the symbolic.

While the film generally neglected Danny's desire to learn how to read, what it did concentrate on was the opposing theme: Jack's insecure and labile hold of his place in the symbolic order. In other words, while Danny was struggling to "master" language, Jack was in danger of losing control over it. "I gave them my word," says Jack early in the film; he means he had made a promise to the corporate owners of the Overlook Hotel, but the interpretation that he had literally given away his word also resonated within a Lacanian interpretation of the film. Jonathan Romney was one critic who appeared to demonstrate an understanding of the subtextual issue at stake here: "By the end of the film he [Jack] has renounced language entirely, pursuing Danny in the maze with an inarticulate animal roar."[33] Romney did not pursue the idea further, but a Lacanian reading in which Jack was losing the symbolic while Danny was racing toward it, toward the symbolic world of language, was present if the viewer wished to perceive of it.[34]

Jack's loss of control over "the word" is perhaps best exemplified in the film's "All work and no play makes Jack a dull boy," a specific aspect of the film's narrative, one not found in the novel. Jack is a writer, but, when we finally discover what he has been writing, all he has produced are hundreds of pages with the same tautological line. Thus Jack *has* become a dull boy, with the implied suggestion that he is regressing toward infantilism. We note at one point, unable to write, Jack appears to revert to childhood by throwing a ball against the walls of the Colorado Lounge; if he cannot write he will play; he will revert from the symbolic world, back into the ludic world of the imaginary. In addition, and perhaps most significantly, at the end of the film Jack loses complete control over language; in the maze, shouting at Danny, his words break down into unintelligible utterances; by the end of the film Jack cannot speak at all. He has, very literally, given the Overlook "his word."

In a contrasting aspect, Danny finally enters the symbolic when he is able to write *Redrum*, which occurs, in the novel, on page 306; although a discerning reader may have worked out the reverse code of the word on its first usage, on page 56. Kubrick made much less use of this idea but when he did use *Redrum*, near the end of the film, it was perhaps pertinent that Danny used his mother's lipstick to write the word, adding not just a sense of horror in its blood red color, but also adding a sense of irony within a Lacanian reading: as what Danny used was, in a sense, a female pen.[35]

A Lacanian reading can also be seen in the use of mirrorings and reflections at use in the film. One of Lacan's most significant concepts revolved around what he referred to as the "mirror stage." This was a time when the young child appears to gain an illusory sense of control over the world by seeing him or herself in a mirror. The young child, not able to speak, identifies with the image of itself it sees in the mirror; identifying with the image by perceiving of the "I" who watches and the "I" who is watched. The child can control the image but is not able to perceive of the split between the two. It is only when the child leaves the comfort of the imaginary world; to enter the symbolic order; the world of conformity, of law, of institution, of order and, most specifically, of language, that this divergence is recognized. (In this sense, language might be seen as offering the promise of recapturing the wholeness of the experience within the imaginary stage. However, this is illusory, as in the sense that the "I" in the mirror is not in a position of unity with the "I" who stands before the mirror. We can never fuse with the "other" even though we might spend our lives in a fruitless search to recapture it — this desire, this "lack," to use Lacan's term, is doomed to remain forever unsatisfied.)

This idea was explored in the film via the consistent ways in which characters and places were mirrored, doubled and reflected. However, what was significant was that the doubling often turned out to be not quite as it first seemed. For example, the two Grady girls were not twins, as often assumed — they were sisters.[36] In a similar sense one notes the confusion between the two Mr. Grady's: Delbert and Charles; it might have seemed they were twinned characters, but they were, in fact, simply the same person with differing first names. Also, there was the confusion between Danny and his alter-ego, Tony; in addition, one might point to the alluring (younger) and the abject (older) versions of the inhabitant of room 237. Finally, there was the supposed twinning of Jack in the present day and Jack in the past, in 1921. Also, there were a number of literal uses of mirrors throughout the film. The very first image of the film was that of a mirror image of an island in a lake; Danny's first conversation with Tony took place in a mirror; when Wendy brings Jack his breakfast in bed the first part of the scene was a mirror image; Jack's conversation with Mr. Grady in the men's bathroom was mirrored; Jack's encounter with the inhabitant of Room 237 occurred in a mirror, and when Jack first "sees" Lloyd in the Gold Room, it is his own reflection he should have been seeing. (There is a custom in the horror film genre that supernatural essences will be revealed via the use of a mirror. Thus a vampire or a ghost will not be reflected in a mirror because of the inherent "holy" quality of the mirror's silvered surface; as, in a similar way, a werewolf can only be slain via a silver bullet. This is a custom subverted in Kubrick's film: Tony shows Danny the truth about the Overlook in the mirror; Jack sees the true nature of the woman in Room 237 in a mirror; and Wendy sees the true nature of *Redrum* in a mirror.)

*   *   *

A discussion of the film in Lacanian terms must, of some necessity, bring Freud (Lacan's precursor) into the discursive arena. This being especially pertinent as it is known (from documentary sources) that Freud's essay, "The Uncanny," was another significant influence on Kubrick in the making of the film. As Diane Johnson commented: "Family hate seemed quite important. We decided that in the case of *The Shining* this was the central element."[37] This is pertinent to the Oedipal conflict of both King's novel and Kubrick's film; wherein the narratives were based around the Oedipal triangle of father, mother and child. In the film the Oedipal triangle was ironically resolved when the father was killed and the child escaped with the mother. In the novel, although the ending was not as explicitly Freudian, a sense of Oedipal rage and aggression was nonetheless clearly apparent. This was expressed insomuch as Wendy is obsessed with her father and despises her mother; while Jack hates his father and venerates his mother. Thus Wendy appears to be continually living in fear of turning into her mother, as Jack is in fear of becoming his father. In contrast to this, Kubrick's film, because of the constraints of the cinematic format, did not include these narrative nuances, but such Freudian references nonetheless operated in the film in the background, demonstrating the sense in which the film had at least an awareness of the novel's Oedipal rages. (In a further example of a Freudian perspective, Geoffrey Cocks has perceived of "anal sadism" in the film. For example, Halloran's remark to Wendy: "You know, Mrs. Torrance, you gotta keep regular if you gonna be happy." In addition, Danny's choice of chocolate ice cream was seen — perhaps somewhat risibly — as being "the color associated with anality."[38] Delbert Grady was seen as "a classic case of the repressed anal type who stresses order and cleanliness."[39] Finally, Cocks saw "anal sadism" in the comment Wendy makes to Danny in the maze: "The loser has to keep America clean." However, it is debatable whether such readings were wholly viable; for example, the final comment, the euphemistic "keep America clean" might alternately have been read as "keeping America white," given the explicit subtext of racism that ran throughout the film.)

Of perhaps greater significance was the way in which the film rejected the innate misogyny implied in the novel, assuming instead what might be described as an almost feminist point of view; perhaps attributable, in part, to Kubrick's co-author of the script, Diane Johnson. In the novel, as in much of King's work, there would seem to have been little awareness of a complex feminist ideology. As writer and critic Chelsea Quinn Yarbro noted, of King's work in general: "It is disheartening when a writer with so much talent and strength of vision is not able to develop a believable woman character between the ages of seventeen and sixty."[40]

In fact, it would seem fair to say that the novel had an innate misogyny, and at times possessed what could be called an overtly sexist discourse. This becomes apparent if one looks at some examples of Jack's internal dialogue in the novel, dialogue that gradually becomes more and more extreme in nature:

> Bitch ... you stinking bitch.[41]
> At times she could be the stupidest bitch.[42]
> You stinking bitch, you'll get what's coming to you.[43]
> Nowhere left to run, you cunt.[44]
> You cheap nickel-plated cold cunt bitch.[45]

All of this culminates in the physical attack on Wendy, which is depicted in the novel in a distinctly sadistic manner. In the novel Wendy is assaulted with the roque mallet, which King recounts with what might be described as a sense of misogynistic relish:

> The mallet came down again with whistling, deadly velocity and buried itself in her soft stomach. The mallet head struck her squarely between her shoulder blades and for a moment the agony was so great she could only writhe, hands opening and clenching.[46]

Kubrick's film did not appear to be as interested in such a level of physical violence toward a female victim. In the film Wendy is terrorized by Jack and verbally abused, but she suffers no actual physical harm; in fact in the film it is Jack who is physically injured by Wendy. In delineating Wendy as something other than a victim of male violence (and as a sexual object, a significant change from the novel) Kubrick was enabled to point the characters of Jack and Wendy in other, arguably more significant directions.[47]

In other words, in avoiding the stereotypical portrayal of a couple within a physical abusive relationship (the violent husband and the beautiful wife), Kubrick was able to depict more convincing characters. For example, Shelley Duvall was deliberately cast, by Kubrick, in this light. Kubrick has commented he wanted an actress who was not overly sexually attractive:

> You certainly couldn't have Jane Fonda play the part: you need[ed] someone who is mousy and vulnerable. The novel pictures her as a much more self-

reliant and attractive woman, but these qualities make you wonder why she has put up with Jack for so long.[48]

One theme Kubrick may have developed, in the light of Jack's lack of subsequent sexual interest in Wendy, might be described as that of the "abject female." This was explored in the film in a variety of ways; the most literal example occurring in the scene in Room 237: a horrifying epiphany, wherein the desirable female form becomes decaying and corruptive. In a more abstract way, the scene in which blood flows from the elevator delineated a similar idea; in a psychoanalytical reading this image representing the "abject female" in a grossly exaggerated manner. This iconic and nightmarish vision could be interpreted from a number of angles, but it specifically put forward fears of the menstrual female, the mother, the womb, the abject entrance to the feminine body.[49] In the novel the elevator looked to Jack "too much like an open mouth,"[50] in the film this could be perceived in a differing symbolic way: the elevator serving as a metaphor for the vagina, a chamber from which torrents of abject menstrual blood flowed. (One might also note how several of the other supernatural visions, experienced by each of the central characters in the film, had a sexual component. For example: Jack and the nude young woman in Room 237, Wendy witnessing the two men having oral sex near the film's *denouement*, and the Grady girls' perverse suggestion to Danny, to "come and play with us.")

Julia Kristeva, in her book, *The Power of Horror* (coincidentally first published in 1980, the same year as *The Shining* was released) argued, from a Freudian and Lacanian perspective, that anything fluid, anything wet about the body, as in the secretions of male and female in coitus, defiles and, hence, were abject. Women's menstrual blood being particularly abject within a patriarchal discourse; perhaps pointing to an unconscious fear of the power of the female body, but also the sense in which the vagina, already redolent of castration anxiety, proved even more problematic when shedding blood. (In this sense it is perhaps interesting to note how our culture seeks to exhibit a fetishistic interest in the underwear women wear. This could be explained by the idea that underwear replaces the genitals as the primary source of erotic excitement, hence managing to evade the underlying phobia towards the female genitals themselves.)

Thus this "strange object," full of moisture and fluidity, associated with unclean and improper connections, becomes the most abject part of the female body.[51] As cultural critic Lynn Segal put it: "The vagina has served as a condensed symbol of all that is secret, shameful and unspeakable in our culture."[52] As far as "unspeakable" goes, it is perhaps relevant to note that the most obscene word in our culture relates directly to the vagina. As to just what the essential reason for this sense of "abjection" might be, one might argue that, as suggested above, a metaphor of castration anxiety was at play.

Thus, *The Shining* was literally a "slasher" movie, exploiting the repressive fears of the vagina as a cut, a wound, a place that had been "slashed," woman thus unconsciously becomes to be seen as a castrated man. In a slightly differing context, the persistent desire in pornography of displaying the so called "meat shot," the open vagina, might — on one level — be explained via Luce Irigaray's idea[53] of the repeated desire to be sure women still have "no thing"; in other words, that women do not possess "the thing," the phallus.

In contrast to this, the film's purposeful neglect of heterosexual desire could be interpreted as deriving from the idea that Jack was either potentially or literally impotent. This idea being supported explicitly by Jack's offhand remark to Lloyd: "Just a little problem with the old sperm bank upstairs." In addition, the idea was further enhanced by Kubrick's adoption of a standard impotence metaphor. To put this somewhat crudely: in a range of Hollywood films male lameness often appeared to be an unofficial pointer toward impotence and symbolic castration. There were numerous examples: in Arthur Penn's *Bonnie and Clyde* (1967) we learned that Clyde was impotent, we also learn that while in prison he has had two of his toes amputated. Alfred Hitchcock used a similar motif in a number of his films, for example, in *Rear Window* (1954) wherein James Stewart had a broken leg and was temporarily marooned in a wheelchair — he was metaphorically if not literally impotent and reduced to voyeurism. In Don Siegel's *The Beguiled* (1970) Clint Eastwood played a Yankee soldier, wounded during the Civil War, and taking refuge in a southern seminary for young women; after transgressing their sexual codes he suffers a brutal revenge — his wounded leg being amputated. In Richard Brooks's *Cat on a Hot Tin Roof* (1958) Paul Newman played one of Tennessee Williams's many repressed homosexuals, his inability to satisfy his wife — Elizabeth Taylor — being symbolized by his spending the whole film on crutches. Finally, in another Stephen King adaptation: Rob Reiner's *Misery* (1990), the character played by James Caan suffered a gruesome attack on his body by his supposed "biggest fan" — Kathy Bates's character, again symbolizing lameness and castration anxieties — her character explicitly stating she has spared the protagonist's "manhood" in attacking his foot instead. In terms of Kubrick's work, there were already a number of men marooned (impotently) in wheelchairs[54]; and in *The Shining*, Jack was symbolically rendered impotent, in this sense, via the injury to his ankle. Thus Jack was lamed, in the sense that the term "Oedipal" ultimately translates as "swollen foot." In *The Shining* such a paradigm was further enhanced via the feminized prison — a pantry — in which Jack was held after being lamed; and, still further to this, the way Jack ultimately regained his dominant masculine potential via the adoption of an aggressively phallic axe.[55]

In a final discursive maneuver within this specific arena, one could speculate that Jack's lack of a heterosexual interest in his wife might potentially point toward a homoerotic discourse. As has been argued in previous chapters, a homosocial and homoerotic discourse runs visibly throughout Kubrick's work; and, in the case of *The Shining*, this was enhanced insomuch as a strong homoerotic theme could already be perceived in the novel, arguably one of the reasons Kubrick was drawn to the book in the first place. On the one hand the novel was inherently homophobic, while on the other one could hardly help but perceive of the barely concealed homoerotic discourse. The homophobic praxis could be seen mostly at the start of the novel, concerning Watson's attitude toward Mr. Ullman. In the novel Ullman is a variant character to Kubrick's pleasantly bland corporate image, in the novel Ullman is a somewhat prissy and repressed character whose sexuality is constantly questioned by Watson, the Overlook's summer caretaker:

> "That fat fairy upstairs would scream all the way to Denver if he saw the water bill."[56]
>
> "Yes, sir," Watson said [talking to Ullman] and Jack could almost read the codicil in Watson's mind: *"you fucking little faggot."*[57]

Later Watson questions Jack's sexuality:

> "Say, you really are a college fella, aren't you? Talk just like a book. I admire that as long as the fella ain't one of those fairy boys. Lots of 'em are. You know who stirred up all those college riots a few years ago? The hommasexshuls, that's who."[58]

Jack's attitude to Ullman is only slightly more subtle. Jack's first thought about Ullman, the opening line of the book, is: *"Officious little prick."*[59] While Jack's second thought about Ullman occurs when he was standing close enough to the hotel manager to sense his cologne, with the narrative imparting this internal thought of Jack's: "All my men wear English Leather or they wear nothing at all."[60] This comment, comes from Jack's mind, "for no reason at all"[61] and while King did not elaborate further, nonetheless, the comment at least offers a certain degree of ambiguity into Jack's way of thinking.

The opening of the novel linked to a later scene, wherein Jack is thinking of George Hatfield, the schoolboy with whom he had lost his temper and assaulted. As the narrative's heterodiegetic voice tells us: "Tall and shaggily blond, George had been an almost insolently beautiful boy."[62] Jack later dreams of George's corpse floating in the bath in Room 217:

> Lying in the tub, naked, lolling almost weightless in the water, was George Hatfield, a knife stuck in his chest. The water around him was stained a bright pink. George's eyes were closed. His penis floated limply, like kelp.[63]

One obvious interpretation would be to perceive of the cause of Jack's dreams as being that of repressed same-sex desire.

In the film Kubrick did not have the narrative scope to include such speculations around Jack's sexuality. The only explicit homoerotic scene is the surreal vision of two men indulging in fellatio, which Wendy "shines" near the end of the film. However, one might, on close attention, have noted Jack is shown reading *Playgirl* at the start of the film, raising at least a certain degree of ambiguity. In addition, the film presented the gentle suggestion, within the characters of Stuart Ullman and Bill Watson, of a same-sex couple.[64] It is possible, with a knowledge of such a clearly defined homoerotic subtext in the novel, that Kubrick purposefully added these homoerotic gestures in the film. While, at the same time, furthering the clear sense of a homosocial discourse that prevailed within the body of his work as a whole.

In a differing context, the inherent sexual tensions within the film could be framed within Eve Kosofsky Sedgwick's ideas on the homosocial basis of male-to-male relationships. As alluded elsewhere in this book, Sedgwick argued that male-to-male desire was legitimized within Western society and culture on a homosocial basis, and that the intense desire felt between men was rigidly controlled within a patriarchal discourse.[65] In the film, Jack's "intense" relationships with men seems to bear this out. For example, Jack's relationship with Lloyd, the sinister, spectral barman, is of significance in a homosocial light. Jack and Lloyd talk to each other as if they are lifelong friends: "I like you, Lloyd, I always liked you," says Jack. He and Lloyd seem comfortable with each other. A Faustian pact may be being struck; Jack is selling his soul, but he still appears very much at ease with Lloyd. In a similar sense, Jack's relationship with Mr. Grady has overt homosocial tendencies, and is especially satiric inasmuch as their main encounter took place, with just the two of them, in a gentlemen's restroom.

The confusion seen within Jack's character, pertaining to his sexuality, is also intertwined in the inherent hatred he appears to feel for the role he is forced to lead within the family, and, by inference, within the capitalist system. This is a significant element in the film, in this sense the horror at the heart of *The Shining* was the horror of the dysfunctional American family and masculinity's displacement within it. One could therefore say one of the most significant differences between King's novel and Kubrick's film resided in their respective outlooks on the American family. In King's novels one perceived of the recurrent idea that the American family, and all its inherent ideological baggage, was "good" and that "evil," in the form of the various supernatural forces King offered, came from without. However, in Kubrick's work, adopting a more cynical, misanthropic and arguably more realistic stance; there was the alternate idea that the American family was flawed, and that "evil" came from within. Thus the film became a critique of the American nuclear family, and, hence, not the horror film Stephen King and many of his fans were hoping for. In Robert Kolker's words the film foregrounded:

the function of patriarchy ... within the context of the family and the explosion of violence inherent within the repression that so often constitutes the family unit.[66]

The key focalizer in this context of the film was obviously Jack. Jack appeared to resent having to conform to being a husband, a father, a breadwinner and a provider. In the film, and to at least some extent in the novel, Jack's resentment was pointed toward his family, rather than toward the exploitative capitalist system to which he was obviously enchained. Thus we can perceive here of a narrative built around the innate hatred of a man's role within the hegemony of a capitalist system, but with that hatred sublimated and aimed elsewhere. Such an idea impacts on poststructuralist concepts of the family representing *the* significant element of a stable capitalist society. As critic Tamsin Spargo, speaking of just this point, argued: "The key unit of this social order was the bourgeois family within which the future work force would be produced."[67]

Jack may have dreamed of a cathartic respite from the relentless domestic assaults on his ideal of masculinity, but he had no way of achieving it. As Kubrick himself put it:

Jack doesn't have very much further to go for his anger and frustration to become completely uncontrollable. He is bitter about his failure as a writer. He is married to a woman for whom he has only contempt.[68]

Within Jack's situation at the Overlook, one perceives of a continual sense of a man striving to escape the snares of responsibility, of marriage and of domesticity. Thus there is a sense in which Jack feared women because of the pernicious compromise they posed in terms of his sense of what it meant to be a man. It is because Jack cannot express his masculinity in a sexual way with Wendy, or express himself culturally via his writing, that a descent into psychosis appears to be almost inevitable. In other words, because there is no other means of actual physical escape, a descent into madness appears to be Jack's only viable option. (We might note, in this context, that Jack was a well-rounded failure: failing as a teacher, a writer, a father, a husband, a hotel caretaker, and even a failure in his final role: as a mad axe man.)

In this light a Marxist reading of *The Shining* might envisage Jack as the job hunter, almost willing to sell his soul in order to survive within a capitalist system. The Overlook Hotel thus becoming a metaphor for exploitation, a symbol for the American capitalist way of life; a contrast to the promise of the American dream that suggested if you work hard you will succeed. In such a context it is clear that issues of class are redolent in the film from the very beginning. One notes, for example, how, after having been shown the opulence of the hotel, the Torrances are taken to their modest servant quarters and are quite literally "put in their place." Furthermore, we later note how Jack appears as very much a working class figure among the jet-set clientele of the ghosts he encounters in the Gold Room. The Overlook thus becomes a repository for American class divisions, encapsulated by Ullman's acerbic phrase: "All the best people."

From the opening words of the film, Jack seems subservient, very much the economic unit in a capitalist system:

Jack: Hi I've got an appointment with Mr. Ullman. My name is Jack Torrance.

We note that Jack is called Jack:

Ullman: Oh, well —come on in, Jack.

While Mr. Ullman is addressed as Mr. Ullman:

Jack: Nice to meet you, Mr. Ullman.

Hence one of the subtle features of Kubrick's intent was to offer an American film with explicit issues of social class. It is sometimes said that American texts are about trying to find oneself in the landscape, while English texts are about trying to find oneself in a social hierarchy. In Kubrick's work, and particularly in *The Shining*, this was arguably one of the most carefully contrived of themes; and here, in this film, Kubrick managed to combine the two most successfully. (In this strict sense, one might argue that *Spartacus* was Kubrick's only authentic Marxist film, attributable most likely to the contributions of scriptwriter Dalton Trumbo and novelist Howard Fast; however, more than any Kubrick film since then, *The Shining* examined the idea that there is little immune to the corrosive implications of capitalism.)

In the novel Jack is continually obsessed with work, and in the film (as previously alluded) Kubrick deftly summarizes and emphasizes this in the repeated and seemingly meaningless logorrhoea Jack turns out to have been typing: "All work and no play makes Jack a dull boy." However, within this line of text, Kubrick could again be seen as delineating a clear Marxist discourse. All work (a unit in the capitalist machine) and no play (no sexual outlet) has made Jack a markedly dull boy, so much so that he has lost his sanity. In many ways this is *the* key line in the film, not least in the light of Marx's celebrated comment: "Constant labor of one uniform kind destroys the intensity and flow of a man's animal spirits." Herein there is a sense in which capitalism had ground Jack down; yet almost with the sense he had accepted it willingly. In other words, the sense in which capitalism prevails by persuading the majority (who it exploits) to narrowly define their interests for the minority (whom enjoy the fruits of such exploitation). In a previous time, this being achieved by simple deprivation; in the present by imposing a false standard of what is and what is not desirable. In other words, the sense in which capitalism encourages us to believe work will provide wealth which will make us happy; this being one reading of the line in the film.

*   *   *

The cause of Jack's descent into madness is not made clear in the film. In the novel Jack's delusional psychosis is explained, albeit somewhat reductively, insomuch as Jack had simply been possessed by the evil spirits of the Overlook. However, the film poses other readings; namely resentment (the curtailing of Jack's belief in his dream of becoming a great writer), alcoholism and intimations of impotency. This arguably leads to the descent into psychosis, a descent into the meaningless ten-word phrase Jack had repeatedly been typing. However, if there is no explicit explanation, there is a metaphor at work; in the film Kubrick uses the hotel's maze (not apparent in the novel) as a metaphorical indicator of Jack's insanity. (Note that along with the use of the hotel's maze, a diverse range of the iconic images in the film did not derive from the novel, for example: the yellow Volkswagen driving into the Rockies; Danny's ride on his buggy around the hotel; the repeated images of the two Grady sisters; Jack's typing of "all work and no play"; the elevator shaft disgorging blood; Jack's cry of "H-e-r-e's Johnny!" the film's ending in a photograph — none of these were apparent in the novel.) The labyrinthine passages of the maze represent the sense in which Jack has lost his sense of awareness within his own conscious being. Jack is blocked, Jack is lost, Jack is adrift, Jack is deteriorating, Jack is sealed within the closed circle of the society and culture in which he finds himself. The corollary being a closed circle of psychosis, from which, like the maze, there is no escape.[69]

For viewers of the film the only escape is via the ambivalent and challenging ending; an ending that still remains at the edge of interpretation. Kubrick was rare among American filmmakers in that he not only respected the intelligence of his audience, but also continually challenged their intelligence, a feature found in the endings of a number of his films. It was apparent, from the start, that Kubrick was unlikely to have used the ending as it appeared in King's novel. The idea of ending the film with the novel's exploding boiler, being rejected by Kubrick at an early stage as clichéd, telegraphed and narratively unsatisfying.[70]

In a spatial and chronological sense, one could state that the film's narrative progressed toward an end point, an end point wherein time and space became regressive, and, significantly, accelerated within their regression. We could interpret the compression of time in the film's structure, in the sense it suggests the ending reaches a moment of singularity, to the extent that Jack appears to revert back to the past. This being represented by the compression of place and time in the film: mountain to hotel to maze to photograph; and then months to weeks to days to hours. As in the film's various sections:

The Interview
Closing Day
A Month Later
Tuesday
Thursday
Saturday
Monday
Wednesday
8 A.M.
4 P.M.

In this way the accelerating of time adds weight to the final image of the film, as if time had compressed into a single point, to what might be called an "Oedipal moment," when all restraints of rational order were let loose, as if time was rushing to a finite end point.

Stephen King claimed that the film's final scene had been used before on *The Twilight Zone*[71]; and Richard T. Jameson also described the film as having "a *Twilight Zone* twist at the end."[72] Whether or not this was wholly factual is difficult to ascertain[73]; however, from a technical and an ideological perspective, the film's ending would appear to have been operating at a different level than that of *The Twilight Zone*.[74] If nothing else, the ending of *The Shining* demonstrated Kubrick's mastery of the camera. The tour-de-force of the long tracking shot into the photograph appeared to offer us a camera with the same ability to travel into the past — as the camera's ability — in the opening title sequence of the film, to offer a god-like perspective on humanity.

In terms of an ideological perspective, the ending offered a range of significant narrative features: Danny's adroit outwitting of his father in the maze, followed by the sudden cut to Jack — frozen in death — and then the enigmatic sense of closure in the photograph from 1921. In the case of the latter feature, the cinematography was of particular importance; for one last time in the film Kubrick's camera was on the move. In one smooth, unbroken "tracking" shot, with the camera moving gracefully through the corridors of the Overlook, finally ending, via a slow and impeccably controlled zoom, into the wholly ambiguous image of the 1921 photograph. (An additional element here was the way the musical soundtrack enhanced the mood during the film's closure. Luis M. Garcia-Mainar has noted the most commonly heard extradiegetic music in the film was "ominous and lack[ed] melody" while the diegetic music, as heard at the ball, was "melodic, soft and friendly."[75] In this way one could see the lush and tuneful music of the film's closure as suggestive of the Overlook tempting Jack to return, pulling him back to the past.)

It was, in Jonathan Romney's words: "An uncanny end to an uncanny film."[76] Romney went on to note the well-known fact (as already alluded to in this chapter) that Kubrick and Johnson had read Freud's essay, "The

Uncanny," while writing the film's screenplay. In such a context Romney quoted Freud's definition of the uncanny as "that class of the frightening which leads back to what is known of old and long familiar."[77] In this sense it was entirely possible that Kubrick's ending was a reference to Freud. The image of Jack, forever frozen in the past, was both familiar and frightening, as it was wholly uncanny. However, in addition the image, wholly enigmatic, contained (as Diane Johnson has commented) all the artistic satisfactions of a fairy tale. Thus we were back within the connotative designs of the fairy tale to find that Jack had always been there, with the corollary that the Overlook was a place where one really can stay "for ever and ever."

Thus the ending of the film pointed toward both endings *and* beginnings, to paraphrase T.S. Eliot: to arrive where we started and to know that place for the first time. As critic P.L. Titterington noted: "In *The Shining* we are concerned with a journey's end, the point in human experience where all journeys come to a halt."[78] In terms of this, the film offered one further clue, one last piece of narrative information. The final moments of the film left us with the inscribed date: July 4th, 1921. A narrative detail that might be seen as a deliberate gesture toward an Oedipal juncture; insomuch as it suggested the date of America's birth, and the film, as we have seen, continually positioned the Overlook as a kind of repository and metaphor for America itself. Thus the final destination might be said to reside in the past, and Jack's final gaze into the camera might be seen as a search toward the past for an answer. As Jonathan Romney put it: "At the Overlook, it's always 4 July 1921—although God knows what happened that night."[79] In this we envisage a true vision of eternal damnation, recalling Mr. Grady's comment: "You have always been the caretaker. I should know, sir. I've always been here." (The film's enigmatic ending was perhaps less confusing if compared to another enigmatic ending from Kubrick's canon: *2001: A Space Odyssey*. The room at the end of *2001* was arguably as ambiguous as the photograph of 1921 at the end of *The Shining*. One notes, for example, how both films ended in similarly baffling hotel rooms; the end of *2001* seemed to speak of man's last night in an ornate hotel room; and there was a sense in *The Shining*, in an albeit different way, that Kubrick was presenting a similar idea.)

*   *   *

The aporic ending of the film also pointed, within a certain context, toward a postmodern reading.[80] In 1979, the year before the release of *The Shining*, Jean François Lyotard had famously defined postmodernism as "incredulity toward metanarratives."[81] In this sense, Lyotard's ideas on postmodernism signaled the collapse of all universal meta-narratives—the way such big stories presented a privileged truth was disregarded in favor of the increasing sound of a plurality of voices from the margins. In the novel, King's somewhat simplistic and sentimental discourse told us that "truth comes out, in the end it always comes out."[82] However, it would seem that Kubrick's film operated within a more skeptical and satiric discourse. One might argue that the film pointed, within a certain discourse at least, toward Lyotardian concepts of postmodern "nihilism." Here, and in Kubrick's work as a whole, one perceives of a stance pointing to the postmodern idea of multiple interpretations within a fluid discourse; as Geoffrey Cocks put it: "*The Shining* is Kubrick's clearest expression of the contingency of human existence in a cold, silent, absurd universe — a hotel empty save for demons — devoid of meaning or purpose."[83] Hence the "truth" did not come out in Kubrick's film, it was more knowingly positioned within a plurality of voices on the margins of interpretation.

If one were to take an overall view of postmodern theory, one of its main arguments was to suggest a fundamental shift in the human psyche occurred at the end of World War II. The Holocaust, and the dropping of the atomic bombs on Japan, caused a belief and confidence in old traditional values, already shaken, to begin to break down altogether. Ideas of providence, progress and truth became harder to uphold. Truth became a relative term; instead there were merely differing kinds of truth; in a Foucauldian sense truth depended on who had the most power in whatever discourse was in question. We were left with an indifferent universe, or worse, a meaningless universe. A universe that needed no moral character (after Darwin), a universe that required no God (after Einstein), a universe that — according to Freud — presented us as subjective identities with no specific aim or purpose, merely a "clutter" of conscious and unconscious desires. The path from providence, progress and truth — to the nihilism of the postmodern world — seems to have been a "one way street," and it is such a world, one might argue, that Kubrick offered in *The Shining.*

It has commonly been suggested that Kubrick had a pessimistic view of the world, but, in terms of the postmodern environment described above, one might differ. Kubrick was an individual and an artist, working within his own time, who merely responded to the world he perceived. The use of the horror genre simply allowed him to respond to what he perceived in a more exaggerated way. Kubrick:

> There's something inherently wrong with the human personality. There's an evil side to it. One of the things horror stories can do is to show us the archetypes of the unconscious: we can see the dark side without having to confront it directly.[84]

A reading of the film in this light, in terms of Kubrick's idea that there is an "evil side" of the human personality, could also be seen as pertaining to issues of racism, both within the film's American setting and without it. *The Shin-*

ing was a film that dealt obliquely but significantly with issues of race. The character of Mr. Halloran is an obvious place to begin; according to Kubrick, Halloran's character was relatively easy to read:

> Halloran is a simple, rustic type who talks about telepathy in a disarmingly unscientific way. His folksy character and naive attempts to explain telepathy to Danny makes what he has to say dramatically more acceptable than a standard pseudo-scientific explanation. He and Danny make a good pair.[85]

One notes the racial implications here, insomuch as Kubrick was portraying, albeit innocently, "the black man" in the stereotypical fashion of "black man" as child.[86] Denise Bingham considered Kubrick's stance to racial issues in the film in this light:

> The presentation of the black character as a collection of deep-seated stereotypes exemplifies the danger of Kubrick's cryptic, elliptical style of exposition and signification, once again moving critics to misread (perhaps) his intentions. Kubrick's confused attitude toward women is compounded with his confused attitude toward blacks: he seems not to have thought very much about either (perhaps the only modern issues he hasn't thought very much about).[87]

How seriously Bingham's opinion should be accepted is open to question. There are certainly few significant female characters in Kubrick's work, and still fewer black ones. However, a more correct assessment might be to suggest that Kubrick's attitude toward "women and blacks" was merely an expression of relative disinterest; given that Kubrick's real interest was always towards men, usually white men.

Nonetheless, while Halloran was, at times, positioned in a stereotypical way, it would seem clear that *The Shining* was a film decidedly unconfused in its attitude toward America's racism. The irony in Jack's comment to Lloyd should not be overlooked: "White man's burden," Jack says, recalling issues of class and racial superiority within a discourse of Kipling's self-righteous Victorian paternalism. One might consider here Jack's conversation with Mr. Grady. Grady refers to Mr. Halloran as: "A nigger, a nigger cook." Jack's incredulity at the utterance of the word is significant; "A nigger?" Jack says with a note of almost complete incomprehension. Jack may be losing his sanity and may soon be contemplating the murder of his family, but his liberal sensibilities were still shocked by the use of such politically incorrect and "murderously" racist language.

In a similar sense, the issue of Native American peoples was positioned within the narrative in an unobtrusive but significant way. Such a theme was already present in the novel if not as strongly expressed; however, it found a clearly delineated ideological intent in the film. For example, the narrative detail that the Overlook was built on a Native American burial ground; one could argue Kubrick included such narrative information in order to further explore one of his primary themes: that of racial exploitation. In addition, within the interior of the hotel we constantly "see" examples of Native American culture: the wall hangings, the designs on the furniture drapes and other cultural objects. Or do we "see" them — one of the subtle strategies Kubrick employed in the film was to show the audience signs of Native America in almost every frame of the film, but to suggest we never really see them, thus, in a sense, we *overlook* them. This acting as a potential, if latent metaphor, for the way in which the Native American has consistently been overlooked and written out of American history.[88] In this sense, one of the most striking and frequently seen of the film's supernatural visions— the flooding river of blood that gushes from the elevator shaft — gains an additional relevance. As discussed above, this operated to symbolize the abject nature with which Jack viewed the female subject; however, it also served in another symbolic way. We have been told the hotel was built on a Native American burial ground, hence the river of blood will presumably sink into the ground itself — it is the blood upon which the nation state was built. The Overlook Hotel, as has been argued, symbolizes the best and the worst of American history, not the least here, and this, one might argue, was Kubrick's clear and present intent.[89]

"Is there something bad here?" Danny asks Mr. Halloran early in the film. There is if we perceive of the Overlook as a repository of America's guilt toward Native American peoples. The film presents us here with the inherent contradictions of a free republic deeply committed to slavery and genocide.[90] The genocide of the Native American peoples (and the enslavement of tens of millions of African-Americans), was the issue at stake here. Thus the (birth) date apparent at the film's closure could therefore be seen as pointing to the birth of one nation and the death of another. In this sense *The Shining* was very much a satiric American film; from the American flag on Ullman's desk at the beginning, to the July 4th caption at the end. In addition, as intimated, it was also a film that purposefully "overlooked" significant elements of American history. In this sense the film was not about the murders at the Overlook Hotel, it was about the murder of other peoples, peoples other than the dominant white peoples (all the best people), and the consequences of those murders.

In the context of racial genocide, some critics, primarily Geoffrey Cocks, have seen the film as having a specific subtextual design. It is suggested that the most significant subtext in Kubrick's film refers to what was arguably *the* most significant event in the history of the 20th century: the Holocaust. In a series of essays, dating from 1987, 1991 and 2003, culminating in the monograph, *The Wolf at the Door: Stanley Kubrick, History and the Holocaust* (2004), Cocks presented an overarching reading of the film in this light. While there is a wide range of circumstantial detail pointing toward this interpretation, it must be said that, at times, such a reading appears in danger of becoming overly extended. For example, Cocks sees a number of clues in the foreboding opening of the film[91]; he finds significance in the change of color in Jack's car, from dull red in the novel to yellow in the film[92]; he also links the adaptive soundtrack by Carlos and Elkind: "Dies Irae" (The Days of Wrath); Cocks notes that Kubrick did not use Krzystof Penderecki's "Dies Irae" insomuch as it was also known as "The Auschwitz Oratorio" which may have been considered as too direct a reference within "his indirect discourse on the Holocaust."[93] (Cocks also noted how much of the soundtrack for the film derived from Eastern Europe "during the era of that region's greatest suffering and tragedy," in other words the Holocaust.[94] Cocks went on to note that both Bartok and Penderecki were "directly affected by the disasters of Nazism."[95] Note, however, that in King's novel Wendy thinks, at one point, of listening to Bartók.[96] Note also, that Penderecki's music had been used previously in horror films; for example, in *The Exorcist*, released a number of years before *The Shining*.) In addition, Cocks also noted such details as the typewriter on which Jack writes his "novel," an Adler, a German machine adorned with an eagle, being reminiscent of a Nazi emblem. In German, the word "adler" meant eagle, and Cocks denoted how an eagle was a symbol of past and present: of latter-day Nazi Germany and present-day America—which Cocks perceived as forging a link between "American 'genocide' of the Indians and Nazi extermination of the Jews."[97] In addition, Cocks perceived of Grady and Jack as symbolic figures who carry out the "dirty work of killing for their social, political and economic masters. The effect here is not so much to invoke the supernatural steering of events as to evoke the horror of the bureaucratic process of modern mass murder."[98] Finally, Cocks concluded that:

> The Final Solution was not a rational system gone wrong; it was a rational system gone horribly right. The message is clear as well as—ironically and appropriately—unheard ... in our century, the century of genocide. For filmmaker Kubrick ... in this century as in all centuries, what haunts us is not the supernatural. What haunts us is history.[99]

It should be noted that Frederic Jameson had previously made a similar point in his discussion of the film:

> The Jack Nicholson of *The Shining* is possessed neither by evil as such nor by the "devil" or some analogous occult force, but rather simply by History, by the American past as it has left its sedimented traces in the corridors and dismembered suites of this monumental rabbit warren.[100]

It is clear that Kubrick had a consistent interest, not to say a mild obsession, with the Holocaust.[101] Kubrick was born in 1928, into a Jewish background, his adolescence coinciding with the unspeakable horrors taking place in Germany. While he seems to have had a relatively happy childhood (his father was a doctor, his mother maintained the family household) the horrors that were occurring in Europe in the 1930s and 1940s, for similarly well-off Jewish families, must have seemed very close to a Jewish child growing up "safe and plump" in America. In the light of this, it is perhaps not too exaggerated a view to place Kubrick as a man haunted by the Holocaust, but who never succeeded in approaching it directly via his work.[102] As Michael Herr put it: "Probably, what he most wanted to make was a film about the Holocaust, but good luck putting all of that into a two-hour movie."[103] The question that thus arises is this: would it have actually been possible? While Kubrick may have been able to avoid the Spielbergian sentimentality of *Schindler's List* and have made a film truthful to the horrors of the Holocaust, one has to ask whether anyone would have been able to attend such a film without averting one's eyes from the horror and hell the "shining" screen would have offered.[104] To cite cultural critic David Lehman:

> The horrors wrought by the Nazis, so singular in their cruelty and so unprecedented in their scope, still defy comprehension even as they demand to be understood.[105]

Perhaps such a task was beyond art, beyond those human values on which art was based, and, hence, beyond even a filmmaker of Kubrick's resources. As alluded to at the start of Chapter 2, Theodor Adorno suggested that we should avoid dealing directly with certain horrors in art and literature, because it is not possible to put them into an aesthetic form. In Adorno's words there is a "holy dread," that precludes the depiction of certain horrors within a cultural discourse. Thus, while Kubrick had been able to approach a holocaust of a certain kind with *Dr. Strangelove,* a satirical, black comedic take on nuclear war and the end of the world, there may simply have been no way he could have approached a depiction of the Holocaust itself.[106]

In this light, Geoffrey Cocks has argued that "the dark heart of *The Shining* lies deeper. The Holocaust ... serves in *The Shining* as the veiled benchmark of evil."[107] However, while there may be a temptation to follow such a beguiling interpretation, it would seem, using a Barthesian model, that this was somewhat reductive. In other words, instead of looking toward authorial intent, each reader/viewer of the film was free to make their own individual reading.[108] Yet, there was arguably at least one authentic allusion to the Holocaust in *The Shining*: that being Kubrick's "beguiling" depiction of the two Grady sisters. Diane Arbus once stated: "A photograph is a secret about a secret. The more it tells you the less you know." One might argue that a real key to understanding a potential Holocaust metaphor in Kubrick's film was to perceive of a semiotic signal toward the director's former colleague at *Look* magazine, photographer Diane Arbus.[109] The image of the two Grady girls resonated throughout the film with an iconic status matched by few other images. The clear reason being that this image resonated upon a previous image, on the 1967 Arbus photograph: *Identical Twins*. This being explained via the sense that the image of the Grady Girls directly related to Arbus's disturbing photograph; which, by inference, could not help but echo, albeit deep in the subconscious, with Josef Mengele's experiments on twins within the concentration camps.[110]

It might be noted that the Grady girls were mentioned only rarely in the novel,[111] while in the film Kubrick deliberately gave them more prominence. This prominence was clearly as sisters and not as twins; however, the fact (as mentioned previously) that a wide range of critics mistakenly referred to them as twins, perhaps reinforces the idea that Arbus's image resonates within the public consciousness. According to Christiane Kubrick, Kubrick did not cast the two girls deliberately to resemble the Arbus photograph; in 2005 journalist Sean Hagen had interviewed Kubrick's widow:

> I asked her if, as some critics have suggested, the girls' image was based on the famous Diane Arbus portrait of two similar looking girls. "No," she replies, "he cast them as he saw them from Stephen King's book. He liked how utterly serious they looked."[112]

This may be the case, but there was, nonetheless, a strong suspicion that such an allusion was a conscious intent on the part of the film, that the film deliberately alluded to Arbus's photograph and that it hence created a sense of unease via the allusion to Mengele's experiments of "holy dread." This is not to say, as a critic from Geoffrey Cocks's perspective might argue, that the film possessed an overarching and deliberately contrived Holocaust subtext. Such a gesture rather confirmed Kubrick's overall view of the world: his pessimistic outlook and his bleak sense of humor.

In a certain sense *The Shining* was a flawed film, as Michael Herr commented:

> *The Shining* ... largely failed as a genre piece but worked unforgettably on [other] levels. [Jack] Nicholson did some of his greatest work, and his very worst in *The Shining*, and the same could be said of the director.[113]

Herr went on to add: "All of Stanley's movies are flawed, along with just about everybody else's.... Flaws can make a masterpiece even more loveable."[114] In a certain context Herr may have been correct; however, in terms of generic expectation, there remains another potential appraisal of the film. In terms of the idea of genre, as expressed at the start of this chapter, one could restate the possibility that Kubrick, deliberately working within the horror genre, was aware of its inherent limitations and, hence, was reconciled into accepting them, while at the same time drawing upon horrors of a wholly different kind. Thus, one might argue, Kubrick was operating within the sense of horror closer to Joseph Conrad's notion of "the horror," at the end of *Heart of Darkness.* The sense in which Conrad's famous phrase: "The horror, the horror," written in 1899, offered a warning of what the 20th century was to bring, horrors of a wholly differing kind to the horrors of Stephen King's haunted hotel. In this way *The Shining* represented at least an attempt to confront such horrors, and, when placed within a variety of theoretical arenas— structuralist, poststructuralist, Freudian, Marxist, feminist and postmodernist — it was possible to conclude that Kubrick's generic film was a further attempt to make sense of the "horrors" of the 20th century. It would be a further seven years before Kubrick offered another film, another attempt to confront similar horrors, a return to the war genre: the film *Full Metal Jacket,* the subject of the next chapter.

CHAPTER 6

Full Metal Jacket

The Law of the Father

Of arms and the man, I sing. — Virgil

Full Metal Jacket was Stanley Kubrick's final foray into the genre of the war film, and, as the opening line of Virgil's *Aeneid* reminds us, that genre continues to have a significant appeal within Western cultural tradition. It was Kubrick's 12th of 13 films; and if those first 12 films had one thing in common, it was this: they all appertained to a dramatic arena in which men killed other men, or, more specifically, to the *joy* achieved in killing these men. Kubrick's 13th and final film, *Eyes Wide Shut,* would be an exception, as it was in so many diverse ways. However, from *Fear and Desire* to *Full Metal Jacket* the one consistent theme one might observe was that of men killing other men and the pleasure derived from so doing.[1]

Kubrick had always had an interest in the military mind, a "fascination with warriors,"[2] and a significant measure of his work, in some sense at least, had dealt with war and the military. His first film, *Fear and Desire* (albeit in a decidedly existential context) was a war film; *Paths of Glory* is now generally regarded as one of the greatest war films ever made; *Spartacus* allowed Kubrick the scope to depict scenes of battle on a scale he would never be able to repeat; *Dr. Strangelove* was a film that interrogated the military mind in an exaggeratedly satiric way; the opening of *2001: A Space Odyssey*, arguably depicted the first armed conflict in human history; in *Barry Lyndon* Kubrick presented Redmond Barry's experiences (on both sides) in the Seven Years' War; and so to *Full Metal Jacket* — Kubrick's last examination of war — an account of the American experience of Vietnam, and the subject of this penultimate chapter.[3]

As in all of Kubrick's films, *Full Metal Jacket* operated on a number of distinct levels and, hence, there are a diverse number of ways with which to enter it. In an initial sense it was a film that challenged the idea of narrative structure itself, the fragmented narrative arc of the film, split into two distinct and almost schizophrenic parts, could be seen as another attempt by Kubrick to extend the conventions of cinematic narrative. On another level the film was concerned with the duality of man, "the Jungian thing," as Private Joker satirically puts it; although it would appear Kubrick's intent had a more serious design within this discursive arena. On still another level the film represented a rigorous interrogation of male sexuality, always one of Kubrick's most frequent subtextual concerns, here treated in what was possibly its most explicit fashion. Finally, the film was concerned with the use and abuse of language, again a generic concern in Kubrick's canon, but again perhaps seen here in its most virtuosic representation. However, as with all of Kubrick's work, the discourse of all these themes was overlaid with what might be described as: "Kubrickian satirical gloss," made all the more potent here given the subject matter: the Vietnam War.

*   *   *

The film begins with a scene of a number of "marine recruits having their heads shaved with electric clippers."[4] This is accompanied by Johnny Wright, singing a patriotic or jingoistic (dependent on your viewpoint) country song, "Hello Vietnam." A satiric subtext is thus immediately implied; we are hearing a song with a right-wing ideological approach, with a simplistic political discourse to the lyric, complemented by a simplistic "country and western" musical backing. However, the ideological maneuvers at play are far from simplistic and point to a noticeable satiric intent; a satiric intent that the film exhibits, in an unfailing fashion, throughout its entire running time.

The shaving of the recruits' heads, aligned with the country song, may, in some viewers' minds, set up the distant cultural reference of Elvis Presley having his hair cut on entering the army, in the late 1950s.[5] Alternatively, and in its own contemporaneous decade, the cutting of the recruits' hair recalls the idea of long hair equating with youthful rebellion in the 1960s. In more general terms, to shave one's head might also be seen as acting as a cultural indicator of preparing for an ordeal, for a journey, for combat. However, the primary act at work here would seem to remove "all traces of individuality,"[6] in having their heads shaved the recruits assumed a conformity, a homogeneity. (It is interesting to note the direct opposition of the homogeneous bald heads, in the first half of the film, with the more varied styles of the second. The recruits, now full-fledged marines, not only have grown their hair back, but now wear diversely adorned helmets designed to establish personal identity — often with an ironic intent. A structuralist reading would thus perceive of the binary opposition of conformity of the first half of the film; contrasted with a sense of rebellion in the second half.) In addition, and on an albeit more repressive level of discourse, the scene also sets up castration anxieties, anxieties that permeate the entire film. The sense in which masculinity is constantly challenged and undermined, the recruits being routinely brutalized by their "castrating father figure," Gunnery Sergeant Hartman (Lee Ermey).

In his opening speech, Hartman proceeds to reduce the recruits to the lowest form of life, a verbal discourse that consistently mixes sexist, homophobic, scatological, racist and blasphemous insults. Hartman's main method in which to belittle the recruits is rendered by attacking both their sense of individuality and their masculinity. Hartman routinely refers to the recruits as "Ladies," and regularly questions their sexuality, "sound off like you've got a pair," being a typically vituperative comment. In addition, Hartman is consistently and overtly homophobic: "Only steers and queers come from Texas," he tells Cowboy, chiming with the subtextual iconography of the "gay" cowboy.[7] Finally, in one of the most famous lines in the film, Hartman comments: "I bet you're the kind of guy that would fuck a person in the ass and not even have the common courtesy to give him a reach-around." (It is perhaps interesting to note that Lee Ermey himself was responsible for much of Hartman's dialogue, according to Kubrick — up to fifty percent of his lines were improvised by the actor; turning him into a "poet laureate of verbal vulgarity."[8] The "reach-around" line, one of the many lines improvised by Lee Ermey, was apparently so perversely obscure as to first need an explanation to Kubrick. However, Kubrick then insisted the line was annotated and used in the final script. In a wider sense Hartman's derogatory comparison of the recruits to a passive femininity recalled General Mireau's comment in *Paths of Glory*: "If those little sweethearts won't face German bullets, they'll face French ones.")

The fact that the film consistently questions and interrogates constructs and contradictions of masculinity, serves to show how intense male-to-male relationships operate here, as in Kubrick's work as a whole. As suggested previously, Kubrick's work was regularly concerned with homosocial relationships; only in his final film, *Eyes Wide Shut*, do we find anything like a genuine interest in a viable heterosexual relationship, only in *Eyes Wide Shut* do we find the lack of an intense homosociality among men. Invariably, the women in Kubrick's universe were almost routinely marginalized and placed peripherally in respect to relationships between men and other men. It is perhaps fair to say that such an observation is not entirely new, but the more interesting question to ask might be: why should this be so and what is the underlying implication in this aspect of Kubrick's narrative discourse?

If all of Kubrick's films were patent critiques of masculinity, then here, in *Full Metal Jacket*, this unquestionably reached its most exaggerated forum. Here there was a sense of extremes in the film's depiction of gender: absolutist masculinity and reductive femininity. Thus, one might argue, there was a sense in which masculinity, as a socially and culturally constructed edifice, was most explicitly exposed. As the recruits trained to become soldiers, to become marines, they were also being indoctrinated to "perform" a version of masculinity that was, in Judith Butler's now famous words: "a free-floating artifice."[9] As Paula Willoquet-Maricondi, writing of *Full Metal Jacket*, put it: "Kubrick's film reveals the profound analogies between the making of the marine and the making of masculinity in general."[10]

Once again the work of Leslie Fiedler, and his influential book, *Love and Death in the American Novel*, was of relevance within Kubrick's canon. Fiedler's book might be described as the first serious attempt to approach American literature with gender as a key issue. It was a controversial book, insomuch as a "vulgar" interpretation might place Fiedler as arguing the basic pattern of the classic American novel involved the homoerotic desire of a white boy and a "colored" man; in critic Charles B. Harris's words, that Huck and Jim were as "queer as three dollar bills."[11] In reality Fiedler was attempting to forge an argument of a much more subtle intent; Fiedler was attempting to demonstrate the immaturity of the American novel, how the chaste and "holy marriage" of male couples freed "the protagonist of classic American fiction from the adult entanglements of heterosexual passion, marriage and domestic obligations."[12] Love and Death — Eros and Thanatos — were the core binary oppositions at the heart of both the American novel and, so Fiedler insists, the American experience itself.[13]

In terms of a homoerotic discourse, Thomas Nelson, while not directly alluding to Fiedler, appeared to suggest that the film operated within what might be defined as a Fiedlerian discourse. Nelson argued that the film expelled or repressed all things female and went on to speculate how Joker's "sweet asexuality" blended into "Hartman's vision of a homoerotic paradise."[14] This description being clearly redolent of a Fiedlerian argument, such a reading being supported by a number of factors throughout the film. For example, the ironical placement of a 1960s soundtrack, with an overtly heterosexual content, set against a strongly homosocial *mise-en-scène*, was both obvious and significant. This was seen markedly in the performance of "Chapel of Love," by the Dixie Cups. This is particularly ironic when one considers the context; the men of Lusthog squad being placed far more securely within Leslie Fiedler's "holy marriage of males"[15] than any actual sense of emotional contact with a female partner.

In addition, a series of ideological inferences, that denoted the broadly homosocial linkage of sex and death, were apparent throughout the film. For example, Hartman, within his typically scabrous discourse, claimed that God (adding blasphemy to his already-loaded linguistic arsenal) was so excited by killing that he had "a hard-on for marines."[16] In a similar way, one might consider the scene in which the recruits, "the privates," are shown marching through the barrack-room holding their rifles in one hand and their genitals in the other: "This is my rifle! This is my gun! This is for fighting! This is for fun!" Finally, in the scene at the end of the film in which the surviving marines of Lusthog Squad are shown standing around the dying sniper, Animal Mother declares: "Fuck her," in terms of killing the young girl, not in a literal context. "Hard core, man, fucking hard core," another member of the squad adds— after Joker has shot and killed the sniper. Once again the literal language of sex/pornography being paraphrased within the context of killing, confirming a clear connection between the binaries of sex and death. (As critic Michael Pursell noted: "The victim lies on the floor, gasping with pain in an obscene parody of sexual excitement while men stand around her."[17] A similar point was made by Paula Willoquet-Maricondi, in a discussion of a different scene in the film: "As Pyle brings the M-14, loaded with full-metal-jacketed bullets, to his mouth in a deadly quasi-sexual embrace and pulls the trigger, he achieves complete unity with the gun."[18] The implications here of Pyle assuming the passive role in another "obscene parody," this time of oral sex, with the gun having the same lethal orgasmic effect.)

Further to this, it was clear that the men depicted in the film often enjoyed killing, almost to the extent of it being sexual in nature. One might note the marine on patrol in Hue, who first misses a number of Vietcong who cross a street ahead of him; the marine "cocks" his rifle and then successfully shoots and kills the next group of Vietcong. The emotion on his face, that of intense pleasure, being of relevance in this context. In addition, one might think of the machine gunner in the helicopter, killing escaping Vietcong, or more likely Vietnamese peasants; the same look of intense enjoyment, the same "euphoric pleasure in the act of killing," being readily apparent. Thus the film appeared to offer the uncomfortable idea that there was a pleasure, a sexual pleasure, in killing. Furthermore, there was the implication that this may have been one reason why men so readily indulge in warfare. As Michael Herr put it: "Take the glamour out of war! I mean, how the bloody hell can you do *that*?"[19] The appeal of war, the film seemed to suggest, is primarily a masculine experience, allowing men to glamorize their existence in a way not possible within the constraints of a civilized society. In other words, war enables men to construct a meaning out of an otherwise mundane and almost meaningless existence. The corollary here would appear to have been that masculinity only finds one of its "real" forums within a warlike discourse. Once again Michael Herr is of assistance; Herr claims to be a pacifist and that there are no excuses to kill people, but that violence is inside us:

It's inside us and we have to get it out. We do it everyday in the streets through millions of small acts of aggression. And when the aggression becomes institutionalized, it results in war.[20]

In the film such a discussion of masculine violence is explored, at least in one sense, via a Jungian discourse. The lines spoken in the film, by Joker, about "the Jungian thing" have become famous and somewhat clichéd; however, one could argue they conceal a more subtle discourse. As with a greater part of Kubrick's work as a whole, the film is built around the concept that man has the capacity for both good and evil. One thinks, for example, of the Manichean heresy explored in *A Clockwork Orange*; however, here in *Full Metal Jacket* the idea is explored in more depth. Here there was the idea that, given sufficient coercive training, anyone is capable of extreme violent activity. In other words we are generally inclined not to hurt other people — but a conflicting side can be revealed via indoctrination. As Kubrick has commented:

> We are never going to get down to doing anything about the things that are really bad in the world until there is recognition within us of the darker side of our natures, the shadow side.[21]

"The shadow side," or "the Jungian thing" was the point at issue here. If one accepts that Kubrick's work has regularly depicted the duality of man, the idea that good and evil exists concurrently in human beings; then it must also be admitted that Kubrick more often turned toward the darker side of humanity, toward at least a partial misanthropy. As Vincent LoBrutto put it:

> Kubrick ... did not believe in Anne Frank's credo that mankind was basically good. Kubrick held that evil was alive and well. A pessimist, Stanley Kubrick was drawn to the dark side of the human experience and found it thriving in armed conflict.[22]

If the "Jungian thing" was seen most clearly in the character of Joker, then his name is perhaps worthy of scrutiny in such a context. As Thomas Nelson noted, Joker's name and ironic personality could be read in association with the Jungian archetype of the "Trickster"; a character who has "the ability to turn that which is absurd or meaningless into something meaningful."[23] In the film, Joker's attitude toward the experience of Vietnam reflected this idea; on the one hand he appeared wholly cynical, while at other times he appeared to believe in the war he was fighting. In addition, Joker's first line in the film: "Is that you, John Wayne? Is this me?" in itself raised questions around the duality of identity; insomuch as it metaphorically questioned whether Joker actually knew who he was, or indeed, why he was preparing to fight in Vietnam. This was especially relevant in the light of Joker's high intelligence; for example, one assumes he would have been able to gain a student deferment in 1967, at this early stage in the war.

Joker's antithesis in the first part of the film was Sergeant Hartman. As part of the military's aim to "breed" brutal killers, it was Hartman's aim to strip the recruits of their sense of identity, one method being to "strip" the recruits "of their names."[24] The act of renaming might be seen as a typical patriarchal measure, a means of enforcing patriarchal superiority. Hartman could thus be seen as the sadistic father, renaming his recruits, bringing them under his patriarchal authority. Thus Hartman renames his surrogate sons, in the same way as he regularly demeans them with his homophobic slurs: "faggots," "ladies," "steers and queers" and so on. However, in addition to this, Hartman went further in employing threats of implied emasculation, thus exaggerating his position as an all-powerful, castrating father. (Hartman's name itself had been changed, in the novel and in early versions of the screenplay Sgt. Hartman was Sgt. Gerheim. It is possible to argue Kubrick changed the name for symbolic purposes, insomuch as "Hartman" resounded with one of the film's intertextual resonances, Joseph Conrad's novel: *Heart of Darkness*. There were a number of intertextual correlations to Conrad's novel, not least the knowledge of Coppola's *Apocalypse Now* and its similar mythic resonances with Jungian thought. In addition, the lyrics of the film's closing song, "Paint it Black," resonated with the film's correlation to *Heart of Darkness*. In the lyric of the song we find the line: "I look inside myself and see my heart is black.")

The film contains constant allusions to castration; for example, Hartman claims he is going to "rip off" Private Pyle's "balls," so he could not contaminate the rest of the world, and that he would motivate him "if it short-dicks every cannibal on the Congo." (Note here the subtle context of Hartman's reference to the Congo, in relation to *Heart of Darkness*.) This is a theme that continues throughout the film; note Animal Mother's aside: "If I'm gonna get my balls blown off for a word ... my word is poontang." Also, and in the film's most literal and brutal attack on male sexuality, Private Eightball appears to be emasculated before our eyes. In what is probably a calculated intent, the sniper (whom we later discover is female) deliberately shoots the unfortunate Eightball in the groin and we seem to see his genitals blown away from his body.[25] In a scene prior to this, the now (seemingly) ironically named Eightball is accused of possessing, in a somewhat stereotypical and racist way (Eightball is an African-American), a large phallic appendage. The young Vietnamese sex worker who touts for business as the Lusthog Squad is resting outside the ruined theatre, being apparently concerned in having intercourse with Eightball; communicating that she wants: "no boom-boom with soul brother," making the point that "soul brother" is "too boo-coo." In response to this, Eightball offers a practical demonstration. To quote verbatim from the published screenplay:

EIGHTBALL: Uh, excuse me, madam. Now what we have here, little yellow sister, is a magnificent ... *(takes out his dick)* ... specimen of pure Alabama blacksnake. But it ain't too Goddamn boo-coo.[26]

The "boo-coo" nature of the "pure Alabama blacksnake" is, however, to prove immaterial; the scene of Eightball being shot depicts the sheer brutality of warfare, while also depicting the soldiers' most innate fear. In Gustav Hasford's source novel we find lines such as:

Then the sniper started shooting off fingers, toes, ears—everything.[27]

Bang. The bullet rips open Cowboy's trousers at the crotch. "No...." He feels for his balls.[28]

In one of the early versions of the film's screenplay, there was the same sense of anxiety over castration, as Joker, under fire from the sniper, checked his bodily integrity:

I put out the word to every part of my body. Dear feet, tiptoe through the tulips. Balls, hang in there.[29]

In *Dispatches,* Michael Herr more explicitly expressed this fear:

Everyone feared the wound of wounds, the Wound.... Take my legs, take my hands, take my eyes, take my fucking *life,* You Bastards, but please, please, please, don't take *those.*[30]

Such a fear corresponding to Freud's concept: that the loss of the genitals was the worst thing in the world. "It is worse than death," says Freud, "because the fear of death is only a shadow of this."[31] (In an intertextual context one might think here of the infamous scene in Samuel Fuller's 1980 film, *The Big Red One,* in which Lee Marvin, the leader of a lost patrol in World War II, infamously castigates one of his troops for cowardice after he had had his testicles shot off. In itself, *The Big Red One,* casts a shadow over *Full Metal Jacket,* most significantly in the way both films challenged Hollywood's approach to narrative. *The Big Red One* was a film wholly lacking a conventional narrative, it is merely a continuous strand of disconnected episodes detailing Lee Marvin and his platoon through a meaningless series of adventures. In a sense this mirrored *Full Metal Jacket*'s purposeful disregard for the conventional "three-act play" of Hollywood narrative. *The Big Red One* is also, from beginning to end, a film that exhibits an almost risible homosocial and phallic obsession, this being clearly apparent from its title on down. An obsession *Full Metal Jacket* continued, albeit in a more subtle fashion.)

To return to Hartman's role as the castrating father, it is interesting to note how such a role was present, albeit in less exaggerated ways, elsewhere in Kubrick's work. In other words, the ways in which real or surrogate fathers were often destroyed by their sons in Kubrick's films. Here, in *Full Metal Jacket,* Pyle eventually kills Hartman; in *The Shining,* Danny outwits Jack in the maze, leading to his father's death; in *Barry Lyndon*, Barry's stepson, Lord Bullingdon, shoots, cripples and ultimately destroys Barry; while in *Dr. Strangelove*, General Ripper (one of the ultimate castrating fathers) is ultimately let down by "his boys." In this sense, Michel Ciment was perhaps correct to speak of Hartman as being "the terrifying and paternal figure" Kubrick was so "fond of representing," Ciment perceiving of Pyle as Kubrick's "latest Oedipal murderer."[32]

As previously suggested, one way in which Hartman constructed his superiority over the recruits was by attacking their sense of masculinity. They were to be trained as killers and, hence, any sense of a feminine side must be erased. Luis M. Garcia-Mainar: "In killing the most feminine aspects of the men's personalities ... the male gains access to the woman precisely by killing the woman in himself."[33] This was a concept that would, incidentally, be challenged at the film's denouement, when the sniper, the most ruthless killer in the film, is revealed to be a young woman. Once again, the association between the binary opposition of sex and death proved significant, herein one notes, for example, that the only women in the film were either killers (the sniper) or sex workers (the two prostitutes). This is an albeit exaggerated but not exactly atypical situation in Kubrick's work. As Robert Kolker commented: "His films are rarely concerned with women, except in a peripheral and usually unpleasant way."[34] Such an argument would seem to be confirmed by noting how, when the female subject was mentioned elsewhere in the film, it was usually within an overtly abject and sexualized context. For example, in the oddly half-hearted sexual fantasies around Mary Jane Rottencrotch, or in Animal Mother's chosen word he would die for "poontang," or in the marching chants that tell us "Eskimo pussy is mighty cold."[35] As Leslie Fiedler once only half-joked: "The only safe woman is a dead woman."[36]

However, this was not to imply a simplistic misogyny, something of which Kubrick's films have often been accused. The situation was arguably more complex, as Dana Polan commented: "Kubrick is simultaneously a sexist director and one of the most interesting depicters of a fundamental sexism in men's treatment of women."[37] In other words, one might argue how Kubrick was interested in the way women were treated within a variety of culturally diverse arenas, correlating with the sense in which they were often feared and hated; seen here in *Full Metal Jacket* and throughout Kubrick's work as a whole. Hence it would appear that Kubrick was a filmmaker aware of his artistic limitations, in this case his treatment of women, this being obvious in the relative lack of significant female characters in his films; but nonetheless Kubrick had an interest in female characters that went beyond a simplistic misogyny. (In this context note that there was little in the way of any sexually explicit scenes in the film, a rarity for Kubrick. However, it is known that Kubrick did shoot a sex scene for the film. In Matthew Modine's book: *Full Metal Diary*, Modine offers the new information that Kubrick shot a scene between himself and Papillion Soo Soo, a graphic sex scene that Kubrick was probably wise to exclude.[38])

*   *   *

In addition to a sense of intense feminization, another significant way in which the men in the film were treated was the manner in which they were subjected to infantilization. This was seen most clearly in the character of Private Pyle (Vincent D'Onofrio),[39] who becomes the main target of Hartman's attention, and under the onslaught eventually descends into madness, therefore adding to the long list of delusional male characters in Kubrick's work.[40] At one point Hartman says to Pyle: "Didn't Mommy and Daddy show you enough attention when you were a child?" In another instance Hartman forces Pyle to eat a jelly doughnut in front of the other recruits; in a similar way Pyle is made to march on parade, with his thumb in his mouth, his rifle the wrong way around and with his trousers around his ankles. One might also observe the way in which Pyle appears to cry like a child after the "blanket party." In Freudian terms Pyle thus regresses to the oral stage of childhood, in such an *imaginary* stage he can no longer cope with the *symbolic* world, hence his subsequent suicide.

On a superficial level this might be seen as suggesting the soldiers were boys fighting a man's war; especially as the age of the average American soldier in Vietnam (as is well known) was only 19. However, one might argue that the film had a more subtle intent, insomuch as it appears to offer a still further extended Freudian context. In other words, it is not only the oral stage in which the recruits are confined; they are also confined within Freud's anal stage of development. This offers one possible explanation for the way the film is so prodigiously and routinely scatological. The word "shit" is probably one of *the* most common epithets used in the film: "You are nothing but unorganized grabasstic pieces of amphibian shit!" says Hartman near the beginning of the film. There are other examples too numerous to list in full: "They shit over us every chance they get"; "I want to get out in the shit"; "It's a huge shit sandwich and we're all gonna have to take a bite"; "You'd better get your head and your ass wired together, or I will take a giant shit on you"; "I am in a world of shit"; and so on, *ad nauseum*. (This even extends to Snowball's mistaken malapropic identification of the Texan Book *Suppository* Building.)

The often-repeated phrase "a world of shit" achieved a literal depiction within Pyle's suicide and his murder of Hartman, insomuch as it took place in the barrack latrine (or "head") itself. Pyle, who had already admitted he was living in a world of shit, hence found his final resting place, his final consummation, sitting on a toilet and firing a rifle bullet into his brain. Thomas

Nelson was one of several critics to equate this to a sexual arena of discourse, describing Pyle's suicide as "erupting in an orgasm of blood and brain all over the white, antiseptic surfaces of Hartman's utopian dream."[41] Thus the extreme scatological discourse of the language used in the film might then, in some senses at least, be connected to the intense homophobic and homosocial discourses at work in the film. As the homosocial is so dangerously parallel to the homoerotic it must be strictly disciplined; containing, as it does, repressed fears of a slippage from a homosocial to a homoerotic discourse. Thus the endlessly repeated fecal epithets could be seen as a homophobic signal, the obsession of living "in a world of shit" pointing to a repressed fear of anality within a same-sex relationship.

In the moments prior to his murder and Pyle's suicide, Hartman asks: "What in the name of Jesus H. Christ are you animals doing in my head?" This points to the sense in which Pyle's suicide had taken place in both Hartman's head and in *the* head. In addition, the fact that Pyle's mental degeneration comes to a head (in the *head*) was of a differing significance, when compared to Kubrick's work as a whole. For example, one notes the way Pyle shoots himself in a bathroom was a direct assimilation to the way General Ripper, another deranged member of the military, had shot himself in another bathroom, in *Dr. Strangelove*. In addition, the bloodstains above the toilet after Pyle shoots himself could not help but recall "REDRUM" from *The Shining*. Private Pyle encoded a different kind of signifier for us to decode, a much more obscure signification, but one that inscribed similar notions of violence, repression and masculinity. (Note that in the novel, and in the initial draft of the screenplay, Pyle's suicide and murder of Hartman (then named Gerheim) take place in the barracks and not in the latrine. Hence, it is clear this change of scene most probably came directly from Kubrick, further delineating the long line of bathroom scenes in his films.)

This sense of repression, coupled with the way in which the recruits were seemingly entrapped within oral and anal stages of development, can also be seen as operating within the linguistic discourses present in the film. As was clearly apparent the film, like much of Kubrick's work, employed a virtuoso use of language. As Michael Herr noted:

> It's always seemed obvious to me that language was one of the most striking things about his [Kubrick's] films, whether cunningly, crushingly banal ... or in manic bursts of frantic satire ... or starkly obscene, utterly cruel, sparing nobody's sensibilities.[42]

In the case of *Full Metal Jacket*, firstly, there was an almost Orwellian misuse of language: "We will defend to the death the right to be misinformed," being just one example. In addition, there was Hartman's use of language; as previously intimated, a lexicon of obscene, homophobic, misogynistic, scat-

ological, racist abuse; what Thomas Nelson described as "a cascade of vitu-
peration rarely heard in life or in a movie theatre."[43] However, in addition
to this, it was also possible to perceive of language in *Full Metal Jacket* as
operating within a more elaborate and cerebral discourse, within Jacques
Lacan's theoretical model of the "Law [or Name] of the Father."

The "Law [or Name] of the Father," was a term used by Jacques Lacan
to signify the phallic order structuring language. As alluded in the previous
chapter, Lacan, taking his lead from Freud, argued that at the time of the
Oedipal crisis the child was forced to separate from the mother — whom Lacan
saw as representing the *imaginary world*— to arrive at a sense of identity and
to enter the social order, the father's *symbolic world*— in other words, the
world of words or language. Thus, Lacan argues, it is a phallic authority that
imposes and determines cultural order, the social and symbolic order, represented by the father, who stands for the phallus; what Lacan described as
the transcendental, universal signifier. In this sense the phallus represents the
symbolic order, preventing the child from lingering within the imaginary
phase. On acquiring language the child then enters the gendered space
assigned to it by the linguistic order. The father is installed in the position of
lawgiver, not so much because he has a superior procreative function, but
merely as an effect of the linguistic system. Lacan's model asserts that human
subjects enter positions within a pre-established set of signifiers (mother,
father, son, daughter) which can only operate within a language system. The
libidinal drives (oral, anal and genital) of infant-hood are brought under the
restraint of the "Law [Name] of the Father," which is strongly connected with
the entry into the symbolic system of language. However, the repressed desires
never go away, their repression maintains a permanently split subject.[44]

The theorist Julia Kristeva (taking her lead from Lacan) envisaged the
child, before entering the symbolic world of language, as existing in what she
referred to as the *semiotic*. The *semiotic* being a world of flowing and fluid
drives, a rhythmic, wordless flow of impulses and appetites which must be
repressed to admit the articulation of structured speech. The utterances which
most approximates the *semiotic* discourse is the "pre–Oedipal babble" of the
child.[45] Kristeva argued that no matter how organized symbolic language may
be, it retains something of this *semiotic* flux. The *semiotic* being a subversive
force within the ordered social world of language, always fertile, always
opposed to the hard outlines of the phallocentric order, perpetually undermining the forces which organize and control our experience. For Kristeva
the *semiotic* was associated with the female body, the free floating sea of the
womb and the enveloping sensuousness of the mother's breast, the environment of the pre–Oedipal experience. Thus, while the *symbolic* was associated
with the "Law [Name] of the Father"— which censors and represses— the
imaginary was associated with the silence of the unconscious which precedes

discourse, standing outside and threatening to disrupt the conscious, rational order of speech.

In attempting to place such theoretical concepts within the film, one might consider a number of issues. For example, the aforementioned reduction of the fully grown recruits within oral and anal stages of development, specifically within the infantilization of Private Pyle. In addition, the choice of several of the songs on the soundtrack (in the second half of the film) seemed to verge toward Kristeva's "pre–Oedipal babble." This can be seen in the almost nonsense lyrics of such songs as "Surfin' Bird"[46] and "Wooly Bully,"[47] both of which suggests the idea of signifiers descending beyond signification.

In a sense, the seemingly meaningless rhyming couplets in the two songs thus seemed to locate with linguistic rhyming patterns of "gruntspeak" redolent throughout the film. For example:

> this is my rifle, this is my gun, one is for fighting, one is for fun
> I love working for Uncle Sam, lets me know just who I am
> in the rear with the gear
> put a nigger behind the trigger
> mother green and the killing machine
> I don't want no teenage queen, I just want my M14
> life takers and heart breakers[48]

While such simplistic rhyming, in some sense, drew attention to the artifice of language itself, it also suggested a return to a childlike state, to a pre–Oedipal discourse. Thus songs like "Woolly Bully" and "Surfin' Bird" threatened to descend into a chain of wholly meaningless signifiers, and, as well as suggesting Julia Kristeva's semiotic babble, they were also saying something about the immature action of the Americans in a war that made no sense to them. The fact that the film ended with the "grown-up" recruits singing the Mickey Mouse song added weight to such a proposition.

If the use of language in the film could be interpreted within a psychoanalytical model, it could also be read within a differing theoretical context, that of structuralism. A structuralist analysis of the film uncovers a diverse range of interpretative issues. For example, it supported the idea of a clear binary opposition between sex and death within the film. This was perhaps most pertinently seen in the use of the ubiquitous signifier "fuck." In the film this continually gestured away from a literal and sexual discourse, toward the metaphorical and homicidal. Thus, the fact that the men in the film spend such a significant amount of their time saying "fuck" to one another was of interest. In a sense the use of this common epithet might be compared to pseudo-sexual mounting among male primates to demonstrate superiority; with the ubiquitous "fuck you" here being perceived in a literal sense.

In a similar way, the contradictory semiotic signals Joker wears in the second half of the film ("Born to Kill" on his helmet and a peace symbol on his lapel) could also be illuminated via a structuralist analysis. In other words, they are simply oppositional elements, representing not just "the Jungian thing—the duality of man," but more literally signifying America's contradictory attitudes toward the war in Vietnam as a whole; what Norman Kagan saw as suggestive of the "split personality of the U.S. in Vietnam."[49] However, what was arguably of more significance, within a structuralist reading, concerned the narrative structure of the film. As previously mentioned, the two distinctly designed halves of the film tended to subvert the three-act play format of the classical Hollywood film.[50] The two halves of the film were unusually distinct insomuch as little in the first half was echoed in the second. For example, Joker and Cowboy are the only common referents, the only characters to prevail from the first into the second half. In this sense, it is significant to note that at no time do Joker or Cowboy directly refer to their experiences at Parris Island. In other words, the denouement of part one, Private Pyle's suicide, appears to have no bearing at all on the events in the second part of the film. Thus the two halves are almost completely disconnected, disturbing the audience's preconception of cinematic narrative. Kubrick's celebrated comment, that he had a desire to "explode the narrative structure of movies,"[51] being particularly appropriate here. Kubrick's primary aim was always to tell a good story, but to tell it in an original way. He may have never been fully aware of what exactly constituted a good story, as he stated:

> You can say a lot of "architectural" things about what a film story should have: a strong plot, interesting characters, possibilities for cinematic development, good opportunities for the actors to display emotion, and the presentation of thematic ideas truthfully and intelligently. But, of course, that still doesn't really explain why you finally choose something, nor does it lead you to the story.[52]

However, one thing Kubrick was alert to was his attempt to continually explore as many cinematic narrative variations as he could. Thus to attempt to displace the narrative of this film, to split it into two such distinct parts, was arguably an authentic attempt to forge a new means of telling a story on film. (Finally, one might note that while the two parts of the film appear to be disconnected, a structuralist reading of the "split narrative" might, nonetheless, reveal certain linkages. For example, how each part begins with an iconic non-diegetic musical interlude and that each part ends in an unexpected and surprising shooting.)

In the novel the Parris Island sequence did not make up such a major proportion of the narrative, only the first 33 of the novel's 180 pages; however, the film gave it a much more equivalent status.[53] It could thus be concluded that Kubrick, in this deliberate rearrangement, was attempting to do something new with the basic grammar of cinematic structure, albeit in a modest way. As mentioned, the lack of scarcely any narrative "connectors," between parts one and two, being a clear demonstration of Kubrick's insistence to explore differing means of telling stories on film. To help facilitate this, Kubrick appeared to find inspiration from his own previous work; note how the jump cut from Pyle's suicide in Parris Island to Joker in Da Nang (albeit probably an ellipsis of only a relatively short period of time — perhaps a few months)[54] could not help but recall the three-million-year ellipsis from bone to space station in *2001: A Space Odyssey*, such was the sense of narrative dislocation.

The corollary of such a narrative device offers a further theoretical dimension; insomuch as the lack of a connection between the two narrative components posed the suggestion that the film deliberately lacked a center. This linking with one of the basic tenets of postmodern theory: that the world, as we know it, lacks a center. This idea was most specifically seen in the second part of the film; in the overarching metaphor that might be called "the lost squad motif." In Hue: Joker, Cowboy, Rafterman, Animal Mother and the other marines lose their way and change direction, leading them straight into the line of fire of the sniper. This could be seen as a grand simile, depicting America's experience in Vietnam, as a whole. In other words, America had no overall strategy, no means of gaining a victory in the conventional sense of warfare, no sense of knowing where they were going in a strategic sense. Thus the film ultimately expressed the futility of the Vietnam War, how there was little if any strategic reason for fighting the war. In the "lost squad motif" three marines die in a brutal fashion, the surviving marines kill the sniper; but nothing has been gained, we are merely left with a number of meaningless deaths.

Hence, the idea of the Vietnam War having no center, of the film itself having no center, corresponds to postmodern and poststructuralist ideas redolent of this concept. In other words, the erosion of meaning within the sense we have of ourselves (in a postmodern or poststructuralist environment) is repeated in the film via its exploration of the erosion of meaning in the context of the war in Vietnam.[55] Thus, within such a theoretical reading, the film appears to offer little in the way of a redemptive discourse, something of a prerequisite in most Hollywood films. Instead all we were offered in *Full Metal Jacket* was a sense of almost unremitting cynicism and irony. At the narrative climax of the film, the killing of the female sniper, the viewer is offered little in the way of compensation. As Robert Kolker noted:

> No other Vietnam film, with the possible exception of *Apocalypse Now* (but without that film's hallucinatory and mythic pretensions), so expresses the hopelessness and confused motivations of that war, its sense of already and always being lost by the United States.[56]

In this sense, one can perceive how Kubrick's film was calculatedly neutral in terms of its moral approach to the war. For example, Kubrick appears to have had no interest in depicting American atrocities in Vietnam; the film appears to merely take this as a given, perhaps best observed in the scene wherein the machine gunner in the helicopter is shown shooting at suspected Vietcong, or, in reality, probably peasant farmers.[57] A comparison to Oliver Stone's *Platoon* (1986), thus is of relevance; in his film, Stone strove to find a sense of hope, a sense that there were at least some "good" Americans in the field of war. The fact that there were no sentimental possibilities of moral equivocation in Kubrick's film adds weight within a poststructuralist reading; insomuch as there was no sense in Kubrick's following Stone's proclaimed intention of "bringing Americans together and healing the nation's wounds."[58] The conventional plotting and characterization of *Platoon* simply do not get into *Full Metal Jacket*. As Alexander Walker noted: "One man [Stone] is recalling his own experiences of battle: the other [Kubrick] is constructing his own universe of the unreal."[59]

This notion of the "unreal," linking with the idea of the film lacking a center, had further significance in relation to a postmodern reading of the film. One might think, for example, in terms of Jean Baudrillard's concept of the *hyper-real*, or most specifically Baudrillard's conception of the "loss of the real." The view that the perverse influence of images from film, television, advertising, the internet and so on, has led to a loss of the distinction between the real and the imagined, between reality and illusion, between surface and depth, between authenticity and simulation. The result is a culture in which these distinctions had been eroded, one where it is now impossible to be sure what is real and what is not. In this context the film might be read as less an attempt to represent an accurate portrayal of Vietnam and more an attempt to offer a *hyper-real* representation of the Vietnam experience.

Kubrick's deliberate use of a television crew, part way through the second half of the film, was one obvious reminder of this. On one level it served to reflect the way in which the Vietnam War was generally perceived as the first television war. However, in another sense it served as what was arguably a parody of Baudrillard's idea of simulation; the idea that the actual war in Vietnam had been replaced by a parodic simulation of the event.[60] In this sense it might again be noted that Kubrick made no genuine attempt at offering a realistic depiction of Vietnam; for example, there was never any intention of photographing the film in an authentic setting. Instead what Kubrick appears to have offered was a cinematic representation of the impression of the war we all have stored in our heads, with the implication that this may have been more "real" than the actual reality. The often-cited fact, that much of the film's vision of Hue City was actually shot at a derelict gasworks in Beckton-on-Thames, might suggest we should look beyond the surface and to question the supposed depth that may or may not have existed in the first place.

Additionally, again within such a postmodernist context, it is interesting to perceive of how Kubrick chose to end his film: with the marines singing
the "fatuous" Mickey Mouse song. This appeared to be potentially relevant
insomuch as Baudrillard would famously view Disneyland as a mythologized,
misrepresentation of the United States. As far as Baudrillard was concerned,
Disneyland was the place where all the values of American society and culture were exalted, albeit in miniature and comic strip form, thus ultimately
idealizing a self-contradictory reality. Therefore, for Kubrick's film to conclude in such a fashion only added further connotations to an interpretation
within Baudrillard's concept of the "hyper-real." (Another way in which
Kubrick increased the artificiality of the *mise-en-scène*, and hence a sense of
the hyper-real, was in the use of slow motion. In previous films Kubrick had
always used slow motion in a relatively sparing fashion, but in *Full Metal
Jacket it* was used to a greater and more telling extent; the primary use occurring in the instances of violent death, for example, Cowboy and Eightball.
In so doing, the process of death seems to achieve an elegiac quality, far from
the actual experience of receiving a gunshot, thus, once again, the film might
be seen as consciously reaching for a sense of "hyper-reality."[61])

On a final note in viewing the film within a postmodern light, the use
of intertextual referencing might be seen as being of interest. As before, the
primary intertextual references in a Kubrick film pertained to Kubrick's own
work itself. For example, there are a number of potential references to *2001
A Space Odyssey*; Luis M. Garcia-Mainar has compared the marines assisting
the dying Cowboy to the apes in *2001*: "Here human beings are shown as still
animals who in their defenselessness seeks comfort in the group."[62] Also,
Hartman's question to Private Pyle: "What is your major malfunction, numb-
nuts?" (a line not found in the novel) could be seen as an internalized
Kubrickian reference to HAL. In other words, Kubrick's ubiquitous theme of
human fallibility and of the perfect scheme going awry. However, of more
interest, and perhaps of more significant intent, are the intertextual references in the film to *A Clockwork Orange*. In both films we share an intimacy
with an autodiegetic narrator, both Joker and Alex take us into their confidence with a similar laconic means of expression and an anti-hero persona.[63]
Also, one might note the same individualistic use of language in both films:
Alex's Nadsat and Joker's "gruntspeak." In addition, the contrasted use of
indoctrination in the two films is of interest; one notes how the idea of men
being indoctrinated to kill in one film, *Full Metal Jacket*, contrasted in the
other, *A Clockwork Orange*, wherein the indoctrination attempts to deny the
killing impulse. "It is a hard heart that kills," Sergeant Hartman tells the
recruits, stating a basic truth, that it is difficult to turn men into killing
machines.[64] Joker isn't born to kill, he is trained to kill.[65] In addition, there
are other examples of intertextuality: Alexander Walker compared the "lost

squad" motif in the film to *Fear and Desire*,[66] while James Howard noted a number of parallels to *Spartacus*.[67] This use of intertextuality, rendered in a purposefully self-referential way, clearly pointed to a postmodernist sense of self-awareness; *Full Metal Jacket* knew it was a film and told us so with a clear metafictional intent.

Gustav Hasford's source novel, in itself, had similarities to *A Clockwork Orange*, at least in the way we can envisage its initial appeal to Kubrick. This can be seen insomuch as both books were relatively short, both were told in a laconic first-person narrative voice and both appeared to lack a conventional moral conscience. Kubrick had apparently become aware of Hasford's novel as early as 1979, but only had time to actually read it three years later. In any case, *The Short Timers* also offered Kubrick that special quality he was continually looking for: a good story, or at least a good story in terms of its potential for cinematic adaptation. Michael Herr had been one of Kubrick's initial contacts in the project, primarily because of his book, *Dispatches*. However, much as Kubrick admired Herr's book, it was clear he couldn't make a film out of it "because he couldn't find a story in it."[68] However, Herr thought highly of Hasford's novel, commenting: "I think that *The Short Timers* may be the best book to come out of the Vietnam War,"[69] and supported Kubrick in his choice of the novel as source material.

It was Hasford's first novel and it was a book that took a long time to find a publisher, in Vincent LoBrutto's words, a book that took "seven years to write and three years to sell."[70] Hasford, like Joker, had been a combat correspondent in the Marines, and his book had a combat authenticity mixed with a surreal nihilistic discourse; qualities that must have appealed to Kubrick's inherently misanthropic disposition. In many ways it was a much more harrowing and disturbing narrative than the one that found its way into Kubrick's adaptation. Hasford's discourse is far darker and far bleaker than Kubrick's; again offering a comparison to the adaptation of *A Clockwork Orange* insomuch as Kubrick chose to avoid some of the more graphically violent scenes of the original novel. Michael Herr wrote of Hasford's novel:

> He was telling a truth about the war that was so secret, so hidden, that I could barely stand it.... It was a masterpiece that absolutely anybody could pick up and read in a couple of hours and never forget.[71]

On reading the novel one can perceive something of Herr's argument. For example, the dialogue within it was vivid and memorable, so much so that a careful reading of the novel demonstrates a significant percentage of the film's dialogue was drawn directly from it.[72] In this sense, *The Short Timers* may have been one of the most faithfully adapted of Kubrick's films, raising, once again, the validity of *auteur* theory. The visual properties of the film were, as usual, all Kubrick's invention; in addition, changes (usually improvements) were made to the plotting, but the essential question still remains: who was the actual author/*auteur*?[73] (Hasford would publish little else of any great significance; only two further books: *The Phantom Blooper* [1990], a sequel to *The Short Timers,* and *A Gypsy Good Time* [1992], a detective story. After being arrested and receiving a six-month jail sentence [in 1988] for stealing some 10,000 library books, Hasford, a diabetic, moved to the island of Aegina in Greece, where he died of heart failure on January 29, 1993. However, his death may not have gone unremarked upon by Kubrick, as his name arguably resonates in *Eyes Wide Shut,* that is if one rejects the somewhat otiose idea that Bill Harford's surname derived from Harrison Ford.)

Kubrick's collaboration with Hasford and Herr was one of his most successful since his work on *2001: A Space Odyssey* with Arthur C. Clarke. In this sense *Full Metal Jacket* arguably represents one of Kubrick's most mature and thoughtful works. It fulfils this quotient in terms of its ideological content, its narrative flair, its originality and its influence on war films that came after it. The film had its discontents, for example, David Thomson thought it was "an abomination, the sort of film Mr. Torrance might have made."[74] However, such views have proven to be unsupported and the film has grown in stature and impact since it was made; as David Hughes commented: "There can be little doubt that *Full Metal Jacket* has, in one way or another, influenced virtually every war movie to follow it."[75]

In this sense, *Full Metal Jacket* was Kubrick's last word in terms of human warfare. Nearly 30 years previously he had ended *Paths of Glory* by offering at least some degree of a redemptive resolution. That film had ended with the assembled soldiers being moved, and humanized, by the singing of a young German girl. However, in *Full Metal Jacket* even the suggestion of a movement toward a sentimental discourse would not be offered. *Full Metal Jacket* also ended with a song, but with a wholly bitter and cynical connotation, with the Marines singing the Mickey Mouse song. As previously alluded, a satiric implication is obvious here — this was a war with little meaning, with little redemption; in other words, a Mickey Mouse war in a Mickey Mouse world.

Thus, in summary, one can see *Full Metal Jacket* was not a war film or an anti-war film; it was simply a film about war. It was a film that explored war via a diverse range of approaches: subjectivity and identity, masculinity and an intense sense of homosociality, the use and abuse of language, Freudian and Jungian discourses, postmodern notions of the hyper-real, further explorations of narrative structures, a further linkage between sex and death and the masculine journey, along with other numerous, disparate discourses. *Full Metal Jacket* might finally be seen as Kubrick's most profound meditation on warfare. The film offered a God's eye view of war, a God's eye view of the masculine experience of combat. On the one hand there was an undoubted intentional ambivalence on Kubrick's part: he was aware of the damage war does to the men who fight it. On the other hand, Kubrick's film was fully aware of the attractions of war, as Michael Herr commented: "He also accepted to acknowledge that, of all the things war is, it is also very beautiful."[76]

It would be a further 12 years until the appearance of another Stanley Kubrick film. A number of false starts (*A.I.* and *Aryan Papers,* being the most prominent examples) together with what might be seen as a mixture of physical fatigue and artistic carefulness, had caused Kubrick to slow down his output even further. However, Kubrick's final film, perhaps the most complex and ambivalent film in his canon, would be *Eyes Wide Shut,* the subject of the next and final chapter of this book.

CHAPTER 7

Eyes Wide Shut

Twelve and a Half

When we are dreaming are we perhaps ghosts in someone else's dreams?
— Arthur Schnitzler

In 1968, shortly after the release of *2001: A Space Odyssey*, the Italian film director, Franco Zeffirelli, forwarded a telegram to Kubrick:

You made me dream eyes wide open Stop Yours is much more than an extraordinary film Stop Thank you Franco Zeffirelli Rome.[1]

Apart from offering a potential source for the title of *Eyes Wide Shut*, Zeffirelli's message, from one director to another, also connoted an authentic description of the cinematic process. A film should make one dream with one's eyes open, something that Kubrick's final film (and arguably all his others) consistently attempted to do. Thus the intent of this final chapter will be to explore Kubrick's 13th and final feature film, and, at least in part, to consider it in the light of Zeffirelli's comment; that "extraordinary" films cause one to dream with one's eyes open. In this sense it would seem reasonable to argue that Kubrick's final film *was* "extraordinary." The fact that it was, once again, largely misunderstood by its immediate and contemporaneous critical response, does not alter this fact. Thus *Eyes Wide Shut* might be reasonably envisaged as Kubrick's final attempt at subverting cinematic form and narrative; herein offering a unique cinematic discourse via a representation of the real world and the dream world; and, in so doing, offering a signpost to an understanding between the two.

The history of Kubrick's fascination with Arthur Schnitzler's 1926 novella, *Traumnovelle* (usually translated into English as *Dream Story*), and

137

his wish to adapt it cinematically, is a long one, and one that can be traced back even further than Zeffirelli's 1968 telegram. It is possible that Kubrick first encountered Schnitzler's work and perhaps *Traumnovelle* itself, via his second wife, Ruth Sobotka, sometime in the mid–1950s.[2] In this sense it is worth noting that in 1957, in the space between making *The Killing* and *Paths of Glory*, Kubrick seriously considered adapting Stefan Zweig's *The Burning Secret*. Kubrick is said, at the time, to have been "extremely enthusiastic about Zweig's sardonic Freudian account of sexual infidelity."[3] In terms of their ideological components Schnitzler and Zweig, one could argue, were closely linked. Zweig, like Schnitzler, was born in Vienna of Jewish parentage in the latter part of the 19th century; his work, like Schnitzler's (and arguably Kubrick's), was strongly influenced by Freud and he had a strong interest in the complexities of sexual relationships; thus there was a sense here of a similarity within literary and cinematic discourses. (In a Freudian context it is perhaps significant to reflect how the 20th century had opened with Freud's publication of *The Interpretation of Dreams* [January 6, 1900] and neared its end with the premiere of *Eyes Wide Shut* [July 16, 1999]. Freud believed *The Interpretation of Dreams* to be his most significant achievement, while Kubrick described *Eyes Wide Shut* as "his best movie ever." In this sense, the fact that two such noteworthy cultural productions, bookending the century, saw dreams as "the royal road to the unconscious"[4] is of obvious interest in any serious consideration of the film.)

The Zweig project did not progress past the development stage, but Schnitzler's work seems to have remained within Kubrick's consciousness.[5] It would appear that *Traumnovelle* primarily appealed to Kubrick insomuch as it offered a psychological insight into the erotic life of a married couple, and thus had the potentiality of exploring a narrative seldom covered in cinema, or anywhere else, for that matter. In such a sense it was a narrative concerned with desire, a narrative that questioned and interrogated the significance of sexual desire and jealousy within marriage, arguably one of the most challenging discourses for a filmmaker to operate within.

In 1960 Kubrick had said of Schnitzler:

> [Schnitzler's] plays are, to me, masterpieces of dramatic writing. It's difficult to find any writer who understood the human soul more truly and who had a more profound insight into the way people think, act, and really are, and who also had a somewhat all-seeing point of view — sympathetic if somewhat cynical.[6]

Once again talking in 1960, and possibly with *Traumnovelle* specifically in mind, Kubrick spoke of his desire to make a film of a contemporary story

> that really gave a feeling of the times, psychologically, sexually, politically, personally. I would like to make that more than anything else. And it's probably going to be the hardest film to make.[7]

In one sense *Eyes Wide Shut* did prove to be the hardest film to make, insomuch as it would be some 35 more years until Kubrick succeeded in beginning to actually shoot the film. (It might be pertinent to note here that the novel had, in fact, previously been adapted for Austrian television in 1969. Directed by Wolfgang Glück, with a script by Glück and Ruth Kerry, it retained its original German title of *Traumnovelle* and featured Karlheinz Böhm, Carlo Böhm and Erika Kambach. Unfortunately, as far as can be ascertained, there is no extant version extant for comparison to Kubrick's adaptation.)

The precise history of the means by which *Eyes Wide Shut* reached the screen is still somewhat unclear. Some sources suggest Kubrick secured the rights to the novella, in 1968, via the assistance of the journalist Jay Cocks. Cocks: "I ... also assisted him in securing the rights to an obscure novel by Arthur Schnitzler that interest[ed] him."[8] Other sources suggest it was Jan Harlan, Kubrick's executive producer, brother-in-law and close collaborator who acted as Kubrick's agency. According to Harlan: "In April 1970, I entered into an option-purchase agreement with S. Fischer Verlag in Frankfurt to acquire the film rights to this novella."[9] In any case, in April 1971, John Calley, of Warner Bros., issued a press release announcing that Kubrick's next film would be an adaptation of Schnitzler's novel and would begin filming in late fall under the title *Rhapsody*. In addition, at around the same time, in an interview with John Hofsess, Kubrick had stated his next project would be a film about Napoleon, followed by "an adaptation of Arthur Schnitzler's *A Dream Novel*."[10] (It is interesting to note, in the light of such a well-publicized intent to adapt Schnitzler's novel in the 1970s, that Kubrick's subsequent preoccupation with keeping the project secret in the early 1990s was thus somewhat undermined. One presumes Kubrick was hoping his initial public interest in the project had simply been forgotten over the course of time.)

However, Kubrick's early plans for such a film were to prove unfounded; the reality would consist of a further two decades attempting to adapt the novel to the screen.[11] There are few details as to how extensive Kubrick's attempts were at this stage; for example, what kind of screenplay, if any, he produced. It is thought that, at a very early stage, Kubrick had decided the novel would be updated. At first he considered transposing the story to London or Dublin[12] before eventually settling on New York City. What is known is that in 1994, after stalling on two other projects: *Aryan Papers* and *A.I.*, Kubrick decided to go ahead with the adaptation of *Traumnovelle*. At some point, in the summer of 1994, it appears Kubrick approached two writers, Candia McWilliam and Frederic Raphael, to collaborate on the project, although it seems neither knew of the other's contribution at the time.

Frederic Raphael's role in the adaptation of the novel is well known, and he would later gain some notoriety via the publication of his polemical memoir: *Eyes Wide Open*.[13] McWilliam's role is less well known; but it is now apparent that she attempted, for a significant period of time, to adapt the book with Kubrick. On Kubrick's death, McWilliam wrote a balanced albeit somewhat cautious and circumspect account of her work on the novel.[14] As to how much of McWilliam's work got into the film — if any — is uncertain. As McWilliam received no co-screenwriter credit, it is possible that Kubrick used some of her work in his rewrite of Raphael's screenplay, but without documentary evidence it is impossible to know what this contribution might have been.

It seems McWilliam was unable to write in her own voice:

> I feared privately that my slight gift was too indirect for him to lean upon and so I wrote increasingly in a way not my own, producing in the end a rank impersonation about which he was far too kind. It was rotten, and I think often of how it should have been had I been older then, and of how generous, tactful, encouraging and kind was this man who gave me such a lot of his time.[15]

McWilliam also noted "the unfailing manners he [Kubrick] always showed me" and added: "It was the closest intellectual contact I've ever known ... he was, if the word has meaning in a debased time, a genius."[16]

McWilliam's contribution pointed to Kubrick's clear interest in offering the script a feminine perspective. This can be seen in the fact that Kubrick also attempted to interest Sara Maitland in the project. Maitland, whom Kubrick had contemporaneously been working (albeit fruitlessly) on the screenplay of *A.I.*, is on record as famously stating that Kubrick needed her to "smear the script" of *Eyes Wide Shut* with "vaginal gel," an obvious if crude signifier of female involvement. Maitland:

> One day he handed me a book called *Viennese Novelettes* by Schnitzler. I must read "Rhapsody," it was a wonderful story, it would make a wonderful film. So I read it and it didn't grab me. That was the end. It had grabbed him. (I now know it had grabbed him 20 years ago, but he spoke as though he had only read it the night before.) It is the basis of *Eyes Wide Shut*. "Pinocchio" was on hold. The cheque for completion of my contract arrived and I never heard from him again.[17]

At some point during the unsuccessful collaboration with McWilliam and the foiled attempt to interest Maitland, it seems Kubrick called Raphael. From his own account Frederic Raphael was approached by Kubrick in the summer of 1994, and then worked, throughout the late summer and fall, on a first draft of the still-untitled screenplay, based on *Traumnovelle*. Raphael delivered the first part of the screenplay just before Christmas 1994, supposedly giving the Kubrick household "the best Christmas they'd had in eighteen years."[18] Raphael completed a first draft of the screenplay sometime between January and March 1995, after which Kubrick reworked this into a prose treatment and then Raphael further reworked this until something close to a shooting script was produced.[19] Kubrick continued to work on the script up until the start of shooting and, of course, beyond it — as Kubrick once stated: "I never stop working on a script."[20] It is thus difficult to be sure how much of Raphael's work survived into the finished film; on consideration, one might possibly suspect that this ultimately resulted in relatively little. This is supported by the report that Kubrick had considered removing Raphael's screen credit, and was only forced to aver under the threat of legal action.[21]

In any case, throughout the rest of 1995 Kubrick then turned his attention to the issue of casting the film, ultimately announcing, on December 15, 1995, in Warner Bros.'s now-famous press release:

> Stanley Kubrick's next film will be *Eyes Wide Shut*, a story of jealousy and sexual obsession, starring Tom Cruise and Nicole Kidman.

The official information that Kubrick was about to shoot a new film, allied with the prospect of two of the world's most famous film actors taking part, aroused a significant level of media interest. However, principal photography on the film would not begin until November 7, 1996, and would not end until late in February 1998, with reshoots taking place in April and May 1998,[22] thus earning the film the dubious honor of being the longest continuous cinematic "shoot" on a major American film in motion picture history. The task of editing the film, together with other post-production work, continued throughout the rest of 1998 and into 1999, with Kubrick delivering what was purported to be "the final cut" of the film on March 2, 1999. Kubrick died on March 7, with the premiere of the film taking place about four months later, on July 13, 1999.

The rationale behind Kubrick's continuing interest (and his obsession with Schnitzler's novel) is uncertain. One might point to some obvious biographical connections: the same Jewish background and familial Austrian ancestors, together with the same fatherly profession (Kubrick's father, like Schnitzler's, was a physician); however, it was arguably the erotic subtext within Schnitzler's work, so closely echoed in Kubrick's, that was probably the most significant factor. In other words, Kubrick's films had the same erotically edged psychological intent as Schnitzler's plays and novels. More specifically, Kubrick's fascination with Schnitzler may have lain in the fact that Schnitzler seems to have considered the issue of sexual jealousy as the ultimate subject for artistic concern. In some ways this perhaps accounts for Kubrick filming it — the novel — so late in his life. (One might note here that Kubrick began work on his film at the same age as Schnitzler published his novel: 64.) It is known that Kubrick's wife, Christiane Kubrick, had not liked the novel, or Kubrick's interest in it. It is possible that Kubrick perceived of the novel as a dangerous subject to approach earlier in one's life, that he was aware of the dangers of art spreading beyond artifice.

Thus the film's primary preoccupation was concerned with "adult material," for once that trite and clichéd phrase being accurate. The concern of Schnitzler's novel was sexual jealousy, perhaps both the most tangible and also the most proscribed of all human emotions. *Eyes Wide Shut* would be routinely misunderstood as being a film about sex (although it might be argued it was cynically marketed in this way); however, the film was, in fact, concerned with something much more significant. Thus one could say that the film was concerned not so much with sexual activity and fantasy, but with the nature of marital fidelity. In other words, the dilemma of maintaining sexual love within a long-term relationship, coupled with the onset of *ennui* and the resultant temptations exterior to the relationship. This may have disappointed a part of the film's audience, who were expecting to see explicit and salacious scenes involving one of Hollywood's most famous couples, but this was to miss the point. As Michael Herr commented, of Schnitzler's original text: "*Traumnovelle* ... isn't the sexiest novella ever written ... [but was] ... one of the most disturbing."[23]

Herr went on: "They even said that it [the film] didn't have a story, but it did, and a good one, the one about the man who loved his wife."[24] This is approaching the core of Kubrick's final film, this was a story seldom told: the story of a happy marriage.[25] However, in addition to this, it was a story that attempted to portray the fragility of a marriage, with the suggestion that all marriages, however strong they may appear on the surface, are open to outside temptation. At the beginning of the film, the Harfords seem to represent the epitome of a happily married couple: the perfect apartment, the perfect family, the perfect relationship. However, as the narrative progresses, the temptations available and the idea of betrayal, even as fantasy, create damaging feelings of sexual jealousy. As critic Janet Maslin noted, for a director who could create new universes with each undertaking, *Eyes Wide Shut* "chose the bedroom as the last frontier" and that, with his final film, Kubrick chose to confront "grown-up sex and its discontents."[26] In this sense the film was a meditation on fidelity, a meditation on the commitments and sacrifices necessary within a monogamous relationship.

In terms of the film's core theme, of monogamous fidelity, critic Charles Whitehouse perceived of a clue in the film's title: "My guess is that the phrase 'Eyes Wide Shut' is shorthand for the most successful attitude a monogamous couple can adopt to viewing each other's inner life."[27] One could argue Kubrick strengthened this idea via his choice of password in the film, the password Bill must know in order to gain entrance to the Somerton orgy. In Schnitzler's source text the password was "Denmark," while in the film it was "Fidelio." Beethoven's only opera, *Fidelio* (with its subtitle: *Married Love*), being the obvious connotative allusion and an obvious reminder of one of the film's central themes. (In this context it is perhaps pertinent to consider how the title, the phrase "eyes wide shut," may have had an antecedent from a quotation by Benjamin Franklin on marriage: "Keep your eyes wide open before marriage, half shut afterwards.")

All of this is not to suggest Kubrick was unaware of the erotic potential of the film. This is especially pertinent if one considers that all his previous films, almost without exception, had had such an awareness. However, Kubrick's previous work had tended to present a sexual discourse within arenas other to that of conventional sex between a man and woman. For example, the erotic subtext of "machine sex" in both *Dr. Strangelove* and *2001: A Space Odyssey,* the pedophiliac discourse in *Lolita,* the linkage of sex with violence in *A Clockwork Orange,* the metaphor of homosocial bonding as a replacement to sexual desire in *Full Metal Jacket,* and so on. In other words, Kubrick's work had previously offered little in the sense of a sexually functioning married couple. One might think of such examples as: Jack and Wendy in *The Shining,* Barry and Lady Lyndon in *Barry Lyndon,* Pee and Em in *A Clockwork Orange,* Humbert and Charlotte in *Lolita;* however, nowhere in any of these cases do we find anything like a sexually viable relationship. (To find another example of Kubrick presenting another viable heterosexual relationship, one has to go back to his second film: *Killer's Kiss,* to the love affair between Davy and Gloria. However, as will be seen later in this chapter, *Eyes Wide Shut* and *Killer's Kiss* have, in fact, a number of other close intertextual connections.) Thus, in a sense, Kubrick's last film was unique in offering a sense of conventional human sexuality, an undisguised and direct view of sexual desire between a man and a woman within a monogamous relationship.

However, one consistent thematic element in Kubrick's work, which was upheld in the film, was the linkage between the discursive practices of sex and death, here presented in what was perhaps its most full-fledged fashion. The correlation between Eros and Thanatos, between sexual desire and the death instinct, was consistently called into question throughout the film. This being first apparent in the scene in which Mandy, after having sex with Ziegler in his opulent bathroom, is shown as being near to death, due, we are told, to the result of a drug overdose. In addition to this, the way in which Marion declares her love for Bill within an hour of her father's death, in the same room as her father's body, demonstrates a similar correlation. Also, Domino, the playful if unrealistic prostitute Bill encounters, is later found to be HIV positive. In a similar sense, Alice speculates whether some of Bill's patients (some with terminal diseases) may, nonetheless, be sexually aroused by him. While the joyless orgy at Somerton appears to offer unlimited sexual opportunities, it also threatens Bill's life when he is discovered to be a trespasser.

Finally, Mandy's later fate — a sexually desirable woman dead on a mortuary slab — and Ziegler's typically caustic comment that she "got her brains fucked out," suggests a clear delineation of sex and death. In fact, the image of Mandy's naked body in the morgue typified the discourse of sex and death running throughout the film: sex, here in *Eyes Wide Shut*, was the "bad, bad thing."

In one way the thematic appropriation of sex and death can be seen as Kubrick simply maintaining a veracity to Schnitzler's source novel. This sense of authenticity, from the beginning to the end of the book, was followed, at times, to an almost pedantic degree. One might note here how the film was consistently adept in the way it translated and enhanced even minor narrative details from the novel. For example, a single phrase, "two dominoes dressed in red,"[28] would appear to have provided both the inspiration for Gayle and Nuala and perhaps Domino's name. In a similar sense the character of Sandor Szavost was seemingly derived from Albertine's brief encounter with "a stranger, whose blasé, melancholy air and foreign-sounding — evidently Polish — accent."[29] In addition, in the novel Albertine states: "I opened a wardrobe ... hanging there: resplendent oriental operatic costumes,"[30] this potentially providing Kubrick with the idea of the two Japanese men in Millich's costume shop. In the same way Fridolin's comment: "Quite obviously the whole thing had been a charade,"[31] in the novel, are Fridolin's thoughts within an internal monologue — but they echo Ziegler's words to Bill in the film: "Bill, suppose I told you that ... everything that happened to you ... was a kind of charade. That it was fake."

∗   ∗   ∗

Dream Story begins with a story within a story: "Twenty-four brown slaves rowed the splendid galley that would bring Prince Amgiad to the Caliph's palace."[32] Fridolin and Albertine's daughter (unnamed in the novel, but named Helena in the film) is reading a story from a text that seems to be deliberately reminiscent of *1001 Nights*. To begin a fictional text with a quotation from another fictional text cannot help but draw attention to the artifice of fiction itself; something to which Kubrick's film also attested. While *Eyes Wide Shut* does not refer to the opening of the novel directly, it nonetheless demonstrates an awareness of it via other symbolic means. Prince Amgiad in his "splendid galley" is "wrapped in "his purple cloak" (red in other translations[33]) and is alone on deck, under the "deep blue, star-spangled night sky." The significant issue here is the fact that these same colors, red and blue, are used and are clearly apparent throughout Kubrick's film.[34] In addition, the way the opening passage goes on is of interest: "But the Prince, wrapped in his purple cloak, lay alone on the deck beneath the deep blue, star-spangled night sky, and his gaze — ."[35] What the Prince gazes upon we never discover, as Schnitzler's text breaks off here with an elliptical hyphen. We never return to the story within the story; Schnitzler's text merely goes on: "Up to this point the little girl had been reading aloud; now, quite suddenly, her eyes closed."[36]

In these opening sentences it is possible to perceive some of the reasons why Kubrick was so besotted by the novella, of how even these first few lines offered a diverse opportunity of cinematic potential. For example, the significance of the masculine gaze, of eyes closing and — subsequently — of the interpretative nature of dreams. Schnitzler writes (and Kubrick reads) "and his gaze," this phrase having a particular significance to both Schnitzler's novella and to Kubrick's film. It is also a phrase that provides a way in which to begin to approach the film from a theoretical perspective. Laura Mulvey's celebrated essay, first published in 1975, "Visual Pleasure in Narrative Cinema," argued that film was primarily addressed to the male viewer, and that women in film were "represented as the passive object of the male gaze."[37] Mulvey's essay inscribed two main features pertaining to women in cinema: she was the object of male desire; and she was also the signifier of the threat of castration. The image of woman, especially when naked, connoted the lack of a penis; hence the threat of castration, the end of pleasure. According to Mulvey, the male figure in film was predominantly active, narrative revolved around him; while the female figure was on the periphery, merely decorative — the locus of male desire — a spectacle to be looked at both by the men in the film and by viewers of the film.

It is possible that, given his choice of title for the film, Kubrick may have been aware of Mulvey's argument. One might suppose that Frederic Raphael (with his self-proclaimed academic credentials) was also aware of Mulvey's work, given that it was one of the most influential essays within film studies in the last 30 or 40 years. However, if this was so, one wonders why Raphael dismissed, so out of hand, Kubrick's choice of title for the film.[38] Raphael's proposed titles: *You and Me* and *The Female Subject* were both rejected by Kubrick; *Eyes Wide Shut* being proposed solely by Kubrick, himself. Hunter Vaughan, in his essay: "*Eyes Wide Shut*: Kino-Eye Wide Open" is one of the few critics to have discussed the use of Mulvey's ideas in the film. Vaughan argued that Kubrick self-consciously employed the male gaze in the film, suggesting that, in a sense, Kubrick attempts to subvert Mulvey's ideas. In a discussion of the film's opening scene, Vaughan wrote: "Not only does this initial image scream of Mulveian scopophilia in the hands of the 'male gaze,' it also supports Mulvey's derivative point about the fetishization of the female star [Kidman]."[39]

From the beginning, the word "gaze," in Schnitzler's novella, was self-evidently a masculine gaze; it was Prince Amgiad's. In the same way, from the beginning of Kubrick's film, the gaze of the camera was predominantly masculine. For example, in the film's opening image we see Alice (gratuitously) undressing before our eyes, a scene having little if any narrative cohesiveness. (The ambiguous nature of the opening scene revolved around the question of when it was supposed to have taken place. It was not the night of Ziegler's party, as Alice is seen wearing a different dress. However, it could be interpreted as a proleptic moment; as though Alice were undressing to prepare to enact the film's final word. Such a reading would therefore complete a Joycean circle of sorts—the film begins with its ending, as in *Finnegans Wake*, the final word begins the story again. This perhaps being not wholly irrelevant, insomuch as the film contains other clear references to Joyce, as will be seen.) Hence, this scene might clearly be read as one of the many obvious signifiers of the masculine gaze in the film. (One notes the classical allusions of the scene: the two classical columns framing Alice as if she was a classical nude; "a body that is complete and idealized,"[40] a body that has "a distinctly Botticellian image."[41] However, the anachronous detail of the two tennis racquets offered a surreal quality, disturbing the effect, a typical Kubrickian motif.) In terms of this opening scene, the screenplay merely tells us: "ALICE, a beautiful woman with her back to the camera, lets an elegant black dress drop to the floor."[42] However, other than the accomplishment of revealing her near perfect body, it was difficult (as suggested above) to perceive of any narrative significance. The scene faded in from black and then faded back to black, offering almost a sense of an eye opening and closing, to reveal Alice disrobing within a purely voyeuristic discourse. A vivid representation of Mulvey's theoretical argument, represented saliently and (one might argue) consciously in the title of the film.

Thus, while it is not possible to be entirely certain, it would appear that Kubrick's film was, potentially at least, aware of aspects of contemporary film theory, especially in terms of voyeurism and scopophilia. In drawing upon the work of such theorists as Mulvey and Jacques Lacan, one can therefore argue that Kubrick's last cinematic work was, in one sense, about the act of looking itself; a critique both about looking; and also about looking and not seeing, most specifically the ways in which men look at women and do not actually see what they are looking at.

"You're not even looking at it." So says Alice, in only the film's fourth line of dialogue, exasperated by Bill, her husband, who says her hair is "great" without actually looking at her.[43] Yet, throughout its length the film was concerned with looking: often with Alice as the focal point. Bill may not have been looking at her in the film's opening, but almost everyone else Alice meets in the film is doing just this. For example, Roz, the baby-sitter, tells Alice: "Wow! You look amazing, Mrs. Harford." Ziegler says: "Alice, look at you! God, you're absolutely stunning." While later, and perhaps most significantly, Alice will tell Bill that the naval officer "glanced at me, as he walked past, just a glance. Nothing more. But I could hardly move." Thus the power of the male gaze, or so one might argue, was explicitly expressed here — a man merely looks at a woman, and his gaze transfixes her.

At times the men in the film commanded women to look at them: "*Look at me. Look at me, Mandy,*" says Bill to Mandy, the young woman who has overdosed at Ziegler's party. Such a concept worked another way around, as when Alice is recounting her dream, she tells Bill: "I was fucking other men, so many ... I don't know how many I was with. And I knew you could *see* me in the arms of all these men." However, for the greater part, the film presented men looking at women for scopohilic pleasure. "I had a very interesting look around," Bill says at the orgy, to the young woman (Mandy) who will "redeem him," and we note the emphasis on "*look* around." In this context, the orgy at Somerton[44] might be seen as the paramount example of voyeurism in this, or in any of Kubrick's films. Here we are offered one of Kubrick's most blatant opportunities for the male gaze: numerous women, young and nubile, with physically perfect bodies, presented in a naked or near naked state. Hence, it would seem reasonable to suggest the film is fully cognizant of the issue of scopophilia: from the first scene, in which we are coerced into becoming voyeurs as we watch Alice undress, to the scene of Bill and Alice beginning to make love in front of a mirror, to the excesses of the orgy, and to the various other voyeuristic scenes in the film. However, the charges of a blatant misogynistic discourse might be countered if one perceives of the film operating within a more theoretically astute arena.

In this sense, the depiction of Alice in the film is of specific interest; on the one hand, it is clear that she is the most compelling character in the film, perhaps the most compelling female character in the whole of Kubrick's work.[45] Yet, on the other hand, her body is depicted in what appears to be a deliberate and wholly exploitative discourse. Alexander Walker called the "pot smoking" scene between Bill and Alice in their apartment: "The most extraordinary and complex sequence Kubrick directed in his later years ... it crosses the white line on the high road of conjugal convention."[46] However, Walker also thought the scenes of Alice's nudity in the film gratuitous: "These shots are hardly necessary — though quite effective in revealing Kidman's anatomy in more explicitly erotic activity."[47]

As previously intimated, the opening scene of Alice undressing had little narrative relevance. Thus one might rephrase the question: why are we shown her undressing in such a provocative and narratively meaningless way; was the scene offered as mere voyeuristic pleasure; or was there something else? In a certain sense the film simply appeared to take a stereotypical approach to nudity, predominantly to female nudity? One might suggest that, like many great artists, Kubrick simply admired the female nude. One might think, for example, of the infamous scene in *A Clockwork Orange,* wherein

Virginia Wetherell tempted Alex with her "perfect pair of groodies"; or one could go all the way back to 1953 and *The Seafarers*, as Vincent LoBrutto noted:

> A cut produces the first example of nudity in a Stanley Kubrick film and shows the director's adolescent sense of sexuality. The screen is filled with a photograph of a young naked woman, a string of pearls draped above her breasts.[48]

Similarly one could think of many other diverse examples from Kubrick's work: the Vietnamese prostitute lifting up her mini-skirt in *Full Metal Jacket*, the nude young woman in the shower in *The Shining*, Major Kong ogling the *Playboy* centerfold in *Dr. Strangelove*, etc., but in *Eyes Wide Shut*, Kubrick seems to have offered himself the indulgence to go almost as far as he wanted.

However, beyond this somewhat obvious observation pertaining to the depiction of the female nude in the film, there were further and perhaps more significant issues at work within an erotic discourse. For example, the representation of Alice's body was of interest within a psychoanalytical light. This might be argued insomuch as it is difficult to overlook the overtones of anality and bodily functions toward Alice's body in the film. At the start of the film we see Alice sitting on the toilet urinating,[49] while at Ziegler's party she again needs the toilet, excusing herself, telling Bill that she "desperately needs to go to the bathroom." In addition, we see Alice wholly nude three times in the film, and it is always from behind, hence with a specific attentiveness to her bottom and, hence, her anus hidden within. Furthermore, in one of Bill's fantasy visions, of Alice making love with the naval officer, Alice raises up her haunches to let her partner remove her underwear and then kneels as if to offer herself to be taken from behind — with the implication that she might be offering herself to be penetrated anally.[50]

Thus, in one context, one might perceive all of this in a scatological light; of Kubrick returning, once again, to the bathroom, to his "favorite locus of corporality."[51] As Alexander Walker commented, referring to *Eyes Wide Shut*: "Bathrooms and their ceramic conveniences occupy a central and ominous place in Kubrick interiors."[52] There were two bathrooms in *Eyes Wide Shut*: Bill and Alice's more conventional environment, compared to the opulence of Ziegler's "rest room," Kubrick's last and most virtuosic bathroom. Kubrick's undoubted interest in such discursive spaces (bathroom scenes, as has been noted, occur in all his films) may simply have been the intent here; on the other hand the deliberate depiction of Alice in this way may be construed within a more grotesque representation of femininity. In a sense such a representation, in some way at least, may help to explain the previously mentioned classical allusions of the opening scene. Roger Horrocks, a perceptive gender theorist, has spoken of the image of woman in classical art as a "sealed container"; whereas, pornography presents a "vessel full of holes," insomuch as the open "display of vagina and female anus" shatters taboos and "demystifies the mysterious."[53] It is perhaps valid to speculate that Kubrick's flirtation with an erotic (and by inference a quasi-pornographic) discourse was pointing, albeit in a significantly subtle way, toward such issues here. Alice, in other words, represents both an idealized erotic female body and the actual physical reality of a female body. The depiction of Alice portrays her as a "vessel" full of holes; thus Alice, like Jonathan Swift's Chloe, also shits.[54]

However, in an alternate context, Kubrick was once again simply following Schnitzler, following the sense of fear and anxiety expressed in the novel over the mystery of the female body. For example, in the mortuary scene, wherein Fridolin looks down at the body of the dead woman he had previously lusted after:

> Unconsciously Fridolin bent lower, as if the intensity of his gaze might wrest an answer from those rigid features.... [He] followed the contours of her lower body, noticing the way the well-formed thighs spread out impassively from the shadowy regions that had lost their mystery and meaning.[55]

The key issue here was the sense in which this film, and arguably Kubrick's work as a whole, appears to have been inherently, if benignly, misogynistic. Aside from Alice, the other women in the film were either prostitutes (Mandy, Domino and Sally), or budding prostitutes (Millich's daughter), or exaggeratedly promiscuous women (Gaye and Nuala). This is not to mention the women at the orgy, whose only *raison d'être* appeared to be that of blatant sex objects. Thus these women were presented in what appears to be a self-evidently misogynistic discourse. The critic Tim Kreider has placed *Eyes Wide Shut* as part of a "thematic trilogy" of misogyny, citing Jack Torrance's hatred of his wife in *The Shining,* "The institutionalized misogyny of the Marine Corps" in *Full Metal Jacket,* and the portrayal of women in *Eyes Wide Shut.*[56]

Yet the complexity of these three films (and indeed, one could extend this to all of Kubrick's canon) suggests a knowingness toward the sexually charged political discourses under discussion. In *Eyes Wide Shut* the women assume roles in which they are little more than sexual playthings for men: but they, and especially Alice, at least seem to have an awareness of a feminist perspective of themselves within the phallocentric and patriarchal discourses they inhabit. One might note how Alice has a confidence to disclose that her dreams consists of men "fucking her," and her last word in the film decidedly points to an awareness of feminine pleasure within the patriarchal and misogynistic discourses expressed.

Thus it might be argued that the film has an awareness of the complexities and ambivalences of the sexual politics at play. On one level the film might appear blatantly exploitative, while on the other hand there is a sense of knowingness to its construct of a sexual discourse. For example, one might point to the fact that while the film continually appears to be approaching a sexual *denouement*, it is continually able to avoid it. Bill never succeeds in consummating his desire with anyone: not with his wife, not with Gaye and Nuala, not with Domino, not with Millich's daughter, not with Sally and not with any of the women at the orgy. One might sum this up by saying there are no actual *money shots* in the film: sexual release is continually withheld. In fact, for the most part, the film seems purposefully unarousing, purposefully un-erotic and purposefully un-orgasmic.

However, this is from a masculine perspective. One might argue that the film possesses a greater sense of depth and subtlety from a feminine point of view. One notes women generally have a dominance and assertiveness in the film; from Marion's declaration of love, to Domino's propositioning of Bill, to Millich's daughter and her unabashed flirting with Bill, to Alice's explicit last word. In this sense one of the film's greatest assets is Nicole Kidman's portrayal of Alice. It has been suggested, by David Thomson, that Kidman could have played multiple roles in the film: "If only someone had had the wit to let her play all the female roles—so that Tom Cruise can't help seeing her everywhere."[57] This was at least suggested in Schnitzler's novel. In one of *Traumnovelle's* most risible lines, a line Kubrick was probably wise not to use, Fridolin says to Albertine: "In every woman—believe me, even though it may sound trite—in every woman with whom I thought I was in love, it was always you I was searching for."[58] It was a trite line, but the women Fridolin/Bill encounter can, in some way, be seen as representations of Albertine/Alice. As previously intimated, the nude women at the masked orgy seem to resemble Alice, at least in the perfection of their bodies. Neither Domino nor Sally is wholly unlike Alice, nor are the two models at Ziegler's party—even Millich's daughter conjures up a younger version of Alice. Such a reading cannot help but set up the suggestion that some, or all, of Bill's encounters may be extensions of his unconscious, and hence that some, or all, of his adventures are the mere extension of a dream. Slavoj Žižek has argued that the events of Bill Harford's nighttime journeys around New York were dreams or fantasies:

> The fantasy of being the passionate love interest of his patient's daughter ... the fantasy of encountering a kind prostitute who doesn't even want money from him ... the encounter with the ... owner of the mask rental store who is also a pimp for his juvenile daughter.[59]

Žižek went on to comment on the behavior of Bill in the orgy sequence at Somerton, at how his behavior was thus explainable and not a "ridiculously aseptic and out-of-date depiction" as "many a critic"[60] had dismissed it. In other words, Bill was dreaming and the anachronistic *mise en scène* was, to some extent, explained by this.

It is certainly accurate to say the narratives of *Dream Story* and *Eyes Wide Shut* both pointed toward the idea of narrative intermingling with dreaming; and since narratives in themselves could be seen, in a sense, as projections of our waking dreams, then the inference here was further enhanced.[61] One might also consider the idea that dreams are routinely interpreted as narratives, as stories; hence the title of Schnitzler's novel becomes more and more worthy of note. In his novel Schnitzler offered continuous references to the shifting relationships between dream and reality:

> Wasn't he perhaps lying at home in bed this very moment — and hadn't everything he had experienced been nothing more than his delirium?[62]
>
> ... one could no longer tell whether one had experience or merely dreamed it.[63]
>
> ... as if everything he had experienced had only been a dream.[64]

In its narrative structure the film can also be seen as resembling a dream, insomuch as, in numerous instances, it has a surreal quality, the same intensity of dreaming. As Marion says, near the beginning of the film: "It's so unreal." While near the end of the film, Alice sums up hers and Bill's adventures by saying: "We've managed to survive through all our adventures, whether they were real or only a dream." All of this is not to suggest we were in the clichéd territory of "It was all a dream!" Instead the viewers of *Eyes Wide Shut* are presented with a subtle discourse that questions the representation of reality or dream that explores the borders of reality and dreaming.

It might also be noted that the film, like the novel, attends to the common anxiety within dreams of being naked when others are fully dressed. Such a scenario is implicit in the order for Bill to undress, by Red Cloak, at the orgy. Freud had something to say about this, speaking of "a dream in which one is naked or scantily clad in the presence of strangers."[65] Freud thought this was common to many people: "I believe that the great majority of my readers will at some time have found themselves in this situation in a dream."[66] Freud went on: "The persons before whom one is ashamed are almost always strangers, whose faces remain indeterminate,"[67] and that "the dreamer's embarrassment and the spectator's indifference constitute a contradiction such as often occurs in dreams."[68] Freud's analysis here seeming to fit precisely into the context of the scene in question, thus adding an opportunity for further oneiric contextualization.

There is also the sense in which characters in the film appear to become interchangeable, and, for want of a better word, dreamlike. For example: Domino for Sally, Carl for Bill, and Mandy for the Mysterious Woman who redeems Bill at the orgy.[69] In a similar sense there is the way in which events repeat themselves in similar ways and different times throughout the film, seen most exaggeratedly in Bill's re-treading of the same nighttime journeys. In addition, there is the idea that Alice's dream, Alice's actual dream, within the film's fictional narrative, seems to correspond, in content, to Bill's "real" adventures in Somerton. In all these ways the film can be seen as a deliberate masquerade, a narrative with intentionally ambiguous levels of dream and reality. As Norman Kagan commented: "[The film represents] an extended Freudian dream grafted onto another dream."[70] Or as Michael Herr put it: "In the case of *Eyes Wide Shut* the camps were made up of people who knew within minutes that they were watching a dream film and those who didn't."[71]

*   *   *

The use of names in the film is of interest in this context. For example, Alice's name: on a simple level it recalls the initial "A" in Albertine, but it also creates allusions to the Alice of Lewis Carroll's stories, hence further enhancing the concept of narrative as dream. (In particular, Alice's name signifies *Alice Through the Looking Glass,* and we might note the instances of Alice looking into mirrors in the film, in particular the "Baby Did a Bad Bad Thing" scene in which she gazes into the looking glass, as if at another reality. It would appear Alice's name might have been a conscious design on Fredric Raphael's part, as an earlier version of the screenplay contained several allusions to Lewis Carroll's Alice. For example, in the scene at the Sonata Café, in an earlier draft of the script, Bill says to Nick: "This is getting curiouser and curiouser." However, it seems that Kubrick, anxious to excise any overly ingenious allusions in the script, removed such references.) In terms of Bill's first name, in full William half-rhymed with Fridolin, but the diminutive may have been a satiric comment on the significance of money in the film. "You're Bill ... *the* Bill," Sally will later tease him. (As to Harford, Bill and Alice's surname, it has been suggested that it derived from a reduction of Harrison Ford's name, the actor at one time apparently being considered for the male lead; however, as suggested in the previous chapter, a more probable echo might have been towards Gustav Hasford, Kubrick's collaborator on *Full Metal Jacket,* who had died just a year before Kubrick was preparing to shoot *Eyes Wide Shut.*) The choice of Ziegler's name is of particular interest; according to Frederic Raphael the name of the character derived from an "unaffectionate memory of 'Ziggy' a garrulous agent who once represented me in California."[72] However, the name arguably also resonated with the only other famous Ziegler of recent times, that of Ronald Ziegler, President Nixon's press secretary in the early 1970s. Ronald Ziegler's most famous contribution to the culture perhaps being to coin the term: "This is an operative statement—all previous statements are inoperative." In a sense *Eyes Wide Shut* was a film concerned with "covering up," in the film Ziegler was wholly corrupt, a man who had "got lost in the labyrinth of his own lies."[73] There were other names of potential interest: Domino's name suggests black and white as against the colors in the rainbow; the name of Sandor Szavost, in one specific sense, potentially points to an SS reference; while it is perhaps significant to note the name doubling of the domestic helps, the babysitter at the Harfords' and the maid at Lou Nathanson's house were Roz and Rosa, respectively. Overall, this echoing and chiming of names adds to a further sense of ambiguity, a further sense of an oneiric discourse within the film.

* * *

While the film could thus be perceived as inhabiting the border between dream and reality, it was also a film very much set in the real world in its adult (to use that word without a euphemistic intent) treatment of marriage. The monogamous relationship and the possibility of remaining faithful within it, being contrasted against the opportunities of the orgy at Somerton. The much-discussed and much-misinterpreted orgy could, in fact, be seen as operating on a number of levels, levels that have been mostly neglected in favor of a discussion of the sexual content of the scene.[74] To begin with, it is clear that the orgy inhabited an ironic discourse. To have "Fidelio" as the password to an orgy would immediately seem to suggest some kind of ironical intent. (In the original shooting script the password was the somewhat awkward sounding "Fidelio Rainbow," possibly a pun by Raphael on his own initials, as if to attempt to furtively insert his authorship into the drama; this idea was dropped by Kubrick in the final shooting script.) Also, to have "Strangers in the Night" as ambient music was clearly another ironic gesture — the overtly romantic scenario of the song had little to do with the wholly carnal and loveless encounters taking place at Somerton. For example, there was little sense of lovers exchanging glances and falling in love at first sight; instead, the viewer is presented with loveless, anonymous, emotionless couplings. Thus what Kubrick seemed to be showing, at least in part, was the way sex has become anonymous and emotionless. Hence, one could argue that Kubrick was looking at the way in which sex has been commodified; the way pornography, via film and video and the Internet, has reduced sex to a loveless exchange of intimate bodily fluids. Bill will later talk of "a fucking charade," in a sense this was exactly what the orgy presented, at least in terms of a comparison to his relationship with Alice. (As Neil Fulwood commented: "It [the orgy] is a vision of sex without intimacy, without love—cold, anonymous, impersonal. It represents what Harford stands to lose."[75])

In a differing context this element of sexuality, in the film, could also be read in connection with issues such as power, money and class. In this light the orgy could be seen as representing a sinister inversion of Ziegler's Christmas party at the opening of the film. As Norman Kagan noted: "The orgy mansion is the upper-class Christmas party stripped of its own masks and conceits, reduced to its naked sexual assertions of power and submission."[76] Thus the orgy portrayed the underside of the polite representation of capitalist wealth at Ziegler's party. One of the underlying themes in Kubrick's work, and especially in *Eyes Wide Shut,* is a consideration of the corrosive effects of power upon society. In *Eyes Wide Shut* power is delineated via the possession of excessive wealth, with money being an ever-present and significant issue, something seen from its opening line, when Bill asks: "Honey, have you seen my wallet?" As Tim Kreider has noted:

> The real pornography in this film is in its lingering depiction of the shameless, naked wealth of millennial Manhattan and of its obscene effect on society and the human soul.... For those with their eyes wide open, there are plenty of money shots.[77]

If the film can be positioned within a postmodernist reading, if it is, as it has been described "a postmodern, erotic tragedy,"[78] then Frederic Jameson's Marxist argument, that postmodernism was "the inevitable cultural logic of late capitalism,"[79] can be seen as resonating throughout the film. One theme Kubrick's film would appear to have been interested in was the excesses of capitalism.[80] Hence the issue of money, and those who own vast amounts of it, was a significant aspect of the film. We might recall the film's aforementioned opening line, or Bill's question to Domino, further on in the film: "Do you suppose we should talk about money?" In a sense, the whole of the film was concerned precisely with talking about money. *Eyes Wide Shut* is a film about those in American society who possess vast amounts of money and those who possess a derisory share. At Ziegler's party we see the most exaggerated expression of capitalist wealth in the film, the guests providing a visual representation of Mr. Ullman's comment, in *The Shining*: "All the best people," or, to go back further, Lord Wendover's comment in *Barry Lyndon*: "People about whom there is no question." At one point Ziegler refers dismissively to "ordinary people," pointing out the difference between himself, and, presumably, people like Domino in her "cozy" apartment a few miles but a different world away.[81] As Kreider put it:

> The slice of that world he tried to show us in his last ... work, the capital of the global American empire at the end of the American Century, is one in which the wealthy, powerful and privileged use the rest of us like throwaway products, covering up their crimes with pretty pictures, shiny surfaces, and murder.[82]

Kubrick's decision to set his film at Christmas, *the* season of consumerism, was perhaps of relevance here; such a setting offering an additional pointer to the blatant consumerism of the society in which Ziegler and the other "best people" inhabited. Once again there is a provenance from

Dream Story; in Schnitzler's novella Christmas was at least suggested as being the time of year, as it was clearly late winter with snow falling on the ground. (Note how, early in the novel after the masked ball, Fridolin and Albertine take a "swift coach ride through the white winter's night."[83] Kubrick did not go the full way and show us a white Christmas—not altogether uncommon in New York—but the idea of a "white winter's night" remains in the Christmas setting.) However, Kubrick's reasoning may have had further resonances, insomuch as the orgy scene thus achieves a sense of the Roman festival of Saturnalia.[84] Its inherent hedonistic excesses thus provide an obvious connection between the Christian and the pagan: the quasi–Christian elements of Ziegler's party and the decidedly pagan elements of the orgy.

There are other aspects linking the film to the festive season; for example, Michel Chion, while accepting that the season in the film is decidedly one of Christmas, noted: "Neither the name of Jesus, nor any crosses or cradles are ever shown or mentioned."[85] An example of this might be observed within the death scene of Lou Nathanson. We might note that although Bill tells Marion that her father had died peacefully in his sleep, and that she was a great comfort to him, he makes no mention of an eternal soul, or of the sense of redemptive hope within any kind of religious discourse. In this sense the world of *Eyes Wide Shut* is decidedly atheistic, appearing to point more toward the pagan, a life of sensual pleasure, a world we encounter, most explicitly, at the Somerton orgy. As Chion pointed out: "It [*Eyes Wide Shut*] is a society in which religion no longer has any power over private life."[86] (One might also note the confirming influence of consumerism in the film's closure; the film ends in a toy shop on what we may presume to be just before Christmas, on the eve of Christ's birth. However, the discourse here relates to the toy shop and consumerism and not to any form of religious content.)

However, in an unadorned contrast to this, the apparent atheistic discourse of the film is undercut by the idea of Bill being redeemed by Mandy at the orgy. This adds a jarring note that points toward an incongruous and paradoxical sense of Christian redemption and sacrifice. Once again a reading of Schnitzler's novel reinforces such an idea; in the novel Albertine dreams of her husband being stripped and beaten and ultimately crucified; at one point Albertine says: "I could see at once that they were erecting a cross for you."[87] The film did not repeat such an explicit Christlike depiction, however there are Christian overtones. Randy Rasmussen noted that Bill was "put on trial by the high priest in front of the assembled guests.... In symbolic terms, the compassionate woman is a Christ figure, sacrificing herself for Bill's sin."[88] Rasmussen noted that in Bill being ordered to remove his clothes some "unspecified bodily harm" was to occur. Rasmussen speculated: "Torture? Mutilation? This bizarre crowd seems capable of anything."[89] There is certainly a sense of there being a ritualistic overtone to the scene. In being ordered to undress Bill is not being invited to have sex, nor is he simply suffering a loss of personal dignity, rather there was a sense he was to be stripped prior to suffering a punishment of some kind. One might speculate that, had he not been redeemed, his fate may have been a gruesome one: as Geoffrey Cocks put it, Bill was "threatened with public undressing, rape, humiliation and death — a modern *auto-da-fé*, the medieval ceremony of the public torture and burning of heretics."[90] Given the nature of his trespass, one presumes castration, followed by death, may be the designated punishment. Several critics have remarked on this; for example, Phillip Sipiora: "Bill ... is forced to confront the 'court' and unmask himself under penalty of great harm."[91] Mark Pizzato: "The mystery Woman ... saves Bill's ego and body from symbolic, imaginary and perhaps real castration."[92] In a manner typical for Kubrick, the film offers a number of satirical intimations of this: for example, Helena (Bill and Alice's daughter) wants to know if she can stay up and watch *The Nutcracker* on television; while at the start of the red billiard room scene, Bill asks if Ziegler had been playing pool, to which Ziegler replies that he has "just been knocking some balls around."

In this sense the orgy scenes at Somerton, while threatening a very literal attack on masculinity, also acts as a critique of masculine anxiety at a more abstract level. "You will kindly remove your mask," Bill is ordered. On an abstract level, this can be read as a statement pointing to an allegorical unmasking of masculinity itself. Bill Harford represents the last example of Kubrickian men who are not wholly confident about their sexual identity. One could point to Joker in *Full Metal Jacket*, Jack in *The Shining*, Alex in *A Clockwork Orange*, David Bowman in *2001: A Space Odyssey*, General Ripper in *Dr. Strangelove*, and so on, back through Kubrick's work.[93] However, in *Eyes Wide Shut* there is also the possibility that Kubrick was deliberately playing on the perceived media speculation around Tom Cruise's sexual identity.[94] Kubrick's use of Cruise and his public persona may have been (albeit probably unknown to Cruise himself) an attempt by Kubrick to use the whispered insinuations about "the star" within a fictional narrative. In this way Kubrick's film interrogated both the part Cruise played in the film and also his iconic cultural status as an actor and world famous celebrity. To state this plainly, Kubrick may have been playing on Cruise's well-known reputation as a so-called "gay" iconic figure; and in so doing saying something about the way celebrity has begun to enhance and even eclipse cultural productions— such as the Hollywood feature film.

While the film does not overplay such references, there is, nonetheless, an ambivalence toward Bill's sexuality. This is exemplified most obviously in the incident wherein Bill is taunted on the street by a group of "rowdy college boys."[95] They accuse him of being gay, seemingly for no other discernible reason than the fact he is a man alone on the street late at night. The "rowdy college boys" question Bill's manhood by asking which team he plays for, suggesting he may play for "the pink team." In a similar sense the hotel clerk at the Hotel Jason, played with suitably "camp" nuance by Alan Cumming, offers another perspective on Bill's sexuality. As Randy Rasmussen put it: "The hotel clerk represents a homosexual option the protagonist does not consciously acknowledge."[96] (In a differing context, Geoffrey Cocks saw the "wildly gay hotel clerk" as Kubrick's "long delayed reaction" to the censorship of the "homosexual banter" between Quilty and hotel clerk, George Swine, in *Lolita*.[97] While Robert Kolker went further, commenting that "the circles traveled round by the central character [Bill] are drawn by an unacknowledged, perhaps unacknowledgable, homosexuality."[98])

Whether such a sense of "homosexuality" was consciously present in the film must remain open to question; however, one might conclude that there is at least a subtextual suggestion, deliberately apparent in the film, of "an innocent homosexuality."[99] In such a context we might recall once again that Bill never succeeds in consummating any of the heterosexual encounters he experiences; and that there is at least the implication that the wish for a real consummation may exist elsewhere. During his nighttime journey, Bill will have a number of adventures, mostly revolving around potential sexual encounters. As intimated previously: he will be tempted by Gayle and Nuala, he will be propositioned by Marion, he will be picked up by Domino (the somewhat implausible prostitute),[100] he will be enticed by Millich's Lolitaesque daughter, and finally, he will experience an orgy full of nubile and near-perfect women. The fact that Bill does not take advantage of any of these opportunities is the point of interest. Throughout there is a sense of a literal *coitus interruptus*, Bill always seems on the verge of being unfaithful to his wife, but never actually achieves fulfillment. Once again, such narrative detail could be explained via a recourse to the sense of a homosocial or even homoerotic desire. In this sense, one might note that the most explicit sexual material in the film derives from Bill's imagining, one might say his obsessive imagining, of Alice's encounter with the naval officer. Bill imagines them making love on five occasions, one assumes he recreates this encounter out of jealousy; however, one could argue it presupposes an erotic interest not just in his wife, but also in the naval officer; as Peter Loewenberg put it: "The handsome officer is not only Albertine and Alice's fantasy, he is Fridolin and Bill's."[101]

In moving away from a homoerotic reading, to a more diverse level of discussion, a homosocial interpretation of the film offers what might be seen as a less polemical way of explaining the actions of the men (most notably Bill) in the film. In the novel Schnitzler repeatedly positioned masculinity within the standard benchmark that men have a fear of domestic space:

He felt ... a remarkable reluctance to go home. [H]ome ... with a slight shud-
der he realized that there was nowhere he wanted to go less.... Going home
like this, as he was on the point of doing, seemed to him positively ridiculous.... Fleetingly, and without any serious intent, he thought of driving to
some station, taking a train to wherever it might be and vanishing from the
lives of everyone who knew him ... and under no circumstances go home.[102]

In the film Kubrick did not dwell upon this issue in such depth, but
there was, nonetheless, a similar subtext, as Thomas Nelson put it: "Like
Nick, Bill has a typical male yearning to 'walk away' from the constraints of
fidelity."[103] We might note that Nick Nightingale has left (if perhaps only temporarily) his wife and four children in Seattle; and when Nick is asked, by
Bill, why he walked away from medicine, Nick says: "It's a nice feeling. I do
it a lot." In this sense such a comment could be seen as alluding to a masculine aversion to familial responsibility. In a similar sense there is the idea that
Bill may have found his obligations to his wife, his family and his professional life as running counter to his actual desires as a man. Note that Bill
seldom shows any real evidence of thinking about his family during his adventures, just as Nick's four children seldom, if ever, appear to be uppermost in
his mind.

"Well, that is the kind of hero I can be," Bill jokes with Gayle and Nuala,
with a kind of falsely modest *braggadocio*. However, one might argue a domes-
ticated man might find it hard to be a hero, at least in the sense Bill seems to
imply. In this light, Bill's journey and adventures may have less to do with
repaying Alice for her sexual indiscretion, and more to do with a desire to
escape the familial space, to journey and adventure beyond that familial home
environment. In other words, to forge a space wherein Bill might experience
a heroic and non-domesticated life. Bill will eventually have no choice but to
return to his wife and family, all masculine journeys (at least in Kubrick's
films) being ultimately circular. Thus, as with a diverse number of other
Kubrickian male protagonists, Bill remains caught up in an endless cycle of
being repelled and attracted toward a female presence and the domesticity
this entails.

*   *   *

It is an apparent fact that Kubrick seldom turned to great literary novels as adaptive sources; he did so only once — with *Lolita*. However, one could
argue that, at least in one specific sense, Kubrick was continually attempting
to embrace one of *the* great literary novels of the 20th century; the text in
question being James Joyce's novel of 1922: *Ulysses*. As is well known, *Ulysses*
(with *The Odyssey* at its back) is a text with a predominantly circular journey, a masculine protagonist traveling both away and toward a feminine environment. In this context, one notes, once again, how a significant number

of Kubrick's films explored the concept of masculine travel, of the masculine journey; always linked to a circular voyage of attraction and aversion around a feminine body.

Thus, in *Eyes Wide Shut*, Bill's journey into New York's dark underworld appeared to recall Leopold Bloom's similar travels around Dublin's Night-town in *Ulysses*. In this sense, the retelling of Joyce's *Ulysses* positioned the film explicitly as a "sexual odyssey."[104] Bill Harford, like Leopold Bloom and Odysseus before him, experiences both an attraction and a sense of alienation to his wife, to the marital home, to familial responsibility. This is asserted by a number of parallels that, at times, seem almost deliberate on Kubrick's part. For example, some of the women Bill encounters seemed oddly coinciden-tal: Nuala and Gaye are clearly representative of the Sirens, Domino is rep-resented as Calypso (or perhaps Nausicaa), and the orgy is a decidedly obvious representation of Bloom's visit to Bella's brothel in Dublin's Night-town. While a small number of critics have commented on the somewhat obvious Joycean connections,[105] few, if any, have commented specifically either on the concept of the masculine journey and its specific ambivalence to the domes-tic environment, or — and this is most significant — on the way Kubrick's film appears to deliberately distort language in a specifically Joycean fashion.

In *Ulysses*, Molly gets to have the last word, this being a sort of Joycean joke, perhaps demonstrating Joyce's awareness of the prejudice women endure within the linguistic system. In *Eyes Wide Shut*, Alice, like Molly, also gets the last word; the point of interest being how these two last words pointed, more or less, to the same thing. The last word of *Ulysses*, the last word uttered by Molly, after her 4,391 word monologue, unbroken by internal punctua-tion, was "yes."

> I put my arms around him yes and drew him down to me so he could feel my breasts all perfume yes and his heart was going like mad and yes I said yes I will Yes.[106]

In *Eyes Wide Shut* the last lines spoken are:

> ALICE: The important thing is we're awake now and hopefully for a long time to come.
> BILL: Forever.
> ALICE: Forever?
> BILL: Forever.
> ALICE: Let's ... let's not use that word, it frightens me. But I do love you and you know there is something very important we need to do as soon as possi-ble?
> BILL: What's that?
> ALICE: Fuck.

The word "fuck" evokes the word "yes," insomuch as Molly's monologue ends with her letting Bloom make love to her. Alice's vocabulary is more explicit, but the meaning is the same. (There are other allusions to Joyce in the film; for example, Nick Nightingale's hotel, the Hotel Jason, has Homeric overtones. Also *Blume in Love*, the film Alice is shown watching at home, could be seen as an oblique reference to Joyce's novel; Leopold Bloom certainly being in love with his wife, Molly. In addition, one might also note the allusions between *Dream Story* and *Finnegans Wake*, insomuch as the latter would also appear to be written in the language of a dream — purporting to be the dream narrative of one H.C. Earwicker, the owner of the Dublin public house in Joyce's novel.)

One could argue that Kubrick's last word was chosen with some care, as it may have proven (as indeed it did) to be his final word of all. To close out the century (and perhaps one's body of work) by uttering such a linguistic term, in a film about sex, was perhaps not such an injudicious decision. As Celestino Deleyto noted: "[Kubrick] aimed to make his ultimate statement (and, if possible, twentieth-century cinema's ultimate statement) on sex."[107] However, Deleyto went on: "But can the single word 'fuck' summarize, Rosebud-like, a whole century of thinking about love?"[108] This is a debatable question; however, the fact that the final word in Kubrick's entire lexicon was one of our culture's most taboo words, was arguably saying something about Kubrick's attitude toward language itself.

In *Eyes Wide Shut* Alice gets the last word, but the question still remains: who was actually in charge of the linguistic system? In a sense, the use of language within the film serves to undermine theoretical concepts — which suggests the masculine voice has a dominance: that language was man-made. Bill, the film's primary masculine voice, does not appear to control language, at least not in the conventional sense of this idea. When Bill receives a phone call from Alice, while he is with Domino, he tells Alice: "It's a little difficult to talk now." This comment might be seen as encapsulating Bill's relationship to language throughout the film. Michel Chion has noted the way in which Bill often "parrots" back what is said to him; Chion counted no less than forty-six separate instances of this.[109] Thus, the way in which Bill constantly repeats what is said to him throughout the film could be seen as suggesting he does not have total authority in terms of the ownership of language. In this light, we might note the film's newspaper story from the *New York Post* — the headline: "Lucky To Be Alive." When viewed on DVD, in freeze frame, the story turns out to be partly nonsense, but in a calculated way. It was an article Jack Torrance might have written, insomuch as the paragraphs were deliberately duplicated, thus recalling Jack's similar loss of control over the word in the "All work and no play" scene in *The Shining*. In a sense Kubrick appeared to be working here with elements of poststructuralist concepts, the idea that the correlation between signifier and signified was wholly arbitrary and that meaning was endlessly deferred. A distrust of language, albeit not conventionally theorized, being apparent throughout Kubrick's work and patently redolent here, in *Eyes Wide Shut*.

* * *

If Kubrick was, as ever, distrustful of language in the film, he *was* willing to operate within another level of linguistic discourse: that of intertextuality. This concept of intertextuality being focused, once again, on Kubrick's own corpus of work; thus the main intertextual references were pointing, not to the world outside, but to the world within. In *Eyes Wide Shut*, perhaps to a greater extent than ever before, Kubrick was deliberately alluding to almost the entire canon of his previous work. For example, to go back to the very beginning, to Kubrick's first published photograph, that of a "dejected" news vendor on 170th Street mourning the death of President Roosevelt. The photograph was published in *Look* magazine on June 26, 1945, when Kubrick was only 16 years old, and marked the start of his professional career. Hence the scene in which Bill buys a newspaper off a newsstand with the "Lucky to be Alive" headline could arguably be seen as a deliberate allusion to this. (Interestingly, James Naremore perceives of another conscious allusion in the film from Kubrick's days at *Look*. Naremore: "In 1949 he [Kubrick] photographed a nude woman modeling for the cartoonist Peter Arno; the woman stands with her back to the camera, her hips slightly cocked, in a pose exactly like that of Nicole Kidman at the beginning of *Eyes Wide Shut*."[110])

In a similar way, Kubrick's first feature film, *Fear and Desire*, although regularly disparaged by Kubrick himself, was also specifically alluded to in *Eyes Wide Shut*. One notes how, in having Alice watch the film *Blume in Love* on the television, pointed directly to *Fear and Desire*. *Blume in Love* was directed, in 1973, by Paul Mazursky — Mazursky having starred in *Fear and Desire*. The allusion was especially apt as Mazursky's film was a game of musical beds much in the manner of Schnitzler's play, *La Ronde*. Hence, one might presume this was not a coincidence and that Kubrick, always meticulous in his choice of background detail, was deliberately drawing attention to such an inference.[111]

The decision to locate *Eyes Wide Shut* within a New York City setting, apart from pertaining to the film's critique of capitalism, can at least be partially explained by pointing to the intertextual gestures made toward Kubrick's second feature film, *Killer's Kiss*, the only other Kubrick film to be shot in his birthplace. In addition to this, *Killer's Kiss* and *Eyes Wide Shut* shared a number of intriguing similarities; for example, each film has a narrative duration of three days. Also, each film has similar beginnings — in each a couple, a man and a woman in New York apartments — are depicted as preparing to go out for the evening. The type of apartments are different: in *Eyes Wide Shut*

Bill and Alice are together in their opulent Central Park West apartment; in *Killer's Kiss* Davy and Gloria are in separate and more modest apartments, presumably somewhere in downtown Manhattan. However, the scenarios are the same, and a perceptive student of Kubrick's work may see deliberate gestures here. (In addition, the narrative detail that Nick Nightingale is from Seattle, and has supposedly returned there, provided a clear correspondence to Davy; in *Killer's Kiss*, Davy is making just the same journey: escaping New York for Seattle.)

In addition, there are a number of various pointers in *Eyes Wide Shut* to *2001: A Space Odyssey*. These have been appositely noted by Michel Chion; for example, Chion points to the way in which a child is depicted at the end of both films: the Star Child and the imagined child resulting from *Eyes Wide Shut*'s finally uttered word. Also, Chion saw the toy shop scene at the end of *Eyes Wide Shut* as a recreation of the scene deleted from *2001: A Space Odyssey*; the scene in which Squirt, Heywood Floyd's daughter, achieves her wish of having a bush-baby for her birthday; Chion sees the final scene in *Eyes Wide Shut* as fulfilling this wish:

> If we see it this way, then Kubrick spent no less than thirty years, between 1968 and 1999, trying to come through on a promise of a gift to a child. It is as if he regretted having left the promise of a bushbaby toy — a baby after all — up in the air, and that this had haunted him the whole time.[112]

Chion pointed to a number of other connections: noting there are waltzes in both films, in *Eyes Wide Shut* the triumphal major key of Strauss being replaced by the minor key of Shostakovich. Chion also noted that *Eyes Wide Shut* was completed close to, and was quite possibly set in, the iconic year of 2001. Finally, Chion commented on the similarities, in both films, between the scenes of dead men lying in bed: David Bowman and Lou Nathanson. Once again, it is possible to perceive of at least some conscious intent, by Kubrick, in these references. There are, however, further intertextual allusions; for example, David Hughes observed a pointer toward *A Clockwork Orange*, noting that the mortuary room, visited by Bill, was located on floor C, room 114, which echoes the experimental serum Alex was injected with in *A Clockwork Orange*. (This claim may be somewhat dubious: while Hughes claims to see Floor C and Room 114, careful observation of the DVD of the film, while clearly depicting a Floor C, would not seem to depict a Room 114. Perhaps Kubrick missed a trick here, a trick Hughes aims to re-insert.) One might also note how Gayle and Nuala, the two models who attempt to seduce Bill, directly quote the scene of Alex and the two girls in the music store in *A Clockwork Orange*. In terms of *The Shining*, there are a number of allusions: Alice and Helena watching television recalls Wendy and Danny watching television; the dual elevators at the Nathanson apartment recalls the dual elevators of the Overlook; and both films find a naked (abject) woman in differing bathrooms. It is even possible to see how Kubrick may have incorporated elements of his unused screenplay, *Napoleon*; for example, Josephine's infidelity causes Napoleon to seek comfort with a "young prostitute" on a "cold, dark street," recalling Bill's encounter with Domino, after which Napoleon attends an orgy where couples "copulate spiritedly in plain sight of the other guests."

One might question: what does all this tell us? A sentimental explanation might lead one to suggest that Kubrick, suspecting the film may have been his last, deliberately chose to look back on his career in a retrospective fashion, offering an autobiographical tracing — albeit one carefully embedded and disguised. In this sense (albeit remaining within a sentimentalized reading), the film's narrative could thus be seen as pointing to an alternate world, one in which Kubrick, had he been born a generation later and had he stayed in New York, may have become — like his father — a doctor.

However, one significant way in which Kubrick was determined not to incorporate a personal or autobiographical element in the film, was his exclusion of the overtly anti–Semitic discourse found in Schnitzler's novel. In his memoir, *Eyes Wide Open*, Frederic Raphael expresses puzzlement in Kubrick's wish to elide any suggestion of Jewishness in the film. However, a knowledge of Kubrick's work as a whole might suggest either an inability or an unwillingness, on the part of the filmmaker, to approach this subject directly. Once again, one could argue that Kubrick's work was concerned — at least in part — with a struggle of coming to terms with anti–Semitism and, at the back of this, the problematical issue of the Holocaust. One could argue one of the appeals of Schnitzler's novel was its clearly delineated anti–Semitic subtext, but nonetheless it was one Kubrick chose not to approach directly.

In this context, it is interesting to note that among the only direct guidance Kubrick gave to Raphael, about the character of their "New York doctor," was that he should "not be (manifestly) Jewish."[113] Raphael originally offered the name Bill Scheuer, Kubrick balked: "Give him some name that doesn't identify him, OK? It could be Robinson, but ... we don't want him to be Jewish."[114] Within his memoir of his contribution to the film Raphael painted a picture of Kubrick as relentlessly obsessive about anti–Semitism, but nonetheless determined not to include such ideological gestures in his work. Raphael:

> It is, however, absurd to try and understand Stanley Kubrick without reckoning on Jewishness as a fundamental aspect of his mentality, if not of his work in general. He himself was known to have said that he was not really a Jew, he just happened to have two Jewish parents. Jews are not featured in any of his films; he seemed to expose, or at least dwell on, many ugly aspect of human behavior, but he never confronted anti–Semitism.[115]

Raphael went on, concluding:

> The capacity of the camera to confront the unspeakable without blinking: its
> mechanical ability to distinguish between the human and the inhuman ... my
> glib suspicion is that the only serious scandal for him is the Holocaust, which
> is why he will not, or cannot, deal with.[116]

Thus there was the contradiction of a novel by a Jewish novelist (Schnitzler), influenced by a Jewish psychoanalyst (Freud), co-written with a Jewish
screenwriter (Raphael), directed by a Jewish filmmaker (Kubrick); nonetheless eliding any sense of Jewishness. To take just one obvious instance: the
attack on Fridolin in the novel, blatantly racist and anti–Semitic, was altered
into a homophobic attack in the film. This provides a clear example of Kubrick's adaptive technique: at the same time as eliding one unwanted ideological maneuver, he deftly embraces another.

* * *

In this light, the film's ability to forge, in such subtle ways, a less than
literal adaptation of its primary source might be positioned within a wider
discursive arena. This might be asserted insomuch as the viewer of the film
might therefore be advised not to take all its components too literally. For
example, it has been suggested that the New York locations lacked authenticity: "It's difficult to make a movie about a city you last set foot in 35 years
ago,"[117] was one, somewhat typical comment, on the film. However, this was
to perhaps misunderstand Kubrick's intention. It could be argued that Kubrick was not so much interested in offering an authentic and contemporary
New York City, but rather a vision of New York City that applied to his particular and specific interpretations of Schnitzler. In this way, Kubrick seems
to have been more interested in using his version of New York City, an idealized New York, a metafictional New York, to compare its decadent way of
life to the decadence of Schnitzler's Vienna, a century before. As Tim Kreider noted, describing just this issue as blurring "the distinction between Mil-
lennial Manhattan and *fin-de-siècle* Vienna, another corrupt and decadent
high culture on the brink of an abyss ... in the champagne haze of Victor's
party the 1990s and 1890s become one, just as the "1970s and the 1920s merged
in one evening at the Overlook Hotel."[118]

As part of a wider discussion, a deliberately anachronous subtext might
thus be perceived as operating throughout the film. For example, *Eyes Wide
Shut* may notionally be seen as being set in the present day of its making, but
it consistently pointed back to an earlier age, whether it be the music Nick
Nightingale played (hardly cutting-edge jazz) or the sexual *môres* of its characters.[119] In addition, Sandor Szvost seems to have escaped from a time almost
as far back as the world of Schnitzler's original novella, while the two models,

Gayle and Nuala, appear to have come straight from the 1960s. In a similar sense, the attitudes expressed by Bill and Alice, toward sexual fantasy, seem to place the narrative before the so-called sexual revolution of the mid–20th century. Would, for example, Bill and Alice have reacted in the way in which they do with a knowledge of such celebrated authors as Nancy Friday or Shere Hite? All of this does not seem to add up; but then a lot of things in the film do not add up: the Harford's home has been criticized as being beyond their financial means,[120] Marion's attitude to Bill appears oddly pre-feminist, the orgy at Somerton appears almost bizarrely anachronistic, and so on.[121]

A sense of such purposeful ambiguity can be seen in the so-called Red Billiard Table scene, with Bill and the avuncular Victor Ziegler. The majority of contemporary reviewers questioned the scene's validity:

> This scene is a grotesquely vivid parody of all the unsatisfying scenes in movies where shrinks tell their patients the ultimate truth.[122]

> This laboriousness kills the story's climax.[123]

> The scene has been criticized as clumsily done, an awkward tying up of plot details.[124]

> [It feels like] boilerplate Agatha Christie.[125]

In other words the scene could be read as being merely a "clumsy" device to tie up the narrative's unresolved plot lines. (However, to Michael Herr it was somewhat different: "Though it's an incredibly interesting scene in many ways. I don't even know what it's supposed to be about, unless, as I suspect, it's really about the red pool table. You could always count on Stanley every time to vote for Beauty over Content, since he didn't think of them as two separate things."[126]) It is said that the scene was originally scheduled for four days shooting, but ended up taking seven weeks, which could be seen as pointing to the premise of the scene itself, prompting the elementary question: does the scene, in fact, work? One could argue it does not, and even argue that, had Kubrick lived, he may have cut the scene, either in part or perhaps entirely, from the film. All of which raises a key and fundamental question: was this a finished film?

The answer must be an unequivocal one: *Eyes Wide Shut* was not a finished film. At least not the (finished) film Kubrick would have offered the world, had he lived to witness its release. It has been commonly stated that the film was Kubrick's "final cut," that Kubrick delivered the "final cut" of the film to Warner Bros. on March 2, 1999, four days before his death on March 7. Terry Semel of Warner Bros. stated: "The film is totally finished ... [except for] a couple of color corrections [and] some technical things ... what he showed us was his final cut."[127] However, how final was the "final cut?" How finished did "finished" mean? J. Hoberman, for one, disagreed:

Kubrick had made "his final cut." From a semantic point of view, this last statement is undeniable — the director *had* made his last cut, at least on this earth. But *Eyes Wide Shut* may be scarcely more Kubrick's film than *Juneteenth* is Ralph Ellison's novel.... The ponderous Temple of Doom orgy, crassly matched location inserts, reliance on cross-cutting, and atrocious mixing (most obviously in the orgy's dreadful dubbing and oscillating hubbub level) all suggest the movie was quite far from completion when its notoriously perfectionist author passed away.... It requires but the barest familiarity with *Lolita* or *Dr. Strangelove* to see how *Eyes Wide Shut* might have been cut by 45 minutes and played for East European black comedy.[128]

Hoberman went on to question who had actually finished the film, pointing to rumors of Steven Spielberg or Sydney Pollack or even Tom Cruise supervising the film's completion:

Someday some dogged cine-archaeologist will get to the bottom of this corporate restoration and, figuring out just who did what to whom, sort the potential film from the apparent one ... this two hour and 39 minute gloss on Arthur Schnitzler's phantasmagoric novella feels like a rough draft at best.[129]

Hence the claim that the film was "finished" must be seen as being somewhat disingenuous, such claims having more to do with commercial considerations than any accurate appraisal of the film as a cultural entity. As is well known Kubrick had previously chosen to edit several of his other films up until the very last moment of their release. One notes that *Dr. Strangelove, 2001: A Space Odyssey, The Shining,* and possibly others, were significantly edited up to (and in some cases beyond) their openings.[130] In the case of *Eyes Wide Shut,* it would seem fair to suggest that Kubrick would have given the film greater focus by reducing its length considerably, perhaps not to the extent Hoberman suggests, but to a substantial degree. In other words, it is highly unlikely that Kubrick would have left the film untouched for those four months, from the time of his death on March 7 to the planned release date on July 16. Michael Herr's appraisal of the film as a finished product is perhaps apposite here. While perceiving of the film as a "masterpiece," Herr noted that it was both a flawed and unfinished masterpiece: "No matter what was said at the time of Stanley's death. He would have fiddled ... with it right up to the time of its release and beyond, if he thought he could tune it any finer."[131]

David Cronenberg, who, as a fellow director, was perhaps better able to comment, made this observation just before the opening of the film:

I think his movie was not finished because he had the sound mix still to do and the looping with the actors, where you add dialogue and so change performances. It's only people who don't know about film making who think it will be Stanley's movie, because a huge part of it won't be.[132]

Finally, critic Robert Kolker offered this opinion:

I am still left with the sense of a film somewhat incomplete or unthought out, weak in subject and lacking the usual Kubrickian visual and narrative energy.... I would like to stake a claim for *Eyes Wide Shut* that it is an unfinished, perhaps unfinishable film.... The resulting film is very long, very flat. It seems almost inert, and its editing structure is as conventional as Kubrick has ever done.[133]

In this context, one might consider whether Kubrick had the powers to complete the film; that he had been attempting to bring Schnitzler's novel to the screen for too long (nearly four decades); that he had undergone the longest shoot in motion picture history, and that his energy was simply failing. Insomuch what remained was arguably a mere rough-cut, an overlong, unfinished film, a mere suggestion of the film it might have been.

* * *

One other way of assessing the film's overall quality might be to consider its casting. It has been suggested that the film was flawed from the outset, because of its casting, or rather its miscasting. While some critics, Michel Chion for example, had high opinions of the cast Kubrick assembled: "*Eyes Wide Shut* is both the best-acted film in Kubrick's work and one of the best-acted films in the entire history of cinema."[134] On the other hand, it is clear that others did not, and that for once in his career Kubrick may have made significant and serious errors in the casting of a film. In the case of *Eyes Wide Shut* the selection of the cast was more complicated than usual, insomuch as it is clear that Kubrick had decided, early on, he had to cast a married couple for the two main roles in the film. Furthermore, it would seem that commercial reasoning was a significant factor in Kubrick's selection of Tom Cruise and Nicole Kidman.[135] At that time Cruise and Kidman were the most famous and most "bankable" couple in Hollywood; but for some critics Cruise was simply incapable of portraying the complexity of the character he was being asked to play. Richard Alleva:

Cruise is good in any role that requires old-fashioned, all–American ... macho élan ... trying to convey a sensitive man's complex doubts, he's in over his head.[136]

J. Hoberman:

Playing out of his depth, Cruise is as blatantly miscast as his character is incoherent. The role of this self-deluded doc might have made more sense if Bill were unhappily Jewish, as Rafael [sic] wanted, or a closeted gay, as Kubrick sometimes hints.... [Cruise is] the most boyish, least likely, doctor in New York City.[137]

Molly Haskell:

The sexual insecurity and introspective bent of the protagonist in Arthur Schnitzler's novel ... is something Mr. Cruise simply can't project. The reflective spirit of an intellectual, self-doubting man, anxious about middle age, is not in his repertory.... The director wanted to have it both ways: a mood art film with a Hollywood marquee star to boost the budget and bring in the crowds.[138]

In support of this one might note how, in his scenes with Nicole Kidman, it was clearly apparent that Cruise was routinely out-acted. This was also apparent when Cruise's acting was measured against the quality of almost all the supporting cast, in his scenes with: Rade Sherbedgia, Alan Cumming, Marie Richardson and even Leelee Sobieski.

However, all of this was perhaps to miss the point; in other words, there was arguably a clear, albeit somewhat subversive motive to Kubrick's (deliberate) miscasting of Cruise. In other words, it is conceivable to conclude that Kubrick was intentionally playing with the nature of Cruise's celebrity, with his limitations as an actor, along with (as previously alluded) the rumors of his ambiguous sexuality. All of this engendering the film with a deliberately more subtle and more ideologically profound discourse.[139] Thus in terms of an overall consideration of the film; herein lays one potential reading: the film was (by necessity) unfinished, Cruise was (deliberately) miscast: but beyond these considerations the film may still be judged as late, high Kubrick.

In approaching a summation, one might begin by saying that *Eyes Wide Shut* is a significantly flawed film; but flawed only because it was unfinished. In other words, it is a film whose creator had simply stopped work, for the overwhelmingly persuasive reason that he had simply ceased to be — the inopportune and altogether unfortunate demise of Stanley Kubrick. In this sense, and with these diverse pre-conditions, *Eyes Wide Shut* nonetheless represents one of Kubrick's most mature and thoughtful works. In a significant way the film might thus be seen as an attempt to engage seriously with sex, specifically sex within marriage; issues seldom considered anywhere within Kubrick's work, or indeed, without it. On the one hand the film seems to be suggesting that the intensity of the sexual relationship within marriage is partly tied to the possibility of infidelity. (The idea that "sexual gratification is at its best when we have a diverse array of sexual partners," that our sexual desires cannot be embraced within monogamy, that "sexuality is darker and less controllable than we typically care to admit, let alone seek to understand."[140]) On the other hand the film, faithful here to the novel, seems to suggest that monogamy is one of the underlying ways of surviving in the hostile environment of the modern world. Thus it might be seen as a film that offers a radical exploration of male and female sexuality within a marriage. In this sense, *Eyes Wide Shut* remains an oddly hypnotic film, a film that is "deliberately deliberate" throughout. In one sense Kubrick appears to be taking things very seriously, in another sense it was satiric to an almost exaggerated degree. However, fundamentally, the film attempted to look at sex, at marital sex, in a serious way.

The critical reception was generally negative; nothing new for a Stanley Kubrick film on its initial release, but perhaps here it was even more exaggerated, with this, his last film. There were some perceptive (mostly later) readings:

> For one last time Stanley Kubrick had flouted genre expectations, and once again, as throughout his career, critics could only see what wasn't there.[141]
>
> Kubrick's thirteenth and ... last film proved that his long search for a new subject had not sapped his capacity to surprise.[142]
>
> Eyes Wide Shut remains a film that had never been made before and is unlike any other, including the previous films of Stanley Kubrick.[143]
>
> Eyes Wide Shut is one of the most moving, playful and complex movies I have ever seen.[144]

However, the film had numerous detractors, Peter Bradshaw, writing in *The Guardian,* represented the average response to the film from the broadsheet press in the U.K.:

> Stanley Kubrick's extraordinary last testament ... a certain type of classic ... best described as Manhattan porn gothic. It has left the global critical community uneasily aware of the possibility that this was not a masterpiece, but rather a grotesque, preposterous flop that embarrassingly damages one of the most unimpeachable reputations in world cinema.... Kubrick's last film works only if its satirical mischievousness is fully appreciated as an essay on the nature of sexuality ... it is vulgar and pretentious, but taken as a bizarre black comic fable about married life, it is plausible and enjoyable. The technical and visual command of the movie is captivating — but it is minor Kubrick![145]

While in the U.S.A., Pauline Kael, the esteemed film critic of the *New Yorker* but hardly a Kubrickian champion, raised herself from retirement to declare Kubrick's final film was a "piece of crap."[146] David Thomson, perhaps not unexpectedly, described *Eyes Wide Shut* as "a travesty." Thomson closed his estimation of the film by commenting: "Kubrick was always a 'master' who knew too much about film and too little about life — and it shows."[147]

However, one might argue such criticism now appears somewhat limited and biased, based in the main on a prejudiced personal aesthetic. *Eyes Wide Shut* is not "Manhattan porn gothic," it is not a "piece of crap," it is not a "travesty." One might note, for example, the way in which some elements of the film seem to have scarcely been considered. To take just one example, to perceive of the film positioned as a "Hitchcockian thriller." This would seem relevant insomuch as the complex plotting reveals minor narrative details that seem purposefully suggestive of a mystery waiting to be solved. A case in point being the ambiguities surrounding Amanda's death: the newspaper report refers to her body being found in a hotel room, at the Florence Hotel to be specific. In contrast to this, Ziegler claims her body was found in her locked home.[148] This is a key issue, no doubt planted there deliberately by Kubrick. One might question if this provides a specific clue that Ziegler is lying, something a casual viewer of the film might have overlooked. In a similar sense we might ask just how did the mask get onto Bill's bed? This is a crucial aspect of the film; Kubrick makes great play over this, emphasizing this narrative detail. We note that Bill is holding the mask when we last see him at the orgy. But what happens next? He carefully hides his costume when he returns home, but it is not possible to know if the mask is with his cloak. What we do know is that the mask is not with his cloak when he returns to Rainbow Fashions. Does Bill leave it at the party — or does Alice remove it from the bag — or do unseen hands, from Somerton, deliberately break into the Harford's apartment, leaving the mask on the bed as a kind of warning? All of these questions remain ambiguous. Hence there is a clear sense of the narrative of *Eyes Wide Shut* having an altogether more complex plot than has previously been acknowledged.

The film would eventually speak to a much wider constituency; specifically, the more considered response to the film coming from an academic perspective, from the inordinate body of academic attention the film has received within the years since its release. (One apt demonstration of this being Graham Roberts and Heather Wallis's book, *Key Film Texts,* published in 2002. The book strove to establish a cinematic canon of the 20th century, listing 50 films, of which D.W. Griffith's *Intolerance* (1916) was listed first — with Kubrick's *Eyes Wide Shut* (1999) as the final entry.) In the years that have followed, the response has proved to be kinder to Kubrick's reputation than his immediate mainstream critics suggested. If one takes, for example, the work of Michel Chion, one of Kubrick's more intuitive critics, Chion considered the film among Kubrick's three masterpieces: *2001: A Space Odyssey, Barry Lyndon* and *Eyes Wide Shut.*[149] In a similar sense, Thomas Nelson, author of *Kubrick: Inside a Film Artist's Maze,* believed the film was "one of his [Kubrick's] greatest achievements."[150] While, from a non-academic perspective, to fellow director Martin Scorsese *Eyes Wide Shut* was the fourth best film of the 1990s.

In a final summary, *Eyes Wide Shut* was at once typical and atypical of Kubrick's work. It possessed many of the attributes of previous Kubrick films, but it was atypical insomuch as it was one of the few Kubrick films to offer the viewer the prospect of a happy ending. Orson Welles once commented: "Happy Endings are only possible if you don't tell the rest of the story."[151] In a rare instance Kubrick took advantage of this, stopping the story at a significant moment: Bill and Alice together again, about to consummate their desire for each other. Thus while Kubrick was renowned for possessing a bleak view of humanity, here, in choosing to end the film (and his life's work) at this point, he seemed to be suggesting that happy endings can sometimes be found.[152] As Michel Ciment noted: "Kubrick, shortly before his death, for the first time in his career, offers us a glimpse of the light at the end of the tunnel, the dawn at the end of the nocturnal journey."[153]

Thus the film might be read as that of a visual genius taking one last look at the world, turning "his fixated gaze upon a conjugal arrangement composed of trust and complacency in equal measure."[154] As William Arnold put it:

> Love it or hate it, there's not a single moment in this two hour, thirty-two minute film in which we don't feel we're in the hands of one of the cinema's great virtuoso directors, indeed, completely in his world. Frustrated and puzzled, maybe, but also privileged.[155]

Such a comment pointed to the idea of *Eyes Wide Shut* possessing a rare quality in American cinema, a film that possessed a "grown up" attitude toward sexuality; a film that possessed that "almost unheard of phenomena, a serious major studio film that contemplates grown-up sex and its discontents."[156] Insomuch, the film might finally be defined as a sardonic, Freudian account of the ambivalences of a "happy" marriage; expressing a rare critique of erotic desire within a monogamous and non-illicit relationship.[157] Insomuch *Eyes Wide Shut* might, in the end, be perceived as a mature, radical, provocative and at times deliberately playful film; complex, diversely layered, atmospheric, satiric, meticulously crafted and intellectually aware. However, it is also a film in which Kubrick's usually misanthropic and bleak view of the world is tempered by the idea that a certain kind of optimism and happiness might be available, for a time at least, within a relationship of two people who love one another.

Afterword: *A.I.*

A Real Boy

For the world's more full of weeping, than you can understand.[1]—W.B.
Yeats

It is generally assumed that *A.I.* would have been Kubrick's 14th film;
and that, had he lived, the film would have gone into production after the
completion of *Eyes Wide Shut*.[2] Whether this would actually have occurred is
open to speculation; the more likely scenario, given Kubrick's increased age
and his reduced physical energy, may have been that Steven Spielberg would
have directed the film in any case, albeit with Kubrick producing within a
more active capacity.[3] However, in whatever scenario one might envision, it
would appear that *A.I.* would have been a significantly different film — had
Kubrick not died when he did. In a sense, all of this is speculation, in reality we are left with Spielberg's interpretation and, without direct and detailed
access to Kubrick's original script and preparations, it is largely a matter of
detective work to decide how much the Spielbergian version of the film dif-
fered to what one might call the "ur" Kubrickian version.[4]

It is possible that Kubrick had had some sense of adapting Brian Aldiss's
short story, "Super Toys Last All Summer Long," almost as far back as its publication in 1969, not long after the release of *2001: A Space Odyssey*. (The fact
that Aldiss wrote his short story in 1969, just a year after the release of *2001:
A Space Odyssey*, might suggest his interest in artificial intelligence may have,
in some sense, been inspired by this source — thus creating an intertextual
circle of sorts.) However, substantial work on the project appears to have
started in 1982, when Kubrick optioned the rights to the story and shortly
thereafter began to work on a treatment and script with Aldiss. In any case,

the collaboration eventually reached a stalemate and Kubrick turned his attention to the project that would become *Full Metal Jacket.* In 1988 Kubrick once more returned to *A.I.*, working (separately) with two acclaimed science fiction writers, Bob Shaw and Ian Watson.[5] But once again Kubrick could not find a way to proceed and turned toward other projects, one being the development of the subsequently unmade film, *Aryan Papers*. Then, in 1994, Kubrick returned, for one more time, to *A.I.*, working with author Sara Maitland, who would famously comment that Kubrick chose her as he needed some "vaginal gel," presumably to coat the otherwise "macho" content of both this project and what would become *Eyes Wide Shut*. Maitland tried her utmost, but once again the collaboration did not bear fruit, vaginal gel or no vaginal gel.

    Nonetheless, the combination of working, over the years, with Aldiss, Shaw, Watson and Maitland (not to mention additional help from others as diverse as Leon Vitali and Arthur C. Clarke) allowed Kubrick, in May 1994, to assemble an 87 page treatment. (This was together with a reported thousand drawings and storyboards by artist Chris Baker. Baker [a.k.a. as Fanghorn] began his involvement with the project in the winter of 1993, eventually producing over a thousand drawings. On Kubrick's death and Spielberg's appropriation of the project, Baker was invited to continue work, thus seeing many of his original ideas developed into the finished film. This can plainly be perceived in the drawings that have thus far been published.)[6] This would be the nature of the project Steven Spielberg would eventually inherit, after Kubrick's death. It has been said Kubrick procrastinated because he did not believe the special effects he envisaged for the film were at a sufficient level of sophistication[7]; however, it is possible there were other more substantial and more significant reasonings behind Kubrick's unwillingness to proceed with the project.

    Firstly, there was the issue of repetition. *A.I.* would have been a return to the science fiction genre, and the envisaged film did have a degree of similarity to *2001: A Space Odyssey*, a potential problem for a filmmaker like Kubrick, who was consistently determined not to repeat himself. For example, one might think of David and HAL, both of whom were artificially intelligent beings, both possessing an inherent desire to prevail and a desire to be loved — one potential definition, albeit a sentimental one, of consciousness. (There were other interesting similarities; for example, the room at the end of *A.I.* was built from David's memory — much in the same way as the room at the end of *2001* was built from David Bowman's memory. There was also the sense in which human beings, in both films, seldom seemed able to demonstrate the emotional depth of the artificial life forms depicted in each narrative: David and HAL. One might also note the perceived jokes in the film (possibly inscribed by Spielberg); for example, Professor Hobby — whose name in itself was already something of an inside joke — talks at one point of "primitive monsters who could play chess," a not so subtle reference to Hal's character and abilities.) Secondly, another perhaps more significant reason, may have been the realization that the film did not accomplish anything markedly innovative in the way it told its story. One component of each of Kubrick's later films (from *Lolita* onwards) was a sense of being able to do something original with cinematic narrative itself. However, in the case of *A.I.* it would appear Kubrick never quite managed to find a way of doing this, of finding a means of telling a story in a new way.

In terms of the film's ideological content, it is perhaps true to say that the film would have been Kubrick's most Oedipally obvious narrative. The most pertinent, and most poignant, aspect of the narrative is arguably the fact that David is alone, and hence the theme of the only child seemed to reach its zenith here in *AI*. (In fact, this may have been one of the most appealing aspects to Spielberg; insomuch as it directly echoed the recurring theme of a lost child searching for home, a theme found throughout a significant part of *his* work.) In terms of the overtly Oedipal content in the film (found most extremely in the film's final scene, wherein mother and son lie idyllically in bed — almost like lovers[8]), this was tempered and somewhat offset by the positioning of the narrative within the genre of fairy tale. This was clearly a genre Kubrick's work had always had an awareness of and *A.I.* was (or would have been) one of Kubrick's most explicit uses of this generic convention.

In terms of the fairy tale motif running throughout the film, Kubrick's assistant, Leon Vitali, is often cited as the source for the "Pinocchio" allusions in the film. This arguably represented one of Kubrick's few serious miscalculations, and a fact that may have doomed the project's successful adaptation; as Sara Maitland put it: "You can't load two and a half thousand millenniums onto the poor little Pinocchio story."[9] However, from an opposing perspective, the retelling of the Pinocchio story, as intimated above, would have allowed Kubrick his most explicit use of fairy tale so far in his career.[10] One might think of the allusions apparent in Spielberg's version: how Monica abandons David in the middle of a wood; how Monica can live again only for one day; the use of Teddy as a non-human companion; and finally (in typical Spielbergian fashion), the happiest of happily-ever-after endings. In other words, Kubrick's explicit use of the fairy tale allowed him the opportunity to tell a story he may otherwise have been unable to tell.

In contrast to this, Spielberg's film appears to have retained at least some of Kubrick's more cynical thematic patterns; for example, that pertaining to a skepticism toward established religious faith. This concept finds a linkage within the metaphor of the absent father; David's overwhelming desire to find his maker, his "father" in Professor Hobby, pointing toward one of the core tenets of the Abrahamic religions: Judaism, Christianity and Islam. In the same light, the idea of David praying (for 2,000 years) in front of the Blue Fairy had obvious resonances. The Blue Fairy seems to purposefully resemble Our Lady of the Immaculate Heart; thus pointing to the idea that Catholics have been praying before similar statues, for the same span of time, and meeting with a similar response.[11] As has been noted, conventional religion was routinely satirized in Kubrick's work — and so it was here, within this element of Spielberg's interpretation.

However, it would seem fair to suggest that Kubrick's interpretation would have been a considerably darker endeavor. If a Kubrick film grew more uncompromising as its narrative progressed, then a Spielberg film would seem unable to avoid becoming more and more sentimental, as its narrative progressed. (As Alexander Walker put it: "Spielberg's sentimentality often hits the right place in the heart for the wrong reasons."[12] Walker was writing in a more general context, different to that of *A.I.*, but the underlying inference still applies.) In this sense, one might presume, for example, that Kubrick's version of *A.I.* would most probably have included Kubrick's predilection for nudity and aberrant sex — one can only speculate what Kubrick's film might have made of Gigolo Joe. In a similar sense, one presumes the violence in the film would have been more explicit, receiving a higher certification than the "12" the film received in the U.K. Thus, within a Kubrickian discursive arena, it would seem fair to say that *A.I.* would undoubtedly have been a very different film.

In conclusion, one must accept that, in the end, it was Spielberg who actually made the film. *A.I.* thus remains one of the key unmade Kubrickian cinematic texts,[13] but the relationship between the "ur-movie" and the Spielbergian reading remains unclear. Nonetheless, the Spielberg reading does offer at least a suggestion of what Kubrick's film might have been; and, in addition, it arguably remains one of the most thoughtful science fiction films made in recent times, perhaps since *2001: A Space Odyssey*. (Note here the irony in the film's release date, as Jason Sperb put it: "The last trace of Kubrick appropriately debuted in the calendar year 2001."[14]) In this sense, Spielberg's film preserves one of the key issues Kubrick appears to have been most interested in, namely to raise the question: what is consciousness, and "what constitutes a sentient 'being?'"[15] Such a question is one of the current key issues of interest to both scientists and artists alike. The conundrum of consciousness: "What it means to be 'real,' and how this intangible idea gives meaning to human life, existed at the heart of Stanley Kubrick's original concept of *A.I.*"[16] Thus one might finally decide that it was probably better to have some sense of what Kubrick's vision might have looked like, albeit diffused within Spielbergian excesses of optimism and sentimentality. It was in this sense that the film represents at least a semblance of what Kubrick's (unmade) 14th cinematic text might have been.

Conclusion

On Sunday, March 7, 1999, only a few days after "completing" what was to prove to be his final film, *Eyes Wide Shut*, Stanley Kubrick suffered a heart attack and died in his sleep. He was 70 years old. One could adopt a sentimentalist attitude: in other words, to suggest that Kubrick, aware he had finished what was literally to be his final film, was therefore finished with life. For a man who had lived and breathed the art and craft of filmmaking, the knowledge he would never complete another was perhaps too great a challenge to his sense of self-preservation.[1] Alternatively, and perhaps more pragmatically, one could simply presume that Kubrick had an undiagnosed heart condition (not entirely uncommon) which resulted in a heart attack at a purely coincidental time. In any case, the funeral took place on the following Friday, on the afternoon of March 12, on the grounds of Kubrick's home at Childwick Bury, with such luminaries as Tom Cruise, Nicole Kidman and Steven Spielberg, along with business associates and friends Terry Semel, James B. Harris, Mike Leigh, Alan Yentob, and Alexander Walker, together with Kubrick's close family.

Thus far this book has continually refrained from looking at Kubrick's work in terms of Kubrick himself. The reason for this being relatively self-explanatory: the poststructuralist argument that a writer or an artist's life has no relevance to a reading of their work. A random glance at the stereotyped portrayal the media has most often assumed in relation to Kubrick would seem to bear this out. For example, it is often said Kubrick was a recluse, notwithstanding the obvious fact that Kubrick was *not* a recluse, at least not in any acceptable sense of the word. It is true that he preferred to work from a home base, that he disliked traveling,[2] that he had a strong family commitment. However, it is self-evident that Kubrick regularly communicated with the outside world. For example, he did speak (albeit on his own terms) with the press; Kubrick knew it was essential that the press were granted access to provide the required publicity for each film as it came out. If Kubrick was a recluse then one has to ask how one describes actual recluses, such as, for example, a J.D. Salinger or a Thomas Pynchon? In a similar way, the ubiquitous claim that Kubrick had a cold, misanthropic and cynical view of the world may have a limited accuracy, but it hardly gets one very far in a greater understanding of Kubrick's films. Kubrick was no more cold, misanthropic and cynical than anyone with a reasonable grasp of the post-war world. As Michael Herr put it: "He [Kubrick] wasn't exactly a cynic, but he could have easily passed for one."[3]

To perceive of Kubrick's work within such a partial and imbalanced perspective merely obscures a reading of his films. Perhaps of marginally more use, if one were to choose to take a biographical stance, would be the opinions of some of Kubrick's contemporary filmmakers. For example, Steven Spielberg, who called Kubrick: "The grand master of filmmaking. He copied no one while all of us were scrambling to imitate him."[4] Another contemporary, John Landis, admitted: "Kubrick has influenced every living director."[5] Oliver Stone commented: "He was the single greatest American director of his generation. He influenced me deeply."[6] From a prior generation of film directors, Billy Wilder: "Kubrick was a wonderful director. I love all his movies. These are pictures any director would be proud to be associated with, much less to make."[7] Orson Welles: "Among the younger generation Kubrick strikes me as a giant."[8] And finally, Luis Buñuel:

> I'm a Kubrick fan, ever since *Paths of Glory.* Fabulous movie; that's what it's all about: codes of conduct, the way people behave when the codes break down. *A Clockwork Orange* is my favorite. I was very predisposed against the film. After seeing it, I realized it is the only movie about what the modern world really means.[9]

However, to move from the reductive constraints of a biographical reading of Kubrick's work, to a more analytical and theoretical approach, one might begin by restating some of the main thematic elements that have been observed, and to offer an overall evaluation of how they may be assessed. As has been previously argued, these themes were wide-ranging and diverse in content. In no particular order they included: diverse issues of human sexuality, the masculine journey, the significance of masculine violence, spatial components both vast and intimate, the failed plan, an intense interest in the deconstruction of varied cinematic genres, historical factors such as the Holocaust, the complexity of narrative discourse, and so on.

Perhaps the clearest conclusion to draw in relation to Kubrick's preoccupation with human sexuality is to comment upon his undeniable reliance on the ideas of Sigmund Freud. What is refreshing about Kubrick's work is that it is so unashamedly Freudian, at least from certain specific interpretative perspectives. To be more exact, one can perceive of a "strong Oedipal theme"[10] throughout many if not all of Kubrick's films. Such a conclusion is not wholly original — several critics have had similar opinions; for example, Hans Feldman:

> His view of man is clearly Freudian: the primal facet of the human personality is the id, the completely self-orientated structure that demands immediate gratification of its instinctual urges for food, shelter and the propagation of itself. It is not moral or intellectual or sensitive to the needs and feelings of others. It simply is.[11]

However, within this context an issue that has not been commented upon, at least not to any great extent, is what might be described as the issue of the "only child" in Kubrick's work. It would seem clear that one can find recurrent patterns of such a thematic element throughout Kubrick's films, in both realized and unrealized projects. To take a number of examples: in *Eyes Wide Shut* Bill and Alice's daughter, Helena, is an only child; as is Danny in *The Shining*; as is Bryan in *Barry Lyndon;* as is Alex in *A Clockwork Orange*; as is Squirt, in *2001: A Space Odyssey*; as is Lolita in *Lolita*. In addition, Spartacus has only one son, the one held up to him as he is being put to death on a cross. In the unmade *Napoleon*, the narrative would no doubt have revealed that Napoleon had only one legitimate child — to Marie-Therese — the so-called King of Rome. In a similar sense, in the unmade *Aryan Papers*, Maciek was an only child, this being a significant part of the narrative. Finally, in *A.I.*, David was a decidedly only child, a unique and only child in more ways than one.[12]

One might then ask: why the only child? How do we explain Kubrick's attraction (whether conscious or unconscious) to such an arena of discursive intent; why do so many dark Oedipal tales about the only child provide such a core narrative facet in so many films? In one sense, such narratives cut down on complications allowing a clearer story to be told; in other words, sibling rivalry is bypassed and familial relationships are rendered less complex. In addition, of interest in what might be called these "mono-sibling tales" is the slanted Oedipal scenarios that therefore resulted: most typically the issues of dysfunctional mothers and absent or monstrous fathers. For example, one might note the absent fathers in *Lolita* and *Barry Lyndon*, or the sense in which such characters as Victor Ziegler, Gunnery Officer Hartman, Jack Torrance, General Ripper, General Broulard (not to mention Professor Hobby), are seemingly representative of corruptive father figures. In contrast, fathers elsewhere in Kubrick's work, often appear weak and inadequate; for example, in *A Clockwork Orange* Alex's father is so wholly ineffectual as to be scarcely a credible character; in *Eyes Wide Shut* Bill Harford seems to have relatively little interest in his daughter; and finally, in *A.I.*, David's "father,"

Henry, is a "marginally developed character, having no authority and rarely an opinion of his own."[13]

Kubrick's concern with Oedipal junctures: the only child, the dysfunctional parent, and the complex sexual relationships between them, may partially be explained via Jacques Lacan's poststructuralist re-treading of Freudian thinking. To be specific, one of Lacan's central tenets was the idea that we are born into a condition of "lack" and that we spend the rest of our lives trying to overcome this. Lacan suggests we never attain this, as a fundamental essence of being a human subject is to experience such a sense of "lack." In a more explicit sense, Lacan proposes this sensation is suggested by the impossibility of ever recreating a union with the mother, the moment of plenitude, before the fall into "lack." Instead we console ourselves with a diverse range of displacement strategies: culture, religion, sex and so on. However, such a search is endless and unbroken, meaning cannot be found in culture, sex, religion — or indeed in anything else — because being a human subject, being an "I," having an individual identity is, in itself, founded on loss and separation. To read such a theoretical model into a number of Kubrick's films, within the constantly present Oedipal crisis, might be said to offer at least a potentially persuasive reading. In essence, Kubrick's work tells us one truth: we are alone.

However, while it might be argued that one of the main preoccupations of Kubrick's "fiercely intelligent" discourse was that of human sexuality, it is important to acknowledge that he rarely attempted to show his audience the *why* of his characters. In other words, Kubrick was rarely interested in offering psychological explanations of characters such as Humbert, Ripper, Bowman, Alex, Jack, Joker, Bill and so on. (Perhaps a key issue here is the sense in perceiving of Kubrick's work as being primarily existential. In this sense, one might note Camus's claim that our most important task is not to discover the meaning of life, but to recognize that it is, in fact, meaningless. "For Camus, to live and die with honesty is the central challenge of being human. The task of being human involves asking oneself what one's life is about and being honest about the answer, even if there is no answer at all."[14]) Such an understanding is key in interpreting Kubrick's work. Here a further theoretical reading potentially illuminates our appreciation of Kubrick's cinematic texts, as the *why* seldom gets one very far in any case. If we, with the amount of knowledge we possess about ourselves, cannot answer such questions, then what are the chances of understanding characters outside of ourselves? Kubrick was consistently accused of offering characters that were cold and remote and even "inhuman." However, one might argue that this is precisely what makes them real characters; they are human because as humans we cannot read ourselves. Therefore, to show an explanation of the *why* of a character is to invent and sentimentalize something we have no way of ever really knowing. In this light such a reading might be said to be once again responding, in some sense, to a Lacanian reading of the human subject.

One other way of looking at the issue of human sexuality, within Kubrick's work, might be to consider the spatial considerations on display in the *mise-en-scène* of the films—in other words, the locations in which such scenes occur. In this sense, one might assume the bedroom was the obvious place to start; however, on a cursory examination of the films, it immediately becomes apparent that the bedroom has relatively little importance in Kubrick's work. The narrative spaces of Kubrick's films operate in a more ironic and at times almost "perverse" way. Namely, this is either within the grand and malevolent spaces of the great house or within the lesser and more corporeal spaces of the bathroom.

In the case of the bathroom, the ubiquitous use of such scenes in Kubrick's films, serves to offer a reminder, in metaphorical form, of the clear linkage between sexuality and intimations of mortality.[15] To work backward through Kubrick's canon: the bathroom in *Eyes Wide Shut* first operates as an intimate space for Bill and Alice, but later, in Ziegler's opulent bathroom, death is prescient in terms of Mandy's drug overdose. In *Full Metal Jacket* the discursive arena of the bathroom encloses both sex and death—in one scene Joker and Cowboy discuss potential sexual partners (mopping the floor between the somewhat disturbingly exposed rows of toilet bowls), while the same bathroom is also the chosen site wherein Private Pyle commits first murder, and then suicide. In *The Shining*, Jack Torrance's encounter with the inhabitant of Room 237's bathroom, first promises the opportunity for sexual pleasure and then something much worse. In *A Clockwork Orange* Alex, bathing in Mr. Alexander's bathroom, gives himself away by unconsciously reprising "Singin' in the Rain." The zero-gravity toilet is the one solitary joke of *2001: A Space Odyssey*, although the bathroom at the end of the film, the somewhat incongruous modern *ensuite* to the so-called Louis XIV room, having more ominous overtones of death and mortality. In *Dr. Strangelove*, the fact that General Turgidson is in the bathroom when news that World War III has started provides a comic interlude, while General Ripper will later choose to commit suicide in another military bathroom. Death is also present in the scene in *Lolita,* wherein Humbert Humbert learns of Charlotte's demise while he is lounging in his bath. In *Spartacus,* sexuality is apparent in the famous oysters and snails scene, while Crassus is helped in his bath by Antoninus—the master-slave relationship offering both a homoerotic discourse, together with the inherent threat of potential coercion and violence. There is even an obligatory bathroom scene in the post–Kubrickian and Spielbergian *A.I.,* a brief homage to this spatial tradition, wherein David and Teddy surprise Monica sitting on her futuristic "orga" toilet, a scene resplendent in unique forms of Oedipal tension.[16]

Therefore, the locus of the bathroom — as a space in which significant narrative events occur—can be perceived in Kubrick's work, events which routinely demonstrate an underlying concern with sex and death. The specific question is *why*, why do Kubrick's films appear to operate within such a discourse? This is another matter entirely; however, the preoccupation of Kubrick's work with Freud might perhaps offer a pointer, an indication. Freud, who argued sexuality developed through oral, anal and genital stages, could be perceived as influencing a potentially scatological discourse, one in which Kubrick's films found a significance. In other words, because the sexual organs are placed so closely to the organs of excretion, then sexuality is connoted as being linked to "dirt" and "corruption," and hence to death. However, this would seem a somewhat cursory explanation. It might be more astute to allude either to a Joycean honesty toward bodily functions, a Rabelaisian exuberance with the obscene, or simply a preoccupation with sexual function in such an authentic way as to be unable to avoid a scatological approach.

In contrast to this, the great spaces in Kubrick's work, the great houses, the so-called citadels,[17] also had their importance. One might think of the chateau in *Paths of Glory,* Quilty's mansion in *Lolita,* the War Room in *Dr. Strangelove,* the *Discovery* in *2001: A Space Odyssey,* "Home" in *A Clockwork Orange,* Castle Hackton in *Barry Lyndon,* the Overlook in *The Shining,* the sniper's building in *Full Metal Jacket,* and the Somerton mansion in *Eyes Wide Shut.* These spaces, these "grand and malevolent spaces,"[18] of Kubrick's films also had a significance in representing a common thematic pattern of tropes in Kubrick's *mise-en-scène.*[19] Once again a biographical reading is available, albeit one that arguably leads to what is ultimately an interpretative dead-end. One might note, to take one instance, how in *A Clockwork Orange* "Home" is envisaged as a civilized, middle-class, bourgeois environment that is overwhelmed by outside malignant forces. In this sense it might be tempting to read an autobiographical reverent here; in other words, the way in which Kubrick himself inhabited a kind of citadel—"Castle Kubrick," as biographer, John Baxter, would have it—first at Abbot's Mead and then at Childwick Bury.[20] However, in more meaningful terms the trope of "the citadel" in Kubrick's work demonstrates a clear thematic pattern; one that might be seen as pointing toward the notion of public and private spaces, the private space of the bathroom, the public spaces of the great houses. For example, one might suggest that Kubrick saw the great house within a Marxist context (a symbol of power), or within a Gothic context (a site of repression), or that it simply became a common trope because of its cinematically visual potential. This being purposefully and consistently contrasted against the much smaller, the much more intimate and the much more corporeal space of the ubiquitous bathroom.

One of the other key elements in Kubrick's work was that of narrative itself. If narrative is considered as one of our most important cultural facets, one of the tools by which we have tried to make sense of the world, then this would appear to have a logical reasoning. One might argue that narrative underpins all our writing, all our thinking, all our forms of knowledge. In other words, narrative is how we understand the world.[21] To paraphrase Roland Barthes, narrative is an enigmatic code, a code with a cluster of subtle and barely discernible conventions—but a code that always keeps us asking the fundamental question: what happens next? Thus, from stories around the campfire in prehistoric times to the present diverse range of narratives in our culture, narrative might be said to be fundamental to our understanding of ourselves.

In this sense, one might argue that the way in which Kubrick told his stories was, in itself, a key issue. It would seem fair to say that Kubrick was obsessed with narrative, with what constituted a good story, with finding out what a good story was, with finding differing and diverse ways in which to portray "good stories" within a cinematic discourse. As Kubrick commented to Michel Ciment in 1976:

> You can say a lot of "architectural" things about what a film story should have: a strong plot, interesting characters, possibilities for cinematic development, good opportunities for the actors to display emotion, and the presentation of thematic ideas truthfully and intelligently. But, of course, that still doesn't explain why you finally choose something, nor does it lead you to the story.[22]

The topic would appear to have been a consistent preoccupation, as Kubrick would comment elsewhere:

> Finding a story which will make a film is a little like finding the right girl. It's very hard to say how you do it, or when you're going to do it.[23]
>
> A very good plot is a minor miracle.[24]
>
> The hardest thing for me is finding the story.... Just as actors have nightmares that they'll never get another part, I have a recurring fear that I'll never find another story I like well enough to film.[25]

In Robert Kolker's words, Kubrick had "a lifelong experiment with narrative"[26]; however, it was clearly a continual challenge, as Alexander Walker put it: "For Kubrick, finding a story he wanted to film was probably the most important yet least successfully dealt with part of his work."[27] This may be the case, and it is certainly true that Kubrick did not have the abilities to originate his own source narratives. However, perhaps the significant point to bear in mind is that, although Kubrick may have struggled in finding narratives; nonetheless, he was relentless in finding new ways in which to make use of cinematic narrative forms.

On a cursory examination, Kubrick's films may appear to have had a conventional and linear design; but, nevertheless, he was constantly pushing forward the ways to tell his stories within a cinematic discourse. (For example, the concept of narrative as dream in *Eyes Wide Shut,* the deliberate fracturing of narrative in *Full Metal Jacket,* what at least appeared to be a deliberate use of Vladimir Propp's formalist/structuralist ideas of narrative and the folktale in *The Shining,* the unreliable narrator in *Barry Lyndon* deliberately disclosing dramatic narrative detail to dispel narrative tension, the use of first-person villain as protagonist in *A Clockwork Orange,* the virtuoso use of narrative ellipsis in *2001: A Space Odyssey,* and so on.) Kubrick had an "underlying passion for narrative,"[28] and may, as has been argued herein, have possessed at least some degree of interest in a theoretical understanding of the subject. Kubrick's ideas (on cinematic narrative) seem to have been formed at an early stage, as far back as 1960, wherein he summed up his approach:

> I think the best plot is no apparent plot. I like a slow start, the start gets under the audience's skin and involves them so that they can appreciate grace notes and soft tones and don't have to be pounded over the head with plot points and suspense hooks.[29]

However, it is possible that Kubrick's initial sense of storytelling technique derived from still earlier. For example, Kubrick's use of montage, in his work as a still photographer for *Look* magazine in the late 1940s and early 1950s, might be seen as offering some illumination on his later cinematic style. Kubrick's work on *Look* at times appeared to allude to his often-quoted idea that (narratively speaking) a film needs only a specific number of "non-submersible units."[30] If one considers Kubrick's assignment for *Look* in May 1950: "Dailies of a Rising Star: Betsy von Fürstenberg," then such a concept becomes readily apparent.[31] One can see herein, in Kubrick's photographic study of a "teenage socialite and aspiring actress,"[32] a clearly defined story told via a montage of pictures—what would have been the non-submersible units; what Rainer Crone calls, in his later commentary of these photographs: "Kubrick's unique way of dealing with fragments of reality."[33] We see Ms. von Fürstenberg overacting and preening herself in what appears to be her agent's office, sitting in a restaurant with a "beau," dancing at a party, lounging on a sofa with a drink and a cigarette, and finally, a series of shots sitting, scantily clad, in a window of a New York apartment, learning lines for a part that was, likely or not, never to be.[34] While it is unlikely Kubrick would ever have considered making a film based on such meager material, nonetheless, one can perceive here of his approach to narrative via a visual method of storytelling.[35]

Perhaps one of the other most significant influences on Kubrick's approach to cinematic narrative, at such a formative stage, was the radio.[36] Kubrick had grown up in a generation before the advent of television, one in which radio was therefore a narrative form of some cultural importance. One specific influence to be perceived here was Kubrick's use of voice-over, a technique used strategically throughout his work.[37] "There is an old screen adage," Kubrick would comment, "that says if you have to use voice-over it means there's something wrong with your script. I'm quite certain this is not true."[38] In this sense one might conclude that a number of Kubrick's films (along with his first three short documentaries) benefited from the influence of radio, at least in terms of specific issues pertaining to narrative structure.

In a more esoteric arena, Kubrick's interest in narrative might be further illuminated if one perceives of the potential linkage between narrative to both life and death. Aldous Huxley once commented that we live our lives "behaving as though death were an unfounded rumor."[39] While Wim Wenders, the German film director, commented:

> Stories give people the feeling that there is a meaning, that there is ultimately an order lurking behind the incredible confusion or appearances and phenomena that surrounds them. Stories are substitutes for God. Or maybe the other way around.[40]

To link these two comments together: it could be argued that stories are, in fact, substitutes for death — or maybe the other way around. In other words, it could be suggested that there is an unconscious connection between the closure in the span of cultural narratives and the closure in the span of our own lives. To put this specifically, one underlying appeal and attraction toward narrative, albeit mostly unconscious and unspoken, lies in the idea that within narratives we unconsciously rehearse our own endings; metaphorically dodging the certainty of our own closure via the closure of cultural narratives. Fictional narratives tend to close with the words "The End" — but this does not signal the actual end, the narrative merely reaches a cessation, the characters within the narrative do not necessarily die, they merely cease to operate within the construct of that narrative. Therefore, in some unconscious way, our preoccupation with narrative might be seen as a method of sidestepping an inevitable reality, *the* inevitable reality. Thus narrative might be seen as a way of comprehending death, a means of rehearsing for death. One might therefore argue that we experience narratives not merely in an attempt to achieve a greater understanding of our existence, but to make an attempt to come to terms with our own mortality. In this sense, narrative is a secular religion, and like religion narrative is a way of coming to an understanding that we are all going to die. To paraphrase cultural theorist David Lodge: the ultimate aim of life is death, just as the ultimate aim of all narrative is to abolish itself in endings.

If we were to strip away all our social and cultural trappings, then human beings have always been ruled by two things: Love and Death — Eros and

Thanatos. We have a desire to be loved — often expressed via a need for sex. We have a fear of death — often expressed via a need for religion. In terms of love and death within narrative structures one can make a direct correlation between these most fundamental of discourses: the majority of narratives have an explicit love element, and the majority of narratives have implicit references to our own mortality. Our own narratives, the stories of our lives, always end in one definitive way. In such a sense death is the one universal constant; every human being who has lived will die. Thus Huxley's original comment finds additional contextual currency; narrative is important to us because it enables us to personify the way we love, while also, at the same time, enabling us to understand and to come to terms with our own mortality. It is in this sense that one might read the cinematic texts of Stanley Kubrick. As such it is perhaps arguably correct to perceive of Kubrick's specific interest in narrative, his lifelong experiment with narrative, as a key to understanding his films.

However, to move from a theoretically weighted discussion to one of a differing but equal significance, to Kubrick's mastery of cinematic technique, in all its varying aspects. As such it is important to note how Kubrick was one of the relatively few directors to enter filmmaking via photography; for example, he had no prior background in theatre or television, one of the more usual routes into filmmaking. Rainer Crone said of Kubrick that he was "first and foremost a cinematographer and photographer."[41] One notes here Kubrick's depth of knowledge of cinema, he knew how the camera worked — both technically and aesthetically. In addition, he had a breadth of comprehension of cinema rarely matched; as he once claimed: "I try to see every movie ... I try to see everything."[42] In this way it is clear that Kubrick possessed an assured understanding of his craft and his art that was hard to dismiss. There is a sense that all of Kubrick's work, however diverse, had a signature; in other words there was seldom any doubting one was watching "a Stanley Kubrick film."[43] As to why this should be is hard to define, in a technical sense it might have had something to do with the use of lenses (often wide-angle), the depth of field, the meticulous framing, the precision of cutting,[44] the use of sound, the exactitude of the *mise-en-scène*, together with a diverse range of other factors. As Steven Spielberg commented: "The craft is impeccable."[45] In addition to this there was also the issue of the sheer amount of work Kubrick was willing to commit to a film. In 1966 he told Jeremy Bernstein: "I never stop working on a script"[46]; however, this remark would appear to correspond to all other aspects of filmmaking as well.

Also of significance was the way in which Kubrick was one of the few filmmakers able to operate with complete artistic independence within the Hollywood system of filmmaking. It must not be overlooked that, as well as being an artistic and cultural endeavor, filmmaking is very much a business, at times little else than a blatant capitalist enterprise in accumulating as much profit as possible. Steve Southgate (a Warner Bros. executive who had worked with Kubrick from *A Clockwork Orange* onwards) commented: "He [Kubrick] was the one person in the film industry who knew how the film industry worked."[47] In an evaluation of Kubrick's work this is a key observation. Kubrick's success as an artist cannot be separated from his success as a "businessman." It was as much Kubrick's astute understanding of the film industry as it was his greatness as an artist that enabled him to make the films he made. Kubrick lived "in splendid isolation from the dream factory,"[48] in more ways than one. (In other words, it was not the fact that Kubrick "isolated" himself in Hertfordshire; he was also isolated from the numerous pressures and constraints the vast majority of Hollywood film directors were forced to operate within.) This sense of "splendid isolation" was one factor enabling Kubrick to operate in an industry wherein artworks cost tens of millions of dollars, while at the same time retaining complete artistic control and independence. One might argue that this contributed to the reason Kubrick made so few films—it may have been because such a significant part of his time was addressed toward securing the autonomy he required that his artistic output was reduced.

In a final sense, in a summation of the ways into seeing and interpreting Kubrick's work, one must accept that interpretation is, in itself, an ambivalent enterprise. The detailed examination of a text does not reveal a central meaning. Instead, it releases a polysemantic range of latent, fragmentary and often contradictory meanings, invariably with little relationship to what the author (filmmaker) had originally intended. Thus the interpretations of Kubrick's work, offered within this book, merely represent one individual point of response, there being as many responses to Kubrick's work as there are viewers of his films. In addition to this, there is also the issue of the act of interpreting a text; in itself, having an effect on the way we "read" a text. As Gary Rhodes, in his interpretation of *2001: A Space Odyssey*, pointed out: "The very act of interpretation skews the results."[49] Thus a simplification of Heisenberg's Uncertainty Principle would appear to suggest that, for example, the film *2001: A Space Odyssey* has changed by the sheer weight of the critical attention it has received.[50] Nonetheless, this should not prevent us from interpreting whatever we wish to interpret—Edmund Husserl's phenomenological argument perhaps being redolent here—the proper object of philosophical enquiry being the contents of our own consciousness, not the objects of the world.[51]

It is said Kubrick made films as if he were a chess player playing without out a clock. Of course this is absurd. There was a clock ticking; there always is, as Ziegler says in *Eyes Wide Shut:* "Life goes on. It always does, until it doesn't." In this sense perhaps one of the hardest conclusions, as intimated above, is to reconcile oneself to how few films Kubrick made. However, in drawing toward a final summation, this would appear ultimately unimportant in terms of the artistic *oeuvre* we actually possess. For even within such a restricted arena it is possible to argue that Stanley Kubrick was conceivably America's greatest and perhaps last *auteur*. The films he made, few as they were, "represent a gallery of indelible images that will last as long as the cinema,"[52] each film being a "total, witty, and profound comic paradox of the modern and postmodern condition,"[53] possessing a "complexity, irony and awareness of history, politics and culture that we expect from the strongest of imaginations."[54] In this sense, and in the way of all great art, Kubrick's films would appear to have the ability not to date; they are "classics," insomuch as they seldom seem to stop saying what they have to say. Hence the films of Stanley Kubrick might be said to have a continuing relevance. In these films the rectangular space of the screen is consistently filled with a diverse range of political, aesthetic, social and cultural materials, offering a seemingly endless supply of hermeneutic discussion surrounding the human condition. Thus Kubrick may, in a final conclusion, be seen as one of *the* great cartographers of the human condition, at least as it prevailed within his era — the latter half of the 20th century. Hence the films of Stanley Kubrick succeed in telling us about ourselves and our times. It may well be, as time progresses, that these films will be seen as offering future eyes as accurate an explanation of what it was like to live in the second part of the 20th century, as any other artist of that time, both within and without cinema.

Appendix 1

The Early Films

Kubrick's three early documentary films, *Day of the Fight* (1950), *Flying Padre* (1951) and *The Seafarers* (1953), offer a significant indication of the ways in which his career would develop. In a sense, the documentary beginnings of Kubrick's work can be traced throughout his career, throughout all his 13 features. Dana Polan:

> Kubrick began filmmaking in the area of documentary, and even in his most interventional moments in his later films, there is frequently the impression of a dispassionate, even antiseptic study of a found world.[1]

In such a documentary format it is possible to perceive of a wide range of ideological concepts, all redolent within the rest of Kubrick's work. One key thematic concern found in these early short works often revolved around an intensive homosocial discourse. This is significant insomuch as such a discourse would be apparent throughout the whole of Kubrick's work, from its beginning to its end. An obvious example of this being the boxing scenes in *Day of the Fight*, the spectacle of boxing being a prime example of homosociality, its ritualized and fetishized violence being simultaneously homoerotic and homophobic. The environment of a boxing match is one wherein a predominantly male audience, often in a state of some excitement, watches two near naked men, often black, always young and well muscled, in close and violent contact with each other. (Peter Schaesberg, in a discussion of Kubrick's photographic interest in boxing, cited Joyce Carol Oates's comments on the implicit homoeroticism of boxing: "The fighters stripped to the waist, oiled and sweating; the fights that resemble half dancing, half mating; desperate clinches like embrace."[2] Schaesberg went on to note the parallels between boxing and pornography, insomuch as both promote the breaking of social taboos via public spectacle.)

It is perhaps pertinent to note how Kubrick had always had an interest in boxing; in his *Look* assignment of December 1949 he had presented what might now be seen as an almost overtly intimate portrait of Rocky Graziano. In some of the more explicit photographs, although not photographs used at the time, Kubrick offered images that would not be misplaced within so-called gay erotica.[3] In this light, it is perhaps of interest to note that when commencing work with Marlon Brando, in 1958, on the film that would become *One-Eyed Jacks*, Kubrick had initially proposed "a boxing picture, exploring the Terry Malloy character Brando created in *On the Waterfront*."[4] Brando declined saying he was interested in something more sensitive; however, it is interesting to note Brando's version of *One-Eyed Jacks* had a strong homoerotic subtext: from the acutely masochistic scenes it contained, to the obvious phallic connotations of its title.

In addition, another ubiquitous theme in Kubrick's work, found in the three early documentaries, was an interest in organized religion, albeit from an outsider's perspective. It is interesting to note that all three of the short films had a Roman Catholic content: the boxer, Walter Cartier, was a Catholic (the film showed him attending Mass just prior to the big fight), the Reverend Fred Stadtmueller, the *Flying Padre*, was a Catholic priest at St. Joseph's Church in Mosquero, New Mexico; and finally, in *The Seafarers*, the union membership was made up notably of Irish Catholic workers. An interest in organized religion, significantly always from the outside, would be a recurring feature in nearly all of Kubrick's later feature films.[5]

In the case of Kubrick's first feature, *Fear and Desire* (1953), here one is presented with a singular film for discussion, insomuch as there is no recognizable way of gaining access to it. The film is not commercially available on either videotape or on DVD, it is obviously not available in projected format and, needless to say, it has had no discernible television broadcast. In fact the film is not thought to have been generally available since its initial theatrical run in 1953.[6] At the time of its release the film was relatively well received; it was reviewed in *Time, Newsweek,* the *New Yorker,* the *New York Times, Variety* and *Saturday Review.* However, Kubrick would consistently disparage the film,[7] and hence it eventually came to be excluded from the official canon of his work. In contrast, some critics have demurred; for example, Jason Sperb (one Kubrick scholar to have seen and studied the film at length) has argued that Kubrick's attempts to suppress the film had less to do with it being a pretentious apprentice piece, because it revealed too much of the "major creative strategies of the director's oeuvre."[8]

Kubrick's subsequent film, *Killer's Kiss* (1955), *is* available for critical appraisal and some critics have spoken highly of it. Alexander Walker went so far as to describe it as one of "the most perfect shortish films ever made."[9] Kubrick himself had a more equivocal opinion of the film's value:

While *Fear and Desire* had been a serious effort, ineptly done, *Killer's Kiss* ... proved, I think, to be a frivolous effort done with conceivably more expertise though still down in the student level of filmmaking.[10]

The film contains a number of ubiquitous thematic patterns; as with *Fear and Desire* it is concerned with masculine violence, having "one of the most vicious boxing matches ever put on the screen."[11] Also thematically present is the idea of the perfect plan going wrong — a familiar plot mechanism in Kubrick's work. In addition, the film offers an initial suggestion of the circular narrative told in flashback, the film ending with its beginning is a feature ubiquitous in Kubrick's work. In another ubiquitous facet, the film includes female nudity, albeit in the shape of human mannequins. Finally, the narrative of the film, already suggestive of the simplicity of a fairy tale,[12] has a deceptive complexity typical of Kubrick.[13]

The Killing (1956) marked another step forward in the canon of Kubrick's work, the first sense, for want of an expression, of a discernibly "Kubrickian" Kubrick film. As Thomas Nelson put it: "*The Killing* was the first film that bore 'the unmistakable imprimatur of Stanley Kubrick.'"[14] In addition, it was the first Kubrick film to have had significant lasting influence upon other cultural discourses. According to Vincent LoBrutto, the time-shifting narrative structure of the film would "influence generations of noir crazed filmmakers."[15] As is well known, Quentin Tarantino's *Reservoir Dogs* (1991) had an obvious and an acknowledged influence from *The Killing*. In fact, Tarantino is on record as claiming he would have cast Sterling Hayden in the Harvey Keitel role from *Reservoir Dogs*, had the actor still been alive.[16]

The Killing, with its complex, non-linear narrative, was based on the novel, *Clean Break,* by Lionel White and would be the first of Kubrick's many adaptations from novel to film. Once again there were redolent thematic tropes apparent: the perfect plan that fails; the recurrent theme of the circular journey; the opening scenes of the racehorses on the track being an obvious allusion to one of Kubrick's most common subtextual motifs.[17] Kubrick's interest in narrative itself can also be discerned in the film, the circularity of the narrative and the repetition of events from differing perspectives demonstrated a sense of the ways Kubrick would explore cinematic narrative variations in films to come. In addition, the film had obvious homosocial and homoerotic allusions, especially in the relationship between Johnny and Unger. (This was made almost explicitly clear in some of the film's dialogue. For example, Johnny to Unger: "We'll probably never see each other again after tonight ... but in my book you'll always be a stand-up guy." Unger to Johnny: "Wouldn't it be great if we could just go away, the two of us, and let the old world take a couple of turns.") In a wider sense the film was an early example of Kubrick reworking generic conventions. As with *Killer's Kiss,* many of the classic *film noir* ingredients are present: the male voice-over, the

almost clichéd female predator, the chiaroscuro lighting, even the existen-
tialist ambience of the film's last line, Johnny Clay's: "What's the difference?"
However, there was also an awareness, in *The Killing*, of the limitations of
the genre and a willingness to take advantage of this to tell a more compelling
story.

Kubrick had apparently first read Humphrey Cobb's novel *Paths of Glory*
when he was 15, reputedly one of the few works of fiction he read in his youth.
In 1956, with a view to making a war film, Kubrick had acquired the rights
of the novel, from Cobb's widow, for just $10,000.[18] The film dealt with one
of Kubrick's most exaggeratedly ubiquitous themes: that of war and man's
predilection to kill. In such a context, Winston Churchill's comment, that
the film came closest to portraying the experience of the First World War,[19]
is perhaps pertinent — as is the film's claim for being "the best film ever made
about World War I."[20] In a sense the theme of war, the enigma of why men
are so willing to kill one another, was arguably Kubrick's predominant thematic concern.

However, there were other significant thematic details in the film worthy of comment, one being the idea of a citadel, of a "high place" separate
from the generic *mise en scène*. Thus, in *Paths of Glory*, the chateau in which
the generals plan their "murderous" campaigns, made a grim contrast to the
trenches in which their men are fighting and dying. As such the chateau —
the citadel — offered an early sense of a pattern of great houses of "high
spaces," a pattern that would be repeated throughout a number of Kubrick's
subsequent films.[21] An additional thematic element in the film worthy of note
was — once again — a distinct and manifestly homosocial component. In *Paths
of Glory* this was clearly apparent insomuch as it was a film almost wholly
populated by men, the only exception being the "German girl" (played by
Susanne Christian — the stage name of Kubrick's wife to be, Christiane Harlan) who sang the plaintive song to the troops at the end of the film.

Spartacus was Kubrick's "first and last big-budget Hollywood assignment,"[22] and at a cost of $12 million it was possibly, at least taking inflation
into consideration, the most expensive film of his whole career. In fact, within
its own time of making, the film is said to have been the most expensive
motion picture that had then been made.[23] However, as is well known, it was
not an artistically satisfying experience for Kubrick, insomuch as it was the
one film he made in which he did not have complete artistic control, the one
film on which he was little more than a "hired hand," the one film on which
he was not the *auteur*.

One of the most significant areas over which Kubrick lacked control was
the story, the narrative of the film. As Kubrick succinctly put it: "I am disappointed in the film. It had everything but a good story."[24] Kubrick's emphasis on the importance of narrative is pertinent, insomuch as all of his films

told "good stories," or perhaps to be more precise, told a "good story" that did something new or significantly different in terms of cinematic discourse. It was the fact that Kubrick lacked the power, the control, the overall authority to tell the story he wanted to tell — that proved to be the greatest failing of *Spartacus*.

The film's narrative, based on Howard Fast's allegorical novel with a script by Dalton Trumbo, might now be seen as merely something of "a simplistic left-wing polemic about the power ... and the corruption of the ruling classes."[25] However, Kirk Douglas's interest in the project may have had less to do with moral or political reasoning and more to do with the fact he had recently lost the leading role in *Ben-Hur* to Charlton Heston.[26] In this sense the film represented something of a vanity project for Douglas, in his role as both star and executive producer he had overall control of the film.

In the succeeding years it appeared, to some extent at least, as if Kubrick had disowned *Spartacus*. However, contradicting this idea, it is of interest to note that in 1991 Kubrick took the trouble to partake in the preparation of a new print of the film, one that included previously deleted scenes — most pertinently the infamous "oysters and snails" scene — wherein, in Neil Fulwood's phrase: "Bisexuality [was] rendered in culinary terms."[27]

On the one hand, Kubrick's experience on the film, his lack of artistic control arguably "cemented his disenchantment with the Hollywood studio system."[28] On the other hand, Kubrick's decision to take on the project to direct *Spartacus* might more accurately be seen as a strategic move. This might be argued, insomuch that demonstrating he could efficiently direct a major motion picture of this scope, enabled Kubrick to attain greater influence and stature in the film industry. Thus the experience on *Spartacus* could be seen as ultimately enabling Kubrick to attain sufficient financial and creative independence for his later projects. In a sense the final eight films of Kubrick's career (*auteur*-driven, all) derive from the success of *Spartacus*.

APPENDIX 2

Lolita

In 1995 the screen rights of *Lolita* returned to the Nabokov estate. Shortly thereafter it was reported that Caroloco Pictures had paid a reported $1 million for the renewed screen rights, and not long after this it was announced Adrian Lynne would direct a remake of the film.[1] Lynne, whose previous films had included *Fatal Attraction, Flashdance* and *9½ Weeks,* released his version of *Lolita* in 1997.

Lyne's adaptation followed Nabokov's novel more faithfully than Kubrick's; not that this was necessarily a contributing factor in accounting for its stature as a film. As part of his desire for authenticity, Lyne set his film in the same era as the novel: in late–1940s America. Nabokov's novel had notionally been set within the era 1947 to 1952; however, Kubrick's film had elided verisimilitude and simply let the various time periods blur, with his film set in a notional present day of the early 1960s.[2] However, Lyne decidedly presented his film as a period piece, something he was not always able to render in a wholly convincing manner. For example, Dominique Swain, in the title role, would appear to have seldom suggested anything other than the sensibilities of a contemporary 1990s teenager.[3]

In terms of its faithfulness toward its literary source, it is of interest to note that Lyne's film appears to have made use of at least some elements of the Nabokov screenplay Kubrick had left mostly unused. For example, the scene in which the highway patrol officer draws up alongside Humbert and Lolita shortly after Humbert has collected her from camp, and the scene wherein Lolita escapes on her bicycle into the rain in Beardsley — these were used, almost verbatim, from Nabokov's original screenplay.

One facet of Lyne's version of the film that was of interest was his re-insertion of the novel's flashback to the 1920s and Humbert's first love,

Annabel. Herein Lyne's adaptation was able to offer at least some sort of a plausible reason for Humbert's sexual fixation on young girls.

In addition, Lyne's ability to portray a greater sense of eroticism toward Lolita's body was arguably more compelling when seen in contrast with Kubrick's original version. If one compares, for example, the opening shot of Lolita in the garden. In both films we find a parallel *mise-en-scène* from Humbert Humbert's point of view, his first image of his object of desire. However, Kubrick's film (given the restrictive period in which it was made) was simply not able to portray the same erotic charge Lyne was able to render, albeit overlaid with a (curious) sense of pop-video fetishization.

Numerical Patterning in Nabokov's Novel

It is known that Nabokov deliberately constructed a coincidental patterning of numbers throughout his novel. For example, the number 342 consistently reoccurs: the Haze household resides at 342 Lawn Street; Humbert and Lolita sleep together for the first time in Room 342 of the Enchanted Hunters; in their first year on the road they register at 342 different motels. The number 52 also reappears consistently throughout the novel: on their first trip Humbert and Lolita spend exactly a year on the road — hence 52 weeks; Humbert, Quilty and Lolita all die in the year 1952 — Lolita dies on Christmas Day, the 25th (52 in reverse); Humbert tells us it takes him 56 days to write his memoir in prison — however, if one counts up Humbert's actual time in jail from when he is arrested on September 25, to when he dies on November 16, we note that this adds up to only 52 days; the poem Humbert writes to Lolita is 52 lines long; the numbers of Quilty's two license plates (which Humbert carefully denotes) are Q32888 and CU88322 the letters are self-explanatory — however, the numbers on both plates adding up (29+23) to 52; one could go on. Dates are also significant in the text; we note that Quilty contrives to ensnare Lolita away from Humbert on July 4th, Independence Day, linking to the phone number of the Haze household — which is 1776. However, whether there was anything further beyond Nabokov's usual trickery is open to speculation. If nothing else, the coincidental nature of numbers draws our attention to the presence of an author greater than Humbert writing the text. Finally, in such a context, one might note that Kubrick, to a certain extent at least, was aware of the numerological patterning in the novel, insomuch as he chose to have Quilty say, at the start of his film: "I have fifty-two successful scenarios to my credit."

Intertextual Elements in Lolita

As is well known, Nabokov's novel offered a diverse range of intertextual references, too numerous to mention here in full. However, to offer a
mere sampling, the novel's subtitle: "Confessions of a White Widowed Male,"
could be read as a possible allusion to another "notorious" work of erotica:
John Cleland's *Fanny Hill*, with its subtitle: "Memoirs of a Woman of Pleasure." Throughout the novel there were in-jokes of a similar nature, sometimes overtly blatant, sometimes exaggeratedly obscure. In the case of the
former, the section of the book wherein Humbert discovers Lolita has been
missing her piano lessons can be read as a direct parallel to Emma Bovary
missing her piano lesson in *Madame Bovary*; insomuch as (in *Lolita*) the piano
teacher is called Miss Emperor, while Emma Bovary's teacher is called Mlle
Lempereur; and in both cases the reason for the piano lessons being missed
were to disguise illicit sexual liaisons.

Kubrick was obviously aware of these facets in the novel, and hence
played a similar game in the film. Note, for example, the intertextual play in
the scene of Humbert in his bath just after the death of Charlotte. The scene
could be read as deliberately mirroring Jacque Louis David's 1793 painting;
Death of Marat Sade, the Nabokovian/Kubrickian joke being that Marat was
murdered in a bathtub by another Charlotte — Charlotte Corday. From a differing perspective, *Lolita* would later project itself into Kubrick's work in a
range of disguises. In *The Shining*, when Jack taunts Wendy on the staircase:
"Wendy, light of my life," this would seem both a direct reference to the same
shot of Humbert climbing a similar set of stairs in *Lolita* and, in addition, it
also alluded to the first words in Nabokov's novel: "Lolita, light of my life."
Likewise, it is well known that, in *Lolita*, Kubrick refers to his previous film,
Spartacus. This occurs when Quilty addresses Humbert's question: "Are you
Quilty?" by replying: "No I'm Spartacus. Have you come to free the slaves or
something?" The joke being embellished in Quilty draping himself in a large
sheet to look like a senator in a toga, going on to say: "Let's have a lovely little game of Roman ping-pong, like two civilized senators." Thus it was possible to perceive of Kubrick attempting to translate some of the complexities
of the source novel he was adapting — offering some degree of intertextuality within the cinematic discourse in which he was working.

Dr. Strangelove

It has become clear that this sequence survives in the British Film Institute archives: Ed Sikov, in his biography of Peter Sellers, offers a detailed description of the deleted scene. Sikov appears to have viewed the sequence, which was apparently shot in color. His description is as follows:

> With all hope lost, Strangelove, having fallen out of his wheelchair, rolls around on the lustrous black floor while President Muffley demands a search of the Soviet Ambassador's body cavities. "The seven bodily orifices!" Buck Turgidson cries, whereupon George C. Scott points directly at the camera ... Buck ducks, causing the President ... to be struck. Muffley collapses into Turgidson's arms, a modern *pieta*. Turgidson then says, "Gentlemen, our beloved president has just been struck down by a pie in the prime of his life! Are we going to let this happen? *Massive retaliation!*" Then, in jittery fast motion, everyone begins to hurl cream pies — to the tune of speeded-up silent movie music. Suddenly a gunshot. It's Strangelove firing into the air. Kubrick cuts to a high angle shot. Strangelove: "Gentlemen! Ve must stop zis childish game! There is verk — *verk* — to do." We then see a high angle shot of a physically recovered but mentally stricken Muffley sitting on the floor opposite De Sadesky amid a lunar landscape of custard craters and crust ... happily building meringue mud pies and sandcastles. Strangelove speaks: "Zis is regrettable, but I think their minds have snapped from the strain!" Peter bites down on every word: "Perhaps they Vill Heff To Be In-Stit-Utiona-Lized!" Buck Turgidson responds by calling for three cheers for Strangelove, at which point Kubrick brings Vera Lynn onto the soundtrack.[1]

The custard pie fight took a week to film, and would have occupied eleven minutes of screen time. Some 2,000 custard pies, mostly made of shaving foam, being used for each day of shooting, producing what would have been: "one of the most extraordinary custard pie battles ever filmed."[2] Thus the lost scene, what might have been the ultimate custard pie fight, acts to demonstrate Kubrick's ruthlessness in excising material from his own work.

Casting Decisions

It is said that Kubrick — upon realizing that Peter Sellers either could not or would not play the role of Major Kong — had approached John Wayne for the role. Wayne is said — not surprisingly — to have immediately declined. Kubrick then looked around for an equivalent cowboy actor. Dan Blocker of television's *Bonanza* fame was approached but he, too, turned down the role. It would appear likely that Kubrick then remembered Slim Pickens from his work on *One-Eyed Jacks* and thus ultimately cast him in the role of Kong.

In the other main roles, Kubrick cast George C. Scott as Turgidson and Sterling Hayden as Ripper. Kubrick had seen George C. Scott playing Shylock in *The Merchant of Venice*, at a performance in Central Park — probably in the summer of 1962. James Earl Jones was also in the play and was apparently cast by Kubrick at the same time. Sterling Hayden was obviously known to Kubrick via his starring role in *The Killing*. In an ironic twist of fate, Hayden had been a member of the Communist party and avoided being blacklisted by serving as a "friendly witness," one of those witnesses who informed on other supposed Communist sympathizers. Robert Kolker notes the inherent irony in having Sterling Hayden playing such a rampant anti–Communist, insomuch as "he was a HUAC informer during the anti-communist purges of the fifties and suffered from despair over that act."[3] Hayden later regretted "naming names: "I don't think you have the foggiest notion of the contempt I have had for myself since the day I did that thing."[4]

2001: A Space Odyssey

One of *2001's* most innovative and significant features can be found in the choice of its soundtrack. In fact, the choice of music for the film is something of a story in its own right. As is now well known, during the making of the film Kubrick had made use of so-called "temp tracks" to accompany the various scenes as he filmed them. Alex North, who had previously composed the soundtrack for *Spartacus,* was hired to compose a score for *2001,* which he subsequently accomplished. It appears it was North's idea to give the soundtrack a consistency and homogeneity by composing music that would respond to Kubrick's "temp tracks" in a more inclusive and general fashion. However, none of North's compositions would, in fact, be used. It appears that Kubrick may always have had the intention of retaining at least some of these so-called "temp tracks," which by then consisted of Richard Strauss's *Also Sprach Zarathustra,* György Ligeti's *Requiem for Soprano and Mixed Choirs, Lux Aeterna* and *Atmospheres,* Johann Strauss's *The Blue Danube*[1] and the "Adagio" from Aram Khatchaturian's *Gayne Ballet Suite.* It is speculation, but it is possible that Kubrick had originally planned to use at least part of North's music, but then came to realize that he had no use for a conventional score at all. Alternatively, Kubrick may have gone through a knowing "charade," for reasons of a more tactical and political nature with MGM. It has been inferred that North attended the premiere of the film unaware that not a note of his score was to be used. Whether this is strictly accurate is open to question. In any case, North's original music for the film went unused and unheard.[2]

That is until 1991, when North, (somewhat in the manner of Vladimir Nabokov later publishing his version of the screenplay of *Lolita,* or Stephen King later making his own film version of *The Shining*) would eventually release his score for *2001*—albeit posthumously—in 1993. Robert Towson, in a somewhat hyperbolic set of sleeve notes[3] claimed that Kubrick never intended to use an original score, but having had his "request" to MGM of using classical music excerpts rejected, began a "charade of monumental proportions."[4]

Towson refers to the recording of North's score (on January 29 and 30, 1993) as finally realizing "one of the most important pieces of film music ever written."[5] However, a knowledge of the music actually used in the film and access to the now extant recording of North's intended soundtrack, suggests the reality to be somewhat different. North's music appears as little more than a poor simulation of Kubrick's "temp tracks," his attempts to provide alternatives to Richard Strauss, Johann Strauss, Ligeti and Khatchaturian belonging to the conventional and somewhat clichéd genre of Hollywood film scores. A selection of somewhat bombastic and ultimately forgettable pieces lacking the artistic quality of the originals, any sense of homogeneity would have been lost in the sheer indifference of the music.

What is perhaps of significance here is Kubrick's awareness of the way a musical soundtrack affects the reception of a cinematic text. The "typical Theramin inspired electronic score"[6] of science fiction films, or North's conventional Hollywood fare, was discarded here in favor of a significantly different approach. Kubrick's decision to maintain his choice of music for the film, specifically *Also Sprach Zarathustra* and *The Blue Danube*, has proved prescient; both pieces have become synonymous with the concept of outer space and space exploration, the two pieces now being iconically embedded within the culture in a way North's music could not have hoped to achieve. The "utter exhilaration," of *Also Sprach Zarathustra* and the way *The Blue Danube* depicted "grace and beauty in turning,"[7] was something Alex North's music could not come close to reproducing. As Kubrick commented:

> He [North] wrote and recorded a score which could not have been more alien to the music we had listened to, and much more serious than that, a score which, in my opinion, was completely inadequate for the film.[8]

In 1972, Kubrick made the comment: "The thing a film does best is to use pictures with music."[9] This perhaps explains Kubrick's desire to go beyond the conventional methods of a Hollywood epic, to look to new ways of creating pictures with music. Insomuch, the musical soundtrack might be seen as one of the key elements in the success of *2001* as a cultural entity. The music is considerable and material to the narrative operation of the film, and Kubrick's decision to drop North's conventional score had a significant affect on the way audiences have responded to the film's narrative discourse.

Special Effects

An obvious innovative feature of the film was the groundbreaking use of special effects. In a defined sense, the special effects, as used in the film, have yet to be surpassed. This is true, even now when we have moved beyond the predicted year of 2001 itself. The clarity and sharpness and authenticity of the special effects in *2001* offer a quality that is not present even in the most sophisticated computer generated images (CGI). The four main members of the special effects team (Wally Veevers, Tom Howard, Con Pederson and Douglas Trumbull), working in England with British technicians, managed to produce effects of almost total verisimilitude and authenticity. The models of the spacecraft were the most precisely detailed for any film thus made, and the almost perfect smoothness of movement was achieved by slow exposures, scenes lasting only a few seconds often taking several hours to film. In addition, practical — if sometimes vastly complicated — effects were also created. For example, Floyd's "weightless" pen; the revolving set to enable the stewardess to climb the wall in the Orion; and, famously, the centrifuge on board *Discovery*. Kubrick also used the technique of front projection, particularly in the Dawn of Man sequences. This was a previously well-known technique from the earliest days of cinema, but one Kubrick used to almost virtuoso effect.[10] The use of front projection and other special effects in *2001* saw Kubrick as a director interested in technological innovation; this would continue in films to come. In *A Clockwork Orange* via the use of pin-on microphones, in *Barry Lyndon* with the development of ultra-fast lenses to enable filming by candlelight, and in *The Shining* wherein the Steadicam camera was first used to major effect.

The Cultural Relevance of the Film's Title

One specific issue that was to prove influential was the way in which the film gave us a means of uttering the name of the historical year in question. The fact that we have called the first years of the 21st century *two thousand and one, two thousand and two* and so on, (instead of twenty-oh-one and so on) is arguably because of Kubrick's film. Fred Ordway, a scientific consultant on the film, commented:

> Stanley asked me if we should say "two thousand and one" or "twenty o one" like we say "nineteen o one," ... and we decided that "two thousand and one" sounded better. We often wondered among ourselves whether the fact that the film was called "Two-Thousand-and-One" would have an influence on the English language when we got into the twenty-first century.[11]

The title itself was not selected until April 1965, a year into work on the film. Previously it had had the somewhat parochial title: *Journey Beyond the Stars*. Arthur C. Clarke admitted that the title: *2001: A Space Odyssey* was completely Kubrick's idea.[12] However, one possible genesis for the film's title may have derived from Clarke's non-fiction book of 1958, *The Challenge of the Spaceship*, which included the line: "For somewhere in the world today, still unconscious of his destiny, walks the boy who will be the first Odysseus of the Age of Space."[13] As a side point, Jerome Agel cites Allen Ginsberg, on June 8,1965, saying: "Tonight, let's all make love in London, as if it were 2001, the year of thrilling God."[14] In this context, it would be interesting to know just how Ginsberg had uttered the words, 2001.

The Original Prologue

Kubrick's original intention was to have begun the film with a prologue, consisting of a number of interviews with scientists discussing a wide variety of the issues the film would deal with — these interviews were filmed and Jerome Agel's book published some of the transcripts. The footage of the 21 interviews was planned for inclusion in a re-release of the DVD of *2001*, in 2001, but it could not be located. The footage is believed to exist as, according to Anthony Frewin: "Kubrick never threw anything away."[15] Fuller versions of the transcripts of the interviews were published in 2005: *Are We Alone? The Stanley Kubrick Extraterrestrial Interviews*, edited by Anthony Frewin. Among the 21 interviewees were Isaac Asimov, Margaret Mead, Jack Good, Constantine Generales, Freeman Dyson, etc. In Frewin's book, Arthur C. Clarke refers to the plan as "one of Stanley Kubrick's few really bad ideas … much in the manner of Herman Melville collecting quotations on whales and whaling from various authorities at the beginning of *Moby Dick*."[16]

APPENDIX 5

Napoleon

I expect to make the best movie ever made.[1]— Stanley Kubrick

It would seem clear that it was Kubrick's intention, after the release of *2001: A Space Odyssey*, to create an even more ambitious and an even more epic film. That film, had it been made, would, of course, have been *Napoleon*. The fact that Kubrick did not succeed in realizing this ambition was perhaps one of the most significant turning points in his career. On the one hand, it prevented Kubrick from making what has often been thought of as his potential masterpiece.[2] On the other hand, the cancellation, by MGM, of *Napoleon* could be seen as having a significantly positive outcome. One of these being the fact that this decision took Kubrick to Warner Bros., where he would stay for the rest of his filmmaking career, solidifying his artistic independence. In addition, Kubrick's next two films, *A Clockwork Orange* and *Barry Lyndon*, would most probably not have been made had *Napoleon* gone into production.

In the case of the former, *A Clockwork Orange,* this was both one of Kubrick's most productive and most controversial films; insomuch as Kubrick made it with great efficiency (in terms of both time and money) yet it is a film still capable of raising both a polemic and a disturbing debate.[3] In the case of the latter, *Barry Lyndon,* one might argue that this was, quite simply, the most significant of all the films Kubrick made. It was, arguably at least, his masterpiece, or at least the masterpiece to which he managed to assert a signature. In this way it is perhaps a valid argument to suggest that *Barry Lyndon* was a ciphered paradigm for the unmade *Napoleon,*[4] and that, in many ways, *Barry Lyndon* fulfilled the ambition Kubrick was unable to achieve in his unmade *Napoleon.*[5]

In any case, it is known that by September 29, 1969,[6] Kubrick had completed a screenplay of *Napoleon*, although documentary evidence suggests Kubrick may have begun work on the project as early as July 1967. Kubrick had written the script himself, loosely basing it on Felix Markham's biography, of which Kubrick had previously secured the rights. In this sense, the film would seem to have been the only instance of Kubrick wholly authoring a screenplay without recourse to a literary source. The screenplay followed Napoleon's life from early childhood, through military training, his love affair with Josephine, his military campaigns, his ascension as emperor, his divorce from Josephine, his marriage to Marie Louise, the early life of their (only) son, the King of Rome, the failure of the Russian campaign and, ultimately, downfall and exile.[7] The film, had it been made, would thus have continued one of Kubrick's most common themes, that of human frailty and of the most carefully laid plans ultimately resulting in failure.

The screenplay (which for some time has been freely available on the Internet) would have offered an overtly explicit film; Kubrick was aiming for "maxima erotica"[8] as the screenplay puts it. As previously mentioned, a number of scenes demonstrated this: a prostitute — Lisette La Croix — picks Napoleon up on the street much in the way Domino picks up Bill in *Eyes Wide Shut*. In addition, there is a scene in which three "actresses" and three "desperadoes" strip and have sex in front of an audience of distinguished French society — again recalling *Eyes Wide Shut* and its orgy scene. There is also a scene in which Napoleon and Josephine make love in an "oval bedroom," with mirrors that encircle them from "floor to ceiling." The script also includes an "openly bisexual" character, Barras, which would thus have contributed a further homoerotic element to Kubrick's *oeuvre*. In addition, the film would also have had scenes of explicit violence; for example, there is a dramatic scene wherein Napoleon executes Verlac, a revolutionary leader, by shooting him through the head in front of a riotous crowd. Overarching this would have been Kubrick's fascination with the military mind, contributing to the narrative scope of the film: "Strategy is dramatic," as Kubrick is once cited as saying.[9] A further familiar feature the screenplay possesses is the consistent and almost comforting use of a third person narrator, again a comparison to *Barry Lyndon* being readily apparent.[10]

In terms of casting, it is often stated that Jack Nicholson was always Kubrick's first choice to play the title role, at least in the initial plans for the film.[11] It is also reported that Kubrick was considering, again in an early stage in preparation, Audrey Hepburn for the role of Josephine.[12] As time progressed these plans changed, but Kubrick apparently never completely gave up hope of making the film.[13] As late as the early 1990s, Kubrick is said to have had the idea of rewriting the project as a multi-episodic television series, with Al Pacino positioned as a strong possibility for the title role; Christiane Kubrick: "He had plans to make it into an 18-hour television special ... that's why he saved all the books and stuff."[14] However, as is now known, none of these plans ever came to fruition. Upon Kubrick's death, Martin Scorsese expressed an interest in *Napoleon,*[15] as did other directors such as Ridley Scott and Michael Mann; however, as of the time of writing, the film that would perhaps have been Stanley Kubrick's masterpiece, remains both unsigned and unmade.

APPENDIX 6

A Clockwork Orange

It is known that Terry Southern had already attempted to write a film treatment of Burgess's novel,[1] and, when Kubrick acquired the rights to the film, it seems Southern, as a previous collaborator, was enthusiastic to work again as a screenwriter. However, Kubrick declined, seldom having the inclination of returning to an old collaborator, perhaps with a view of not repeating himself.

What is less well known is the fact that Anthony Burgess himself had also written a screenplay of the novel. This was at the behest of Si Litvinoff and Max Raab, the owners of the film rights. At this stage the film was apparently set to be directed by Nicholas Roeg, who had then recently directed the critically acclaimed *Performance* (1970).

Burgess's original screenplay, which had been lost for several decades, was eventually rediscovered in 2004. Anthony Biswell, author of *The Real Life of Anthony Burgess*, described its content as being "an elaborate reworking" rather than "a straightforward adaptation."[2] Biswell notes that Burgess's screenplay was more violent than either the novel or Kubrick's subsequent film:

Armed with a razor and a bicycle chain, Alex slashes and swishes and dances his way through a gaudy fantasy world, sexually aroused by the screams and moans of his victims, and urged on to further atrocities by the classical soundtrack which plays constantly in his head. His bedroom cupboard is full of horrors: chemicals, syringes, weapons, sadistic instruments, human bones and the skull of a small child. Burgess's stage-directions make it clear that this cinematic Alex is intended to represent the suppressed violent desires of the audience. As in the novel, the true villain of the film is the authoritarian, technological society, which seeks to "cure" him of the impulse to do evil. Disregarding the redemptive twenty-first chapter entirely, the ending of Burgess's film script follows the American edition of the novel. "I was cured all right," says the deconditioned, post-clockwork Alex.... The script ... has an intensity of violence which is largely missing from Stanley Kubrick's more euphemistic interpretation.[3]

Barry Lyndon

The fact that Stanley thinks the picture will gross in nine figures is reassuring.[1]

Barry Lyndon, of all Kubrick's later films, is perhaps his least well known, but equally it is the film that may prove to be his most lasting legacy. As intimated elsewhere, there is a temptation to see the film as a response, as a surrogate, as a substitute to Kubrick's unmade *Napoleon*. In this sense it might be viewed as a "stand-in" for the major work Kubrick could not, for all his influence in the film industry, engineer a means of making. Thus, there is a sense that in *Barry Lyndon* Kubrick was able to use at least some of the multitudinous research he had undertaken for *Napoleon*. However, within this frame of reference one might also forge, might frame, might fabricate the claim that the film represents Kubrick's greatest work; that it is, for want of a better word, his masterpiece.

In this light a significant issue to consider might be the personal quality of the film. In the case of *Barry Lyndon* it was as if, just for once, Kubrick allowed himself to make the film he wanted to make, without his habitual astute and prudent concern over the issue of commercial considerations. Up until this time Kubrick seems to have possessed, in Robert Kolker's words:

> An unerring ability to seize upon major cultural concerns and obsessions—the cold war, space travel, the ambiguities of violence—and realize them in images and narratives so powerful and appropriate that they became touchstones, reference points.[2]

Thus it might be argued that, just for once, Kubrick eschewed the *zeitgeist*; just for once Kubrick was not concerned with the timing of his film in relation to world events. However, in choosing "a largely unread Thackeray novel"[3] and attending to the construction of an almost wholly convincing depiction of the 18th century,[4] it would appear that Kubrick was also setting out to make his most ambitious film. It has been noted that Kubrick revisited the past in *Barry Lyndon* with the same authenticity as he had visited the future in *2001*[5]; but, if anything, Kubrick was working on an even larger creative canvas with *Barry Lyndon.*[6]

In this light, *Barry Lyndon* found Kubrick at his most convincing as an *auteur.* Kubrick worked on the adaptation of Thackeray's novel alone and, it might be noted, many of the key scenes in the film were not, in any case, to be found in the novel. For example, Barry's encounter with Gretchen, his stealing of the clothes and horse from the "gay" officers in the river, the duel between Barry and Bullingdon, and so on — none of these scenes were to be found in the novel. In addition, if one takes the film's closing epilogue: "It was in the reign of George III that the aforesaid personages lived and quarreled; good or bad, handsome or ugly, rich or poor, they are all equal now." While the lines did derive from the novel, Kubrick's use of them enabled a much greater significance. In Thackeray, the lines derive from very early in the book, eight pages into the first chapter, and were expressed in an almost offhand way — as James Naremore noted, of these lines: "The film utterly transforms its source."[7] Also, although the film necessitated Kubrick's biggest crew — upwards of 170 people — it was, nonetheless, a very personal artistic endeavor: Kubrick was in control of the photography, of the music, of the script. He was the primary editor and, as usual, he had a significant influence in terms of the cinematography, he had selected the cast (with almost impeccable judgment) — the film was his vision. Here, with *Barry Lyndon*, he was as close to an *auteur* as it is perhaps possible to get.

As might be expected, the film contains a diverse range of Kubrickian tropes. However, of perhaps most interest, at least in the space available here, was the way in which Kubrick, once again, had an interest in forging new ways of telling a cinematic story. In other words, there was a specific interest in the way narrative operates within a cinematic discourse. Robert Kolker:

> The film [*Barry Lyndon*] is an advanced experiment in cinematic narrative structure and design and attests both to the strength of Kubrick's commercial position (no other director could have received the backing for such a project) and the intensity of his interest in cinematic structures.[8]

Thus, once again, Kubrick was attempting something new in terms of cinematic narrative. The key figure here was perhaps Michael Horden, the film's omniscient third-person narrator. What is of interest is the way in which Kubrick used his narrator to undermine conventional suspense. Throughout the film Horden's seemingly authoritative voice consistently informs of what is to occur; giving us, the audience, advance warning of pivotal plot events; thus seeming to purposefully undercut narrative suspense and, hence, to deliberately subvert some of the dramatic conventions of film narrative. The change from the novel's first person, autodiegetic narrator, to an anonymous, heterodiegetic narrator in the film (while seeming to offer Kubrick a cipher for Thackeray himself, or at least a late 18th century Thackeray-esque voice) also enabled a more remote and detached way of telling the story. On the one hand, the narrator appears to know everything that is to occur in the story, thus placing him on a level with the author of the text. On the other hand, Michael Horden's world-weary, melancholic, dispassionate and, at times, sardonic voice seems to be merely commenting on Barry's rise and fall, as if from the outside, with no actual influence on the story he is telling. Bille Wickre has commented how "the narrator never comments on the visual text"[9] as if, as Robert Kolker suggested:

> The narrator of *Barry Lyndon* is part of another discourse, the teller of another tale, often parallel to the narrative seen on the screen, though as often denying what is seen, or telling a great deal more than contradicts what is seen.[10]

Hence there is an interesting range of subtle storytelling techniques in play, techniques that might be missed in a casual viewing of the film. For example, it is perhaps worth noting, in this sense, that the epilogue (the title card at the end of the film) is not spoken out loud by the narrator, as if to suggest this derived from a different and perhaps more authorial source.[11] A final indication that the narrator, seemingly omniscient, was, in fact, in less than total control over the narrative he was telling.

In terms of narrative design, a structuralist analysis of the film proves beneficial. It might be noted, for example, that the film begins and ends with two very different dueling scenes, one very short, one very long, both concerning either death or injury to "the father." In a similar way, the film is "bookended" by two very different card games, the provocative and innocent game between Redmond and Nora at the start and the "desolate game between the legless Barry and his mother at the end" of the film.[12] Similarly, the second half of the film begins with a triumphant and newly married Barry — driving, in a carriage, to Castle Hackton with his wife — and ends with an "unmanned" Barry climbing into another carriage, traveling alone into defeat and exile.

Aside from a structuralist reading, the film might also be seen as pointing toward a potential psychoanalytical interpretation. One might note how the film begins with the death of Barry's father and ends with Barry in the care of his loving mother, perhaps by purposeful intent on Kubrick's part, given the proliferation of Oedipal imagery throughout the film. In addition to this, a psychoanalytical reading is perhaps enhanced by positioning the film within an intertextual arena, specifically by reading the film's narrative as a retelling of *Hamlet*. However, this was a retelling of *Hamlet* from a reverse angle, one in which we viewed the world from Barry's point of view: as

Claudius, the wronged stepfather. Hence, with the story told from this perspective, our sympathy resides with Barry/Claudius, while Lord Bullingdon/Prince Hamlet is always viewed from an exterior position. Of obvious significance here is Bullingdon's close relationship to his mother, Lady Lyndon/Gertrude. For example, one recalls Bullingdon's comment after the Reverend Runt has suggested he should be happy his mother has remarried. "Not in this way and not in such haste and certainly not to this man."[13] The line is Bullingdon's, but it could just as easily have come from Prince Hamlet's mouth. Thus Bullingdon hates Barry not so much for reasons of class,[14] but for Oedipal reasoning. Bullingdon: "Madam ... it is not only the lowliness of his birth and the general brutality of his manners which disgust me, but the shameful nature of his conduct toward your Ladyship." Bullingdon, like Hamlet, cannot accept another man in his mother's bed, suggesting the premise of an incestuous desire, something perhaps also mirrored in Barry's close and intimate relationship with his own mother.[15]

In addition, both texts, *Barry Lyndon* and *Hamlet,* reach their *denouements* with dueling scenes, with both scenes having crucial narrative import. In a specific context, here in *Barry Lyndon* (and to a certain extent in *Hamlet*), a duel between two men might be seen within a homosocial arena. The duel, like the boxing ring, presents an arena in which two men, within an intense encounter, have the ultimate aim of penetrating each other's bodies, albeit in a violent way. One might also note how the duel in *Barry Lyndon* is loaded with sexual symbolism: Lord Bullingdon — as the offended party — is seeking "satisfaction," Bullingdon is told to "cock" his pistol, Barry is asked if he is ready "to receive" Lord Bullingdon's fire, and so on. Insomuch, within the idea of a psychoanalytical reading, the duel becomes a metaphor for male-male intercourse. Such a clearly delineated homoerotic discourse being supported by a previous scene in the film, one in which Barry is shown beating Bullingdon with a cane on his buttocks, a potential metaphor for pseudo-mounting.

In summary, *Barry Lyndon* could arguably be viewed as Kubrick's most significant film; hence the decision not to attempt to fully embrace it within this volume, the film perhaps deserving of a monograph in its own right. In this sense one might comment that perhaps the most significant and compelling aspect to the film was its visual appeal, here arguably reaching the zenith of Kubrick's cinematic authority. A diverse number of critics have commented on the film's visual virtuosity. For example, Vincent Canby found it "inordinately beautiful."[16] Adding that while

> [it was] not a warm film — Kubrick's never are — but it is so glorious to look at, so intelligent in its conception and execution, that one comes to respond to it on Kubrick's terms.[17]

Richard Schickel commented that:

Kubrick has assembled perhaps the most ravishing set of images ever printed on a single strip of celluloid.[18]

James Howard described the film as being

one of the most astonishingly beautiful movies ever made.[19]

Playboy called *Barry Lyndon*

one of the most breathtakingly beautiful films of all time.[20]

Rodney Hill declared:

Barry Lyndon stands among his most beautiful and arguably most perfect cinematic achievements.[21]

James Naremore described the film as being

one of the most remarkable and unorthodox costume pictures ever produced ... one of his most impressive artistic achievements.[22]

Even Frederic Raphael was forced to admit that

to find *Barry Lyndon* boring is to admit to having no eye.[23]

In this sense, *Barry Lyndon* is a work of significant visual appeal; of all of Kubrick's work, this film is a piece of pure visual cinema. However, it is also a film in which Kubrick offered a remarkable honesty, specifically in the way the human beings who inhabited the narrative were so clinically dissected. Here was a depiction of human beings lacking either the sentimentalized gloss of religious belief, or a recourse to Enlightenment ideals. Instead, as the epilogue tells us— good or bad, handsome or ugly, rich or poor — here was a representation of human beings as they actually are. Hence, while *Barry Lyndon* is a film of significant visual appeal, it also represents a significantly bleak view of humanity, perhaps the zenith of Kubrickian misanthropy. But this, Kubrick would no doubt have insisted, was a truthful representation. In this sense, and in a diverse number of other ways, *Barry Lyndon* might fairly be said to mark the epitome of Kubrick's work — the epitome of his craft and his art.

APPENDIX 8

The Shining[1]

1. One of the members of a family absents himself from home.

This is Jack, whom we see at the start of the film, driving up into the Rockies, for his interview at the Overlook Hotel.

2. An interdiction is addressed to the hero.

The hero of *The Shining* is Danny, an interdiction is a prohibition, an order forbidding a certain act; hence it is clear that this could be interpreted as Tony telling Danny he should not go to the Overlook.

3. The interdiction is violated.

Danny has no means of obeying the interdiction; he has to go to the Overlook with his parents.

4. The villain makes an attempt at reconnaissance.

The villain in *The Shining* can be seen as the embodiment of the Overlook Hotel's evil. We see this on Closing Day with the appearance of the two Grady girls in the games room. They look at Danny, they do not speak, but they certainly attempt what might be interpreted as a reconnaissance.

5. The villain receives information about his victim.

The Overlook learns of Danny's ability of the "shining."

6. The villain attempts to deceive his victim in order to take possession of him or his belongings.

The Overlook wishes to possess Danny and his belongings—in other words his gift of "shining." Here the villain operates through Danny's father. Lloyd, the spectral barman, deceives Jack and fools him into giving up his most precious belongings: his wife and child.

7. The victim submits to deception and thereby unwillingly helps his enemy.

Here Jack is the unknowing victim. He submits to deception and starts to become possessed by the hotel.

8. The villain causes harm to a member of the family.

In the novel this refers to the episode in which Danny is stung by the wasps; in the film it refers to the injuries sustained to Danny's neck by the woman in Room 237.

8a. One member of the family either lacks something or desires to have something.

The member of the family is Jack and he lacks and desires alcoholic drink.

9. Misfortune or lack is made known; the hero is approached with a request or command, he is allowed to go or is dispatched.

Danny (via Tony) learns of Jack's situation — his need for a drink, his selling of his soul, his danger to Wendy and himself. Danny is not dispatched, he does not leave the hotel, but Tony tells him to send a message to Dick, and, via his special talent of "shining," Danny is able to "leave" the hotel and the telepathic message is sent to Mr. Halloran.

10. The seeker (that is, the hero in "quester" mode) agrees to or decides upon counteraction.

Danny decides he and Wendy need help if they are to survive; now the hotel has succeeded in turning Jack against them.

11. The hero leaves home.

As suggested, Danny does not literally leave home — but his message does leave the hotel — his message "shines" to Mr. Halloran in Florida.

12. The hero is tested, attacked etc., which prepares his way for his receiving either a magical agent or helper.

The hotel is "shining" images into Danny's mind; he will be attacked in Room 237. Only his gift, his magic agent, "the shining" helps him.

13. The hero reacts to the actions of a future donor.

Danny tries to get Tony to help him.

14. The hero acquires the use of a magic agent.

This refers to Danny's "shining," at this point in the narrative he is able to use his "magic agent" and at last solve the riddle of REDRUM.

15. The hero is transferred, delivered or led to the whereabouts of an object of search.

The object of search is Danny's solving of the riddle of REDRUM.

16. The hero and the villain join in direct combat.

Danny and the Overlook

17. The hero is branded.

Danny's injuries in Room 237.

18. The villain is defeated.

Danny and Wendy manage to survive Jack's and the Overlook's attacks on them.

19. The initial misfortune or lack is liquidated.

Jack's desire for alcohol is no longer a significant factor in the story.

20. The hero returns.

Danny returns to the maze.

21. The hero is pursued.

Jack chases Danny in the maze.

22. The rescue of the hero from pursuit.

Danny outwits Jack in the maze and escapes.

23. The hero, unrecognized, arrives home or in another country.

This is only implied in the film, in the novel Danny and Wendy are living anonymously in a resort in the Western Maine mountains.

24. A false hero presents unfounded claims.

Unwritten.

25. A difficult task is proposed to the hero.

Unwritten.

26. The task is resolved.

Unwritten.

27. The hero is recognized.

Unwritten.

28. The false hero or villain is exposed.

Unwritten.

29. The hero is given a new appearance.

Unwritten.

30. The villain is punished.

In the novel the hotel explodes and burns down; in the film the Overlook does not manage to kill Danny and Wendy; however, Jack dies in the maze.

31. The hero is married and ascends the throne.

Unwritten, but we might imagine a future for Danny, wherein he would grow up and marry and succeed where his father has failed.

The 1996 TV Movie Remake of The Shining

The 1996 television mini-series/TV movie of *The Shining* — apparently shot from King's "unread" script of 1977 — was nearly five hours long and featured Steve Weber as Jack, and Rebecca De Mornay as Wendy; it was directed by Mick Garris who had previously made *Sleepwalkers* (1992) a film based on a Stephen King short story. The mini-series was filmed between February and June 1996 and premiered from April 27 to May 1, 1997, on ABC television, in the United States.

The King/Garris version was faithful, for the most part, to the novel; with a nearly five-hour running time it had sufficient scope in which to do this. However, it remains a somewhat sentimentalized account of the narrative, replete with a coda, new to the novel, in which the grown-up Danny sees the ghost of his dead father at his high-school graduation — a scene that was, according to James Howard, "cringingly awful."[2] Anthony Magistrale, author of a number of books on King, made a similar point, talking of the "regrettable indulgences" and the "maudlin excesses" of King's version of the film.[3] Magistrale quoted King as saying: "I am a sentimentalist at heart,"[4] and made the point that the emphasis of the mini-series was "almost exclusively on plot."[5] Magistrale went on to make the point that the King/Garris version did not have "the complexity of forces" of Kubrick's film, lacking the "symbolic layering and ambiguity" of the Kubrick film.[6]

The main problematical feature was arguably King's screenplay, insomuch as scriptwriting would not appear to have been his strongest literary proficiency. One notes, for example, David Cronenberg's comment, in a discussion of his film adaptation of another King novel, *The Dead Zone*: "I got five scripts that had already been written, including one by Stephen King which was the worst one by far."[7] In addition, King and Garris were obligated to side-step Kubrick's iconic inventions: the maze, Jack's repeated phrase of "All work and no play," the Grady girls, Lloyd and the Gold Room, Grady and the Frank Lloyd Wright bathroom, the final photograph and so on. Instead King's script reinstated many of the narrative nuances of his novel, the animal topiary, the roque court, the wasp nest, the use of multiple flashbacks and so on.

In this way the film was more ideologically simplistic; however, there were some points of interest, for example, Danny's struggle to read was preserved; the repressed violence — traced to Jack's childhood — was present here; also, the handling of tension in the Room 217 scene was more compelling in this version, living up to the fact that this was the most frightening part of King's novel.

Numerical Symbolism in The Shining

The use of a numerical design to *The Shining* has been commented on by a number of critics, most significantly Thomas Nelson[8] and Geoffrey Cocks.[9] While retaining some sense of skepticism, insomuch as numerical patterns can and do arrive via coincidental chance, it seems possible that Kubrick *may* have injected a purposeful numerical design into the film. We might note, for example, the following numerical patterns surrounding the number 7 and multiples thereof:

- the hotel was built in 1907
- Charles Grady killed his family at the hotel in 1970
- the film ends with the date of July 4, 1921 (the 7th month and 21 being a multiple of 7)
- the number 42 appears on Danny's t-shirt
- a television report speaks of a $42 million appropriation
- Wendy watches the film *Summer of 42*
- on the television we hear of a 24-year-old woman who is missing— 24 being 42 in reverse
- 7 is a factor of 42 — linking 1907, 1921, 1970
- 42 is 21 doubled
- 42 is the sum of multiplying the digits of Room 237
- 12 (21 in reverse) is the sum of adding the digits of Room 237
- there are 21 pictures in the tableau of images we see in the final scene— three rows of 7
- the radio call sign is KDK (12–21 in reverse)
- Danny is 7 years old in the film
- Jack drinks Jack Daniel's No. 7

Geoffrey Cocks provided an ingenious thesis as to the use of numbers in the film. Cocks believed Kubrick was deliberately "leaving tiny clues in the form of numbers throughout the film,"[10] thus serving both as a link from past to present and also recalling the Nazi habit of tattooing their victims with a number. How much of this was down to coincidence or to design is open to question. Cocks went on to link the recurring use of the number 42 in the film, to the January 20, 1942 meeting at Wannsee, at which the Nazis decided upon the "Final Solution."[11] Cocks argued this was Kubrick's implied intent, but whether it actually was Kubrick's intent remains somewhat speculative; especially when one moves to anything like a reader response or reception theory approach to the film. Kubrick may or may not have enclosed ambiguous numerical symbolism in the film, but ultimately it was the readers (viewers) of the film who constructed the many and varied interpretative readings of the text.

Intertextual References in The Shining

There were numerous intertextual gestures in the film: a complex mosaic of quotations from other cultural sources. For example, the bathroom scene of Room 237 was, in a certain sense, a retelling of the infamous shower scene in *Psycho* (1960), although here it was the masculine intruder who was threatened by a feminine persona. In a parallel sense, as a further reference to the bathroom scene in Room 237, Alexander Walker cited Henri-Georges Clouzot's film, *Les Diaboliques* (1954), in which "a living corpse" was depicted rising out of the bath.[12]

The film might also be compared to Henry James's novella, *The Turn of the Screw* (1897). One notes, for example, how both texts began with a job interview, how both texts were concerned with a haunted "country house," how both texts focused on children and possession by evil spirits, and how both texts had purposefully ambivalent endings.

Geoffrey Cocks perceived of an intertextual resonance between the film and Thomas Mann's novel, *The Magic Mountain* (1924); denoting a number of symbols shared in both texts: the idea of a *doppelganger,* a hedge garden, snow, the uncanny, the symbolic use of the number seven and the same use of color imagery.

Kubrick himself compared the film to a Stephen Crane story, *The Blue Hotel* (1898), in the way the text attempted to persuade its reader that its central character was mentally disturbed, a paranoid individual — but how, at the end of the story, we discover he really was being conspired against. Kubrick: "I think *The Shining* uses a similar kind of psychological misdirection to forestall the realization that the supernatural events are actually happening."[13] Finally, critic, Richard Jameson compared the end of *The Shining* to Michael Snow's "underground" film, *Wavelength*:

> I've no doubt that Kubrick had seen *Wavelength*. His new film ends with a shot that moves down a corridor and into a photograph, after which we dissolve for still closer scrutiny of the photo's elements.[14]

Snow's forty-five minute film, made in 1967, had consisted of one single continuous zoom shot down an 80 foot loft — culminating in a close-up of a photograph on the far wall, and it would seem likely that Kubrick at least had an awareness of this.

Deleted Closing Scene

As is commonly known, Kubrick deleted the closing scene from the original version of the film, shortly after the initial screenings in America. *New York Times* critic Janet Maslin believed this was "mildly damaging," stating that while the deleted scene imparted little narrative information it "helped maintain the film's languid, eerie rhythm."[15] It is known that this scene consisted of Mr. Ullman visiting Wendy and Danny in the hospital. Ullman and

Wendy discuss the tragic events at the Overlook, with Ullman explaining how Jack's body has not been found, thus raising a number of somewhat intriguing narrative implications. (For example, if Jack's body has not been found, then one has to ask: where is it? One possible speculation being that it has reverted back into the past, back to 1921, to the July 4th party, to endlessly recycle the same events.) Finally, as Ullman walks into a hallway, he sees Danny playing with some toys on the floor. Ullman says, "I almost forgot, I have something for you," and throws a yellow ball to Danny, thus suggesting Ullman may be a part of the evil presence in the Overlook. As Shelley Duvall later commented: "There was a Hitchcockian side to this resolution, and you know that Kubrick was crazy about Hitchcock.... I think he was wrong [to delete the scene] because the scene explains things that are obscure ... like the importance of the yellow ball and the role of the hotel manager in the plot."[16] Finally, the stage actress Robin Pappas played a nurse in the excised coda, but she is still listed, to this day, in the cast list. Ms. Pappas can be seen in continuity Polaroids in *The Kubrick Archives*, page 457.[17]

Incongruous Supernatural Elements

Of *The Shining* Diane Johnson claimed: "The film must be plausible, use no cheap tricks, have no holes in the plot."[18] However, there were apparent holes in the plot, holes in the original novel, holes that Kubrick may have deliberately allowed to persist in his adaptation.

This was most pertinently seen via the manner in which Jack escaped from the pantry, thus raising the question as to whether the ghosts in the hotel were real or not. Mr. Grady would appear to have either been a ghost — a supernatural being — or else a figment of Jack's delusional imagination. However, as soon as Mr. Grady *physically* enabled Jack to escape from the pantry, unbolting the door via a physical act, such ambiguities disappeared. Insomuch one might then presuppose the following: if the supernatural presences in the hotel had control over material and physical forces, then why would they have need to work through Jack in order to have him kill his family. If the "spooks" could unbolt a pantry door, could they not have simply killed Danny in order to possess his supernatural talent? This was a flaw which at least appeared to serve in lessening our confidence in the logic of the narrative.

In addition, there would appear to have been another significant flaw (in both the novel and film) insomuch as it was clear that there was a bolt on the door of the pantry and not a lock. This was a clear and pivotal part of the plots of both the novel and the film. In the film Wendy knocks out Jack, drags him into the storage room and then *bolts* him in. The flaw residing here was the fact that there was no logical or coherent reason to have a bolt on the *out-side* of a pantry. A bolt being designed to stop someone entering from the other side of a door, one might envisage having a lock, to avoid inventory shrinkage by hotel staff, but why a bolt? The risible element in King's original plotting demanded there was a bolt on the outside of the pantry door; if there had been a lock, Wendy would presumably have removed the key, thus negating Mr. Grady's spectral ability to free Jack from his prison. In King's novel one could have put this down to general plot inconsistency, of which there are a diverse number of other examples. However, the fact that Kubrick kept this inconsistency in the film requires further thought. One might argue that Kubrick was fully aware of the absurdity and inconsistency of this pivotal part of the plot, but deliberately included it in order to add weight to the idea that he was making a conscious parody of the horror genre, a genre that often entailed plot inconsistencies.

Continuity Errors

As with all films, *The Shining* had its share of minor continuity errors. For example, in the scene wherein Jack is axing his way through the door to "correct" Wendy and Danny, two panels instead of one suddenly appear to have been splintered away. These were minor issues; however, some of the other, more significant so-called continuity errors, may, in fact, have been deliberate on Kubrick's part. For example, it has been suggested that the fact there were seemingly two Mr. Grady's in the film was an error on Kubrick's part. However, such an obvious and simplistic discrepancy would be hard to account for in a filmmaker as pedantically exacting as Kubrick. It would seem more likely that a deliberate ambiguity was created, thereby providing an additional sense of mirroring and twinning. Charles and Delbert Grady may have been one and the same person, or they may have been two very different people, the ambivalence serving to add to the sense of unease in the film. Finally, it was perhaps of significance that Kubrick offered a deliberate discontinuity in the final shot of the film, the photograph from 1921, in which Jack is imprisoned. This showed a room, a large open space, that existed nowhere within our previous knowledge of the Overlook. Thus, in all these instances such disruptions of narrative detail, far from being careless mistakes, appeared to add greater subtextual and perhaps subconscious anxieties in the minds of the viewers of the film.

The Making of The Shining

Vivian Kubrick's[19] television documentary, *The Making of* The Shining, remains the only significant extant record of Stanley Kubrick at work.[20] It was first aired on BBC television on October 4, 1980. Apparently the crew of the documentary had unlimited access to the set of the film; but as to whether Vivian Kubrick had unlimited control when it came to editing the footage is a different matter; one cannot help but think Kubrick himself may have had some influence here. It is thought that Vivian Kubrick shot some 60 hours of footage on the set of the film — together with some formal interview footage, set up by Leon Vitali and Iain Johnstone.[21] The DVD version of *The Making of* The Shining, had a slightly longer running time and included a commentary by Vivian Kubrick herself. (From the commentary we learn a diverse range of information: the snow used outside the Overlook was apparently salt; Jack Nicholson had worked as a fireman and, hence, was something of an expert with the fireman's axe; Margaret Adams— Kubrick's long serving secretary — was given the job of typing up the pages of script in the "All work and no play" scene; Jack Nicholson and Shelley Duvall spent a year dressed in the same house clothes, apparently having five duplicate pairs each.)

The Use of Multiple Takes in The Shining

It is reported that Kubrick shot 1.3 million feet of film on *The Shining* — a ratio of 100:1, whereas most films would rarely go above a ratio of 15:1. Patrick Robertson, in his book *Film Facts,* noted: "The record number of takes for a dialogue sequence is claimed to be the 127 demanded by Stanley Kubrick of a scene with Shelley Duval in *The Shining.*"[22] Vincent LoBrutto went further, claiming that the scene in the kitchen between Halloran and Danny ran up to 148 takes.[23] In addition, LoBrutto noted that Anne Jackson, who played the pediatrician at the beginning of the film, claimed that after multiple retakes of her first scene in the film, Kubrick, in fact, used the original first take. While according to Shelly Duvall, the scene on the Overlook's main staircase, wherein Wendy hits Jack with the baseball bat, took three weeks to shoot — with each multiple take taking approximately 16 minutes to play. Finally, Garrett Brown has commented that the scene with Harry Derwent and his "strange doggy companion" was a "fabulous shot" even though they photographed 36 takes.[24]

Perhaps all of this simply demonstrated the way in which Kubrick chose to work, the way in which he was in a position to take as much time as he wanted in which to make his later films. This being facilitated by the use of relatively small crews with low shooting costs; hence, enabling Kubrick a greater sense of freedom and scope than most (if not all) filmmakers operating within commercial cinematic production. Kubrick famously claimed he shot such a high number of takes "invariably because the actors don't know their lines, or don't know them well enough."[25] However, this raises the question of what Kubrick actually meant; as Matthew Modine noted: "When Stanley told me he did a lot of takes because actors didn't know their lines, he wasn't talking about words."[26] In the same light, Frederic Raphael observed:

> A studio photographer will often take shot after shot until the subject is too exhausted to keep up a veil of charm. Only then does his or her real face appear. This may account, in part, for Stanley's notorious method of asking actors to do a movie scene over and over again.[27]

Thus Kubrick's reputation for multiple and high number takes may have had the underlying intent of pushing an actor further and further in the hope that some previously unexpected performance may occur.

One way to ascertain Kubrick's working methods would be to have access to view the range of repeated takes to see how the work in progress developed. Of course, it is problematical to conduct such research or whether, in fact, such material has survived. The front and end pages of *The Stanley Kubrick Archives* offers a suggestion that such material might still exist. In addition, Alexander Walker offered evidence that, in the case of *The Shining*, at least, this was the case. Walker described visiting Kubrick, at his "command post" in Elstree Studios, the night before *The Shining* was to open: "Stanley sat in a pool of light, hemmed in bunker-like by rack upon gleaming rack of bright film canisters containing every single take he'd shot, whether used in the film or not."[28]

However, in an interview given by Leon Vitali, sometime in 2006, a differing account was given as to what had happened to such outtakes:

> **Interviewer:** Obviously Kubrick shot cans and cans and cans and cans and reels and reels and reels of film for each of his films. Has that work been archived and is it being saved so that at some point people can be able to get a window into his creative process?
>
> **Vitali:** I'll tell you right now, okay, on *Clockwork Orange, The Shining, Barry Lyndon,* some little parts of *2001,* we had thousands of cans of negative outtakes and print, which we had stored in an area at his house where we worked out of, which he personally supervised the loading of it to a truck and then I went down to a big industrial waste lot and burned it. That's what he wanted.[29]

For the present such questions seem equivocal, one presumably has to take Vitali's word for this, disregarding the often-accepted line that Kubrick "never threw anything away." Thus, as to whether such material has been preserved and, if so, whether researchers of Kubrick's work will ever gain access to it, remains—for the moment—uncertain and open to question.[30]

Full Metal Jacket

An early version of the screenplay, dated August 15, 1985, 115 pages long and credited only to Kubrick and Herr, is readily available on the Internet.[1] It was written in prose, rather than the usual screenplay format of dialogue and directions; and, in many ways, bears a strong similarity to the final shooting script. However, the early version did have a significant degree of extra material. For example, it included a much greater use of voice-over than was eventually used. By way of illustration, the following catalogues Joker's original 16 instances of voice-over in the first half of the film, against the more limited number of voice-overs that made it into the film itself:

> Beatings, we learn, are a routine element of life on Parris Island. And not that I'm-only-rough-on-um-because-I-love-um crap in Mr. John Wayne's *The Sands of Iwo Jima.*

> For the first four weeks of recruit training Leonard continues to grin, even though he receives more then his share of the beatings. Even having the shit beat out of him with calculated regularity fails to educate Leonard the way it educates the other recruits in Platoon 30-92. Leonard tries harder than any of us. He can't do anything right.

> I teach Leonard everything I know, from how to lace his black combat boots to the assembly and disassembly of the M-14 semi-automatic shoulder weapon. I teach Leonard that Marines work hard. Only shitbirds try to avoid work, only shitbirds try to skate. Marines are clean, not skuzzy. I teach Leonard to value his rifle as he values his life. I teach him that blood makes the grass grow.

> During our sixth week, Sergeant Gerheim orders us double-time around the squad bay with our penises in our left hands and our weapons in our right hand.

Leonard falls off the slide-for-life repeatedly. He almost drowns. He cries. He climbs the tower. He tries again. He falls off again. This time he sinks.

The first night of our seventh week of training the platoon gives Leonard a blanket party.

On the third day of our seventh week we move to the rifle range and shoot holes in paper targets.

By the end of our seventh week Leonard has become a model recruit. Day by day, he is more motivated, more squared away. We decide that Leonard's silence is a result of his intense concentration. His manual of arms is flawless now, but his eyes are milk glass.

Leonard cleans his weapon more then any recruit in the platoon. Every night after chow Leonard caresses the scarred oak stock with linseed oil the way hundreds of earlier recruits have caressed the same piece of wood.

Leonard improves at everything, but remains silent. He does what he is told but he is no longer part of the platoon. Sergeant Gerheim is careful not to come down too hard on Leonard as long as Leonard remains squared away.

Graduation day. No words can express the way we feel. The moment the Commandant of the Marine Corps gives us the word, we will grab the Viet-Cong guerrillas and the battle-hardened North Vietnamese regulars by their scrawny throats and we'll punch their fucking heads off.

After graduation Sergeant Gerheim forms us into a school circle to read out our orders.

Our last night on the Island. I draw fire watch.

One hundred young Marines breathe peacefully as they sleep — one hundred survivors from the original hundred and twenty.

The civilians will demand yet another investigation, of course. But during the investigation the recruits of Platoon 30-92 will testify that Private Pratt, while highly motivated, was a ten percenter who did not pack the gear to be a Marine in our beloved Corps.

Sergeant Gerheim was a fine drill instructor. Dying, that's what we're here for he would have said, blood makes the grass grow. If he could speak, Gunnery Sergeant Gerheim would explain to Leonard why the guns that we love don't love back. And he would say, "Well done."

As might be seen, much of this material was omitted insomuch as Kubrick may have finally considered it too literal, that the film itself communicated sufficient narrative information without the need for further elaboration.

The original screenplay also contained a limited number of extra scenes, most of them pointing toward a more extreme level of discourse than the final shooting script. For example, the mistreatment of Pyle was more sadistic: there was a scene in which the recruits were ordered to urinate into a toilet after which Sgt. Hartman (still named Gerheim at this stage) half drowned Pyle in the "yellow pool." (A scene that linked the homosocial and scatological in a specific and literal way.)

In addition, there was a deleted scene in which a recruit, Private Perkins, attempted suicide by slitting his wrists, after which Gerheim tells him to get a mop and clean up the mess before double timing to sickbay. Likewise, the scene in the helicopter, as Joker and Rafterman are on their way to Hue, was extended to include an Arvin Captain and Arvin Sergeant interrogating two VC prisoners—whom they eventually throw out of the helicopter to their deaths.

Also, this early version of the screenplay included a scene in which a character, called Captain January, played Monopoly with real money. January retained some of the more aphoristic of the unused lines from Hasford's novel: "This is the only war we've got," January says. "History may be written with blood and iron but it's printed with ink." The scene would have been placed just before the mass graves scene, hence, acting to offer more narrative depth to Joker and Rafterman's journey into battle.[2] At the scene by the mass grave, the "Jungian thing" was also given greater depth. Joker: "The dual nature of man, you know, sir, the Jungian thing about aggression and xenophobia on the one hand, and altruism and co-operation on the other."

Finally, at the end of this version of the film, Animal Mother apparently did cut off the head of the sniper: "Animal Mother spits. He takes a step, kneels, zips out his machete.[3] With one powerful blow he chops off her head. He picks up the head by its long black hair and holds it high. He laughs and says, 'Rest in pieces, bitch.'" After which the script, in another final change in plotting, depicted the death of Joker, intercutting it with an eight-year-old version of his character, armed with a plastic rifle, running in a field. Thus offering one further gesture in the direction of the infantilization of men in the film.

Dispatches— *Textual Influences on* Full Metal Jacket

Michael Herr's celebrated memoir of his experience in Vietnam, *Dispatches*, had led him to work on *Apocalypse Now* (writing Willard's internal narration) and from there to his work with Kubrick on *Full Metal Jacket*.

While *Dispatches* lacks a sufficiently tangible narrative structure, a means of telling a coherent story, a number of elements were used in Kubrick's film. For example, specific lines of dialogue:

I just can't hack it back in the World.[4]
We are definitely expecting rain.[5]
You really had to sound off like you had a pair.[6]
No more boom-boom for that mamma-san.[7]
...told me to get with the programme, jump on the team.[8]

In addition, the scene in the film in the helicopter, wherein the door gunner is indiscriminately shooting at Vietnamese peasant farmers, was drawn from Herr's book:

> There was a famous story, some reporters asked a door gunner, "How can you shoot women and children?" and he'd answered, "It's easy, you just don't lead 'em so much."[9]

The character of Handjob in the film was influenced by a character called Greene, mentioned in Herr's book:

> Greene was all fixed to get out. He's jerkin' off thirty times a day.... He was waitin' outside to see the major about getting sent home, an' the major comes out to find him an' he's just sitting there jerkin' off.[10]

In a similar way, the opening scene in the second half of the film, in which Rafterman's camera was stolen, derives from Herr's book; as were the symbols of duality Joker wears. Herr: "'Born to Kill' is placed in all innocence next to the peace symbol."[11]

In addition, Herr had already provided Hasford's original title for his novel:

> It's the Short-Timers Syndrome. In the heads of the men who are really in the war for a year, all tours end early.... Like every American in Vietnam, he had his obsession with Time. No one ever talked about When-this-lousy-war-is-over. Only "How much time you got?"[12]

At times Herr's writing was both grimly realistic and poetic; there were lines in Herr's book that did not make it into the film, but nonetheless informed it:

> Even the incoming was beautiful at night, beautiful and deeply dreadful.[13]
> Sunsets that would change the way you thought about light forever.[14]
> It was a bad place, the wrong place, maybe even the last place.[15]
> Choppers fell out of the sky like fat poisoned birds a hundred times a day.[16]
> It was one of those days that I realized that the only corpse I couldn't bear to look at would be the one I would never have to see.[17]
> I think that Vietnam was what we had instead of happy childhoods.[18]

Finally, a section of Herr's book, in which he described an Army surgeon operating on a young Vietnamese girl, served to suggest the overall cynicism and yet, at the same time, the underlying humanity of Kubrick's film:

> One of the Vietnamese nurses handed me a cold can of beer and asked me to take it down the hall where one of the Army surgeons was operating. The door of the room was ajar, and I walked right in. I probably should have looked first. A little girl was lying on the table, looking with wide dry eyes at the wall. Her left leg was gone, and a sharp piece of bone about six inches long extended from the exposed stump. The leg itself was on the floor, half wrapped in a piece of paper. The doctor was a major, and he'd been working

alone. He could not have looked worse if he'd lain all night in a trough of blood. His hands were so slippery that I had to hold the can to his mouth for him to tip it up as his head went back. I couldn't look at the girl.... He placed his hand on the girl's forehead and said, "Hello, little darling." He thanked me for bringing the beer. He probably thought he was smiling, but nothing changed anywhere in his face. He'd been working this way for nearly twenty hours.[19]

Appendix 10

Eyes Wide Shut

The final draft of the screenplay of *Eyes Wide Shut* did not have a voice-over narration, a feature redolent of much of Kubrick's work. In Schnitzler's novel the characters' interior monologues, especially Fridolin's, were crucial to an understanding of their actions; but in the film the only sense of gaining access into Bill's internal thought processes was through his "daydreams" of Alice making love to the naval officer. However, an earlier version of the final shooting script, available on the Internet,[1] did make extensive use of voice-over narration. While it is not possible to be sure of this source's complete authenticity, or to ascertain its exact relationship to the final shooting script of the film, nonetheless, it provides an interesting means of looking at some of the other narrative strategies Kubrick appears to have been considering in his adaptation of the film.

In this earlier version the first voice-over occurred in the scene wherein Alice and Bill make love in front of the mirror, after Ziegler's party:

> V.O. That night they were more blissful in their ardent love than they had been for a long time.... The gray of morning awakened them only too soon. And Bill had a number of early appointments. So the evening hours passed in the predetermined daily routine of work, and the events of the night before began to fade.[2]

What was of interest was that this voice-over — and all the others in this version of the screenplay — was adapted, almost word for word, from Schnitzler's novel. In the case here the corresponding passage of the novel was as follows:

> A grey morning awoke them all too soon. The husband's profession summoned him to his patients' bedsides at an early hour.... And so the time had passed

228

predictably and soberly enough in work and routine chores, and the events of the previous night from first to last had faded.[3]

The next example of a planned voice-over came during Bill's scene with Marion:

V.O. I certainly do remember Carl. So she's going to marry him, Bill thought to himself. I wonder why? She surely can't be in love with him. He's nothing to look at, and he hasn't got any money.... He's just an assistant professor of something or other.... But then it's none of my business. Still ... if she were my mistress, her hair would be less dry and her lips would be fuller and red.[4]

The voice-over then followed Bill, immediately after leaving Marion's:

V.O. The image of the tramp made him think of the dead man he had just left, and he shuddered and felt slightly nauseated at the thought that decay and decomposition had already begun their work in the body he just left. He was glad he was still alive and in all probability that these ugly things were still far removed from him, and that he was, in fact, still in the prime of life, had a beautiful wife and could have several women in addition, if he wanted to, although doing so would require more free time than he had.[5]

And then continued, following the homophobic attack on Bill in the street:

V.O. Had he become a coward, he asked himself, and noticed his knees were shaking a little bit. Ridiculous! Why should he get involved in a street fight with some drunken college student who had five friends with him.... He, a man of thirty-five, a practicing physician, a married man and father of a child. He might wind up in the hospital or worse and tomorrow be in the same position as the man he just left. Then he thought about his profession? There were dangers lurking there, too, everywhere and at all times—except that one usually forgets about them. Surely, it had been nothing but common sense to avoid a ridiculous fight with the student ... but if he ever meet [sic] the Naval officer with whom Alice.... But what insanity! After all, nothing happened.... What was he thinking about.... But then, wasn't it really just as bad as if she had actually fucked him — she might just as well have. Wasn't it even worse, in a way. What a joy it would be to teach "him" a lesson.[6]

There was a further voice-over as Bill approached the Sonata Café:

V.O. Where shall I go now, he asked himself? The obvious thing was home to bed. But he couldn't persuade himself to do that. He thought of going back to the girl but that somehow seemed ridiculous now. He was overcome with a sense that he was moving farther and farther away from his everyday existence into a completely different world.[7]

And then another voice-over, as Bill considered the written note from Somerton:

V.O. Second warning? Why the second warning—and not the last? The tone of the note was strangely reserved and seemed to show that the people who sent it by no means felt secure. The note disappointed him, though, in a way, it reassured him, just why he couldn't say. But, at least, he now felt the woman had come to no real harm, and that it would be possible to find her if he went about it cautiously and cleverly.[8]

The final voice-over came near the end of the film, in the scene of Bill at home with Alice and Helena:

> V.O. He had gone home, feeling a little tired but surprisingly cheerful, with a strange sense of security, which somehow seemed deceptive. He was in an excited and cheerful mood and he felt unusually fresh and clear in spite of spending the last two nights without sleep. At the same time, he felt that all this order, this normality, all the security of his existence, was nothing but deception and delusion.... And, he thought, there she sits with an angelic look, like a good wife and mother — the whore of her dreams who made love to a hundred men the preceding night and laughed when he was crucified, and to his surprise he didn't hate her.[9]

While adhering to a degree of skepticism as to the screenplay's complete authenticity, one might nonetheless speculate whether Kubrick was correct in dropping the voice-overs in this early draft. On balance it would seem that the film, although of necessity more ambiguous, benefited from the lack of a voice-over and the inherent narrative transposition.

Finally, there were a number of other details of note to be found in this early version of the screenplay. For example, Ziegler's wife, Ilona, was described as "a Hungarian beauty" thus providing a further added relevance in terms of the film's original Austro-Hungarian source. In this version Alice had been an editor at a publishing house — rather than having previously run an art gallery — the finished film thus offering an additional emphasis on the visual media. The "end of the rainbow" line was not apparent; nor was there any mention of Rainbow Fashions; thus lacking the subtle references to color symbolism the final version of the film possessed. As to the sexual content, the early screenplay was more explicit; for example, Domino undresses completely: "She stands naked before him with her arms outstretched." In a similar way, in a scene additional to the finished film, Bill begins to make love to Marion, undressing and kissing her. Alice's description of her dream was much longer, drawing more on the novel, it included the section wherein she sees Bill stripped naked and about to be crucified. Other details included the precise location of Somerton, it being at Sands Point, Long Island, although here the name of the mansion was Bletchley Manor. Lastly, the closing scene did not take place in a toy shop, but followed the same closing scene from the novel — the script ending in the Harford's bedroom — with Helena running in and a "new day beginning."

Color Symbolism

"It's not quite so black and white," so says Bill, part way through *Eyes Wide Shut*. A perceptive viewer of the film might thus have been minded of the disciplined use of color within the film's *mise en scène*. It is sometimes said that we dream in black and white, and Bill certainly appears to imagine Alice's erotic dalliances with the naval officer in black and white — or at least in differing shades of blue and grey. However, in the main body of the film, Kubrick made use of a specific spectrum of color, luring the viewer into the narrative via an elaborate system of color symbolism. This was self-referentially indicated by two specific references: to Rainbow Fashions (all the colors) and by Domino's name (black and white). In addition and as suggested previously, Kubrick, ever striving for fidelity to Schnitzler's source text, seems to have consciously made use of the colors: blue, red and gold. (The opening page of *Dream Story* refers to the deep blue, star-spangled sky, to the reddish glow of the lamps and to the flaxen (golden) hair of Albertine and Fridolin's daughter.)[10] Once again a perceptive viewer of the film might note how these were used as the main colors within Kubrick's palette. For example, blue is the primary color wherein Bill imagines Alice making love to the naval officer, blue is also the primary background to Alice in her confessional scene with Bill; red relates to the orgy and Red Cloak, and to the red billiard table; gold being reminiscent of the Ziegler party and often directly associated with Alice herself.[11] Thomas Nelson[12] has noted how the final scene, in the toy shop, seems to bring all the colors together — and thus, in a sense, the couple reaches the rainbow's end.

Soundtrack Recordings of Eyes Wide Shut

Kubrick is reputed to have considered some 600 classical works for use in the film, among the music considered and not used: Wagner's *Tristan und Isolde*, Satie's *Gnossienne No. 1*, Brahms's *German Requiem*, Schubert's String Quintet in C, and John Tavener's *Protecting Veil*.

However, as with several of his other films, Kubrick was open to the inclusion of original music alongside existing material. Of interest in this context was Kubrick's collaboration with Jocelyn Pook. It is reported that Kubrick became aware of Pook's work via the Orange mobile phone television commercial which featured a sample of Kathleen Ferrier singing "Blow the Wind Southerly." This led to Kubrick's use of material from Pook's (1997) album *Deluge*, as background while rehearsing the orgy sequences in the film. Pook had never written a film score before *Eyes Wide Shut*, but Kubrick appears to have been confident in her abilities. (One notes here how Kubrick's final three films all made use of music by relatively inexperienced female composers: Jocelyn Pook, Abigail Mead and Wendy Carlos.) According to Pook, Kubrick was "very musically literate"[13] and entrusted her to compose the music without direct knowledge of either the script or any of the footage thus far shot.

The final score — with its signature piece — Shostakovich's Waltz 2 from his *Jazz Suite*, Gyorgy Ligeti minimalist piece: "Musica Ricercata II,"[14] together with Chris Isaak's "Baby Did a Bad Bad Thing" and a sampling of easy listening and jazz standards — was as eclectic as usual; however, it was Pook's original elements of the score that perhaps retain the most interest in terms of the innovative aspects of the soundtrack.

Gary Goba's role as the Naval Officer *in* Eyes Wide Shut

The contribution of Gary Goba, the actor who played the role of the naval officer in *Eyes Wide Shut*, has seldom been the center of great attention; however, James Dickerson, one of Nicole Kidman's biographers, interviewed Goba, hence providing some pertinent and otherwise untold information concerning his contribution to the film. Goba, who had not appeared in a film role prior to *Eyes Wide Shut*,[15] was auditioned in the summer of 1997, then, in December 1997. Kubrick's assistant, Leon Vitali, called him to say they were ready to shoot his scenes.[16] Goba was not given a script, and on the first day of shooting was shown into what was referred to as, "the Cape Cod suite." Here Goba met with Nicole Kidman and Kubrick. The latter of which Goba described as being: "A super nice guy, completely normal. It was like meeting somebody's parents or something."[17] Goba related that there were usually only three people on the set, himself, Kidman and Kubrick — who was operating the camera. The shooting of the scenes are said to have lasted six days, during which time (according to Dickerson): "Goba and Nicole engaged in sexual activity, everything short of actual penetration.... Goba estimates that they probably acted out fifty different sexual positions."[18] Dickerson went on: "The most intimate scenes never made it into the film. In ... one Kubrick had Nicole stand nude against a wall, one foot propped up onto a tabletop and her leg flared open so that everything was exposed."[19] Kubrick then reportedly "instructed" Goba "to go down on her." Goba explained that a "wig" was glued over Kidman's "private parts" — somewhat risibly recalling Merkin Muffley — after which Goba presumably simulated cunnilingus. Dickerson noted:

> One of the aspects of the film that attracted attention was the different level of interest and passion that Nicole showed in her sex scenes. With Tom, she was

cool and distant, almost passionless—and there seemed little physical chem-
istry between them. With Gary Goba she was just the opposite—passionate,
totally engaged in the encounter, oozing with hot-blooded sexuality.[20]

However, Nicole Kidman is on record as suggesting the film had to be explicit:

> Stanley wanted it to be harsh and gritty, almost pornographic.... The film
> deals with sex and sexual obsession, and the scenes could not have been of me
> in a bra and panties pretending to have sex with someone. It has to have a
> graphic quality to it.[21]

In contrast to what might be seen as a somewhat prurient angle, perhaps a more significant aspect of these scenes was the viewpoint from which
they derived. In other words, deriving wholly from Bill's imagination, they
corresponded to the dichotomy of men watching pornography. That is, just
who is the masculine viewer actually interested in; the woman having sex with
a man, or the man having sex with a woman?

Frederic Raphael's Eyes Wide Open

Frederic Raphael's *Eyes Wide Open* remains an intriguing and controversial book: intriguing because it purports to offer one of the most detailed
accounts of Kubrick's working methods; controversial because its veracity
has been challenged by Kubrick's friends, colleagues, and, most pertinently,
by his family.[22] The veracity of Raphael's book must also be questioned by
the general reader, the fundamental question being: how did Raphael reconstruct his conversations with Kubrick so accurately? Such conversations were
presented verbatim almost as if they were being transcribed from a recording. However, it was scarcely credible to suppose that Raphael would have
"bugged" Kubrick. One supposes Raphael may have kept detailed notes of
the conversations, and reconstructed transcriptions from these. Yet if this was
the case one has to speculate how much license was taken in their reconstruc-
tion. For example, at one point in the book Raphael quotes Kubrick's thoughts
on working with Marlon Brando, the direct quotation lasting for an entire
page,[23] one must question how accurately Raphael could have reproduced
this, word for word.[24]

There was also the issue of privacy. It is clear that Kubrick, in his conversations with Raphael, presupposed he was talking in private and hence was
able to talk freely, as anyone might do, within the confines of such a discourse. It is unlikely that Raphael would have considered publication had
Kubrick lived, insomuch as Kubrick would have been able to challenge the
authority of the quoted material attributed to him. However, if one party to
the conversations was no longer alive and could no longer challenge their

veracity, one must therefore ask how ethical it was to reconstruct the supposed private verbatim conversations of a dead man — a man no longer in a position to confirm or refute what he is claimed to have said.

Film critic Iain Johnstone noted: "Frederic Raphael was, in some way, a curious choice for a collaborator since his best work had been done thirty years previously."[25] Raphael had earned an Oscar for his script of John Schlesinger's 1965 film, *Darling*; he had scripted *Two for the Road* (1966) for Stanley Donen, and had then written the screenplay for *Far From the Madding Crowd* (1967) again directed by John Schlesinger. However, Raphael's output since that time had been less significant.[26] Hence, when asked by Kubrick to collaborate on the script of what was to become *Eyes Wide Shut*, a sense of an unacknowledged inferiority complex appears to have come to the fore. Throughout his book Raphael could not help but attempt to continually accentuate his intellectual superiority. The cover of the book already presenting a clue before it had been opened: proclaiming its author as "an Oscar winning screenwriter." Kubrick was, of course, never awarded a major Oscar.[27] In this light, it is interesting to note how, throughout his book, Raphael lay stress on Kubrick's lack of a formal university education: "When I told him that I had been reading a foreign author ... he would ask apprehensively what language I was reading him in."[28] Insomuch, Raphael appears to have been continually concerned about his notional competition with Kubrick, at one point claiming: "I have little fear that he is intellectually beyond my reach."[29]

Raphael would later claim: "By some clerical oversight, I was the only person Kubrick ever employed who was not embarrassed from writing about his experiences with him."[30] This being a somewhat puzzling statement as it appeared to overlook the numerous written accounts of the likes of Michael Herr, Diane Johnson, Arthur C. Clarke, Terry Southern, Vladimir Nabokov, Calder Willingham, Jim Thompson; not to mention Brian Aldiss, Sara Maitland, Candida McWilliam and Ian Watson — all of whom wrote of their collaborative experiences with Kubrick.[31] While each of these writers, at times, pointed to the aggravations involved in working with a director as demanding as Kubrick, all, in different ways, offered more sympathetic accounts than Raphael's.

In this light it is hard to wholly understand Raphael's motivation for writing his book. When Kubrick unexpectedly died it would seem Raphael discovered there was no silencing clause in his contract, and hence he was free to write whatever he pleased, perhaps the more controversial the better. As to whether Raphael was deliberately trying to lessen Kubrick's reputation — as Kubrick's family seemed to imply — is not as clear. However, Raphael's book was not greeted with excessive acclaim, as already stated, its veracity was questioned. Michel Chion:

This [*Eyes Wide Open*] is a source to be used with caution. The title somewhat treacherously suggests that Raphael clearly saw things that Kubrick did not.... However the veracity of this book, in which details of conversations between Kubrick and his co-writer are ostensibly recorded, is disputed by the dead director's wife and brother-in-law.[32]

In an interview in July 1999, Raphael sought to defend his book:

I didn't think my book was the least bit offensive to anybody, and it was certainly not intended to be. There is nothing on God's earth that would make me embarrassed to tell the truth, and people who don't tell it should be embarrassed.[33]

Of course, the problem in adopting such a stance lay in the question of just whose version of truth was at issue. Of still further controversy was the question of Kubrick's alleged anti–Semitism; exaggerated by the now-infamous headline for a piece in the *New York Post*, by Raphael: "Stanley Kubrick, Self-Hating Jew."[34] According to Raphael:

The *New York Post* behaved disgracefully. They put that headline on, which had nothing to do with the piece. I never said that Kubrick was a self-hating Jew.[35]

It is clear Raphael was misquoted; however, the general discourse of his book was arguably not so far away from such a summarizing headline. As critic Roger Clarke put it, cynically, but perhaps with some degree of correctness: "I think what Raphael really can't work out is whether he was being hired as a Jew, by a closet Jew, to de–Jew a Jewish novel."[36]

Perhaps one of the other most regrettable revelations of the book occurred when Raphael quoted Kubrick (allegedly) commenting on Nicole Kidman's body. Raphael's presentation of this came across as a somewhat grubby conversation, that of two sixty-plus-year-old men discussing a young woman's body in an almost debased light. Raphael quoted Kubrick as saying: "She's agreed to give me a couple of days when she takes off her clothes ... might be a good day to happen to drop by the studio, if you wanted to."[37] Whether or not Kubrick actually said this remains uncertain; however, the fact that Raphael chose to reveal such a conversation so soon after Kubrick's death speaks for the level of Raphael's discourse.

Nonetheless, Raphael's book was a revealing document, although perhaps not in the way Raphael intended, insomuch as the author of *Eyes Wide Open* arguably revealed more of himself than he did of Kubrick. To be specific, one of the most interesting elements in the book was Raphael's relationship to Kubrick in terms of the sexual content of the film. It could thus be argued that Raphael's book was, in a sense, a love story, albeit an unacknowledged and deeply repressed one.[38] Throughout the book and within Raphael's "obsessive" discourse, there were clear homosocial issues and even a sense of an innocent homoerotic element. Raphael's portrayal of two men, each in their sixties, each married for several decades, discussing sex with each other, what Raphael referred to as "erotic fireworks,"[39] was at once comic and revealing. Raphael's text was littered with remarks that seemed directly pointed to an almost risibly repressed desire:

> But beyond eroticism, what does he [Kubrick] want of me?[40]
>
> I have the whore's consolation: whatever I am, he *chose* me: he chose *me, he* chose me.[41]
>
> I told myself that Stanley would be seduced into believing that I knew what I was doing.[42]
>
> I had been like Penelope who had decided to complete the tapestry.[43]
>
> S.K. was startled, and a little excited, to find that he had access, on his new computer programme, to a catalogue of world-wide sexual services ... the list began with the simplest item on the menu: One-Shot Cunt Fuck.[44]

In describing his work on the film's screenplay, Raphael often used the metaphor of fertilization and birth. For example, in his covering letter with the screenplay's first draft, Raphael described the writing of it as being "like producing a quarter or fifth of a baby."[45] Talking of the credit sequence (in an early draft of the film, one not subsequently used) Raphael perceived it as a way of displaying ideas of his own and commented: "They could provide evidence of my fertility."[46] Finally, going on to comment: "The screenwriter plays the traditional woman's part ... there is a kind of freedom in such 'feminine' subjection."[47]

This consistent preoccupation with sexualized metaphors was explored elsewhere in the book. For example, when Raphael pondered upon Kubrick's imagined interest in Kirk Douglas's sexual prowess, he speculated: "Whether or not Kirk *stiffened* Stanley's resolve."[48] In a similar vein, in his first draft script Raphael had written a scene in which Bill performed a rectal examination on "a plump lawyer called Harry" and went on to comment how "two guys can talk about ... the meaning of life and then one puts his finger up the other one's ass."[49] Similarly, at one point Raphael has Kubrick asking: "You ever go to an orgy?"[50] Raphael hasn't. He asks Kubrick if he has, Kubrick doesn't reply. Instead Raphael has Kubrick asking: "How about whorehouses?" Raphael says he was "too scared,"[51] and then goes on:

> As if to prove what buddies we now are, he uses the word "cunt" a lot. He talked of a "shaggy-cunt story" when I outlined my role-playing scenario for the orgy.[52]

Later, Raphael revealed:

> Stanley had Tony Frewin send me a batch of Helmut Newton's erotic photography in order, I suppose, to prime my imagination. It was curious (and appetizing) how many of them featured women fondling other women. Yet

when, in one of the scenes between Alice and Bill, I had her ask him if he had ever imagined her being a boy, Stanley rejected the exchange with something like disgust.[53]

Such barely disguised references continued throughout the book:

> I cannot even be sure whether, when I tell myself that I like him, I feel affection, interest or merely hopeful relief that he seems to like me.[54]

> There was between us an intimacy without commitment and, at times, heat without warmth.[55]

> I have never met anyone for whom I had less consistent feelings.[56]

And finally:

> I felt spasms of almost protective affection.[57]

In this sense the book might be read as a means of documenting Raphael's misfortunes within the world of movie making; pointing to the unstated jealousy felt by one man toward another; toward a man who was able to make a number of meaningful cinematic texts, on his own terms, as an *auteur*, within the Hollywood system.[58] In effect the book could perhaps best be read more as a work of fiction; one in which a lesser artist desperately attempted to place himself on the same level as a greater one. The critic D.K. Holm, in his review of *Eyes Wide Open*, noted:

> As presented in the book, Raphael's relationship with Kubrick, that of an ambitious, conceited, but not particularly distinguished *métier en scene*, consulted by, yet also spurned by, and jealous of in a Salieri-like manner, a naturally superior artist, would make a great story — by Martin Amis.[59]

This was a trenchant observation, the Mozart/Salieri subtext to *Eyes Wide Open* perhaps encompassed Raphael's greatest fear: that he would ultimately be most well known as a screenwriter who once worked with Stanley Kubrick.

It was perhaps Michael Herr who best "nailed" Frederic Raphael's memoir, noting, cynically, but accurately:

> It wasn't just that it was so antagonistic to Stanley, or even that it was so bitter and self-humiliating, but that it was so unfailingly patronizing. Stanley, we gather, hadn't been sufficiently deferential to Raphael's credentials, to his academic attainments and his immense store of knowledge, his often unfortunate command of foreign words and phrases and the insolent presumption of superiority that came along with it all, however unentitled ... it's always painful to see a great artist belittled by fools.[60]

Overall, the claim that the book represented an act of betrayal may have been too outspoken. One is nonetheless left with the idea that Kubrick placed his trust in Raphael but that that trust was not returned. What Raphael, perhaps, could never accept was the fact he *was* a "mechanic" for hire, something that appears to have rankled with him, something his sense of esteem found difficult to deal with. As Raphael himself stated: "He does not want, and never wanted a collaborator, but rather a skilled mechanic who can crank out the dross he will later turn to gold."[61] It would seem clear that Kubrick could not tell his stories without assistance; he needed collaborators/mechanics, but he was always the *auteur*, always determined to preserve his own overall vision of the film in question. Thus, a more accurate appraisal might be to read Raphael's book as an essay in which a scriptwriter attempts to come to terms with his own lack of importance, a realization of the lack of significance of a scriptwriter — in film — and especially in terms of a Stanley Kubrick film.[62]

Auteur Theory

One man writes a novel. One man writes a symphony. It is essential for one man to make a film. — Stanley Kubrick

There is a joke about *auteur* theory, one of the few jokes about *auteur* theory, which goes as follows: "In the film world the director is God — but, unfortunately, the actors are atheists." This is perhaps an appropriate position to assume, insomuch as *auteur* theory has always been a fundamentally questionable school of thought. In one sense it succeeded in bestowing cinema an enhanced artistic status. In other words, in recognizing the significance of the director as a creative artist it thus avoided film being seen as the product of an anonymous, industrial, commercial conglomerate. In such a sense, for cinema to be considered as great art, a serious object of study, it had to have a creator, an author. Hence, the notion of "the great director" was important to the way cinema was received and understood. In this light, *auteur* theory could perhaps be better understood as the wishful thinking of a handful of French film critics, of the 1950s and 1960s, who, for reasons of their own, needed to consider directors as authors of their films.[1]

A significantly discomfiture for *auteur* theory came about, in 1968, via the publication of Roland Barthes's influential essay "The Death of the Author."[2] In this short essay, an essay that arguably marked the beginnings of poststructuralist thought, Barthes questioned the very concept of authorship itself, never mind the precarious idea of a cinematic author. However, this has never stopped commentators claiming "*auteur*-ship" for Kubrick:

Stanley Kubrick is a director to whom the term *auteur* can be applied without hesitation.[3]

Kubrick was the closest auteur study got to an image of the filmmaker as a lone artist in a garret.[4]

Kubrick would be treated as a European auteur who just happened to have a Bronx accent, even if at times he might go slumming for satiric effect in mainstream Hollywood genres.[5]

He was a premier auteur among film directors.[6]

He is one of the few "auteurs" in contemporary cinema....[7]

Of all American filmmakers, he works in the most non–American fashion.... He is as close to the European standard of the film *auteur*, in complete control of his work, overseeing it from beginning to end.[8]

If evidence of personal involvement and consistency of theme and style over an apparently heterogeneous range of projects distinguishes the true *auteur*, then Kubrick certainly qualifies.[9]

From the very outset Kubrick was Kubrick: an *auteur*.[10]

Perhaps the contradiction here is that Stanley Kubrick, more than any other filmmaker of his (or any other) generation, could fairly be described as an *auteur*. In 1958, Kubrick had told journalist Jay Varela: "Writer, director and editor: you should try to be one solid entity just like the art you are creating is an individual entity."[11] In a similar vein, in 1960 Kubrick told Eugene Archer: "The director is [the] only one who can authentically impose his personality onto a picture, and the result is his responsibility — partly because he's the only one who's always there."[12] And finally, Kubrick talking to Terry Southern:

> I feel that the director, or the filmmaker as I prefer to think of him, is wholly responsible for the film in its completed form. Making a film starts with the germ of an idea, continues through script, rehearsal, shooting, cutting, music projection, and tax accountants. The old-fashioned major-studio concept of a director made him just another color in the producer's palette.... Formerly it was the producer who ... blended the "masterpiece," I don't think it so surprising that it should now fall to the director.[13]

In a sense, the question comes down to the way in which films are discussed within a general discourse. One might note that the majority of Kubrick's films are adjoined to Stanley Kubrick; when we speak, for example, of *2001: A Space Odyssey,* we generally speak of "Stanley Kubrick's *2001.*" In much the same way we may likely speak of Orson Welles's *Citizen Kane* or Alfred Hitchcock's *Vertigo,* but are we so aware, for example, of Michael Curtiz's linkage to *Casablanca,* or Victor Fleming's to *The Wizard of Oz*?[14] Nonetheless, whether Kubrick, Welles and Hitchcock actually were authors of their films remains another question entirely.

In terms of Kubrick, on the one hand it might be noted how he routinely relied on existing primary narratives for most of his films, ten of his 13 films being based on previously published novels. Also, Kubrick often worked with co-writers on his adaptations; the list here is a long one, but one might ask how much contribution might be offered to Terry Southern in terms of *Dr.*

Strangelove, to Arthur C. Clarke with *2001: A Space Odyssey*, to Michael Herr and Gustav Hasford with *Full Metal Jacket* and so on. To consider a specific film: *The Shining*, based on the novel by Stephen King, with the screenplay co-written with Diane Johnson. King created the main characters, the setting and a semblance of the plot; Johnson contributed a significant proportion of the dialogue. In addition, Jack Nicholson and the other actors provided specific material to the development of the screenplay.[15] Similarly, Wendy Carlos and Rachel Elkind were largely responsible for the assemblage of the soundtrack. John Alcott's photography was a significant element, as was Garrett Brown's operation (not to mention its initial development) of the Steadicam camera. One might also think of Greg MacGillivray's aerial photography in the film's opening,[16] Ray Lovejoy and Gordon Stainforth's contribution to the editing, all the way down to Douglas Milsome's contribution as focus-puller.

On the other hand, it might be noted that, in all of his films, almost every artistic decision was either made by Kubrick or had a significant contribution by him. He influenced all creative and all non-creative aspects of the work: the initial financing, the casting, the scripting process, the design of the sets, the camera angles and movement,[17] the editing, the use of music, together with a diverse number of other aspects involved in the making of a film. In Jack Nicholson's words: "Kubrick is, let's face it, The Man. He is the one director working who commands absolute authority over his project from conception to release print."[18]

It might be observed, in drawing toward a summation on the issue of *auteur* theory, that film is a wholly collaborative venture; that the making of a film is a co-operative effort often containing the combined work of tens or hundreds or even thousands of individuals. To return to *The Shining*; it is said it cost Stephen King $24 to write the book — the cost of paper, typewriter ribbons and postage; while it cost Stanley Kubrick $19 million to make the film, with all the myriad collaborators and technologies at his disposal. Thus the central question is, perhaps, whether the overseer of the complex methods of making a film is as much a creative artist as an author who sits down at a table with a pen and paper. This exchange between Kubrick and Frederic Raphael sums up the point:

S.K.   You don't think directors are artists, that's what you're saying?

F.R.   I don't know. And it doesn't matter.

S.K.   You mean it does, and we're not.

F.R.   I just know that before even you can be the kind of artist you are you need actors and sets and lights and cameramen and tons of money and all kinds of stuff and all I need to be an artist ... is a pencil and a piece of paper.[19]

However, one might argue that there is still a sense in which we can envisage one mind making the creative decisions, no matter how complex and numerous they may be. Mario Falsetto:

When I say Kubrick is the author of his films, I am speaking primarily of the creative decisions and logistical organization involved in their making. I am not claiming that Kubrick is the only creative artist with significant input into the final film. I am arguing instead that Kubrick's overall contribution is the most significant and that his creative input essentially guides the other contributors. This is how I have always understood the idea of a film auteur.[20]

To return to a theoretical model; as previously alluded, in 1968 Roland Barthes had argued (many would say convincingly) that it is language that speaks not the author, and that "a text's unity lies not in its origin but in its destination."[21] The weight of Barthes's argument might thus be seen as dismantling much of the basis of *auteur* theory, albeit in a wider sense to that of cinema. This might be argued insomuch as "Death of the Author" was much more sophisticated than a mere simplistic dismissal of biographical intent. At its most radical it called into question the way we view not only authors but also so-called "individuals." It spoke of a fundamental questioning of the notion of personality, of the self. In what sense can an author, or indeed anyone, be said to be an autonomous, coherent individual? On a slightly less esoteric level, Barthes's ideas pointed to a consideration of the moment when an author sits down to create a literary text. One might note that she or he has only a minimal awareness of what they are, in fact, about to write about. Barthes argued that the author was only "minimally aware" of all the myriad complexities of conscious and unconscious thoughts at work in their minds, as they submitted words to paper. Hence in any text, there is no sacred meaning, rather it will be the Barthesian reader who will create a myriad of potential meanings, a text having as many interpretations as there are readers to read it. Thus each time we read a novel, or view a film, so Barthes argued, we are changed in a small way — our way of thinking being either challenged or reinforced. Barthes would appear to argue that meaning is, in fact, recreated anew in every encounter between a reader and a text. Thus intertextuality would seem to be all embracing, as Barthes says of the author: "His only power is to mix writings, to counter the ones with the others."[22] The text thus has no authorial "authority" — there is nothing to constrain a reader constructing any meaning she or he wishes. The author is simply one voice and there is no reason why hers or his is any more relevant. The author is no longer considered as central to a text's production, the sole arbiter of meaning — the author is no longer thought of as the originator or creator — rather as a synthesizer, someone who draws together and orchestrates raw linguistic materials into a "mosaic of quotations."[23] Finally, Barthes's argument seemed to suggest meaning is endlessly deferred — that a text is merely a tissue of signs whose ultimate meaning is forever unattainable; as Barthes concluded: "The birth of the reader must be at the cost of the death of the author."[24]

Unmade Projects

Kubrick, like most filmmakers, had a large and diverse number of unrealized film projects, some more significant than others, some better known than others. The following list aims to depict the main examples; some specific dates and some precise details are open to speculation.

- *Along Came a Spider* (1953) — an early project that was apparently rejected by the Production Code Administration because of the script's treatment of rape, violence and explicit sexual content — perhaps demonstrating, at the very start of Kubrick's career, some of the provocative preoccupations that would follow.[1]

- *The Snatchers* (1955) — another early unused project, based on a then unpublished novel by Lionel White that would later be filmed, in 1968, as *The Night of the Following Day,* directed by Hubert Cornfield and starring Marlon Brando.

- *Lunatic at Large* (1955) — a screenplay by Jim Thompson concerning an American soldier (or former carnival worker — depending on the documentary source) and a woman with "psychopathic" tendencies. This may ultimately have been the basis of Thompson's novel, *The Getaway,* which would later be filmed twice by Hollywood: by Sam Peckinpah in 1972 and by Roger Donaldson in 1993. The lost manuscript of the film was rediscovered in 2007, by Philip Hobbs, Kubrick's son-in-law; it was reported that a film would be directed by Chris Palmer with Colin Farrell in the lead role.

- *So Help Me God* (1955) — a film based on Felix Jackson's novel concerning the anti–Communist witch hunts in post-war American society, few other details are known.

- *Moseby's Rangers* aka *The 7th Cavalry Raider* aka *The Down Slope* (1956) — a script by Kubrick in collaboration with Civil War historian Shelby Foote; it was set at the end of the American Civil War and based on the experiences of Confederate officer John Singleton-Mosby. In a letter, dated June 30, 1956, Foote had written to his lifelong friend, the writer Walker Percy: "Finished the filmscript this week and am going home tomorrow.... It has the makings of a movie ... a true picture of war in its last stages.... Stanley Kubrick is the director; the only authentic genius to hit Hollywood since Orson Welles, they say. I believe it. He'll do a good job if anyone will."[2] In retrospect this project may come to be regarded as one of the most significant lost opportunities, one of the great lost Kubrick films. Shelby Foote might have proven to be one of Kubrick's most successful collaborators; his knowledge of the Civil War (later to be acknowledged via his contributions to Ken Burns's seminal television documentary, *The American Civil War* [1990]) may arguably have accorded Kubrick a war film equal to *Paths of Glory*.[3]

- *The Burning Secret* (1957) — Kubrick's planned adaptation of Stefan Zweig's novella is well known and documented. The screenplay, written by Kubrick and Calder Willingham, seems to have been seriously considered as a viable project. The film would eventually be made, by former Kubrick associate Andrew Birkin, in 1988. The plot concerned: "an Oedipal story about a boy who tries to protect his mother when his father discovers she has been having an affair,"[4] had obvious overtones pertaining to Freudian connotations surrounding the issue of the only child, as discussed — a ubiquitous facet of Kubrick's work.

- *The Last Parallel: A Marine's War Journal* (1957) — Kubrick and James Harris apparently took out an option on Martin Russ's book on the Korean war, what stage of development the project reached is uncertain.

- *I Stole 16 Million Dollars* aka *The Theft* aka *God Fearing Man* (n.d., probably late 1950s) — a script by Lionel White, based on the life of safecracker, Herbert Emerson Wilson — the true story of a priest who became one of the biggest bank robbers in America.

- *The German Lieutenant* (1958) — it is said Kubrick considered following up *Paths of Glory* with another war film, this being based on a screenplay Kubrick and Richard Adams (a former paratrooper in the Korean War) had written, which apparently reached something close to a completed stage of development. The film was set in World War II and was concerned with the experiences of the eponymous Lieutenant Paul Dietrich, during the last days of the war.

- *Natural Child* (n.d., probably late 1950s) — Kubrick apparently considered an option on Calder Willingham's 1952 novel, set in Manhattan, dealing with issues of "abortion and illicit sex."[5]

- *One-Eyed Jacks* (1960) — as is well known, Kubrick spent a considerable amount of time in 1958 developing this film with Marlon Brando. It would have been a Kubrickian venture into one of the few significant cinematic genres Kubrick did not explore: the Western. However, Brando went on to direct the film himself.

- *Henderson the Rain King* (n.d., 1961?) — it is said Kubrick and James Harris may have been interested in adapting Saul Bellow's novel of 1959.

- *The Passion Flower Hotel* (n.d., probably mid–1960s) — it is claimed that James Harris and Kubrick talked of collaborating once again, on a project with a mutual attraction, this being *The Passion Flower Hotel*, a somewhat prosaic story about a group of girls in a boarding school who sell their "services" to a nearby boys' school. The novel by Rosalind Erskine had been published in 1962 and was eventually filmed in 1978, by André Farwagi, starring Natassia Kinski.

- *Napoleon* (1970)—Kubrick's most famous unrealized project—see Appendix 5 for further details.

- *Blue Movie* (1970)—it appears Terry Southern's intent in this project was to present an alternate universe in which a 34-year-old Stanley Kubrick (the protagonist in the narrative, Boris Adrian, being an obvious cipher for Kubrick) makes the first "big-budget pornographic flick." Not unsurprisingly Kubrick declined the offer to make the film; nonetheless, Southern published the idea as a novel (in 1970) dedicating it to "the great Stanley K." Subsequently, elements of the film would eventually end up as part of Blake Edwards's 1981 film: *S.O.B.*, starring Julie Andrews in one of her least typecast roles. In addition, there would also be obvious (albeit wholly independent) coincidental resonances within *Eyes Wide Shut*.

- *Inside the Third Reich* (1972)—Andrew Birkin had been commissioned (by film producer David Putnam) to write a screenplay, based on Albert Speer's then-recently published memoirs. Birkin approached Kubrick with a view of him making it into a film, but Kubrick, after some thought, eventually turned down the project. As yet the film has not been made.[6]

- *The Queen's Gambit* (n.d., mid–1980s?)—a perhaps wholly apocryphal but nonetheless plausible rumor—it is said that Kubrick briefly considered making a film of Walter Tevis's 1983 novel about an orphan who grows up to be a chess champion. Tevis's work had often been filmed: *The Hustler, The Man Who Fell to Earth, The Color of Money*; this more obscure novel would have offered Kubrick a narrative that enveloped both the ubiquitous theme of the only child and also one of his great obsessions: the game of chess. Tevis's early death, in 1984, may have been one potential reason for the curtailment of this project.

- *The Saga of Eric Brighteyes* (n.d., 1980s?)—Anthony Frewin has suggested Kubrick was interested in adapting Sir Henry Rider Haggard's 1891 novel as a film. According to Frewin: "The book haunted SK. And it is a haunting story."[7] However, whether Kubrick had any serious intention of actually adapting the novel to the screen is open to question.

- *All the King's Men* (n.d., late 1980s)—according to Jan Harlan, Kubrick came close to making a film based on Robert Marshall's book, an account of intrigue within the British Intelligence Services. It might have provided Kubrick with another cinematic genre to explore, but it is uncertain what degree of development the project actually achieved.

- *Perfume* (n.d., late 1980s/early 1990s)—it is said that sometime in either the late–1980s or the early–1990s Kubrick had expressed an interest in adapting Patrick Süskind's celebrated novel *Perfume*. However, the veracity of this claim has remained uncertain and it is unclear how much development, if any, was carried out on the book; according to Michel Ciment the project was soon abandoned.[8] However, once again Andrew Birkin appears to have picked up an unused Kubrick project. Birkin would go on to write a screenplay of the novel, which would eventually result in Tom Twyker's film of

2007.[9] (One might note that the protagonist of the novel and film, Grenouille, he of the highly developed sense of smell, was an abandoned and hence an only child.)

- *Shadow on the Sun* (n.d., early–1990s)—this was a BBC radio drama Kubrick had apparently heard in the 1960s—reportedly Kubrick considered using it as potential source material in the early 1990s, no further details are known.
- *Aryan Papers* (1993)—as is well known, Kubrick seriously considered adapting Louis Begley's novel *Wartime Lies,* a novel with the Holocaust as its overt theme and setting. The novel also had personal resonances with Kubrick, as it appears to have been located in parts of Poland, wherein members of Kubrick's family had previously lived. A completed screenplay,[10] casting[11] and significant levels of pre-production work had been carried out: it seems Kubrick was almost ready to begin shooting; the filming was planned to shoot from February 7 to July 5, 1994,[12] and to be filmed—mostly—within the Czech Republic. However, in November 1993 Kubrick and Terry Semel agreed that the production of *Aryan Papers* should be discontinued and work was abandoned in favor of *Eyes Wide Shut.* The usually quoted reason given is that *Aryan Papers* would have come out, most probably at least a year after *Schindler's List*—however, one wonders if this would have had such a significant effect—and that Kubrick simply did not have the faculties to approach the Holocaust "head on." It is also possible that Kubrick came to believe the Holocaust was, in itself, beyond the bounds of narrative. A sense of this can be seen in Alan Clarke's 1989 television drama about sectarian killing in Northern Ireland: *Elephant,* a play Kubrick may possibly have been familiar with, insomuch as it used Steadicam to such telling effect. Clarke's play, without dialogue to speak of, was essentially the bleak repetition of 18 murders, framed without narrative coherence, portrayed without the slightest sense of compassion, one death after another, after another, after another—18 times. A gunman gets out of a car, he walks into a factory/shop/home, shoots his victim and leaves—leaving us, the viewer, looking at the dead body for an uncomfortable period of time. Form here becoming content, the meaningless random nature of events in the minimalist and repetitive narrative—pointing ultimately towards a metaphor for the pointless nature of sectarian killing. One could argue that the Holocaust was similar to these events, in the sense of meaningless murder being committed over and over again, albeit on a still larger canvas. Clarke's play seemed to tell us that there were events beyond narrative—perhaps suggesting to Kubrick there was no sense in which the Holocaust could be translated into a viable narrative structure. (Finally, one might note that Maciek, the young boy who, with his "beautiful" Aunt Tania, is the main protagonist—was another orphaned child—another only child.)
- *A.I.* (2001)—possibly Kubrick's second most famous unrealized project. As is well known the film was subsequently made by Steven Spielberg. See Afterword for fuller details.

APPENDIX 13

Remakes and Reworkings

When a filmmaker creates an original cinematic text he or she has little control in the way this cultural production might be reworked within the culture at large. Stanley Kubrick has thus far been relatively fortunate in this respect. While a number of his films have been subjected to reworkings of various kinds, the main body of his work has remained "sacrosanct." Kubrick's films have retained their own individual integrity and have not been supplanted or superseded by subsequent remakes. However, the following notes attempt to detail the ways in which a number of Kubrick's films have been "reworked," within a diverse category of cultural arenas.

- *Killer's Kiss* (1955) — was deliberately echoed in Michael Chapman's 1983 film, *Stranger's Kiss*, which has been described as an ingenious reworking of Kubrick's film: "A speculative 'history' of the circumstances surrounding the making of [Kubrick's second feature film]."[1]
- *The Killing* (1956) — Quentin Tarantino's 1991 *Reservoir Dogs* has generally been seen as a thinly veiled homage to Kubrick's film; Tarantino himself admitting: "While I was making the movie [*Reservoir Dogs*], I was kinda like sorta saying, 'This is gonna be my *The Killing*.'"[2] In addition, a remake of *The Killing* was announced by Warner Bros., in 1999, with Mel Gibson cast in the role of Johnny Clay — the Sterling Hayden character. To date this project has not materialized.
- *Spartacus* (1960) — was remade in 2004 under the same title, directed by Robert Dornhelm, with a screenplay by Robert Schenkkan — again based on Howard Fast's novel. However, the film was not of any great artistic quality. Of more interest was Ridley Scott's *Gladiator* (2000), Scott being on record as admitting *Spartacus* was one of the main reasons for — and one of the greatest influences on — his making of the film.
- *Lolita* (1962) — was remade by Adrian Lyne in 1997. Lyne's film was both more explicit and more faithful to Nabokov's novel, although neither of which was necessarily advantageous. Thus while Lyne's film was of interest,

247

Kubrick's earlier adaptation would appear to remain the more authentic and authoritative rendition.

- *Dr. Strangelove* (1964) — has yet to be remade; however, Stephen Frears's 2000 remake of Sidney Lumet's *Fail-Safe* (1964) was not without interest; an authentic reworking of Lumet's original — perhaps reminding the viewer of how far Kubrick's film satirically enhanced an almost identical narrative.

- *2001: A Space Odyssey* (1968) — was succeeded, in 1984, by Peter Hyams's *2010: The Year We Make Contact*, a workmanlike sequel that faithfully followed Arthur C. Clarke's second novel in the series, Clarke would go on to write two further sequels: *2061: Odyssey Three* (in 1987) and *3001: The Final Odyssey* (in 1997), each of which is, as yet, awaiting adaptation to film.

- *A Clockwork Orange* (1971) — several earlier adaptations of Burgess's novel had been made before Kubrick's film. For example, it is known that Andy Warhol had produced his own adaptation: *A Clockwork Orange, Vinyl*, in 1965; while the BBC had made a partial television adaptation sometime in the early 1960s. In addition, in 1990 a stage performance of the novel: *A Clockwork Orange — 2004*, was presented at the Barbican in London, with music by U2 and starring the actor Phil Daniels as Alex.

- *The Shining* (1980) — was remade in 1997, a 260-minute television miniseries directed by Mick Garris. It was faithful (perhaps overly faithful) to Stephen King's novel, and was apparently based upon King's original script, the script unused and perhaps even unread by Kubrick in the late 1970s.

- *Eyes Wide Shut* (1999) — it is a little known fact that Arthur Schnitzler's novel had previously been adapted for the screen, albeit the smaller screen, an Austrian television version of *Traumnovelle* had been produced in 1969, directed by Wolfgang Glück, in color, with a running time of 75 minutes. (See page 139 for further production details.)

Published Screenplays

In terms of studying Kubrick's work, access to the screenplays of his films is obviously a useful device. However, of the 13 films only four screenplays have officially been published. These are as follows:

- *Eyes Wide Shut*, published in 1999, as a "tie-in" with Schnitzler's *Dream Story.*
- *Full Metal Jacket*, published in 1987, as a glossy, large-format edition, with numerous color stills from the film and a foreword by Michael Herr.
- *A Clockwork Orange*, published in 1972, in what Kubrick himself described as "a complete, graphic representation of the film, cut by cut, with the dialogue printed in the proper place." However, the book had no pagination, even though it was an estimated 360 pages in length; hence causing a certain amount of difficulty in its use as a scholarly and referenced text.
- *Lolita*, published in 1974; this was not to be in any way identified with the screenplay of the 1962 film; it was Nabokov's version of the screenplay as submitted to Kubrick and Harris, in 1960, before shooting of the film, a version that would go, for the most part, almost entirely unused.

In addition to this, significant elements of the script of *2001: A Space Odyssey* were included in Jerome Agel's 1970 book, *The Making of 2001.* Also, Peter George's 1963 novelization of *Dr. Strangelove* used large portions of the dialogue from the film's screenplay. These aside, no other screenplays are officially available in published form; however, other screenplays are obtainable via the Internet. These include entire shooting scripts of *2001: A Space Odyssey* and *The Shining,* and also earlier draft versions of both *Full Metal Jacket* and *Eyes Wide Shut.* These online screenplays at least appear to be authentic, although their actual provenance must, of necessity, remain uncertain. What is of most interest is the case of *Barry Lyndon,* in what was perhaps Kubrick's most literate screenplay. It appears that there was a specific reluctance to provide any sense of a published script, perhaps with the assumption that a publication of the screenplay would, in some sense, lessen the visual impact of the film. Finally, as to Kubrick's other, earlier films, from *Fear and Desire* to *Spartacus*, as far as research can ascertain, none of these screenplays are available in any format.

APPENDIX 15

Academy Awards

The fact that Stanley Kubrick did not win a major Academy Award, that he did not win, for example, the Oscar for Best Director or for Best Film, seems, on the surface, an anomaly. In the middle section of his career, from *Spartacus* in 1960 to *Barry Lyndon* in 1975, Kubrick's films were regularly nominated and Kubrick himself was nominated for Best Director on no less than four occasions. However, for reasons that remain unexplained and perhaps even inexplicable, Kubrick's final three films (*The Shining, Full Metal Jacket* and *Eyes Wide Shut*) received only one nomination between them.[1]

If one were to take a cynical stance, to argue that the Oscars have always been about commerce and internal Hollywood politics rather than artistic and creative excellence, then this might go some way into explaining this apparent anomaly. As critic Ted Mahar commented:

> Academy Awards are gross travesties. They are blatantly commercial awards given to con yokels into believing that some kind of final word has been delivered on the relative quality of a movie.... They defy artistic expression and reflect the waning dinosaur groans of a movie generation sinking into senility and richly deserved oblivion.[2]

Thus Kubrick's exclusion from the Academy perhaps speaks more of the disparity between aesthetics and commerce, than the quality of his films. As Michel Ciment noted:

> The reaction of the Hollywood community at Oscar time perfectly illustrates the ambivalence of Kubrick's status. Because of his ambition and commercial success they are obliged to recognize him, but his refusal to become one of the "family" and the distance which he maintains from Hollywood have wrecked his chances of being honored.[3]

In a still more pertinent sense Ciment went on to note that Kubrick shares with Charlie Chaplin, Josef von Sternberg, Orson Welles and Robert Altman (rebels, all of them!) but also with Fritz Lang, Alfred Hitchcock, Howard Hawks and Ernst Lubitsch, the unique distinction of never once having received an Academy Award for Best Direction."[4]

In this sense, one might ask whether Kubrick was in better company outside of the Academy than within it. Frederic Raphael once raised the question: "Does he [Kubrick] care that the best director has never been Best Director?"[5] Kubrick's response is not known; he rarely commented on the subject of Academy Awards in any context. However, we might assume that, in an overall sense, given the astute film business brain he possessed, Kubrick fully understood why he did not accord with the Academy and hence why he and his films did not attain the accolades they deserved.

A Kubrick Miscellany

In the course of the research for this book, a diverse range of minutiae —
a wide compass of seemingly trivial information pertaining to Kubrick and his
work — has been unearthed. While such information would not appear to have
been directly applicable to the primary discourse of the book; it would seem
nonetheless eligible of at least some sort of inclusion — presented here within a
randomly noted and appendicized context.

Early Years Kubrick's parents: Jacob Kubrick and Gertrude Perveler, were married on October 30, 1927; Stanley Kubrick was born on July 26, 1928. Hence there was a period of exactly nine calendar months between Kubrick's conception (perhaps on his parents' wedding night) and his birth. This information is arguably reductive and indeed meaningless; however, it echoes similar numerological patterns that have been perceived in relation to Kubrick's life and work. For example, it echoes some of the material at the end of this appendix — and also in some of the wider criticism of Kubrick's work. See the chapters on *Lolita* and *The Shining* as particularly pertinent examples.

Fear and Desire *Fear and Desire* was provisionally entitled: *The Trap* and then *Shape of Fear.*

Killer's Kiss The original title for *Killer's Kiss* was *Kiss Me, Kill Me*, an earlier title having been *The Nymph and the Maniac.*

The Killing *The Killing* had several working titles: *Day of Violence, Bed of Fear* and *Sudden Death.* Andre Previn was the pianist on the soundtrack of *The Killing. The Killing* was filmed within a schedule of just 24 days, making it the quickest-ever Kubrick shoot. The famous quotation from *The Killing*, in which the character of Maurice (Kola Kwariana) compares gangsters to artists, routinely attributed to Kubrick in books of quotations, was apparently all Jim Thompson's work and had no contribution from Kubrick at all.[1] Lionel White, author of the novel *Clean Break*, the source narrative for *The Killing*, included an "in-joke" in his novel of 1960, *Steal Big*. In White's novel something called the "Kubric Novelty Company" turned out to be a front for a gang of black-market arms dealers. Whether this was an ironic comment on White's experience with the adaptation of *The Killing* is open to question.

Paths of Glory At the end of *Paths of Glory*, as is well known, Christiane Kubrick (then Christiane Harlan) provided a kind of redemptive epilogue by singing "Der treue Husa" ("The Faithful Hussar"). One might speculate what changes to Kubrick's career might have occurred had he not met and married Christiane. They were both of the same pre–World War II generation: Kubrick (July 28, 1928) a Jewish American, born in New York, with an intense preoccupation with the Nazis and the Holocaust; Christiane (May 10, 1932) a German national, born in Braunschweig, growing up at the height of Nazi Germany. Vincent LoBrutto: "Like so many German children, Christiane was forced to be part of the Nazi youth movement.... 'I remember we had lovely uniforms ... but all this Heil Hitler thing was really tongue in cheek.'"[2] In the hope of not intruding upon a private relationship, one presumes there may have been certain silences in such a long-term marriage. But one wonders, had Kubrick not married Christiane, would his work have been less veiled in terms of what he no doubt saw as the 20th century's most significant event: the Holocaust?

Spartacus In the titles sequence, at the start of *Spartacus*, when Kubrick's name appears on the screen, the statue of a classical face cracks and breaks. Saul Bass was responsible for the titles of the film — whether there was some collusion here to offer a symbolic metaphor is open to speculation.[3] In *Spartacus*, for some of the sound effects, Kubrick recorded 76,000 football fans at Michigan State University, all chanting: "I am Spartacus." In November 1960, the newly elected President Kennedy deliberately crossed the picket lines to attend a screening of *Spartacus*, in Washington, D.C. Kirk Douglas's distinctive hairstyle for his role in *Spartacus* was created by Jay Sebring; Sebring would be murdered a decade later — in August 1969 — along with Sharon Tate and others, by the Charles Manson family.

Lolita The last book Adolph Eichmann read, while in custody in Israel awaiting his execution on May 31, 1962, was *Lolita*. Eichmann left it unfinished, declaring: *"Das ist aber ein sehr unerfreuliches Buch."* ("This is quite an unwholesome book.")[4]

As to the inspiration for the coinage of the name, Lolita, Nabokov always denied any connection between his choice of name and the fact that Charlie Chaplin's second wife, Lillita McMurray, was only 16 when she married Chaplin. However, Kubrick may have been aware of this, insomuch as the scene of Humbert attempting to put up the cot with the black bellhop, in the hotel room at the Enchanted Hunters, seemed to have clearly intentional Chaplinesque overtones.

It has been suggested that Nabokov may, in some subsidiary way, have based the novel on the case of Sally Horner. In 1948, around the time the novel was notionally set, Florence Sally Horner, a girl of 12 from New Jersey, was abducted by Frank La Salle, an automobile mechanic, and then spent 21 months living and traveling with her abductor before she managed her escape. La Salle was subsequently jailed for 35 years for kidnapping, while Horner herself died in an automobile accident in 1952, the same year in which the fictional Lolita dies.[5]

In terms of casting, it is said that Kubrick had originally wanted Joey Heatherton for the title role of Lolita, but Heatherton's father, Ray Heatherton, declined for fear his daughter would be typecast as a "promiscuous sex kitten." As is well known, Tuesday Weld was briefly considered for the role, but was assessed as being too old. It seems Sue Lyon was chosen for the title role partly due to the size of her breasts. Kubrick had been warned that censors felt strongly about the use of a less-developed actress to portray "the sexually active nymphet;" Lyon apparently being sufficiently developed to fulfill these strictures.

Bob Harris, James Harris's brother, composed the so-called "Lolita" theme, a significant part of the film's soundtrack. Kubrick and Harris went so far as to commission the celebrated songwriter, Sammy Cahn, to write what were "perhaps wisely omitted, verses."[6]

Dr. Strangelove The opening titles of *Dr. Strangelove* contained a misprint: instead of "Based on the Book" the credits read: "Base on the Book." In the light of the controversy over the authorship of the screenplay (between Kubrick, Southern and George) one might speculate whether this was something of a Freudian or perhaps deliberate slip on the part of Kubrick and titles designer, Pablo Ferro.[7]

Two Kubrickian actors would make up the character of Darth Vader in the *Star Wars* films: James Earl Jones, Lothar Zogg here in *Dr. Strangelove*, would provide the voice, while David Prowse, Mr. Alexander's "companion" in *A Clockwork Orange*, would provide the body.

Werner von Braun has often been cited as a possible model for Dr. Strangelove, in a satiric context Kubrick may have been aware of Mort Sahl's joke about Von Braun: in 1959 a film had been made about Von Braun's life, the title had been: *I Aim at the Stars*, to which Sahl added the subtitle: "But sometimes I hit London."[8]

Dr. Strangelove may have suffered from agonistic apraxia, also known as alien hand syndrome. This being a neurological affliction caused by a stroke or other brain injury that causes damage to the nerve fibers that connect the two hemispheres of the brain, often resulting in the arms of the individual behaving as if outside of their control.

The *Playboy* magazine that Major Kong (Slim Pickens) is reading in the film has been identified as the June 1962 issue, hence something of a collector's piece. In addition, it has been noted[9] that Henry Kissinger (then Henry A. Kissinger) had published an article ("Strains on the Alliance") in the January 1963 edition of *Foreign Affairs*, the particular edition Kubrick chose to "palimsestically" drape Tracy Reed, Miss Foreign Affairs. This may have been a coincidence, but perhaps more likely it was a conscious reference by Kubrick.

General Ripper's paranoia about water fluoridation may have been based on a conspiracy theory held by the John Birch Society — a far right-wing organization, founded in 1958, that was prominent in conservative politics, for a short time, in the early 1960s.

In contrast to what was to come in the case of special effects in *2001: A Space Odyssey*, the cost of the B52 models of "Leper Colony" — large and small — was only £750.[10]

In the unused custard pie sequence, it is reported Peter Sellers was hit by 89 pies, while George C. Scott was struck a mere 63 times.[11]

The code, CRM 114, would become a running joke, both inside and outside of Kubrick's work.[12] According to Vincent LoBrutto, CRM stood for "critical rehearsal moment,"[13] while Alexander Walker described it as Kubrick allowing himself "a private joke."[14] In fact CRM 114 may have derived from a factual source. According to Ken Adam, the B52 bombers had a "CRN115 secret box."[15]

2001: A Space Odyssey Some of the Star Gate sequences were the first images of the film to be shot, these being accomplished in New York, before shooting of the film moved to England. In the novel Clarke had placed the Star Gate in orbit around Saturn rather than Jupiter, as in the film. Apparently the special effects team was unable to achieve a believable version of the rings of Saturn. This was something of a loss to Clarke, as in the novel he had been able to suggest that the rings of Saturn — which he dated, coincidentally, as being three million years old — and, hence, presumably caused by the monolith builders in their construction of the Star Gate.

As to overall authorship of the film, Arthur C. Clarke, in a posture of unusual modesty, commented that it broke down as follows: "Ninety percent Kubrick, five percent special effects crew, five percent Clarke."[16]

Gary Lockwood would appear in another iconic science fiction production of the 1960s, *Star Trek*. However, the *Star Trek* connection does not stop here. Gerard Fried, composer for several of Kubrick's early films, would later go on to write incidental music for several episodes of *Star Trek*. Also, Alexander Singer, one of Kubrick's early compatriots and collaborators, would go on to direct a number of episodes of *Star Trek: The Next Generation.*

The chess game played in the film was a real one: "Played by two undistinguished players (Roesch-Schlage) in Hamburg in 1913."[17]

As is well known, Malcolm McDowell received a specific injury to his eyes during the making of *A Clockwork Orange*. However, Keir Dullea also risked potential eye trauma during the filming of *2001*, in the scene of the extreme close-ups of Bowman's eyes during the Star Gate sequence. Dullea: "That was a little scary, because I didn't know if I was going to get blinded or not. They used an arc light and it was close to me. I mean nobody ever gets that close to an arc. There are things that I would never do for anybody else that I would do for Stanley."[18] Dullea also did his own stunt in his explosive re-entry into the *Discovery*; uncharacteristically for Kubrick the scene took only one take.

The stewardesses' "hats" in the film, resembling futuristic bathing caps, seemed somewhat superfluous—if one were cynical, one might comment this was more a way of avoiding the long hair underneath behaving in a way not quite appropriate to zero gravity.

2001: A Space Odyssey was relaunched at the beginning of 2001, the European premiere taking place at the Vatican in Pope John Paul II's own cinema. The invited audience included Kubrick's widow, Christiane, and her daughter, Anya Kubrick.

It is perhaps interesting to note that Arthur C. Clarke's follow-up novel to *2001: A Space Odyssey* — *Rendezvous with Rama* (1972), began on the morning of "11th September in the exceptionally beautiful summer of 2077" when a "dazzling fireball" hits the Earth in the guise of a meteorite. The precise date would later interest conspiracy theorists, especially as Clarke was even close with the time the meteorite hits—09.46—just one hour from the time the first plane hit the South Tower.[19] It has been suggested that Osama Bin Laden, a keen science fiction fan in his youth, had taken the name of *al-Qaeda* from the *Foundation* novels of Isaac Asimov, one of Clarke's direct contemporaries. As to whether Bin Laden chose the date of his most infamous attack on the West from another fictional source is even more speculative, but perhaps one not entirely absent of some potential interest.

Leonard F. Wheat's book, *Kubrick's 2001: A Triple Allegory*, must be seen as one of the most entertaining yet published on the film. The book made a number of extravagant interpretations, putting forward a somewhat eccentric and, at times, tenuous argument that the film was, in fact, constructed around a number of deliberately contrived messages that related to Homer's *Odyssey* and Nietzsche's *Thus Spake Zarathustra*. Wheat continually perceived of hidden messages planted in the film. For example, TMA1, or TMA ONE, supposedly related anagrammatically to NO MEAT. However, this and other anagrams, no matter how ingenious and engaging, would appear to have been wholly coincidental and to have had no significance outside of Wheat's imagination. The book would appear to have been published without the work of an editor, thus a potential anagram of Leonard F. Wheat's own name: ED., ANOTHER FLAW, would seem as valid as any of the other spurious examples found in the book.

Note, that although Kubrick made no Hitchcockian personal appearances in his films, it is documented that the breathing heard in the *Discovery* section of *2001* was Kubrick's own respiration.[20]

In the film Hal talks about human error and how there has never been a computer error. This would become an ironic idea in the actual year of 2001, wherein the phrase "Microsoft Works" was often seen as an oxymoron by modern computer users. In itself the film has a number of "mistakes." For example, there is the famous error of the liquid in Floyd's straw falling back down, in what is supposed to be zero gravity. In addition, there was a lack of moon-like gravity in the conference scene at Clavius. In the same way there was a curious lack of zero gravity in the pod bays on the *Discovery*— one presumes Bowman and Poole may have been wearing the same "grip-shoes" as the stewardess, but they appear to walk in a much more carefree manner. (Later space travel has demonstrated how astronauts maneuver themselves by floating from location, rather than using such artificial gravity devices.) Also, if one looks closely, an ankle zipper was visible on one of the man-apes; and, if one looks closely enough, a cameraman (possibly Kubrick himself) can be seen reflected in one of the astronaut's helmet visors in the TMA1 scene. In addition, the videophone camera apparently tracks Squirt as she squirms about in her seat — the camera would most probably have been static. Finally, the centrifuge, famously built by Kubrick at a cost approaching $1 million (almost a tenth of the film's total budget), this would, in fact, have been too small to work. It was 38 feet in diameter, rotating at three miles an hour, but according to scientific advisor Fred Ordway, it would have needed to have been many times larger or the "Coriolis effect" in the inner ear would have caused uncontrollable nausea in the crew members.

Napoleon Writer Ray Connolly's 1994 novel, *Shadows on a Wall,* is said to have been based on Kubrick's non-making of *Napoleon.*

In the early 1990s a United Artists executive named Jeff Kleeman is said to have found the original manuscript screenplay of *Napoleon*— legend has it — in a salt mine near Hutchinson, Kansas, the reputed home of United Artists archival materials.

The most commonly available Internet version of the screenplay is split into two halves, the first half ending on page 62, with "the final moves" in Napoleon's rise "to supreme power," at St. Cloud on November 10, 1799. It is interesting to speculate that Kubrick might have been better placed to make the film had it been more modest and concerned only with Napoleon's early life. One could go further and speculate how Kubrick could have then made the sequel, perhaps 15 years later, using the same cast who themselves would have aged at an equivalent rate. Thus two *Napoleons*, of more modest length, might have better sufficed Kubrick's ambition, like Napoleon himself, Kubrick may have strategically blundered and overreached himself.

It is interesting to note that some of the most ambitious cinematic projects (other than Kubrick's *Napoleon*) did not come to fruition either. One might think of Erich von Stronheim's *Queen Kelly*, Sergei Einsenstein's *Que Viva Mexico*, Orson Welles's *Don Quixote*, Alfred Hitchcock's *Kaleidoscope*. Hence, Kubrick was not entirely alone in his inability to complete what may have been his masterpiece.

A Clockwork Orange *A Clockwork Orange* was one of only two films given an X-rating in the USA, to be nominated for Best Picture at the Academy Awards— the other being *Midnight Cowboy* (1969).

One of the first violent incidents in *A Clockwork Orange*, the attack on the librarian, as taken from the novel, had already been shot (at a location in Aylesbury); however, the actor involved was not available for the "retribution" scene; hence Kubrick was required to reshoot the scene in the subway, with Paul Farrell as the Irish drunkard.

The two popular music groups— Sparks and Heaven 17 — are said to have derived their names from the record boutique scene in *A Clockwork Orange.*

The shot of the bride falling through the gallows trapdoor (during Alex's masturbatory daydream) was reputedly footage from *Cat Ballou* (1965).

In the scene where the reformed Alex is taken into the woods by his ex-droogs Dim and Georgie, one can see the officer numbers on their uniform lapels: 665 and 667, possibly implying that Alex, in the middle, was number 666, the number of the beast.

A further numerological pattern in the film might be found in Alex's prison denominator, in Julian Rice's words "his appellation becomes a diminishing number, '6554321.'"[21] However, Kubrick had taken the number almost directly from Burgess's novel (it had originally been 6655321), hence undermining any supposed numerological referent.

Steven Berkoff appeared in *A Clockwork Orange* and also in *Barry Lyndon*[22]; however, it appears Kubrick repeatedly had Berkoff in mind for future work. Berkoff auditioned for a part in *The Shining*, he was contacted with an enquiry about his availability for *Aryan Papers*,[23] and was almost cast as Sandor Szavost in *Eyes Wide Shut*.

In *A Clockwork Orange*, Mrs. Alexander (Adrienne Corri) was left wearing only red socks at the close of her scene; there is a story (perhaps apocryphal) that she thereafter sent, every Christmas, a present of a pair of red socks to her ex-director.

According to Malcolm McDowell, the speeded-up sex scene was originally filmed as an unbroken take lasting 28 minutes.

Gillian Hills, one of the actresses who appeared with Alex in the *ménage à trois* scene, had also appeared in another famous *ménage à trois*, in Michelangelo Antonioni's *Blow-up* (1966).

While it is clear that there was some acrimony over Kubrick's cultural appropriation of *A Clockwork Orange*, it is perhaps significant to note that Burgess would dedicate his 1974 novel (his first published novel subsequent to the film) *Napoleon Symphony*, to Kubrick.

Note: Malcolm McDowell incurred minor scratches on his corneas during the filming of the "lid-lock" scene; in addition he also sustained cracked ribs after being stamped on in the Lardface (John Clive) scene, together with a throat infection as a result of the horse trough scene.

Barry Lyndon It seems Kubrick made use of at least two incidents from Thackeray's *Vanity Fair:* the reading of Sir Charles Lyndon's obituary and Lord Wendover's speech about his friends—during the writing of his screenplay of *Barry Lyndon*.[24]

Barry Lyndon is said to have featured the biggest lens aperture in film history—f 0,7.

The actor Brian Blessed was cast in *Barry Lyndon*, but his part was apparently cut from the final print.

The film featured Golden Labradors, one of Kubrick's favorite breeds; however, it did so somewhat inaccurately as this breed of dog did not appear until the end of the 19th century.

In terms of the film's soundtrack, Mark Crispin Miller claimed: "*Barry Lyndon* may be the most visually beautiful film ever made ... perhaps no selection of musical pieces has ever been so aptly and movingly integrated into the action of any film."[25] Leonard Rosenman, who adapted and conducted the soundtrack, demurred. Rosenman, whose career would cover scores for films as diverse as *Rebel Without a Cause* (1955) and *Robocop II* (1990), was hired to supervise — but not compose — music for the film. Rosenman seems to have found the task beneath him: "When I saw this incredibly boring film with all the music I had picked out going over and over again, I thought, 'My God, what a mess!' I was going to refuse the Oscar."[26] Rosenman's dissatisfaction recalls Kubrick's relationship with other conventional film composers, such as Alex North. It appears Kubrick required help with the technical issues of arranging certain elements of his chosen pieces, but had no need for a conventional film composer, perhaps explaining Rosenman's dissatisfaction.

The Shining When John Calley sent Kubrick galley proofs of *The Shining*, in 1977, before publication, it was entitled *The Shine*. It has been suggested that it was Kubrick's idea to call it *The Shining*; given Kubrick's penchant for wordplay the available anagram: "Highest Inn," thus may not have been wholly coincidental.

Diane Johnson's only previous experience of screenwriting before her work on *The Shining* had also concerned a hotel, a screenplay for a remake of *Grand Hotel* Johnson had written for Mike Nichols; however, the film has yet to be made.

The helicopter shadow, seen briefly at the start of *The Shining*, may have resulted from video and DVD releases of the film not respecting the original aspect ratio of the theatrical release. (In *Full Metal Jacket*, one notes the obvious and deliberate use of a helicopter shadow, this perhaps being a reference to the "mistake" in *The Shining*.)

One notes that the maze, in the opening establishing shot of the Overlook, was nowhere to be seen. The maze only existed in the mock-up of the Timberline Hotel, constructed on the Elstree set. One presumes Kubrick did not think viewers of the film would have noted this inconsistency; or, if they did, that it simply offered a further edge to an already "edgy" film. There were other perhaps deliberate inconsistencies; for example, the incongruency of the excessive amount of the Torrance's family baggage and the capacity of the Torrance's Volkswagen. In a similar sense, Kubrick would probably have been aware that the song played during the 1921 ballroom scene, "Midnight, the Stars, and You," wasn't recorded until 1932, eleven years after the scene purportedly took place.

It is well known that outtakes from the opening sequence of *The Shining* were used, by Ridley Scott, for the "happy ending" of *Blade Runner*. What is perhaps less well known is that The Beatles used aerial outtakes from *Dr. Strangelove* for their television film of 1967, *Magical Mystery Tour*.

In an earlier version of the screenplay, Jack's "writing project" was entitled: *Tales of a Winter Caretaker*.[27]

The shot of the blood pouring from the elevator was accomplished in just three takes, although each take is said to have taken several days to set up, and apparently the scene's shooting spanned an entire year of filming. The fact that Kubrick expended such time and effort on the scene perhaps supports the argument that this scene retained a key and significant facet to a reading of the film.

Kubrick's first choice to play Danny Torrance is said to have been Cary Guffey, the child-actor from *Close Encounters of the Third Kind* (1977). However, Guffey's parents apparently turned down the offer due to the film's subject matter.

The role of Lloyd is reported to have initially been cast to feature Harry

Dean Stanton; however, he was not available due to his commitments on Ridley Scott's *Alien* (1979), hence, Kubrick brought in the veteran Joe Turkel.

Wendy Carlos and Rachel Elkind wrote and performed a full electronic score for the film, but Kubrick chose to use only a limited selection. Instead he used a soundtrack consisting of mostly existing 20th century music: specifically Penderecki and Ligeti. Only the adaptation of Hector Berlioz's *Symphonie Fantastique* during the opening credits, and a few other brief moments of the Carlos/Elkind score, survived into the final version of the film.

The Shining's subtextual use of television as artifice was of interest. This attended all the way from Jack Nicholson's inspired burlesque on Ed McMahon's introduction of Johnny Carson, to Wendy's predilection for watching television throughout the film, to Jack's sarcastic comment on Danny's knowledge of cannibalism: "He saw it on the television." However, close attention to the use of television reveals a number of significant indicators. For example, in one of the news broadcasts Wendy watches, we hear that a convicted murderer has been given a "life sentence." Thomas Nelson pointed out how this was "an indirect allusion to Jack's subsequent desire to join the Overlook's immortals."[28] All of this relates to the general sense of reality as artifice in the film. "It's just like pictures in a book," Danny thinks, remembering Mr. Halloran's advice, but the line also resonates toward the filmmaking process—the adaptation of a book—King's novel—and making pictures out of it. We might note that the title of the film and book points toward cinema, which is, in itself, a kind of shining—we see the images shine on the screen from the projector. We might also note that spectral images as presented in the film suggest artifice rather than reality. For example, we see the Grady girls frontally as if they were an image; we see the bloodied partygoer and also the blood flowing from the elevator—all seem to be artificial/projected images rather than images of reality.

Jack Nicholson may have worked harder for Kubrick than any other director; however, he was well rewarded—earning "$1.25 million plus a percentage of the gross."[29]

Full Metal Jacket As previously intimated, Kubrick did not make Hitchcockian appearances in his films; however, his voice is reported to have been apparent in a number of instances. Here, in *Full Metal Jacket*, Kubrick is said to have voiced the role of Murphy, in the scenes wherein Cowboy calls base on the "walkie-talkie," during the confrontation with the sniper.[30]

Although the chosen location for *Full Metal Jacket* allowed Kubrick to return home at the end of each day's shooting—it was not without its problems. In a conversation with Frederic Raphael, talking about security problems on the set, Kubrick would comment: "And what happened was, locals came in and vandalized the battlefield."[31] This remark has a self-conscious humor insomuch as vandalizing a battlefield sounds rather like fighting in the War Room in *Dr. Strangelove.*

Vincent D'Onofrio is said to have gained almost 80 pounds for his role as Private Pyle, exceeding Robert De Niro's weight gain — just 60 pounds — for his role in *Raging Bull* (1980). To create a realistic "battlefield" documentary effect during the combat scenes, Douglas Milsome, the lighting cameraman, experimented with a camera with a shutter deliberately put out of synchronization, a similar effect would be used in Steven Spielberg's *Saving Private Ryan* (1998).

To achieve the iconic shots of the recruits having their hair removed, it was found that animal grooming clippers were the best kind of implements to use.

Aryan Papers *Aryan Papers* was based on Louis Begley's novel *Wartime Lies.* As is known, the film was never made; however, another of Begley's novels *was* later successfully adapted to the screen: *About Schmidt* (2002), directed by Alexander Payne, with Jack Nicholson in the title role.

Eyes Wide Shut Billy Wilder, who had been a journalist and crime reporter in Vienna in the 1920s, had wanted to adapt *Dream Story,* but was apparently "unable to crack it."[32]

It has often been claimed that *Eyes Wide Shut* was in production for more time than any other film, that it was "the longest shoot on record for a major studio production, a distinction previously held by *Lawrence of Arabia.*"[33]

Raphael's proposed working titles — *You and Me* and *The Female Subject* — were rejected by Kubrick. *Eyes Wide Shut* was proposed solely by Kubrick; other working titles included: *American Dreams, Dear Ones* and *A Woman Unknown.*[34]

In the Bedroom might have proved a potential alternate title for the film; in 2001, Todd Field, the actor who portrayed Nick Nightingale in *Eyes Wide Shut,* made a film with this title, based on a short story by Andre Dubus. It remains an engrossing cinematic text, a film, on one level at least, that resonated and responded towards Field's work with Kubrick.

Tim Kreider has spoken of "money shots" in *Eyes Wide Shut.* This seems ironical, primarily because of the censorship issues particular to the USA. In this sense, it is interesting to note how European art cinema, just before and then after Kubrick's death, was beginning to move toward a more unambiguous sexual discourse. One might think of the explicit depiction of sex in films such as *The Idiots* (1998), *Romance* (1999), *Intimacy* (2000), *The Piano Teacher* (2000), *Baise Moi* (2004) and *Nine Songs* (2004) — how these films presented the portrayal of actual sex: penile erection, vaginal/anal penetration and so on. This might be seen as European film's response to Hollywood's cultural domination of cinema via special effect spectaculars and blockbusters.

There were rumors (unfounded, as it happens) that Kubrick played a cameo role in the film.[35] However, it might be noted that Kubrick's daughter and grandson do appear in the film; this can be seen in the short scene in Bill's consultation room wherein Bill examines a young boy with a sore throat; the uncredited actor being Alexander Hobbs, Kubrick's grandson, while his mother was played by his actual mother (Kubrick's daughter) Katharina Hobbs. Also, Emilio D'Alessandro, Kubrick's longtime assistant and chauffeur, is said to appear in the film, as the newspaper vendor from whom Bill buys the *New York Post*; likewise, Leon Vitali (Kubrick's personal assistant since the making of *Barry Lyndon*) makes an appearance as Red Cloak.

The line of poetry Helena recites: "Before me when I jump into my bed" was taken from Robert Louis Stevenson's "My Shadow."

There was a significant element of secrecy to the project; this may have been because Schnitzler's novel was out of copyright and, hence, open to adaptation to film by anyone. Michael Herr talking of *Traumnovelle*'s obscurity, commented: "The reason I'd probably never heard of it ... was that he'd bought up every single existing copy of it."[36] However, all of this was somewhat contradicted by a press release, published in *Kine Weekly* (then the most important trade paper of the British film industry) on May 8, 1971,[37] a release that clearly stated Kubrick was planning to adapt the novel. One presumes Kubrick had hoped the passage of time would have cloaked such previous publicity.

The reasons for Harvey Keitel's replacement (he left the film in May 1997 and was replaced in the role of Ziegler by Sydney Pollack) have always been unclear. Keitel has never commented publicly about this.

Tom Cruise's character of Dr. William Harford was the final instance in a long line of physicians in Kubrick's work. The others being:

Doc Jay	John Stafford	*Full Metal Jacket*
Doctor	Anne Jackson	*The Shining*
Dr. Broughton	Geoffrey Chater	*Barry Lyndon*
Dr. Brodsky	Carl Duering	*A Clockwork Orange*
Dr. Heywood Floyd	William Sylvester	*2001: A Space Odyssey*
Dr. Strangelove	Peter Sellers	*Dr. Strangelove*
Dr. Keegee	Cec Linder	*Lolita*

The opening lines of the film, whether they were written by Kubrick or Frederic Raphael, would appear to have had an unexpected provenance. In the 1983 television series *Kennedy*, there was an early scene in which President-elect Kennedy (Martin Sheen) and Jacqueline Kennedy (Blair Brown), in their apartment, are preparing to go out for the evening, while having the following exchange:

Jackie: How do I look?   Alice: How do I look?
Jack: You look fine.   Bill: Perfect.
Jackie: You never even looked at me.   Alice: You're not even looking.

This dialogue being almost identical to the opening lines of *Eyes Wide Shut*.

A.I. Teddy bears are not unknown in Kubrick's work, note that *Napoleon* was to begin and end "with Napoleon's childhood 'teddy bear.'"[38] A soft toy, resembling a teddy bear is present, albeit in a somewhat gruesome context, in *Full Metal Jacket*. A teddy bear is present in *Eyes Wide Shut*'s final scene, and by proxy, via the bush baby, it is present in *2001: A Space Odyssey*. *A.I.*'s Teddy might thus be seen as completing an albeit very minor thematic pattern in Kubrick's work.

Final Years Kubrick's last public appearance of note is thought to have been at the Donmar Warehouse, probably sometime in October 1998, to see Nicole Kidman in a performance of *The Blue Room*. *The Blue Room* was David Hare's stage adaptation of Schnitzler's *La Ronde*. In the play Kidman played all five female roles—with Iain Glen playing all the male roles. Kidman appeared nude in the production, causing the *Daily Telegraph*'s reviewer, Charles Spencer, to famously describe the play as "pure theatrical Viagra."[39]

Pauline Kael, Kubrick's nemesis, one of his most "implacable and unwavering opponents,"[40] would die, somewhat ironically it must be said, in New York City on September 3, just one week before the fall of the Twin Towers, in Kubrick's iconic year of 2001.

A wide range of books on Kubrick emerged, either as updated editions or as new monographs, in the years immediately following Kubrick's death. The most interesting being the Walker, Ciment and Chion; the most painstakingly accurate the LoBrutto; the oddest Leonard F. Wheat's; the biggest and most expensive *The Kubrick Archives*; the most disingenuous the Raphael; the book with the worst grammar the Reichmann and Flagge[41] and so on.

Kubrick died sometime in the early morning of Sunday March 7, 1999, no one else of any great fame died on the same day; Joe DiMaggio had the patience to expire the day after Kubrick's demise. Alexander Walker notes that he was informed, by one source, that Kubrick had died exactly 666 days before the year 2001, a cursory calculation proving this to be true. Whether this means anything is open to question—Kubrick also died 66 days into the year 1999, a year that, in itself, was 666 upside down. Such coincidences probably being as reductive and meaningless as the first point of "trivia" mentioned in this appendix—not to mention the varied numerological patterns in Kubrick's work, alluded to (sometimes grudgingly) in this book.

Finally, and within the reluctant context of approaching a closing note: it is perhaps appropriate for a director often linked with space and space travel, that Stanley Kubrick's grave is clearly visible from space. In the years since Kubrick's death *Google Earth* has photographed the entire planet, including Childwick Bury Manor, Kubrick's home and final resting place. Kubrick's grave, the final resting place of arguably the 20th century's most significant filmmaker, can be seen from space — by all those who choose to look.

Notes

Introduction

1. Kubrick himself is on record as concurring with this latter claim: "I believe very strongly in the cinema, I'm even foolish enough to consider it one of the major expressive forms of our age" (cited in Castle 2005, p. 308).

2. See the "Books on Stanley Kubrick" section in the bibliography for a listing of these items.

3. Luis M. Garcia-Mainar's book, *Narrative and Stylistic Patterns in the Films of Stanley Kubrick*, did offer a theoretical approach to Kubrick's work — but from a somewhat narrow perspective of narrative theory, without the scope of discussion envisaged here. In addition, one should perhaps mention authors such as Thomas Nelson, Michel Chion, Michel Ciment, and others, whose work undoubtedly possesses a depth of scholarship, albeit, not with the specific and dedicated theoretical perspective envisaged here.

4. See, for example, Barthes's *Le Degré zéro de l'écriture* (*Writing Degree Zero*), 1953, passim, and Eagleton's *After Theory,* 2003, passim.

5. See Barry 1995, 36.

6. See Castle 2005, 378.

7. The phrase "cinema of ideas" comes from P.L. Titterington, cited in Falsetto 1996, 10.

8. As Alexander Walker put it: "Without *Fear and Desire* and *Spartacus*— the one film an initial practice piece and the other an assignment picture he virtually disowned — each of the films of Stanley Kubrick has a strong, unifying aspect" (Walker 1999, 44).

9. The key text is Fiedler's book *Love and Death in the American Novel* (originally published in 1960), arguably still *the* most controversial and thought-provoking book concerning American culture and gender written in the latter half of the 20th century.

10. Together with the Western (which Kubrick attempted to make with *One-Eyed Jacks*), perhaps the only significant cinematic genre that did not interest Kubrick was the musical. Although music played a significant part in Kubrick's work, the musical itself did not appear to interest him.

11. This phrase belongs to Robert Kolker — see Kolker 2000, 119.

12. Since 1987, Cocks has published a series of essays arguing this corner, collated in his book *The Wolf at the Door* (2004). In his work, Cocks provides persuasive readings of Holocaust metaphors, as, for example, in *The Shining*.

13. Phillips and Hill 2002, 197.

14. Hughes 2000, xi.

Chapter 1

1. Kolker 2000, 119.

2. In other words, when we speak of *Lolita,* we do not immediately think of Kubrick's film — Nabokov's novel still has a more significant cultural gravitas. This being the exception to Kubrick's other adaptive sources, wherein the cultural gravitas decidedly resides in the adaptation, rather than the original sources.

3. Nabokov 1991, xi

4. Not that other readers and viewers wholly agreed; for example, Susan Bordo: "For me ... and I imagine for many of my generation ... the

movie was the original, the book a palimpsest" (Bordo 1999, 301).

5. Castle 2005, 478. In an interview from 1957, Kubrick seemed to have already worked out a way to elide such a predicament: "I only consider works that are not particularly successful in literary terms ... I'd never try to adapt a good novel, because the world it creates is totally dependent on purely literary means" (op. cit. 308).

6. This information being derived via James Howard: "Nabokov's script underwent various revisions—certainly by the producer/director team and with possible contributions from Calder Willingham" (Howard 1999, 77). Willingham had previously written a draft of a screenplay for *Lolita* in 1959, which Kubrick had rejected. Willingham, who would go onto find screenwriting acclaim with such films as *The Graduate* (a film with a similar sexual discourse), may potentially have provided elements for the finished screenplay—his contributions being incorporated into the ongoing script which Kubrick and Harris devised.

7. Nabokov: "By nature I am no dramatist; I am not even a hack scenarist" (Nabokov 1974, ix).

8. Corliss 1994, 66.

9. Those elements of Nabokov's script which *did* survive included the following: the scene where Charlotte shows Humbert around her house (however, the "cherry pies" comment was Kubrick's addition); some dialogue from the school dance scene was used, as was Charlotte's attempt to seduce Humbert afterwards. Also, Charlotte telling Humbert she is sending Lolita to summer camp was used; as were the stage directions for Lolita's impetuous kiss to Humbert before she leaves for camp; ditto some elements of the lead-up to Charlotte's death and some elements of Charlotte reading Humbert's diary. Nabokov's script was also used—for a few other specific lines—for example, when Humbert recites Poe's "Ulalume" to Lolita; one line of the piano teacher scene survives in the film, as do about ten lines of Humbert being followed by Quilty's car; and, finally, about a page of the nurse's dialogue in the hospital scene.

10. Nabokov 1974, xii.

11. Ciment 2001, 201.

12. Op. cit. 172.

13. Nabokov's comments about his collaboration with Kubrick are of interest; for example: "I did not feel quite sure whether Kubrick was serenely accepting whatever I did or silently rejecting everything" (Nabokov 1974, ix). However, one might note that Nabokov was not wholly absented from compensation; prior to the release of the film, while the novel had been a "best-seller," it had not sold in vast amounts. After the release of the film the novel would go onto sell well in excess of 14 million copies, offering Nabokov a financial security for the rest of his life. In fact, financial security may have been Nabokov's primary concern all along. He would later state: "[M]y supreme, and in fact only, interest in these motion picture contracts is money" (Cited in LoBrutto 1997, 162).

14. Bosley Crowther, "*Lolita,* Vladimir Nabokov's Adaptation of his Novel," *New York Times,* June 14, 1962.

15. Cited in Schwam 2000, 256.

16. Transcribed from the audio CD: "Interview with Stanley Kubrick to Jeremy Bernstein, November 27, 1966," included as part of *The Stanley Kubrick Archives* (2005).

17. Corliss 1994, 73.

18. For a discussion of Adrian Lyne's remake of *Lolita,* see Appendix 2.

19. There was also the issue that while Lolita is 12 years and eight months at the start of the novel, she is 17 at the end, hence Kubrick needed an actress who could span across the range of both ages. Sue Lyon's age of 14 thus managed to offer a compromise in the ages she had to portray. Incidentally, James Mason was 52 when shooting began and 52 when shooting ended; in the novel Humbert was 39 at the beginning and 44 at the end. To no one's surprise, this discrepancy has seldom, if ever, been commented upon.

20. Kubrick attempted to defend his casting of Lyon: "She was actually the right age for the part ... Lolita was twelve and a half in the novel and Sue was thirteen. I suspect that many people had a mental image of a nine-year-old" (Phillips 1977, 112–113). Nonetheless, one is left with the impression that Lyon did not accurately represent the object of Humbert's actual obsession. As James Harris put it: "I don't think anyone sitting in the theatre would think you were a disgusting old man if you found her sexually attractive" (Howard 1999, 79). This is the crux of the matter, in the novel Humbert is sexually interested in very young girls, he is attracted to the innocence of pre-pubescence, while in the film he merely appears to be obsessed with a nubile (if very young) woman.

21. DeVries 1973, 27.

22. Op. cit. 27.

23. Nabokov 1991, 141.

24. Note that Kubrick's film does not specifically allude to this narrative detail from the

novel; however, it is possible to assume that the film was, nonetheless, aware of it.

25. Corliss 1994, 86.

26. For examples of this see the reproduced photographs in Castle 2005, 332, and in Reichmann and Flagge 2007, 66, 70–71.

27. In contrast to this, one can only speculate on the film that might have been made in the previous decade — the 1950s— around the time of the book's original publication. The perfect casting for the film was cited as Errol Flynn as Humbert and Tuesday Weld as Lolita. Richard Corliss comments: "If the film had been made in 1955, the year it was published, [Tuesday] Weld would have been almost too perfect for the title role" (Corliss 1994, 28). As controversial a choice as Flynn may have seemed, there may have been some credence to the story. James Howard reports that a meeting between Kubrick, James Harris and Flynn apparently did take place, shortly before Flynn's death in October 1959 (see Howard 1999, 78). It is also known that Tuesday Weld was at least *considered* for the part. At Kubrick's suggestion, Nabokov met the actress and found she was "a graceful *ingénue*," but not his idea of Lolita.

28. Nabokov 1974, xi.

29. Ibid.

30. Other than Errol Flynn, actors as diverse as Laurence Olivier, Peter Ustinov, David Niven, and Marlon Brando were all connected, at some time, with the role of Humbert Humbert.

31. As Alfred A. Appel comments: "Many readers are more troubled by Humbert Humbert's use of language and lore than by his abuse of Lolita and law" (Nabokov 1991, xi).

32. Nabokov 1991, 32.

33. Lionel Trilling: "*Lolita* is about love. Perhaps I shall be better understood if I put the statement in this form: *Lolita* is not about sex, but about love" (originally published in *Griffin*, VII August 1958: Lionel Trilling, "The Last Lover: Vladimir Nabokov's *Lolita.*" Reprinted in Clegg 2000, 23).

34. In a letter to Peter Ustinov, dated May 20, 1960, Kubrick had written: "I think the most important thing to say about *Lolita* is that it is a love story. A sad tender eventually heart-breaking story of passion-love" (see Chris Hastings, "The Stanley Kubrick Files." *The Daily Telegraph*, July 7, 2008).

35. Castle 2005, 340.

36. Kubrick made just this point to Alexander Walker; Walker noted that the traditional love story had "absolutely no appeal" for Kubrick, and then quoted Kubrick's ideas on the love story

in the novel: "The literary ground rules for a love story are such that it must end in either death or separation of the lovers and it must never be possible for the lovers to be permanently united. It is also essential that the relationship must shock society or their families.... It is very difficult to construct a modern story which would believably adhere to these rules. In this respect I think it is correct to say that *Lolita* may be one of the few modern love stories" (Walker 1999, 24).

37. Nabokov 1991, 270.

38. Op. cit. 308. As Richard Corliss writes of this scene: "In this beautiful reverie of revelation and flagellation, Humbert accuses himself of a crime worse than raping a child: he has killed her childhood" (Corliss 1994, 84).

39. Bordo 1999, 299 and 319.

40. In the case of this interpretation, Charles Rollo would comment that *Lolita* was "a satire of the romantic novel of 'Old Europe' in contact with 'Young America'" (Charles Rollo, "*Lolita* by Vladimir Nabokov," *The Atlantic Monthly*, September 1958, Volume 202, No. 3, 78). While to Leslie A. Fiedler: "Lolita is America, in other words the vulgarity of America to the European mind" (Fiedler 1997, 335). Finally, James Naremore: "The details of suburban Americana are mediated through a European sensibility" (Naremore 2007, 104).

41. In the novel Mona was Mona Dahl: in the film adaptation, by making Mona the daughter of the Farlows, Kubrick was able to create a more subversive and sexualized connotation to the name.

42. In the novel, Nabokov takes sexual innuendo to a still more exaggerated level. At times the tenor of the salacious jokes Nabokov invents threatens to descend into both self-parody and questionable taste. For example, Humbert's joke about the Beaver Eaters (Nabokov 1991, 90), or the joke about Humbert's neighbors in Beardsley — two tweedy professors of English, Miss Lester and Miss Fabian, there is the still more unsubtle wordplay via the naming of two further teachers at Beardsley: a Miss Corn and a Miss Cole. Nabokov is more successful when his wordplays pertain to Lolita's body: "A halter with little to halt" (Nabokov 1991, 73) "where my philter had felled her" (Nabokov 1991, 125); however, at times even these jokes threaten to descend into bad taste, as in the road sign Humbert sees or at least imagines: "Detour, Children at Play, Dangerous Curves Ahead" (Cited in Corliss, 1994, 51).

43. James Naremore notes a potential continuity error in this scene, insomuch as the Gains-

borough portrait, through which Humbert will shoot Quilty, is clearly visible at the bottom of the stairs at the start of the scene, and at the top at the end of it. However, there is the possibility that Quilty, something of a faker and forger himself, may have had more than one fake copy of the same painting (see Naremore 2007, 116). In addition, one might take note that the final line of the novel: "I am thinking of aurochs and angels, the secret of durable pigments, prophetic sonnets, the refuge of art. And this is the only immortality you and I may share, my Lolita" (Nabokov 1991, 309). It is therefore appropriate that Quilty attempts to find refuge from Humbert's gun behind a work of art. This might be seen as one of numerous instances of Kubrick attempting to encapsulate additional elements of the novel into the film.

44. Bordo 1999, 321.

45. See Clegg 2000, 110–114.

46. Nabokov 1991, 284.

47. In the novel the most common act of sex would seem to be masturbatory, or at least that is what might be most likely perceived from a close reading of the text. What is of significance is that there is never a sense in which Lolita gains or receives any pleasure from her multiple encounters with Humbert.

48. Nabokov 1991, 274.

49. Op. cit. 285.

50. Op. cit. 297.

51. Op. cit. 62.

52. Op. cit. 194.

53. Corliss 1994, 12.

54. Op. cit. 40.

55. Krin Gabbard, "The Circulation of Sado-Masochistic Desire in the Lolita Texts," *Journal for the Psychological Study of the Arts*, August 25, 1997.

56. Nabokov 1991, 59.

57. Kubrick's film, because of time restraints, avoids this specific element of the novel: Annabel dead of typhus within months of her brief tryst with younger Humbert. Adrian Lyne's later cinematic adaptation of the novel does include this detail, offering one narrative advantage over Kubrick's film.

58. Nabokov 1991, 44.

59. Op. cit. 49.

60. Op. cit. 126.

61. Op. cit. 151.

62. Op. cit. 242.

63. Op. cit. 116.

64. Within this context it is perhaps worth noting that the novel includes a passing reference to an "undinist" (Nabokov, 1991, 250). An undinist is someone who takes pleasure in watching women urinate. This was one of Nabokov's more obscure jokes, most probably a reference to Havelock Ellis, a pioneer in sex therapy, and also (apparently) an individual who happened to have a predilection towards this unusual sexual practice. However, additional to this, the reference also adds weight to the thinly veiled scatological discourse within the narrative as a whole.

65. Nabokov 1991, 77.

66. The editor of the annotated version of *Lolita*, Alfred Appel, Jr., noted: "The boyish qualities of a nymphet tempt the reader into interpreting Humbert's quest as essentially homosexual" (See Nabokov 1991, lix). However, Appel went on to argue that we be less absolute in our judgment, as this may have been a part of Nabokov's teasing attitude towards "pop psychoanalysis" (ibid.).

67. This is not, in any way, to fall into the trap of confusing pedophilia with homosexuality. It is merely to suggest that in the cultural arenas of book and film, Humbert Humbert's character can be read in such a way.

68. The film opens with Humbert's cry of "Quilty, Quilty," and closes with the caption: "Humbert Humbert died of coronary thrombosis in prison awaiting trial for the murder of Clare Quilty."

69. Fiedler 1997, 46.

70. Op. cit. 363.

71. Note that the dialogue here is quite different from the parallel scene in the novel, wherein Quilty merely taunts Humbert with a variety of wordplays and double-entendres about Lolita (See Nabokov 1991, 126–127).

72. See Nabokov 1991, 193–198.

73. See Castle 2005, 333.

74. Note: Dr. Zemph does not appear in either Nabokov's novel or in his unused screenplay; he is solely an invention of Kubrick/Harris, most probably with the help of Peter Sellers. The Germanic Dr. Zemph, arguably an initial draft of Dr. Strangelove, offered one of many examples of Kubrick's ambivalent attitude towards things Germanic. Here Zemph is portrayed as a blatant Freudian who has Lolita's developmental health as his concern, what he coyly and repeatedly refers to as "the home situation." Insomuch, there is great comedic value; however, at the same time it is difficult not to perceive of the sinister quality imbued in his character, in other words that this fiction within a fiction has at least the potentiality of having Nazi antecedents.

75. Phillips and Hill 2002, 164.

76. In addition, one might go back to *Day of the Fight* (1951) and to the obvious and explicit homosociality/homoeroticism present within the boxing ring; see Appendix 2 for a further discussion of this.

77. Note how in the novel, Charlotte, showing Humbert around the house on their first meeting, says: "Is that Monsieur Humbert?" (Nabokov 1991, 37).

78. However, it is perhaps pertinent to note that Haze is not Lolita's real name, but that (as Humbert tells us in the novel) it only rhymes with her actual surname.

79. One might also note that the narrator of *Pale Fire* (Nabokov's next book after *Lolita*) was called John Shade.

80. Lewis 2004, 499. Lewis later refers to Quilty as functioning as "Humbert's liberated double and id" (op. cit. 781). James Naremore also makes a similar observation, describing Quilty as an "evil twin" (Naremore 2007, 111).

81. Nabokov 1991, 138.

82. Op. cit. 247.

83. Op. cit. 299. In addition, one might note the incidences of twins in *Lolita*. There are four sets of twins in Lolita's class at Ramsdale — the Beales, the Cowans, the Mirandas, the Talbots — a statistically unlikely occurrence, pointing to a potentially deliberate trope on Nabokov's part.

84). This information is drawn from Carl Proffer's book, *Keys to Lolita* (Proffer 1968, 125). Proffer offers a further range of ingenious material on the numerological patterning in the novel. See Appendix 2 for further information on this.

85. Ciment 2001, 92.

86. Quilty's companion (or girlfriend), Vivian Darkbloom, also has an ambivalently gendered forename. As stated, the name was a somewhat obvious anagram for Vladimir Nabokov; however, one might also note a Joycean allusion, allowing Nabokov's character to be read as a cross-gendered if somewhat sinister version of Leopold Bloom from *Ulysses*. One might also observe, in passing, that the name Quilty appears in *Finnegans Wake*, a detail of which Nabokov was no doubt aware. Finally, one might note the way Kubrick's film responded to this and the many other Joycean references in the novel, insomuch as one of the books Humbert brings Lolita, while she is in hospital, was the somewhat inappropriate *Portrait of the Artist as a Young Man*.

87. Nabokov 1991, 139.

88. To offer just one example, one might note how Katherine Ross embodies the same role in *Butch Cassidy and the Sundance Kid* (1969). The genre of the "buddy movie" would eventually descend into near self-parody, with films such as *Lethal Weapon* (1987) and *Fight Club* (1999) offering near-ludicrous accounts of male bonding. However, more recently the film *Sideways* (2004) has revisited the genre with at least some degree of intelligence and subtlety.

89. Corliss 1994, 77.

90. Ibid.

91. LoBrutto 1997, 222.

92. Note that Poe married his cousin, Virginia, when she was just 13 years old, the same age as Lolita.

93. See Appendix 2 for a fuller discussion of the intertextual elements in both novel and film.

94. Walker 1999, 47.

95. Op. cit. 61.

96. Nabokov 1991, 59.

97. Op. cit. 292.

98. Ibid.

99. Op. cit. 294.

100. Geoffrey Cocks notes the opening of the film, an automobile driving towards a large house, as "anticipating the opening sequence of *The Shining*," and notes how these "large residences" are places of "potential and actual terror," thus finding a linkage to the "horror embedded in ... fairytales" (Cocks 2004, 104).

101. Nabokov 1991, 34.

102. We might note how, later in the novel, matters grow still worse, when we hear Humbert saying: "At the time I felt I was merely losing contact with reality" (Nabokov 1991, 255).

103. Jenkins 1997, 38.

104. Garcia-Mainar 1999, 91.

105. This ending, with a captioned epilogue, may appear a somewhat gauche tying-up of narrative threads; it was a technique Kubrick would use with more flair in later films, such as *Barry Lyndon* and *The Shining*.

Chapter 2

1. Adorno's quotation is cited in Peter Watson's *A Terrible Beauty: A History of the People and Ideas that Shaped the Modern Mind* (London: Weidenfeld and Nicholson, 2000), p. 249.

2. In terms of his anxiety surrounding nuclear war, Kubrick is said to have been sufficiently concerned with the safety of himself and his family to "contemplate a move to Australia," Kubrick's perception of Australia as an "unlikely ground zero" for a nuclear war (see Sikov 2002, 189).

3. It is thought that it was Alistair Buchan, director of the Institute of Strategic Studies in Lon-

don, who had originally suggested George's novel to Kubrick (see Howard 1999, 91).

4. In Alexander Walker's words: "*Red Alert* contained two critical ingredients—a powerful story, which characteristically was what first caught Kubrick's interest, and a brilliant premise" (see Walker 1999, 29).

5. George's novelization of the film, published in 1963, closely followed the final screenplay. However, there were differences—perhaps pointing to George's original intent in his concept of the screenplay. In the novelization, the narrative was framed by an introduction and epilogue—a science fiction element—in which alien beings reported on their observation of Earth and its destruction—the entire narrative being contained within an alien meta-text, called *The Dead Worlds of Antiquity*. This perhaps partly informs the air of detachment in the film's opening voice-over, which (in this context) now has the viewpoint of an alien presence, commenting on mankind and the way it has destroyed itself. This is especially relevant in the final words of the film's opening narration: "What they were building or why it was located in a remote, desolate place, no one could say."

6. Rasmussen 2001, 5.

7. Nabokov 1991, 25.

8. Bryant 1961, 7.

9. Op. cit. 9.

10. Op. cit. 10.

11. Op. cit. 19.

12. Op. cit. 44.

13. Op. cit. 20.

14. Op. cit. 26.

15. Op. cit. 29. The CRM 114 code: OPE, obviously points to the HAL/IBM conundrum; at one point, Turgidson even notes that there are 17,000 combinations of the three-letter code. Note that in the novelization, the three-letter code was changed to "Joe for King," an indicator towards Stalin, but also JFK—a still further satirical element (George 2000, 106).

16. Op. cit. 46.

17. It is known that Kubrick was aware of Kissinger, even at this early stage before he found fame within the arena of world politics. In a letter dated November 15, 1961, to his editor on *Lolita*, Anthony Harvey, Kubrick had mentioned Kissinger's book *The Necessity for Choice* (1961) as part of his background reading on nuclear war (see Naremore 2007, 119).

18. Note that in earlier versions of the script Dr. Strangelove was named Von Klutz, perhaps adding weight to the Von Braun theory.

19. Note that Teller also had something of a Strangelovian disability—he had lost his right foot in a transportation accident.

20. According to James Naremore, Kubrick had "cultivated a sort of friendship" with Kahn and consistently "picked his brain for information on nuclear strategy." When the film came out, complete with its reference to the "Bland Corporation," Kahn apparently asked Kubrick for some royalties, to which Kubrick replied: "It doesn't work that way" (see Naremore 2007, 124).

21. In addition, there were intertextual inferences. Kubrick may have been influenced by George Pal's production of the 1951 film *When Worlds Collide,* which ends with a sinister German scientist (a "Strangelovian" figure) who struggles from his wheelchair and makes a few hesitant steps in a futile bid to escape. In addition, Strangelove's gloved hand and general appearance owe an obvious debt to Rotwang, the mad scientist who creates False Maria in Fritz Lang's *Metropolis* (1926).

22. It is interesting to note how Kubrick's film coincided with the rise of the protest song in the early 1960s. Bob Dylan's "Talkin' World War III Blues," released contemporaneously to Kubrick's film, makes a similar satirical point about the bomb and the fear of nuclear war, thus placing it within a comparable realm of black comedic discourse.

23. Falsetto 196, 140.

24. Cited in LoBrutto 1997, 248.

25. For example, see Bosley Crowther, "Kubrick Film Presents Sellers in 3 Roles," *New York Times,* January 30, 1964.

26. As Daniel DeVries put it: "Since Vietnam nobody believes anything the military says anymore ... because the film succeeds so profoundly on a deeper, emotional level, that prefatory note seems like just one more of the film's nasty jokes" (DeVries 1973, 44).

27. However, Southern may not have been Kubrick's first choice; for example, Ed Sikov claims that Kubrick first attempted a collaboration with cartoonist and playwright Jules Feiffer, but it was not successful (see Sikov 2002, 189).

28. It is often claimed that it was Southern's idea to change the title of the project. Kubrick's working titles at an earlier stage of development had been somewhat prosaic: *Edge of Doom* (corresponding to the alternate title to George's novel, *Two Hours to Doom*) and *The Delicate Balance of Power,* being two examples. *The Kubrick Archives* preserves a page of Kubrick's later brainstorming ideas (probably with Southern's

input) for the film's title, one of the most entertaining being *Dr. Strangelove's Secret Uses of Uranus* (Castle 2005, 348).

29. Hill 2000, 112. It is difficult to untangle Terry Southern's contribution to the script, but it is probable that the title, the sexually ambiguous names of the characters and overtly satiric lines such as the president's: "Gentlemen, you can't fight in here, this is the War Room," and Bat Guano's "preversions" derived from Southern's input. However, it is clear that Peter Sellers was also a contributor to the script, a significant if uncredited fourth writer. As with a number of Kubrick's films, precise allocation of screenwriting credits remain unclear.

30. Op. cit. 111.

31. Op. cit. 117.

32. This is Jean Stein's description, cited in Hill 2000, 282.

33. The naming of Leper Colony itself had an intertextual resonance; it would appear to have been named after a plane in the film *Twelve O' Clock High* (1949), directed by Henry King and starring Gregory Peck. In the film, Peck is a replacement officer who is given the task of taking over an exhausted American bomber group based in England. Peck's character segregates the worst misfits and malingerers into a crew known as "The Leper Colony" (see Cocks 2004, 113).

34. In *Gulliver's Travels*, Laputa is a flying island where the inhabitants literally have their heads in the clouds, being obsessed with impractical theories that never work in reality. In addition, Julian Rice makes the point that an earlier version of the *Dr. Strangelove* script had included the conceit of "Nardac Blefuscu Presents" in its opening titles. In *Gulliver's Travels*, Nardac was the highest honor bestowed by the Emperor of Blefuscu — hence it is clear that this was another deliberate acknowledgment of Swift's influence on the film (see Rice 2008, 13).

35. Castle 2005, 359.

36. Miss Scott (aka Miss Foreign Affairs), in her bikini and sunglasses (recalling Lolita's similar attire in Kubrick's previous film) alludes to one of the more subtle jokes in *Dr. Strangelove*. The cover of the issue of *Playboy* that Major Kong is reading announces this issue will be: "A Toast to Bikinis." The satirical wordplay, in its celebration of all things nuclear, points to a toast to bikinis of a different kind: Bikini Atoll, in the Pacific Ocean. This was the site where America had conducted much of its atomic bomb testing in the 1950s— some of these explosions being included at the film's close.

37. In terms of clinical psychology, Strange-

love's condition might be diagnosed as "anarchic hand syndrome"; however, the Nazi salute still appears, in some form, as a parody of an erection.

38. Norman Kagan even perceived of a sexual connotation in the names given to the bombs: "Hi There," which Kagan sees as "a homosexual advance," and "Dear John," "a letter breaking off an affair" (Kagan 2000, 137). Kubrick's nicknaming of the two bombs in this way recalls the nicknaming of the atomic bomb dropped on Hiroshima: "Little Boy." The bombs in George's original novel were called Bim and Bam (Bryant 1961, 31). While in the novelization they were renamed: "Hi There" and "Lolita," thus at the end of the novelization Kong gets to sit astride Lolita, probably an "in-joke" on George's part (George 2000, 134).

39. As Thomas Nelson commented: "Everywhere you look in the film ... there are hints of primal and infantile regression" (Nelson, 2000, 95).

40. In addition, one might also note the spelling errors in the film's opening titles, whether or not these were oversights or deliberate remains uncertain.

41. Located within an Oedipal tryst, Turgidson is literally a turgid son; his rampant male sexuality is linked directly to the mother — or possibly the father. Note, also, that Turgidson was originally called "Buck Schmuck," an "obscene Yiddish word for 'penis'" (Cocks 2004, 109).

42. This is compounded by the childlike pronunciations Major Kong uses, *nuclear* is articulated as "*noo-clear-air*," Russians as "*Roo-skis*," and so on.

43. A "hardcore hetero" was Penelope Gilliat's description of "Bat" Guano; cited in Walker 1999, 145.

44. Mandrake operates in the film as a quasi-representative of what the French refer to as: "*le vice Anglais*," insomuch as Mandrake does not seem quite manly enough for such "hardcore heteros" as Ripper and Guano.

45. Randy Rasmussen, for example, perceived of a Freudian symbolism in the doodlings Ripper makes while recounting his delusional ideas to Mandrake. Rasmussen perceived of "a rather prim, dour looking woman. Ripper's mother? The word 'scour' is highlighted inside a box. Possibly these are veiled clues to Ripper's antagonistic relationship with women and his obsession with purity" (Rasmussen 2001, 37).

46. For example, Geoffrey Cocks noted the fact that ICBM is "an adolescent and alimentary

play on words" (see Cocks 2004, 109). Cocks also noted a still-wider range of erotic implications within the film; for example, he reads a sexual metaphor into the name of the warship *Weathership Tango Delta*, where the crew plans to "ditch" the plane after dropping their bombs. Cocks perceives of a tango as an erotic dance, while delta might be interpreted as a veiled reference to female genitalia (Cocks 2004, 279).

47. The characteristic Kubrickian ruthlessness with which the film was cut is of interest. The custard pie scene in *Dr. Strangelove* may well have been the best custard pie scene in cinematic history, but Kubrick thought the slapstick quotient did not gel with the satirical discourse of his film. One might note here the significance of this to *Eyes Wide Shut*—and the ruthless Kubrickian editing that did *not* take place, but only insomuch as Kubrick did not live long enough to undertake it. For a further discussion of the deleted "Custard Pie" sequence, see Appendix 3.

48. Thomas Nelson notes how each setting in the film becomes a dark cave or womb (Nelson, 2000, 99). John Baxter, also in a Freudian mood, noted that the War Room was "redolent of a claustrophobic love of the warm dark places where the masters of war make their homes" (Baxter 1998, 184).

49. Walker 1999, 129. The set design was the work of Ken Adam, for which he received significant acclaim, going onto design some of the more memorable sets for a series of James Bond films.

50. Kolker 2000, 120.

51. Cited in Cocks 2005, 141.

52. To take one such comment, Kubrick in conversation with Michel Ciment: "I share the fairly widespread fascination with the horror of the Nazi period. Strangelove and Zemph are just parodies of movie clichés about Nazis" (Ciment 2001, 156).

53. For example, to paraphrase the famous one-liner Allen quips in *Annie Hall:* "If I'd been born in Berlin instead of Brooklyn, I'd have been a lampshade by now."

54. Rasmussen 2001, 32.

55. George 2000, 138.

56. Walker 1999, 114.

57. Falsetto 1996, 138.

58. In Robert Kolker's words, "*Dr. Strangelove* is a discourse of death" (Kolker 2000, 124).

59. See Mark Crispin Miller's description of Major Kong's final scene: "The Texas flyboy, blissfully astride the great H-bomb as if it were the ultimate wild bronco, or a huge prosthetic hard-on" (Cocks, 2005, 143).

60. As Randy Rasmussen noted of the film: "Sex and the capacity for mass destruction become intertwined" (Rasmussen 2001, 7).

61. As Robert Kolker commented: "*Dr. Strangelove* is that rarity among American films, a film in which verbal language plays a major role" (Kolker 2000, 121).

62. Op. cit. 124 and 123.

63. Op. cit. 123.

64. See Barry 1995, 61–80.

65. From Derrida's *Of Grammatology*, cited in Barry 1995, 68.

66. Paraphrased from Barry, 1995, 61–80.

67. In addition, there were Oedipal connotations, not only is the base a mere "burp," it is the son of a mere "burp."

68. Hill 2000, 121. Note also Daniel Ellsberg's view of the film; Ellsberg, who was then a consultant to the Defense Department, on seeing the film for the first time, in 1964, commented: "That was a documentary" (Crone 2005, 242).

69. Of course Kubrick's eventual position in the film world would afford him the great advantage of being able to cast almost anyone he wanted. This was a situation that would also apply to other contributors working within the film industry: script writers, set designers, lighting cameramen and so on. As his reputation grew, there were very few people who would not take up the chance of working on a Stanley Kubrick film.

70. The film cost a reported $1.7 million, but it would earn $5 million in the United States alone on its initial release, making it Columbia's top box-office success of the year. The film was the first Kubrick had both produced and directed, affording him a total artistic control he would never again relent.

71. It is known that Kubrick spent the afternoon of November 22, 1963, in his apartment, on Central Park West, talking to Warren Beatty, who was hoping to interest Kubrick in directing *What's New Pussycat?* At what point Kubrick became aware of the assassination of President Kennedy is uncertain, taking into account the different time zones, it was presumably sometime after Beatty left, at which point Kubrick presumably made the decision to cancel the preview of the film. See Suzanne Finstad's biography of Beatty: *Warren Beatty: A Private Man* (London: Aurum, 2005, 314–315).

72. One feels a sense of ambivalence as to where to place the apostrophe in "assassins." In *Full Metal Jacket*, Lee Harvey Oswald is referred to as Kennedy's *killer*; however, it is probable that Kubrick found this as dubious as the majority of informed commentators.

73. See George 2000, 94.

74. Patrick Murray and Jeanne Schuler convincingly argue that Kubrick has continually "surfed" the zeitgeist in his films, "exploring antiwar sentiments, the sexual revolution, space travel, behavior modification, artificial intelligence, cryogenics, the arms race, youth culture, homosexuality, and women's liberation before they surface in the mainstream" (cited in Abrams 2007, 134).

75. Geoffrey Cocks makes a similar, if arguably more overstated case, although in this instance it would seem he was wholly valid in assuming such an interpretative position (see Cocks 2004, 115–116). Cocks is not alone in perceiving such a subtextual reading of the film; James Naremore noted how the "instrumental rationality" which lay behind the design of the Nazi death camps "also lies behind Strangelove's gleeful presentation of his final solution in the closing scenes" (Naremore 2007, 125).

Chapter 3

1. However, the film has perhaps had a more direct influence on the actual year of 2001, namely the way in which we articulate the date, see Appendix 4 for a fuller discussion of this.

2. In this sense, the film might be compared to another significant cultural text that was date specific in its title and apparently seeking to make some kind of prophetic statement: George Orwell's *1984*. Orwell's novel, like Kubrick's film, gets almost all the details wrong, and yet somehow manages to offer an overall prophecy that possessed an overarching meaningfulness.

3. See Walker 1988, 286–287. Alexander Walker, visiting Kubrick's apartment in New York not long after the release of *The Killing*, in the mid–1950s, had noted seeing numerous cans of Japanese science fiction films. Kubrick swore Walker to secrecy, a promise Walker duly kept.

4. McAleer 1992, 191.

5. Op. cit. 205.

6. It is possible that Kubrick may have used *Childhood's End* itself, had it not been previously optioned. David Hughes suggests that *Childhood's End* was of interest to Kubrick, but that the book "was already under option by writer-director Abraham Polonsky" (Hughes 2000, 265).

7. Storey 2001, 61–62.

8. See Arthur C. Clarke: "For what we are trying to create is a realistic myth" (Clarke 1972b, 246).

9. As Clarke commented: "The Odyssean parallel was clear in our minds from the very be-

ginning, long before the title of the film was chosen" (Clarke 1972b, 247).

10. The warrior context can be perceived via the idea of David as the slayer of Goliath; and Bowman as "bowman," a literal archer.

11. The fact that HAL has only a single eye (although he has many "singular eyes" on board *Discovery*) may be of significance. HAL does not have depth of field; this can be seen when HAL asks Bowman to hold one of his sketches closer, hence there is a suggestion that HAL has a lack of true perception. Thus HAL's single Cyclopean eye perhaps suggests he fails to see the whole picture, a metaphor for his ultimate lack of judgment.

12. Note that HAL was at one time envisaged as having a Homeric (albeit female) name: Athena (see Clarke 1972, 33).

13. Some critics went further, and Leonard F. Wheat was one who went further than most; see Wheat's book: *Kubrick's 2001: A Triple Allegory* for further details of this.

14. Ciment 1983, 128. Also, note Thomas Nelson's description of the film's narrative design, as a "frontal assault on the traditional conventions of Hollywood narrative filmmaking" (Nelson 2000, 110). While in Robert Kolker's words the film has "a kind of openness," that was "alien to American film, which traditionally operates according to conventions of narrative completeness" (Kolker 1988, 102).

15. See Falsetto, 2001, 111 and 116. It was in the *Playboy* interview of 1968 that Kubrick claimed the film to be a "non-verbal experience." Yet one notes he was required to use words in order to explain this. Derrida's truism: "There is nothing outside of the text," would thus seem to impact here, as if implying there was, in fact, no such thing as a "non-verbal experience."

16. As Fred Ordway noted: "His purpose was to keep it almost a silent film" (cited in McAleer, 1992, 217). Also, note Kubrick's comments on silent film elsewhere, for example, to Michel Ciment: "When sound came in, movies became plays, and basically still are" (Ciment 2001, 247). One might argue that a significant aspect of Kubrick's cinema (most pertinently here in *2001*) was an attempt to generate narrative power in film that was different from the three-act play, as if to get back to the originality of silent film narrative.

17. See Kubrick's own comment to Maurice Rapf: "The film departs about as much from the convention of the theatre and the three-act play as is possible. Not many films have departed further than that, certainly not the big films" (cited in Agel 1970, 169).

18. As David Stork noted: "Nearly all the crisis points in *2001* occur in silence" (Stork 1997, 237). In addition, Cedric Anger's observation is pertinent: "Each one of Kubrick's films attempted to recreate the visual impact and hallucinatory power of early cinema and to return to the camera all of its expressive power. For Kubrick, films were meant to amaze and to be watched with the mouth and eyes wide open, and he was at his best when his characters were silent and lighting and music were used to their maximum effect" (Anger 1999, 28–29).

19. Agel 1970, 273.

20. Cocks 2004, 10. Cocks puts forward the idea that this "cut" may have been inspired by the Second World War film, *A Canterbury Tale* (1944), directed by Michael Powell and Emeric Pressburger, in which a medieval falcon became a modern Spitfire.

21. Garcia-Mainar 1999, 30. Moon-Watcher looks into space, he hurls the bone into the air, which becomes the orbiting space-craft; thus, in Paul Duncan's words, man leaves his own world "by throwing an even bigger stick into space" (Duncan 1999, 57).

22. Op. cit. 155. It has been suggested that, at a much later stage, Kubrick may have seriously considered restructuring the Star Gate sequence. According to Alexander Walker, Kubrick was planning to rework the Star Gate section for a new release of *2001* in 2001: "As it turned out, Stanley was not granted the time to tinker with his original. I'm not sorry. An allegory as great as *2001* is not dependent on technological advances" (Schwam 2000, 242).

23. Cited in Falsetto 1996, 9.

24. The sources are as follows: Pauline Kael, *Harper's Magazine,* Stanley Kauffmann, the *New Republic,* Renata Adler, the *New York Times,* Andrew Sarris, the *Village Voice,* all cited in Ciment 2001, 43. Pauline Kael, never one of Kubrick's biggest champions, went onto comment in an even more vituperative fashion: "In some ways it's the biggest amateur movie of them all, complete even to the amateur movie obligatory scene — the director's little daughter (in curls) telling daddy what kind of present she wants (Cited in Agel 1970, 246).

25. Ciment 2001, 43.

26. As Kubrick would comment: "The lasting and ultimately most important reputation of a film is not based on reviews, but on what, if anything, people say about it over the years, and on how much affection for it they have" (Ciment 2001, 177).

27. Phillips 1977, 201.

28. Cited in Agel 1970, 275. Note that the film may have been longer still. Kubrick had intended to open with a prologue in which a number of scientists discuss a wide variety of issues the film would deal with — see Appendix 4 for details of this.

29. Op. cit. 170.

30. Op. cit. 266.

31. Op. cit. 231.

32. Schwam 2000, 240.

33. Chion 2001, 131.

34. Cocks 2004, 4.

35. As Mervyn Nicholson has pointed out, in his essay, "My Dinner with Stanley: Kubrick, Food, and the Logic of Images," Kubrick has always been "preoccupied with eating and drinking as symbolic acts" (Nicholson 2001, np).

36. For a full and detailed representation of these instructions see Agel 1970, 103.

37. The fact that the bathroom here seems modern and contemporary, while the room itself seems based on an 18th century style of architecture, is of interest. As Susan White expressed it, "The bathroom's placement in the scene juxtaposes modernity with the eighteenth century in a way that proves to be symptomatic of Kubrick's approach to the problematic notion of progress" (Kolker 2006, 139).

38. Agel 1970, 25, and Schwam 2000, 260.

39. In the novel, Arthur C. Clarke depicts Floyd as a widower; he has three motherless children, his wife having died in an air crash in 1991: "Perhaps for their sake, he should have remarried" (Clarke, 2001, 40). Thus Floyd might remarry, but only for the sake of his children, not because of any desire of his own. In a similar sense, Clarke's novel notes: "Like all his colleagues, Bowman was unmarried" (Clarke, 2001, 106). In addition, the novel alludes, somewhat ambiguously, to the "ship's pharmacopoeia" providing "adequate, though hardly glamorous substitutes" to replace women" (Clarke, 2001, 106).

40. Bizony 2000, 34.

41. Clarke, 2001, 133.

42. Cited in Schwam 2000, 249–250. In a similar sense, in what we would now call a postcolonial approach, the film did not envisage similar cultural and ethnic changes in the coming society of 2001. As Galen Bullard noted: "With the exception of the martial arts competition, everyone in *2001* is of white European descent" (Bullard 2003, 97). Likewise, Penelope Gilliat noted: "There are no Negroes in this vision of America's space program" (cited in Agel 1970, 210). Or as David G. Stork noted: "[The film] doesn't follow modern multiculturalism; it asks

for a 'Christian name' and so on" (Stork 1997, 335).

43. As Susan White puts it: "*2001* depicts space as a homosocial realm ... where women function as serving maids and then disappear entirely. The farther we get from Earth, in fact, the more devoid of the female space becomes" (Kolker 2006, 138).

44. In this precise context, see Carolyn Geduld: "Typically for a Kubrick film, women are absent ... Bowman has no Penelope to flee from or return to" (Geduld 1973, 69).

45. Fiedler 1997, 366.

46. The scene of Frank Poole sunbathing, as he listens to his parents' birthday message, is of interest here. Poole is almost nude, his body is bronzed and muscular, he wears white shorts and white socks; thus, in terms of a homoerotic content, the scene now seems almost fetishistic.

47. Kolker 2006, 72 and 74.

48. Tomkins 1992, 39. Tomkins also argues: "Westerns— set in the 19th century—created a model for men in the 20th century ... a world without God, without ideas, without institutions, without what is commonly recognized as culture, a world of men and things, where male adults in the prime of life find ultimate meaning in doing their best together" (Tomkins 1992, 37).

49. Fiedler 1997, 26.

50. Fujiwara 2007, 432.

51. In Mark Crispin Miller's words, this was "a comic image of advanced detumescence, effective castration, as opposed to the heroic shots of Moon-Watcher triumphing in his ... death defying instrument, his sinewy hand raised high, his grip tight, his tool in place he seems to roar in ecstasy" (Miller, 1994, 18).

52. Ciment 1983, 134.

53. Note how Bowman's name is, in itself, phallic; he is a "bow-man," a masculine figure who projects sharp, penetrating arrows. In contrast, Poole's name — and indeed Squirt's— might be said to be more "seminal" in nature.

54. There were further symbols of birth imagery in the film, if one wanted to see them. For example, the way in which Poole's oxygen line, his symbolic umbilical cord, is cut; or the way in which Bowman imitates birth as he gasps for breath after forcing himself out of the pod and into the main body of the "mother" ship.

55. Geduld 1973, 44.

56. Cocks 2004, 122.

57. Geduld went on to comment: "The film, very typically for Kubrick, is a disguised quest for this kind of masculine self-sufficiency which in-

cludes childbirth without women" (Geduld 1973, 70).

58. In addition, and in common within the discourse of Kubrick's work as a whole, Oedipal issues are at the forefront of the film's discursive practices. For example, such issues are reflected in the number of birthdays depicted in the film: the dawn of humanity, the exact date of HAL's birth, Squirt's birthday, Frank's birthday and finally, the literal birthday of the Star Child.

59. Cited in Agel 1970, 215.

60. Op. cit. 276.

61. Cited in Schwam 2000, 176.

62. Agel 1970, 118. HAL's voice was perhaps one of the key elements in the film, Douglas Rain was ultimately selected for the role and apparently spent nine and a half hours in a recording studio— reciting the lines for HAL — without access to the film's script and without having seen any footage of the film. However, Rains performed to Kubrick's direction and satisfaction and his contribution to the film remains a crucial element of the film's make-up.

63. Cited in Schwam 2000, 172.

64. Kolker 2006, 165.

65. Cited in Phillips 2001, 94.

66. Clarke, 2001, 161.

67. John Baxter, adopting a somewhat reductive biographical approach, claimed that both Kubrick and Clarke "had a streak of homo-eroticism that favored the sort of film *2001* would become: sleek, sexless, preoccupied with style" (Baxter 1998, 203). Baxter went further; pandering to what may have been unfounded rumors, he commented that Clarke was "an amiable Englishman in his forties who, though born in Somerset, lived in Ceylon because of its pleasant climate, both physical and moral" (Baxter 1998, 203).

68. The idea of artificial life having same sex inclinations wasn't wholly absent from some of the initial ideas Kubrick and Clarke considered; Clarke's diary entry for October 17, 1964, noted: "Stanley has invented the wild idea of slightly fag robots who create a Victorian environment to put our heroes at their ease" (See Clarke 1972, 34).

69. Herr 2000, 37. In a similar vein, Andrew Sarris, writing in a later review and with a significant change of heart to his first appraisal, spoke of HAL's death: "I have never seen the death of a mind rendered more profoundly or poetically" (Cited in McAleer 1992, 208).

70. However, note we never actually learn whether the AE35 unit (perhaps Antenna Exterior 35) was broken — Poole is killed before he

can finish replacing it—perhaps it *was* going to fail, perhaps HAL was right.

71. See Clarke 1972b, 230–237.

72. Op. cit. 237.

73. Such a reading would concur with other personal references Clarke makes in reference to HAL. For example, Clarke would later reveal that his mathematics tutor at Cambridge, George McVittie, had moved to America in the 1950s, taking up a post at the University of Illinois in Urbana—hence the derivation of HAL's birth-place.

74. A potential clue to such a conspiratorial subtext may lie in the name of HAL's original instructor, a certain "Mr. Langley." Such a name cannot help but raise connotations surrounding the geographical location of the CIA and all that that implies. There are, of course, other conspiracy theories linked to the film, David Hughes: "Some conspiracy theorists claim that the Apollo moon landing of July 1969 was faked, and that Stanley Kubrick had directed the footage supposedly broadcast from the surface of the moon" (Hughes, 2000, 155).

75. De Vries 1973, 45.

76. Carolyn Geduld has suggested the opening perspective viewpoint belongs to the "unseen alien visitors" who, one supposes, have just buried the monolith on the moon (Geduld 1973, 35). Note the linkage here to the supposed "alien" point-of-view at the start of *Dr. Strangelove.*

77. Kubrick and Clarke were correct in the idea that a computer may defeat a human being at chess; Deep Blue's victory over Garry Kasparov, on May 11, 1997, demonstrated this. (Deep Blue won the match 2–1, with three draws.) However, one must note the differences in chess technique between the factual (Deep Blue) and the fictional (HAL). There are more possible chess positions than there are atoms in the observable universe, Deep Blue's skill lay in the fact that "he" was capable of searching up to 200 million chess positions a second. Hence, computers (like Deep Blue) do not play chess in the way human beings play chess, as Kasparov put it: "Quality has become quantity." However, in the film HAL appears to play chess as if he were human (See Stork 1997, 79).

78. Chion 2001, 125.

79. Paglia, cited in: *2001: The Making of a Myth* Channel 4 Television, U.K., broadcast January 13, 2001.

80. Ibid.

81. This particular scene, of Moon-Watcher discovering the first "human" weapon, has often been described as having particular power. To Keir Dullea it was: "One of the great moments in the history of cinema" (ibid). While Daniel Richter commented: "Over and over, I have heard that the section of the film where Moon-Watcher raises the bone in the air and hurls it into the future is one of the great moments of film history" (Richter 2002, xv). Of the same scene, Arthur C. Clarke stated: "It never fails to bring tears to my eyes" (Clarke 1972, 51).

82. Such a point of view would seem to concur with the optimism of Arthur C. Clarke, but we might recall this comment from Stephen Hawking: "Have we been visited by aliens? I don't believe we have. I think any such visit would be obvious and probably very unpleasant" (cited in Andrews 1996, 18).

83. Although one might note that Bowman's attack was perhaps not wholly fatal, Daniel C. Dennett: "Those memory boxes [of HAL's] were not smashed—just removed to a place where HAL could not retrieve them" (Stork 1997, 363). In the novel's literary sequels Clarke would make use of this detail, bringing HAL back to life.

84. Note that the monolith was not always a blank surface; Kubrick and Clarke had first envisaged (and then abandoned) the idea of having the monolith project images on its surface, to teach Moon-Watcher and his companions (see Phillips 1977, 204).

85. Clarke, 2001, 69. Note also the fact that we are later told that the monolith on the moon was "deliberately buried." While this responds on one level to the "tombstone" imagery, it also responded (self-referentially) towards the "deliberate" ambiguity of the film.

86. Chion 2001, 87.

87. As Chion notes: "It is at once a screen and the opposite of a screen, since its black surface only absorbs, and sends nothing out" (op. cit. 116).

88. Agel 1970, 80. Galen Bullard also links the monolith to the symbolic nature of standing stones, such as the ones at Stonehenge, finding similarities in their mystical and spiritual properties "a standing stone says one thing unequivocally: 'I was placed here by an act of consciousness'" (Bullard 2003, 104).

89. Michel Chion has referred to the monolith as "a Tablet of Law without commandments" (Chion 2001, 143).

90. The Law (or Name) of the Father being a term used by Lacan to signify the phallic order structuring language. Taking his lead from Freud, Lacan argued that, at the time of the Oedipal crisis, the child is forced to separate from the mother Lacan saw as representing the

imaginary world to arrive at a sense of identity and to enter the social order, the *symbolic world*—in other words, the world of words or language, represented by the father. Thus it is a phallic authority that imposes and determines cultural order. As far as can be ascertained, a linkage to Lacan has seldom been appropriated within Kubrickian scholarship, although critic Barry Keith Grant has recently observed: "This obstacle, I would suggest, is phallic masculinity. The monoliths have a firm and solid presence and are seemingly everywhere, like the Law of the Father" (see Kolker 2006, 82).

91. As Kubrick put it: "I tried to work things out so that nothing important was said in the dialogue." Cited in Don Daniels, "A Skeleton Key to 2001," *Sight and Sound,* Winter 1970/1971.

92. See Paul Bizony: "The characters spent most of their time being icily polite to each other, without so much as once saying anything significant" (Bizony 2000, 16).

93. As was seen in the case of *Dr. Strangelove,* in the previous chapter, language is repeatedly an ambiguous issue in Kubrick's work, as Thomas Nelson noted: "Beginning with *The Killing,* his first novelistic adaptation, Kubrick's films repeatedly express an ambivalence towards language ... he constantly undermined and even ridiculed the authority of these verbal 'objective correlatives.' Here and elsewhere, Kubrick's film worlds suggest that understanding and mystery are matters of visual context and perspective, and not of words" (Nelson 2000, 115).

94. Philip French was one of the first critics to suggest this: "I once suggested that all Kubrick's pictures are about plans that go wrong" (Cited in Agel 1970, 239).

95. Agel 1970, 93.

96. Andrew Bailey, "A Clockwork Utopia: Semi-scrutable Stanley Kubrick Discusses his New Film," *Rolling Stone,* January 20, 1972. As Jan Harlan commented on an edition of the *Charlie Rose* television broadcast of June 15, 2001, *2001: A Space* Odyssey was "a big bow to an unknown creator" (http://www.charlierose.com/view/interview/3069).

97. Clarke, 2001, 192. Earlier in the novel, in a discussion of Moon-Watcher's tribe, and their thinking towards the "uplifters" or whomsoever were the makers of the monoliths, Clarke writes: "He was also learning to harness the forces of nature; with the taming of fire, he had lain the foundations of technology ... stone gave way to bronze ... hunting was succeeded by agriculture ... speech became eternal, thanks to certain marks on stone and clay and papyrus. Presently

he invented philosophy, and religion. And he peopled the sky, not altogether inaccurately with gods" (op. cit. 31). However, Stephen Baxter has pointed out how this idea does not bear very much analysis, insomuch as one might go on to ask, "Who uplifted the uplifters?" (Baxter in his introduction to the special edition of *2001: A Space* Odyssey; see Clarke 2001, xv). It is the same question John Allen posed: "If intelligent beings from elsewhere in time and space are needed to effect the regeneration of man, who effected the change for them? Where does the search for the ultimate cause of intelligence lead?" (cited in Agel 1970, 233).

98. Cited in Phillips 2001, 92.

99. Op. cit. 49.

100. Op. cit. 50.

101. Marie-Joseph-Pierre Teilhard de Chardin, born May 1, 1881, was one of the few Catholic intellectuals to attempt (and arguably succeed) in reconciling religion and science, specifically in terms of the nature of evolution. While still believing that the supreme event in the history of the universe was the incarnation of Christ, Teilhard de Chardin was convinced evolution, albeit a potential source of sin, would lead to greater and greater levels of higher forms of consciousness.

102. Hollis Alpert, "*2001*— Offbeat Director in Outer Space, *New York Times,* January 16, 1966.

103. As Renata Adler put it: "There is evidence in the film of Clarke's belief that men's minds will ultimately develop to the point where they dissolve into a kind of world mind" (Cited in Agel 1970, 207).

104. Clarke 2001, 209.

105. As Irving John Good, one of the proposed speakers in the prologue of the film, stated: "I think the ultra intelligent beings, in telepathic communication with one another, might almost be taken as a definition of God" (cited in Frewin 2005, 102).

106. Some of the concepts Kubrick was beginning to point towards might now be described as "anthropic cosmology." What Arthur Goldwag described as "a highly sophisticated brief for intelligent design," one that argues the odds of the Big Bang producing carbon based life was "vanishingly small." As Goldwag puts it: "Life is so unlikely ... that's its hard to believe that it is accidental, the physical laws of the universe somehow conspired to make it inevitable" (see Goldwag 2007, 146).

107. Note John Allen's review of the film in the *Christian Science Monitor:* "After a Last Sup-

per accompanied by bread and wine" (cited in Agel 1970, 233).

108. See Chion 2001, 141. Carolyn Geduld pushed this idea of religious imagery even further, perceiving of: "a corrupted Passion" in the crucifix imagery apparent in the way Jupiter, its moons, and the monolith were configured (Geduld 1973, 59). Geduld also saw an "Old Testament flavor" in the opening scenes of the Dawn of Man section of the film, seeing the arid landscape as suggestive of the third morning of creation: "When the land had been separated from the waters, but before the 'dawn' of even plant life" (op. cit. 36). Geduld also went onto comment: "Everything that happens in the Tyco crater ... is like a ritual, a sort of black mass centered around the altar like monolith" (op. cit. 49).

109. Note how Kubrick and Clarke, even though they were uncertain of the details of how the film would end, had thought out the basis of *an* ending at an early stage in the film's development. Clarke: "October 3, 1965 Bowman will regress to infancy, and we'll see him at the end as a baby in orbit" (Clarke 1972, 38).

110. Cited in Agel 1970, 265.

111. Herr 2000, 71.

112. Note, the title of the final part of the film, "Beyond the Infinite," is oxymoronically absurd — you cannot go "Beyond the Infinite." This was an idea that would be parodied, perhaps purposefully, in *Toy Story* (1995), with Buzz Lightyear's ubiquitous cry of "To infinity and beyond."

113. Garcia-Mainar 1999, 134.

114. Cited in LoBrutto 1997, 313.

115. Leonard F. Wheat speculates the reason so many reviewers have referred to the room at the end as being "a Louis XVI room," was simply because this derived from information in a press kit distributed to contemporary reviewers (See Wheat 2000, 86).

116. As Randy Rasmussen pointed out: "In symbolic terms, the monolith is an open door leading out of an apartment where earlier there had been no visible exit" (Rasmussen 2001, 109).

117. As Mario Falsetto also commented: "The shift from the Star-Gate to the final room sequence also can be viewed as a shift from a high modernist discourse to a more postmodern one. Individual consciousness gives way to a fractured, disengaged point of view, with no original character as origin. The audience's role as observer and participant is invoked as the film plays not only with our sense of logic but with the very concept of subjectivity" (Falsetto 2001, 117).

118. Note that the circular journey has a commonality within Kubrick's work as a whole, but it is perhaps most specifically apparent in *2001*.

119. Geduld 1973, 33.

120. Ciment 1983, 128.

121. Fiedler 1997, 370. Arthur C. Clarke has also cited Melville: "*Moby Dick*, of course has been mentioned many times in connection with *2001*; though it is asking for trouble to make such comparisons, I had this work consciously in mind as a prototype" (Clarke 1972b, 248).

122. However, there were other intertextual allusions, albeit in a less elevated context. For example, Carolyn Geduld noted comparisons between the film and Nigel Kneale's 1960 BBC television serial, *Quatermass and the Pit*. Geduld found similarities toward the Dawn of Man sequence: "In one episode, while excavating to enlarge the London underground, a five million-year-old alien artifact is discovered. Near it lie the ape ancestors of man whose skulls have been surgically modified to increase intelligence" (Geduld 1973, 22).

123. Other than "The Sentinel," five other stories are said to have provided ideas for the film: "Breaking Strain," "Out of the Cradle Endlessly Orbiting," "Who's There?" "Into the Comet," and "Before Eden." In addition, other elements from Clarke's past work informed the film; for example, the space-pods with their robotic arms, derived from Clarke's short story "Summertime on Icarus."

124. Clarke, 2001, xii.

125. Chion 2001, 21. One might note the wide range of literature published on the film, at the time of writing (January 2010) a total of 13 books have been published in English, each solely concerned with the film, probably few films have been the subject of such critical interest; see main bibliography for details.

126. From a textual point of view it is perhaps more rewarding to view the film of *2001* as a separate entity, a self-enclosed textual body that need have no reference to the novel or the several sequels Clarke would subsequently write.

127. See Alexander Walker: "By leaving the huge, serene eyes of the Star-Child fixed on filmgoers, Kubrick compels individual interpretation" (Walker 1999, 192).

128. King 2002, 75.

129. Bizony 2000, 16.

130. Cited in Christiane Kubrick 2002, 10.

131. Clarke 2001, 252.

132. Kolker 2006, 12.

133. Phillips 2001, 73.

Chapter 4

1. Castle 2005, 411. It is significant that Kubrick, at this stage in his career, felt confident enough to adapt Burgess's novel without the aid of a collaborator. He had recently written the script for *Napoleon* on his own, and would subsequently write the script of *Barry Lyndon* without the aid of another writer. However, after this, for what would prove to be his last three films (*The Shining, Full Metal Jacket* and *Eyes Wide Shut*), Kubrick would again seek the collaborative assistance of other writers. These films would be written with Diane Johnson, Michael Herr/Gustav Hasford, and Frederic Raphael.

2. Ciment 2001, 163.

3. Op. cit. 285.

4. Phillips and Hill 2002, 400.

5. Cited in Howard 1999, 80.

6. However, at least a possible inspiration for the "Singin' in the Rain" scene can be found in the novel; in the droogs' attack on the schoolteacher (not depicted in the film) Dim is described as "dancing round [his victim] with his crappy umbrella" (Burgess 1974, 10).

7. The novel did not specifically describe the lid-locks, Alex merely tells us: "[They] put like clips on the skin of my forehead, so that my top glazz-lids were pulled up and up and I could not shut my glazzies no matter how hard I tried" (op. cit. 80–81).

8. Burgess 2002, 26.

9. Ibid.

10. The date of the novel's (and hence the film's) setting was never explicitly specified. However, from the fact the policemen still wear Queen Elizabeth II monograms on their uniforms we might presume it was not too far in the future. The car Alex and his droogs steal (to play "the old hogs of the road") was a Durango 95, which might be seen as pointing to a potential setting around the year 1995. Alternatively, the prison Alex is sent is Staja 84, apart from informing us there are at least 84 state jails (Staja presumably being shorthand for State Jail) also points to another famous future dystopia, George Orwell's *1984* — and pointing to the idea the narrative might be taking place in the year 1984.

11. One might note how the film predates punk by about five years, but how it was arguably influential on the punk movement in its portrayal of Alex; as Marsha Kinder put it, the film "prefigures the punk aesthetic" (cited in Slocum 2001, 75).

12. Burgess was resistant to "any publisher's demand that a glossary be provided" (see Burgess 2002, 38). However, this resistance was generally ignored and most versions of the novel *did* include a glossary; the most comprehensive is to be found in McDougal 2003, 141–149.

13. Burgess was continuously resourceful in terms of linguistic invention. For example, take the term "yarbles"— a common epithet for testicles in the novel and in the film. This appears to have been a subtle conflation of the Russian *yaytsa*, meaning egg, while also offering a "testicular resonance" within the rhyming slang of the English "marbles."

14. The only sets constructed were the Korova Milk Bar, Mr. Alexander's bathroom and the prison reception hall.

15. Litvinoff and Raab were the original owners of the film rights to the novel, which they had acquired in the early 1960s. It proved an astute investment: aside from their credit as executive producers they received $200,000 for the rights and a five percent profit clause —"a potential windfall of around $1.2 million" (LoBrutto 1997, 339).

16. Biswell 2005, 353.

17. Note that Kubrick chose to shoot the attack on the tramp in a long shot, thus refusing to offer gratuitous close-ups of the violence being perpetrated. Throughout the film there was a sense in which the violence was suggested but rarely shown in an explicit way. It was either rendered, as here, in a long shot, or else the camera would cut away before we were forced to witness what was actually happening.

18. Burgess 1974, 16.

19. In Burgess's novel it is clear that Alex forcibly has sex with the two girls, somewhat removed from the consensual *ménage à trois* in the film. Finally, Kubrick disrupts the sexual quality of the scene by choreographing it with fast-motion photography, thus offering a comical rather than dramatic discourse.

20. See Burgess 1974, 72–73.

21. Op. cit. 34.

22. As Robert Kolker puts it: "Individuals— especially those with political power — rarely get upset over violent films. They get upset over films that ask questions about their violence" (Cited in McDougal 2003, 23).

23. On an unattributed television broadcast, sometime in the early 1970s, Anthony Burgess would joke: "If two nuns were raped in Aberdeen, the *Daily Mail* — almost as if out of routine — would ring me up to pass comment." Such a facetious remark chimes with the almost risible context of this argument and it is difficult, after so many years, to give much, if any, cre-

dence to these so-called copycat crimes. Finally, it might be pointed out how the film mysteriously failed to set off so-called copycat crimes on its re-release in 2000; as far as can be ascertained, no such crimes were reported.

24. Cited in Walker 1999, 208.

25. Cited in LoBrutto 1997, 338, and Ciment 2001, 157. See also: "The fact that Alex is the very personification of evil and is still in some strange way attractive is due to several things: his honesty, his lack of hypocrisy, his energy, and his intelligence. I've always compared him to Richard III, and I think it's a very good comparison" (Kubrick, talking to Gene Siskel, in "Kubrick's Creative Concern," *Chicago Tribune*, February 13, 1972 —cited in Phillips, 2001, 122–123).

26. Parsons 1994, 310–311.

27. Note how language (and a mastery over it) more easily allowed an identification with Alex, similar to the audience's alliance with another so-called human monster: Humbert Humbert in *Lolita*.

28. Kolker 2000, 148.

29. In the preface to his book, *Culture and Anarchy*, first published in 1873, Matthew Arnold famously defined culture as "the best which has been thought and said in the world."

30. Burgess 1974, 35.

31. Cited in McDougal 2003, 128.

32. Robert Hughes, "The Décor of Tomorrow's Hell," *Time*, December 27, 1971 (cited in McDougal 2003, 132).

33. In an interview, Kubrick would later add and concur with this argument: "I think this suggests the failure of culture to have any morally refining effect on society. Hitler loved good music and many top Nazis were cultured and sophisticated men but it didn't do them any good" (Ciment 2001 163).

34. We might note that while Alex is intelligent he is not intellectual; there is little sense of him thinking or analyzing. "Thinking was for the gloopy ones," says Alex in the film.

35. Cited in LoBrutto 1997, 356.

36. This was the first Hannibal Lecter novel and it, too, written only a decade after the Manson murders, was arguably influenced by this event in a similar way as the film of *A Clockwork Orange* had been.

37. Walker was writing in an early feminist film journal, *Women and Film 2* (1972), cited in McDougal 2003, 39.

38. Haskell 1987, 361–362.

39. The art critic Robert Hughes pointed out these figures were influenced by the sculptures of Allen Jones, the British pop artist and sculptor

(McDougal 2003, 132). This is probably factually correct as Kubrick would later admit he had seen an exhibition that displayed female figures as furniture, presumably those of Jones. However, the actual modeling of the fiberglass female nudes was the work of designer John Barry and his assistant, Liz Moore.

40. Such imagery in the Korova Bar later takes on a further sadomasochistic discourse: in the scene wherein Dim decants some "Milk-plus" from a model he refers to as Lucy, the model being represented as totally submissive, her wrists enchained, her nipples available, a phallic dispensing handle between her spread legs.

41. Kubrick's wife, Christiane Kubrick, reportedly found the violence in the film to be distressing and some of the sexual imagery misogynistic. According to one of Kubrick's biographers, Vincent LoBrutto, some of the scenes made Christiane physically ill, but then LoBrutto quotes her as saying: "That, of course, is what it's meant to do to you" (LoBrutto 1998, 375).

42. However, one might note how Katya Wyeth, the girl seen having sex with Alex at the end of the film, was "on top," in other words, in the superior position.

43. Brownmiller 1977, 15. (The italics in this quotation are Brownmiller's.)

44. Op. cit. 306.

45. Op. cit. 301.

46. Op. cit. 302.

47. It is known that Kubrick was an avid listener to BBC Radio— hence it is possible the name, Julian, may have been a subtle reference to the famous "gay" couple "Julian and Sandy," played by Kenneth Williams and Hugh Paddick in the 1960s BBC Radio program, *Round the Horne.*

48. The male figures in the mural are muscular and nearly nude — the pornographic graffiti additions suggesting anal intercourse. One might also note that the figure of Christ in the mural has an erection, something seemingly unnoticed in the general plethora of complaint about the film.

49. McDougal 2003, 67. John Baxter also noted this, seeing the film as being "powerfully homo-erotic," seeing Alex's appearance as having clear homoerotic resonances: "Alex, with his pale face, one eye made up with doll-like false eyelashes, his bulging codpiece ... belongs at the heart of gay iconography" (Baxter 1998, 250).

50. Note the extra Kubrickian touch — insomuch it is in his codpiece in which Alex appropriately keeps the rubber balls he uses to gag Mr. and Mrs. Alexander.

51. In this context Margaret DeRosia claims: "In the close-up of Alex's repeatedly beating one of them [one of Billyboy's gang] the angle of the shot, Alex's cries and the obvious pleasure he takes from the event imply that the blows could be read as a form of penetration" (McDougal 2003, 69).

52. In this sense one might note Daniel Shaw's comment: "A pat Freudian psychoanalysis of the behavior of Alexander DeLarge is clearly suggested by the filmic text. His father is precisely the type of weak figure that would have been unable to generate castration anxiety in his son, hence failing to trigger the primary repression from which the super-ego is said to result, according to Sigmund Freud" (See Abrams 2007, 222–223). In a similar sense, in terms of the phallic authority of the text, Alex's name — Alex de Large — deconstructs to the law of the large, which brings to mind (once again) an association with Lacan's Law of the Father, the phallus as the ultimate signifier.

53. Also, note Georgie's comment to Alex in the Flatblock Lobby scene: "Brother, you think and talk sometimes like a little child."

54. Cited in Ciment 2001, 158.

55. Philip Strick and Penelope Houston, "Modern Times: An Interview with Stanley Kubrick," *Sight and Sound,* Spring 1972. Cited in Phillips, 2001, 128.

56. To paraphrase the behaviorist model, for Skinner there were no criminals, no heroes or cowards, no geniuses or fools, there were merely "individuals whose behavior is determined by the environment" (See Stokes 2003, 201).

57. However, Kubrick is on record as citing Skinner as a reference point: "You know the authority on all this (freewill and conditioning) is Skinner and his latest works state the premise that human freedom and dignity have become inconsistent with the survival of our civilization" (Andrew Bailey, "A Clockwork Utopia: Semi-scrutable Stanley Kubrick Discusses his New Film," *Rolling Stone,* January 20, 1972).

58. *New York Times,* January 4, 1972.

59. *New York Times,* January 30, 1972.

60. *Bob Dylan: A Retrospective,* (New York: Morrow, 1972)

61. *New York Times,* January 30, 1972.

62. *New York Times,* February 13, 1972.

63. *New York Times* February 27, 1972.

64. Ibid.

65. It is perhaps pertinent to observe how later criticism saw the film in an exactly opposite way; for example: "There is one major thematic point in Kubrick's *A Clockwork Orange* that mer-

its detailed attention here: the film's unrelenting condemnation of fascism" (see Phillips and Hill 2002, 57).

66. *New York Times* January 30, 1972.

67. Ibid.

68. Cited in Falsetto 1996, 190.

69. Pauline Kael "A Clockwork Orange: Stanley Strangelove," *The New Yorker,* January 1, 1972 (cited in McDougal 2003, 134).

70. Op. cit. 137.

71. Op. cit. 138.

72. Op. cit. 136.

73. Op. cit. 139.

74. Robert Hughes, "The Décor of Tomorrow's Hell," *Time,* December 27, 1972 (cited in McDougal 2003, 131).

75. Cited in LoBrutto 1997, 334.

76. Walker 1999, 223.

77. Note how, in this context, Randy Rasmussen envisaged Alex's droogs as playing, "Goering, Goebbels and Himmler to his Hitler" (Rasmussen 2002, 116).

78. Ciment 2001, 149.

79. McDougal 2003, 6.

80. Note, however, that the tramp's comment about men on the moon was, in fact, drawn directly from the novel. See Burgess 1974, 15.

81. Ciment 2001, 61.

82. There were other inferences; for example, Alexander Walker perceived of a resonance to *Dr. Strangelove* via Mr. Alexander's wheelchair-bound antics. Incidentally, Patrick Magee's "antic" performance in the film was much criticized for belonging to the "carpet chewing school of acting." However, it is possible to argue that this was a deliberate intention, especially as it had some provenance from the novel. Alex describes Mr. Alexander as having "a like mad or bezoomy look in his glazzies ... I could viddy quite clear he was going off his gulliver" (Burgess 1974, 125 and 126).

83. In addition, there were such mirrorings as Alex being forced to watch the images within the Ludovico Treatment as Mr. Alexander was forced to watch his wife's rape; Alex being pushed into the water trough as he had thrown his droogs into the waters of the marina. Also, note how Mr. Alexander's red typewriter in the first scene is mirrored by a blue in the second, with the same opening phrase being spoken by Mr. Alexander: "Who on earth could that be?"

84. Cocks, Diedrick, Perusek 2005, 149. In a similar way James Naremore's recent book *On Kubrick,* clearly if mistakenly states Kubrick was unaware of the omitted last chapter (see Naremore, 2007, 158).

85. Biswell 2005, 353.
86. Op. cit. 354
87. Ibid.
88. Kubrick himself is on record as stating the final chapter was "unconvincing and inconsistent with the style and intent of the book ... I certainly never gave any serious consideration to using it" (cited in Ciment 2001, 157).
89. One might note here that the screenplay Burgess had written for Nicholas Roeg to direct (see Appendix 6 for further details) had also disregarded the 21st chapter, presumably for similar reasons to Kubrick's.
90. Thomas Nelson has described the film as "a Swiftian fable and linguistic *tour de force*" (Nelson 2000, 136).
91. Kolker, 2000, 128.
92. Cited in McDougal 2003, 35.
93. Baxter 1998, 265.
94. Christiane Kubrick 2002, 140.
95. James Howard, "U.K. Clock Ticks Again for Kubrick's Orange," The Kubrick Site, *www. visual-memory.co.uk.* Accessed July 9, 2002.
96. The masculine circular journey was literally played out at various points in the film: in the prison exercise yard scene; and also in the "Music Bootick" scene wherein Alex made a somewhat derisive 360-degree walk around the shop.
97. As Margaret DeRosia noted: "The opening tracking shot of *A Clockwork Orange* has often been discussed as a symbol of Alex's narrative mastery" (McDougal 2003, 65).

Chapter 5

1. Richter 2002, 24.
2. Ciment 2001, 271.
3. See Cocks, Diedrick, Perusek 2005, 10.
4. Baxter 1998, 302.
5. Falsetto 1996, 245.
6. See Fiedler 1997, 135.
7. Hollis Alpert, "2001— Offbeat Director in Outer Space," *New York Times,* January 16, 1966. Diane Johnson has confirmed this intent: "I think Stanley wants to make the best horror film ever made" (Aljean Harmetz, "Kubrick Films *The Shining* in Secrecy in English Studio, *New York Times,* November 6, 1978).
8. One might note, in this context, Robert Kolker's description of *The Shining* as "a broad, loud, perfectly unsubtle film, it is more a parody of the horror genre than a film seriously intent on giving its audience a fright" (Kolker 2000, 99).
9. Diane Johnson had had little previous experience in screenwriting prior to her work on

The Shining. Kubrick may have decided to work with Johnson because of her novel *The Shadow Knows* (1974), a narrative concerned with a solitary woman threatened by a stalker, a book Kubrick briefly considered filming. He may also have been interested in Johnson's role as an academic. As Johnson herself noted, "I think he was also aware of my university baggage — I teach the Gothic novel — and there was a bit of the academic in Kubrick" (Ciment 2001, 293).
10. Ciment 1983, 194.
11. As if to alleviate the believability of the plot, it seems Kubrick and Johnson sought an alternate way of answering the question: do the ghosts exist or do the ghosts not exist? Diane Johnson: "There's a third, more complicated possibility. The psychological states of the characters can create real ghosts who have physical powers. If Henry VIII sees Anne Boleyn walking the bloody tower, she's a real ghost, but she's also caused by his hatred" (Aljean Harmetz, "Kubrick Films *The Shining* in Secrecy in English Studio, *New York Times,* November 6, 1978). Thus the supernatural presences in the hotel have been, to quote Johnson again: "Somehow generated by human psychology, but, once generated, really existed and had power" (Diane Johnson quoted in Cocks, Diedrick, Perusek 2005, 58).
12. Geoffrey Cocks, "The Hinting: Holocaust Imagery in Kubrick's The Shining," *Psychohistory Review,* Autumn 1987.
13. See Appendix 8 for a discussion of the 1996 television movie remake, made from this "unread" script.
14. Ciment 1983, 181 and 185, and LoBrutto 1998, 411. King's lack of revision is well known, as he himself has admitted: "My own schedule is pretty clear-cut. Mornings belong to whatever is new — the current composition. Afternoons are for naps and letters. Evenings are for reading, family, Red Sox games on TV, and any revisions that just cannot wait" (King 2000, 118–119). See Appendix 8 for a further and fuller discussion of King's views on writing and storytelling.
15. Underwood and Miller 1990, 15–42.
16. According to George Beahm, this short story was inspired by Ray Bradbury's "The Veldt": a "story of a child's playroom gone awry" (Beahm 1993, 91).
17. Underwood and Miller 1990, 15–42.
18. King's original manuscript for the novel was apparently even longer, it had a prologue and epilogue, called "Before the Play" and "After the Play," but King was constrained into deleting them for reasons of length. "Before the Play" told

the story of the Overlook's history before the story begins—it was published in *Whispers* 17/18, August 1982. "After the Play" told the story of what happened to the Overlook after the novel's explosive closure; it has never been published and has apparently been lost.

19. Magistrale 2003, 197.

20. Cited in Jenkins 1997, 73.

21. Ibid.

22. Aljean Harmetz, "Kubrick Films *The Shining* in Secrecy in English Studio," *New York Times,* November 6, 1978.

23. As might be seen from a reading of some of his other films, Kubrick always had an awareness of the potency of fairy tale: "I believe fantasy stories at their best serve the same function for us that fairy tales and mythology formerly did. The current popularity of fantasy, particularly in films, suggests that popular culture isn't getting what it wants from realism" (Ciment 1983, 181).

24. Denise Bingham makes a similar observation to this in Falsetto 1996, 298–299.

25. See Roland Barthes, "Textual Analysis: Poe's *Valdemar*," in Lodge 1992, 176.

26. Bettelheim does not mention Propp by name in his book, but the influences are clearly apparent. Maria Tatar, in her book, *The Hard Facts of the Grimm's Fairy Tales*, notes Propp's influence on Bettelheim while also noting his "curious absence" (see Tatar 2003, no page number available).

27. It is possible that Kubrick may have become cognizant of Propp while working with Jim Thompson. Thompson would later state: "There are thirty-two ways to write a story, and I've used every one, but there is only one plot: things are not as they seem." The notable fact here being Thompson's idea of there being 32 ways to write a story; note that there are, in fact, 32 narrative functions in Propp's list (he includes a number 8a) although the common nomenclature is to state 31 functions.

28. See Appendix 8 for details of the way in which the film accomplishes this, a complete listing and analysis of the way the film follows Propp's narratological theories.

29. Clare Hanson, "Stephen King: Powers of Horror," in Docherty 1990, 145–149.

30. King 1977, 82. It is perhaps interesting to note, in this context, that the derivation of the word *infant,* from the Latin, originally meant "unable to speak."

31. Op. cit. 116.

32. Op. cit. 120.

33. Jonathan Romney "Resident Phantoms" *Sight and Sound* September 1999, 11.

34. In the novel, the fact that George Hatfield, an adolescent, partway between the child and an adult, had a speech impediment—seemed to add to the idea of the novel's concern with the difficulties in moving from the imaginary to the symbolic.

35. An untitled photograph, by Kubrick, from 1950, of a girl writing "I Hate Love!" on a door with lipstick, offered a somewhat eerie prediction of this scene (see Crone 2005, 8).

36. A diverse range of critics have mistaken the Grady girls as twins, disregarding their clear and obvious difference in ages. For example, Anthony Magistrale wrote of "a haunting echo to Grady's dead twin daughters" (Magistrale 2003, 97). Similarly, Alexander Walker mistakenly referred to Grady's "twin daughters" (Walker 1999, 285). Michel Ciment spoke of "the apparitions of the twins" (Ciment 1983, 135). Steve Biodrowski alluded to "the twin ghost girls who invite Danny to play with them forever" (see *www.hollywoodgothique.com/shining1980.html*). While Paul Duncan spoke of "the twin girls" Danny sees in a vision (Duncan 1999, 73). There are specific reasons to account for such misapprehensions, and these will be discussed later in the chapter.

37. Baxter 1998, 310.

38. Cocks 2004, 205.

39. Ibid.

40. Underwood and Miller 1990, 49.

41. King 1977, 399.

42. Op. cit. 176.

43. Op. cit. 399.

44. Op. cit. 411.

45. Op. cit. 377.

46. Op. cit. 398.

47. In terms of the horror genre, Wendy can also be seen in a different light—critic Robert Kolker saw her as an early example of the genre's "final girl." See Appendix 8 for a fuller discussion of this.

48. LoBrutto 1998, 415, and Ciment 1983, 189.

49. Geoffrey Cocks has also alluded, albeit obliquely, to this. Cocks perceived of the blood flowing from the elevator as "an image of menstruation," of "the eerie feminine space of human origin" (Cocks 2004, 204).

50. King 1977, 255.

51. As Norman Mailer put it in *The Prisoner of Sex*: "That unmentionable womb, that spongy pool, that time machine with a curse, dam for an ongoing river of blood." Cited in Siann 1994, 122.

52. Segal 1994, 225.

53. See, for example, Roger Horrocks: "Why

do men continually look at naked female bodies, why the constant preoccupation with women's genitals? A Freudian explanation might be that the trauma of castration and sexual difference has to be constantly gone over and over again, because it is never quite believed—do women really not have a penis—let me have another look" (Horrocks 1995, 114).

54. The eponymous Dr. Strangelove, Bowman at the end of *2001: A Space Odyssey*, Mr. Alexander in *A Clockwork Orange*, Sir Charles Lyndon in *Barry Lyndon*. Robert Kolker perceived of a further exploration of this theme in *Barry Lyndon*: "Barry Lyndon, who wanders Europe only to return to be defeated and castrated" (Kolker 2000, 172). In a similar sense Michel Ciment noted: "Bullingdon symbolically castrates his [father] by having him physically mutilated" (Ciment 2001, 117). In a more facetious vein, Alexander Walker noted how the loss of Barry's leg in *Barry Lyndon* was a literal reminder of the presumptions of "social climbing" (Walker 1988, 297).

55. There were other phallic symbols in the film. For example, Wendy's appropriation of the baseball bat to defend herself against Jack. One might also note the carpet in Room 237, which offered a recurring pattern of somewhat obvious erect phalluses and testicles.

56. King 1977, 21.

57. Op. cit. 97.

58. Op. cit. 21.

59. Op. cit. 3 (King's italics).

60. Op. cit. 4.

61. Ibid.

62. Op. cit. 109.

63. Op. cit. 270.

64. Geoffrey Cocks also perceived of a similar interpretation, seeing "a sexual ambiguity" within the characters of Ullman and Watson (Cocks 2004, 298–299). A cursory viewing of the film suggests that Ullman and Watson are leaving together, as a couple, for the winter's break.

65. See Sedgwick's *Between Men: English Literature and Male Homosocial Desire* (New York: Columbia University Press, 1985).

66. Kolker 2000, 164.

67. Spargo 1999, 19.

68. Phillips and Hill, 2002, 265.

69. It has been said that Kubrick substituted the maze in the film because he did not believe that current special effects would have rendered the hedge animals of the novel in a believable way. However, it is also possible that Kubrick was predicated on the idea of a maze metaphor

throughout the film. This motif could be seen, for example, in the mountain roads—winding up to the hotel—at the start of the film; in the maze-like patterns consistently represented in the carpets of the hotel; in the Native American rugs that hung on the walls of the hotel; and in the corridors and interior of the hotel itself.

70. By way of coincidence, King's first four published novels had all ended in conflagrations. In *Carrie* the town was burned down by Carrie's psychic abilities; in *Salem's Lot* the town was burned down to destroy the vampires; in *The Shining* the boiler of the hotel exploded; and in *The Stand*, Las Vegas—a citadel of evil forces—was destroyed by the detonation of a nuclear device. This was not to be the case in Kubrick's adaptation; in Kubrick's ending the hotel remained intact, awaiting future caretakers, in a never-to-be-made sequel. However, note that while Kubrick chose not to re-enact the conflagration that ended King's novel, in a sense Kubrick's hotel *did* burn down. In January 1979, a fire on the set severely damaged Kubrick's Overlook, necessitating major set rebuilding.

71. Cited in LoBrutto 1998, 453.

72. Falsetto 1996, 244.

73. An explicit source from *The Twilight Zone* has not been traced; it is possible that King and Jameson may have been suggesting a generic inference, rather than a specific episode.

74. The ending of the film has often been compared to Michael Snow's 1967 experimental film, *Wavelength*. See Appendix 8 for a fuller discussion of this and of other potential intertextual references in the film.

75. Garcia-Mainar 2000, 56.

76. Jonathan Romney, "Resident Phantoms," *Sight and Sound*, September 1999, 9–10.

77. Cited in Romney 1999, 10.

78. P.L. Titterington, "Kubrick and *The Shining*," *Sight and Sound*, Spring 1981.

79. Romney 1999, 9. One might note, however, that in the final scene, the slow camera movement through the Overlook, that the furniture was draped with white sheets, suggesting either a forward or backward movement in time from the morning after Jack's death in the maze.

80. In terms of a postmodern reading of the film, one might also consider Frederic Jameson's famous comment that postmodernism elicited "nostalgia for the present." As Jameson also commented, "Our entire contemporary social system has little by little begun to lose its capacity to retain its own past, has begun to live in a perpetual present" (cited in Abrams 2007, 203).

81. Jean François Lyotard *The Postmodern*

Condition: A Report on Knowledge (Minneapolis: University of Minnesota Press, and Manchester: Manchester University Press, 1984), p. xxiv. (Note: the original French edition of Lyotard's book, *La Condition Postmodern: Rapport sur le Savoir*, was published in France in 1979, but was not translated into English until 1984.)

82. King 1977, page number untraced.

83. Geoffrey Cocks, "Stanley Kubrick's Dream Machine: Psychoanalysis, Film and History," *Journal of Psychoanalysis 31,* 2003, 35.

84. Cited in LoBrutto 1998, 412.

85. Ciment 1983, 192.

86. See, also, Rasmussen 2001, 246: "With a bald head, bowed legs and an easy manner of speech, Dick Halloran might have supplied stereotypical black comic relief in old Hollywood films contemporaneous with [the] Overlook's so-called heyday."

87. Falsetto 1996, 305.

88. Randy Rasmussen makes a similar point, describing Mr. Ullman's comment on the hotel's beginnings: "His casual manner reduces a once passionate cultural conflict to a trivial footnote in history" (Rasmussen 2001, 245).

89. Geoffrey Cocks notes that Diane Johnson has confirmed the idea that the persecution of the Native Americans had "intrigued Kubrick as a historical basis for the violent curse of the Overlook Hotel" (see Cocks 2004, 245).

90. See Toni Morrison *Playing in the Dark: Whiteness and the Literary Imagination* (London: Picador, 1992), 9.

91. The opening of *The Shining*, with the aerial perspective of Jack's car, also instilled the idea that some malevolent force was watching. This sense of being watched was felt at later points in the film; for example, of something following Danny's buggy, and the perspective of the maze as Jack looks at the model. Thus, throughout the film, there was the overall idea of a malevolently inclined presence observing proceedings. As Robert Kolker pointed out, "Obsessive movements through the corridors of the Overlook Hotel, suggest ... the point of view of an Other, of some monstrous, destructive force that reigns" (Kolker 2000, 163).

92. As is well known, the Volkswagen originated as the Nazis' people's car: literally the car of the folk. Thus the change of color in the film may not have been coincidence. Cocks noted the manifest cultural reference "the medieval practice of making Jews wear *der goldenen Fleck* which was revived by the Nazis in the form of the yellow Star of David ... they forced the Jews to wear" (Geoffrey Cocks, "The Hinting: Holo-

caust Imagery in Kubrick's The Shining," *Psychohistory Review*, Autumn 1987, 127). In addition, Grady's spilling of (yellow) Advocaat over Jack was also positioned as a symbol of the yellow Star of David, with which the Nazis "marked Jews with the stain of prejudice" (Cocks 2004, 246).

93. Cocks 2004, 251.

94. Op. cit. 246

95. Op. cit. 248

96. King 1977, 221.

97. Cocks 2004, 124.

98. Geoffrey Cocks's "Bringing the Holocaust Home: Freudian Dynamics of Kubrick's *The Shining Psychoanalytic Review*, Spring 1991, 120. (Cocks also devised an ingenious way of interpreting the use of numerical symbolism in the film to support his argument; see Appendix 8 for a discussion of this.)

99. Cocks 2003, 38 and 44.

100. Jameson 1990, 90.

101. See, for example, Baxter 1995, 254, Kubrick: "I share the widespread fascination with the horror of the Nazi period."

102. It is well known that Kubrick made detailed preparations to make a film explicitly about the Holocaust; the early 1990s project: *Aryan Papers,* based on Louis Begley's novel, *Wartime Lies* (see Appendix 12). However, Cocks states that much earlier, in 1975, Kubrick had contacted Isaac Bashevis Singer with a view to working on a screenplay "for a Holocaust film" (Cocks 2004, 161).

103. Herr 2000, 7.

104. Some sense of this can be seen in Elem Klimov's *Come and See* (1985), a World War II film not directly about the Holocaust, but at times depicting scenes that were very nearly unwatchable.

105. Lehman 1991, 186. See also, Al Alvarez: "Since what happened to them [Holocaust victims] was beyond the imagination, it was therefore also beyond art and all those human values on which art is based" (cited in Andrews 1996, 96).

106. As Kubrick's wife, Christiane Kubrick, put it: "He knew that the Holocaust was unwatchable" (see Joan Dupont, "Kubrick Speaks, Through Family's Documentary," *International Herald Tribune*, September 15, 2001). An additional reason may have been because Kubrick, given his lifelong interest in storytelling, had concluded that the Holocaust simply did not have a narrative. It may be that there is simply no narrative device that can embrace the murder of six million people.

107. Cocks 1991, 125. However, there were other potential Holocaust references which Cocks does not mention; for example, in a scene near the end of the film Danny escapes from Jack by hiding in what appears to be a gas oven. Steven Spielberg, for one, appears to have been taken with this idea, insomuch as he clearly parodied it in *Jurassic Park* (1993).

108. For example, Cocks goes into the subject of Kubrick's relationship to his Jewish identity in some depth, talking of the absurdity of trying "to understand Kubrick" without a recourse to his Jewishness, but this elides the question of whether we are trying to understand Kubrick or whether we are trying to understand Kubrick's films. Cocks writes, "There in fact was— and is— always one Jew at the centre of every Kubrick film. The one behind the camera: Stanley Kubrick" (Cocks 2004, 32).

109. See LoBrutto 1997, 53.

110. Interestingly, Cocks provided a photograph Kubrick had taken in 1948 of two sisters— Phyllis, aged five, and Barbara, aged eight — who had been saved from carbon monoxide poisoning (see Cocks, Diedrick and Perusek 2006, 210). One therefore has to ask whether Arbus, a former colleague of Kubrick, had in some way — albeit unconsciously — been influenced by Kubrick's original photograph when she took her famous portrait in 1967. However, Arbus committed suicide in 1971 and, hence, never lived to comment on Kubrick's referencing of her photograph.

111. The only apparent reference appearing in King 1977, 352: "My own girls, sir, didn't care for the Overlook at first," says Mr. Grady. "One of them actually stole a pack of my matches and tried to burn it down."

112. Sean Hagen, *The Observer*, April 17, 2005.

113. Herr 2000, 61.

114. Op. cit. 91.

Chapter 6

1. As Michel Ciment comments: "an institutionalized form of violence ... appears in all his [Kubrick's] work" (Ciment 2001, 234).

2. The phrase is Gene Siskel's, cited in Phillips 2001, 187.

3. To this list one might add: *Napoleon—* Kubrick's never made film of one of history's most brilliant military minds; and also, *Aryan Papers—* the World War II film with the Holocaust as its background, a film that Kubrick, for a time at least in the early 1990s, fully intended to make.

4. Kubrick, Herr, Hasford 1987, 3. The quoted words are taken from the stage directions in the published screenplay, most likely Kubrick's own, unadorned, prose, these "stage directions," at times, enhancing an understanding of the film's discourse.

5. Elvis Presley was inducted into the U.S. Army on March 24, 1958, at which time his hair was cut off to worldwide publicity (See Coffey, 1997, 156).

6. Garcia-Mainar 1999, 199.

7. For a discussion of the homoerotic appeal of the Western, see Jane Tomkins' *West of Everything* and Michael Wood's *America in the Movies*.

8. See Rodney and Hill, 2002, 159.

9. Cited in Bristow 1997, 211.

10. Cocks, Diedrick and Perusek 2006, 218.

11. Charles B. Harris, in his introduction of the 1997 edition of *Love and Death in the American Novel* (Fiedler 1997, vi).

12. Ibid.

13. Op. cit. vii.

14. Nelson 2000, 246.

15. See Fiedler 1997, 350–351.

16. Hartman's discourse veered still further towards the blasphemous later in the film; in describing the cleanliness of the barracks latrines, Hartman famously declared: "Even the Virgin Mary herself would be proud to go in there and take a dump!"

17. Michael Pursell, "*Full Metal Jacket:* The Unraveling of Patriarchy," *Literature/Film Quarterly,* 16, no. 4 (1988), 218–225 (cited in Falsetto 1996, 324).

18. Willoquet-Maricondi 1994, 5.

19. Herr 1978, 199.

20. Ciment 2001, 250.

21. Penelope Gilliat, "Mankind on the Late, Late Show," *The Observer*, September 6, 1987.

22. LoBrutto 1997, 490.

23. Nelson 2000, 245.

24. Op. cit. 242.

25. The use of frame-by-frame DVD technology shows that a significant amount of tissue explodes from Eightball's body when he is shot; we appear to see the bloodied remnants of his genitals cascading in slow motion through the air.

26. Kubrick, Herr, Hasford, 1987, 87. The dialogue is exactly as written in the published screenplay, hence it is interesting to note the lack of any attempt to un-colloquialize the background directions, as in, for example, "takes out his dick." This is especially marked as elsewhere the screenplay becomes poetic and almost lyrical, for example: "Hartman looks suddenly calm. His eyes, his manner are those of a wanderer who

has found his home" (op. cit. 46) The former perhaps suggesting Kubrick's hand, the latter Herr's.

27. Hasford 1985, 109.

28. Op. cit. 176.

29. www.visual-memory.co.uk/amk/doc/0065.htm (accessed September 13, 2005). See Appendix 9 for a more extensive discussion of the earlier draft of the film's screenplay.

30. Herr 1978, 110.

31. Cited in Easthope 1986, 19.

32. Ciment 2001, 234.

33. Garcia-Mainar 1999, 202. It is perhaps significant to note that although the recruits possessed the phallus in a literal sense, they did not, in reality, control the libidinal economy. In the film, as we have seen, the recruits' rifles were equated with their penises: one (the rifle) was "for fighting," while the other (the penis) was "for fun." However, as Garcia-Mainar also pointed out, this was: "a sexuality based on the phallus" that was "turned into an object of attack by the Vietnamese girl" (op. cit. 233). In other words, we might note that while the sniper may not have a phallus she does have a gun, which she uses to devastating effect.

34. Kolker 2000, 106.

35. In passing it is perhaps interesting to note Gustav Hasford's novel *The Short Timers* was clearly influenced by the earlier Vietnam novel — Tim O'Brien's *If I Die in a Combat Zone,* published six years before, in 1973. For example, the song chanted by the recruits as they were marching/jogging — was still more obscene in O'Brien.

36. Fiedler 1997, 267.

37. Falsetto 1996, 94.

38. See Matthew Modine *Full Metal Diary* New York: Rugged Land, 2005, 242. (Note: Modine's text has no pagination; to locate this source, the reader will be required to count the pages.)

39. Gomer Pyle was originally the "simpleminded" gas station attendant from the American television series *The Andy Griffith Show,* played by Jim Nabors, who continued playing the role in the show, *Gomer Pyle, U.S.M.C.,* from 1964–1969; hence contemporaneous with the time frame of *Full Metal Jacket.* In the latter show Gomer was a foil to a "hard-nosed" drill instructor, Sgt. Vince Carter, played by Frank Sutton.

40. The other obvious examples were General Ripper, HAL and Jack Torrance. In this light it is interesting to note how their delusional states often had a repressive sexual reasoning: General Ripper believed the communists were polluting his precious bodily fluids; HAL's problems arguably derived, at least in part, from a "same-sex" jealousy; Jack Torrance problem could be argued as ultimately deriving from impotency problems with Wendy.

41. Nelson 2000, 247.

42. Herr 2000, 45.

43. Nelson 2000, 242.

44. See Barry 1995, 108–115 and Selden 1993, 224–227.

45. Selden 1993, 226.

46. "Surfin' Bird," performed by The Trashmen, written by Al Frazier, Carl White, Turner Wilson, Jr., and Sonny Harris.

47. "Wooly Bully," performed by Sam the Sham and the Pharaohs, written by Domingo Samudio.

48. The earlier draft of the screenplay had a number of other rhyming phrases. For example: Lieutenant Lockhart's: "I've had my ass in the grass"; Sergeant Gerheim's: "You queer for Private Cowboy's gear?"; The Vietnamese prostitute's: "Fuckey, suckey, smoke cigarette in pussy."

49. Kagan 2000, 227.

50. See Nelson 2000, 239: "The two-part structure of *Full Metal Jacket* seemingly violates the three act paradigm found in most mainstream films."

51. Cited in Nelson 2000, 229.

52. Ibid.

53. The novel had three sections: "The Spirit of the Bayonet," 1–33; "Body Count," 35–140; and "Grunts," 141–180. The published screenplay showed a more delineated structure of two halves: Part 1, 1–51, and Part 2, 52–129.

54. The precise chronology is probably not entirely relevant; however, we know the second half of the film begins just before the Tet Offensive of January 1968; furthermore, we know Christmas is celebrated near the end of the film's first half; in addition, Joker tells us, at the end of the film, he is "short," meaning he has served something close to his allocated one-year's duty in Vietnam. Thus, in an overall sense, we can presume the first half of the film takes place in November and December 1966.

55. Penelope Gilliat noted that the film's version of Vietnam was a world without "compass points ... a young black American turns a map round and round in vain and finally says, 'I think we should change direction.' 'Yes, but where to?'" ("Mankind on the Late, Late Show" Penelope Gilliat, *The Observer,* September 6, 1987).

56. Kolker 2000, 116.

57. As in the case of *The Shining* and the use of Diane Arbus's photograph, "Identical Twins," the image of the machine gunner in the helicop-

ter may have been consciously referencing another famous still photograph: Larry Burrows's
celebrated picture "On *Yankee Papa 13*, Vietnam
1965."

58. See Bill Krohn, in Jonathan Crary and
Sanford Kwinter (eds.) *Zone 6: Incorporations*
(New York: Urzone, 1992), 428–435.

59. Walker 1988, 295.

60. Note here Baudrillard's famous (if misunderstood) claim that the first Gulf War had
not happened and was a mere simulation. The
hyper-reality of *Full Metal Jacket* could thus be
compared to the way Kubrick depicted New York
City in *Eyes Wide Shut*, or to the way he depicted
outer space in *2001*, or to the way he depicted the
18th century in *Barry Lyndon*. As Thomas Doherty put it: "*Full Metal Jacket* is not Vietnam As
It Really Was, but as Kubrick realized it ... the
tableau functions mainly as a hallucinatory
dreamscape, not a geographical space" (cited in
Falsetto 1996, 315).

61. See Falsetto 2001, 95, for a further discussion of this issue.

62. Garcia-Mainar 1999, 200–201. (Other
critics have often perceived of other potential
visual references to *2001: A Space Odyssey*; for
example, to the monolith-like structure apparent
in the closing scenes in Hue City.)

63. Alexander Walker wrote of "Hasford's
first-person storyteller, a 'wise-guy' ex-college
kid, [who] possess[ed] the same demonic energy, survival talents, and flagrant but 'cool' in-
subordination of Burgess's anti-hero" (Walker
1999, 317).

64. See Reichmann 2007, 210.

65. Other critics have commented on this
connection; for example, Thomas Nelson saw
the training of the troops as a "Ludovico Treatment in reverse" (Nelson 2000, 238); Norman
Kagan saw the film's depiction that "killers are
made not born" as "reversing" the perspective in
A Clockwork Orange (Kagan 2000, 227).

66. See Walker 1999, 317.

67. Howard 1999, 169. Howard noted how
both films begin with a training program, which
then climaxes with a murderous assault on a drill
instructor, after which the hero "is launched
upon the world" (ibid).

68. Cited in Ciment 2001, 250.

69. Ibid.

70. LoBrutto 1997, 459.

71. Herr, Kubrick, Hasford 1987, vi.

72. However, some of Hasford's best lines
were not used; for example: "If the meek ever
inherit the earth, the strong will take it away
from them" (Hasford 1985, 14). "It takes a lot of

guts to do what Winslow did. I mean, you can see
Winslow's guts and he sure had of lot of them"
(op. cit. 73). "History may be written with blood
and iron but it's printed with ink" (op. cit. 62).
"If you kill for fun, you're a sadist. If you kill for
money you're a sadist. If you kill for both, you're
a Marine" (op. cit. 158).

73. Note how in addition to Hasford's source
novel, the script of the film also included diverse
and significant elements from Michael Herr's
book, *Dispatches*; see Appendix 9 for comprehensive details of this.

74. Thomson 2002, 480. Thomson also criticized Kubrick for pandering to the tastes of the
audience's appetite "for sensation and vulgarity
in the guise of importance" (op. cit. 479).

75. Hughes 2000, 235. The film also proved
to be a commercial as well as a critical success, albeit in a relatively modest way. The filming of
Full Metal Jacket had begun in August 1985 and
ended in September 1986, costing only an estimated $17 million; it was released in the United
States on June 26, 1987, grossing $38 million in
its first 50 days of release.

76. Michael Herr, cited in *Stanley Kubrick: A
Life in Pictures* (Jan Harlan, 2001).

Chapter 7

1. Cited in Agel 1970, 171.

2. See Baxter 1998, 60, and Phillips and Hill
2002, 338 for further details of this association.

3. Nelson 2000, 260.

4. See Watson, 2000, 14.

5. Note: Andrew Birkin, an assistant of
Kubrick's in the 1960s and 1970s, would eventu-
ally make an adaptation of Zweig's novel. See
Appendix 10 for further details.

6. Cited in Hughes 2000, 263.

7. Cited in Nelson 2000, 261.

8. Cited in Schwam 2000, xvii. Also note:
The *Kubrick Archives* includes a hand-written
file card, by Kubrick, dated May 22, 1968, stating: "*Rhapsody* ... Jay Cocks' agent says $40,000
but obviously high" (See Castle 2005, 482).

9. Castle 2005, 512.

10. First published in *Take One* May/June
1971, reprinted in Phillips, 2001, 105–107.

11. From sporadic indications it is known
that work on the *Traumnovelle* adaptation was
ongoing. For example, in 1979 Steve Martin visited Kubrick to discuss the possibility of starring
in the potential film. In 1983 Kubrick's past collaborator Terry Southern was involved in the
project for a short time; see Hill, 2001, 259, for
further details of this.

12. Michel Chion: "At first Kubrick was thinking in terms of a 'period movie' transposed to London or even Dublin ... to the society described by James Joyce's short story 'The Dead'" (Chion 2002, 16).

13. See Appendix 10 for a full discussion of Raphael's involvement in the development of the film.

14. See Candia McWilliam, "There was an Atmosphere Nicely Poised Between a Séance and a Game of Chess," *The Guardian,* March 13, 1999.

15. Ibid.

16. Ibid.

17. Sara Maitland, "My Year with Stanley," *The Independent,* March 12, 1999.

18. Raphael 1999, 92.

19. See Appendix 10 for a discussion of the initial shooting script and its comparison to the finished film.

20. Cited on the recorded interview with Jeremy Bernstein, on the CD included with *The Kubrick Archives* (Castle 2005).

21. The source of this information derives from Kubrick's dependable biographer, Vincent LoBrutto; see Cocks, Diedrick, Perusek 2006, 48. Raphael himself makes no comment on this issue in *Eyes Wide Open.*

22. It appears that Kubrick was subsequently dissatisfied with the scene between Bill (Tom Cruise) and Marion (Jennifer Jason Leigh) and hence decided to reshoot it. Cruise flew back to England to do this; however, Jennifer Jason Leigh was not available, as she was working by then on *eXistenZ* (1999) with David Cronenberg. Nonetheless, Kubrick was not deterred and took the decision to recast the role with Marie Richardson — an actress known primarily for her work with Ingmar Bergman. These scenes, filmed in April and May 1998, were most likely the last time Kubrick was "behind the camera" on a film set.

23. Herr 2000, 82–83.

24. Op. cit. 83.

25. As Frederic Raphael put it, quoting Kubrick: "[Kubrick] pointed out how movies always portray sudden passion and rushes of blood in the elevator, but they never deal with married sex" (Raphael 1999, 42).

26. Janet Maslin, "*Eyes Wide Shut:* Danger and Desire in a Haunting Bedroom Odyssey," *New York Times,* July 16, 1999. Cited in Kagan, 2000, 241.

27. Charles Whitehouse, "Eyes Without a Face," *Sight and Sound,* September 1999. Note also that the novel offered several allusions to Kubrick's choice of title: "Then she looked up at him with wide open, wild, agonized eyes"

(Schnitzler 1999, 125); "Fridolin opened his eyes as wide as he could" (Schnitzler 1999, 156); "Wearily her eyes opened wide" (Schnitzler 1999, 157).

28. Schnitzler 1999, 115.

29. Op. cit. 116.

30. Op. cit. 159.

31. Op. cit. 169.

32. Op. cit. 115.

33. Ibid.

34. Michel Chion has also made just this point: "The two colors mentioned in the story the little girl is reading, the red of the prince's coat and the blue of the sky, are to be found everywhere in the film" (Chion 2002, 15). See Appendix 10 for a further discussion of the use of color symbolism in the film.

35. Schnitzler 1999, 115.

36. Ibid.

37. Laura Mulvey, "Visual Pleasure in Narrative Cinema," in *The Sexual Subject: A Screen Reader in Sexuality* (London: Routledge, 1992), 22–34.

38. See Raphael 199, 133.

39. Hunter Vaughan, "Eyes *Wide Shut:* Kino-Eyes Wide Open," *The Film Journal* http://the filmjouirnal.com/issue8/eyeswideshut.html (accessed March 20, 2007).

40. Rhodes 2008, 182.

41. Lombardi 2004, 211.

42. Kubrick and Raphael 1999, 3.

43. In a sense the words "You're not even looking at it" could also be seen as a warning to the viewers of the film — perhaps *we* were not even looking at *it,* at the film itself, at least not with the intention that the film demands. Mario Falsetto makes a similar point in his book, *Stanley Kubrick: A Narrative and Stylistic Analysis,* of looking and not seeing; perceiving of this as a metaphor for the way the first viewers of *Eyes Wide Shut* approached the film, looking only at the surface and not at the depth that lay beneath (see Falsetto 2001, 130–141).

44. In *Eyes Wide Shut* the citadel is obviously represented by Somerton. In a Marxist sense this house, like the other great houses in Kubrick's films, represents power: Somerton, the Overlook Hotel, Quilty's mansion, the chateau in *Paths of Glory,* and so on — all represent power. However, here, in *Eyes Wide Shut,* this perhaps reached its most exaggerated form — here capitalism and its corrosive and corruptive properties were most pertinently expressed.

45. Thomas Nelson has described Alice as: "the strongest female presence created by Kubrick in any of his films ... the most psychologically

complete character found in any of his films, one whom he allows to speak in his voice. In a way unique in Kubrick's work" (Nelson 2000, 296).

46. Walker 1999, 354–355.

47. Op. cit. 356.

48. LoBrutto 1997, 74.

49. Miriam Jordan and Julian Jason Haladyn see Alice's body as both classical and grotesque; claiming the sound of Alice urinating can clearly be heard over the background music in the opening scene of the film (see Rhodes 2008, 184).

50. See Appendix 10 for background information on Gary Goba's role as the naval officer in the film.

51. Lombardi 2004, 212.

52. Walker 1999, 352.

53. Horrocks 1995, 108–109.

54. See Swift's poem of 1731: "Strephon and Chloe."

55. Schnitzler 1999, 182–183.

56. Tim Kreider, "Introducing Sociology: A Review of *Eyes Wide Shut*," *Film Quarterly* Vol. 53, no. 3, 2000, p. 46 (reprinted in Cocks, Diedrick and Perusek 2006, 280–297).

57. Thomson 2002, 468. Such a notion had obvious antecedents in Kubrick's own work, Peter Sellers in *Lolita* and *Dr. Strangelove* being the notable example. In a sense, Kidman would go onto do this in *The Blue Room*, David Hare's stage adaptation of Schnitzler's *La Ronde*, in which Kidman appeared in October 1998, shortly after finishing work on *Eyes Wide Shut*; the play, directed by Sam Mendes, had Kidman playing all five female roles.

58. Schnitzler 1999, 120.

59. Žižek 2001, 173.

60. Ibid.

61. The titles of both works point to this: *Dream Story* being self-evident, while the title of the film could refer to dreaming — in which one's eyes are closed in sleep, but open in dreaming. (See Hans-Thies Lehmann's analysis of this in Reichmann and Flagge 2007, 234.)

62. Schnitzler 1999, 156.

63. Op. cit. 175.

64. Op. cit. 185.

65. Freud 1997, 137.

66. Ibid.

67. Op. cit. 138.

68. Ibid.

69. For reasons not wholly made clear, two actresses played the role of Mandy in the film: Julienne Davis played the part in Ziegler's bathroom and in the morgue, while Abigail Good (billed as "Mysterious Woman") played the part in the orgy sequence. Interviewed in *The Inde-*

pendent on August 27, 1999, Good claimed that she had spent a year working on the movie: "I was the one at the wrap. My scenes with Tom were the last Stanley ever shot and I got a credit as the mysterious woman." The writer of the piece, Charlotte O'Sullivan, commented: "In splitting Mandy and the mysterious woman in two, maybe Kubrick wasn't letting himself get sloppy, wasn't trying to get away with anything. Maybe he just wanted to check we were keeping our eyes wide open, so we could enjoy a final, profound in-joke."

70. Kagan 2000, 241.

71. Herr, 2000, 83. Herr went on: I have no idea how much of *Eyes Wide Shut* is meant to be taken literally as a dream, or a string of occurrences on the road running in and out of a dream, or a story with no logic but dream logic" (op. cit. 84).

72. Raphael 1999, 116.

73. Chion 2002, 56.

74. The general critical reception of the orgy was to see it as out of touch and out of date, it was seen as recalling sources as meretricious as: Pauline Reage (author of *Story of O*), Roger Corman, outdated 1970s erotica, a mock Gothic imitation of a Hugh Hefner fantasy, etc. It would seem many of the film's contemporary critics were so caught up in the hyperbole of the film's release publicity as to miss the subtle, ironical intent of this part of the film.

75. Fulwood 2003, 124.

76. Kagan 2000, 243. Note that the masks worn by the participants at the orgy (modeled directly from the Venetian carnival) have eyes that are wide open, but they do not see anything. In a similar way, the use of masks enabled Kubrick to depict a number of other metaphorical gestures; for example, critic Janet Maslin noted that the scene of two masked figures kissing was a perfect metaphor for the dislocation of marital relationships (Janet Maslin, "*Eyes Wide Shut*: Danger and Desire in a Haunting Bedroom Odyssey," *New York Times*, July 16, 1999).

77. Kreider in Cocks, Diedrick and Perusek 2006, 280–281.

78. McGowan and Kunkle 2004, 87.

79. See Jameson 1990 passim.

80. As Frederic Raphael commented: "Love was never his theme, though desire — not least for money — went right back to his earliest work" (Raphael 1999, 106).

81. "It's a cozy place," Bill says diplomatically, commenting on the smallness of Domino's apartment, echoing Jack's comment: "It's homey," when seeing his family's "servant quarters" in *The Shining*.

82. Kreider in Cocks, Diedrick and Perusek 2006, 296.

83. Schnitzler, 1999, 116.

84. Saturnalia would traditionally begin on December 17 and end on December 23, thus spanning the winter solstice. It is said that, in a sense, the modern Christmas office party resembles Roman Saturnalia, a temporary release from rigid social restriction via alcohol and abandonment.

85. Chion 2002, 58.

86. Op. cit. 88.

87. Schnitzler 1999, 162.

88. Rasmussen 2001, 348.

89. Ibid.

90. In Cocks, Diedrick and Perusek 2006, 265.

91. In Rhodes 2008, 203.

92. McGowan and Kunkle 2004, 100–101.

93. Thomas Nelson saw such ambivalences in the part of Bill: "Like other Kubrickian males ... Bill eventually realizes a fuller humanity by responding to a latent female ... sensitivity in his character" (Nelson 2000, 296–297).

94. As Mattias Frey commented: "The popular press ... have long dogged Cruise with rumors of homosexuality" (Frey, "Fidelio: Love, Adaptation of *Eyes Wide Shut*," *Literature/Film Quarterly*, 2006). Hunter Vaughan also noted how Tom Cruise was perhaps "the best example of a male movie star over whom the heterosexual female (or homosexual male, bisexuals and perhaps heterosexual male and homosexual female, if it fits their mood) spectator swoons" (Vaughan, "*Eyes Wide Shut*: Kino-Eyes Wide Open," *The Film Journal* http://thefilmjournal. com/issue 8/eyeswideshut.html, accessed March 20, 2007).

95. Kubrick and Raphael 1999, 36.

96. Rasmussen 2001, 350.

97. Cocks 2004, 90.

98. Kolker 2000, 172.

99. The phrase is Leslie Fiedler's, used in his book, *Love and Death in the American Novel*.

100. One of Domino's books, deliberately placed on view, was *Introducing Sociology*. This was most probably Murray Knuttila's book of that name, a core text primer at undergraduate level. In an earlier draft of the screenplay it was revealed that Domino was a university student, studying at NYU. Without this narrative detail Domino's sense of implausibility in having such a book, already at a high level, was further increased.

101. In Cocks, Diedrick and Perusek 2006, 269.

102. Schnitzler 1999, 127, 144, 155, 177.

103. Nelson, 2000, 281.

104. Hughes 2000, 242.

105. For example, see Phillip Sipora: "The night begins as Bill, not unlike Leopold Bloom, wanders through the streets of a city" (in Rhodes 2008, 201).

106. James Joyce, *Ulysses* (Oxford: Oxford University Press, 1993), 732.

107. Deleyto 2006, 29.

108. Op. cit. 35.

109. Chion 2002, 71.

110. Naremore 2007, 7. Note, a reproduction of the photograph can be found in Reichmann and Flagge 2007, 18.

111. James Naremore has made a similar point to this, see Naremore 2007, 226.

112. Chion 2001, 169.

113. Raphael 1999, 68.

114. Op. cit. 87.

115. Op. cit. 105–106.

116. Op. cit. 148.

117. J. Hoberman, "I Wake Up Dreaming," *Village Voice*, July 21–27, 1999.

118. Kreider in Cocks, Diedrick and Perusek 2006, 284.

119. Note that Schnitzler's novel, although published in 1926, reads as if it were taking place some years in its own past, perhaps two decades earlier.

120. For example, Stephen Hunter questioned the Harfords' financial viability: "[They] live on New York's Central Park West in an apartment that must have cost $7 million" (Stephen Hunter, "Kubrick's Sleepy *Eyes Wide Shut*," *Washington Post*, July 16, 1999).

121. Stephen Hunter, in a typical criticism of the film, claimed: "*Eyes Wide Shut* turns out to be the dirtiest movie of 1958. It feels creaky, ancient, hopelessly out of touch, infatuated with the hot taboos of [Kubrick's] youth and unable to connect with that twisty thing contemporary sexuality has become" (ibid).

122. Larry Gross, "Too Late the Hero," *Sight and Sound*, September 1999.

123. Richard Alleva, "Final Curtain: Kubrick's *Eyes Wide Shut*," *Commonwealth*, September 10, 1999.

124. Kagan 2000, 244.

125. Vaughan Hunter "*Eyes Wide Shut*: Kino-Eyes Wide Open," *The Film Journal* http://the filmjournal.com./issue 8/eyeswideshut.html (accessed March 20, 2007).

126. Herr 2000, 92.

127. Bernard Weintraub, "All Eyes for a Peek at Kubrick's Final Film," *New York Times*, March

10, 1999. This was the officially accepted version, although other more accurate details would later emerge; for example, Jan Harlan would reveal that much of the music for the film was recorded *after* Kubrick's death: "We knew what Stanley wanted and carried out his wishes: we recorded Jocelyn Pook's and Ligeti's compositions" (Castle 2005, 513).

128. J. Hoberman, *Village Voice*, July 21–27, 1999.

129. Ibid.

130. Michel Ciment has noted how "ruthless" Kubrick could be in cutting out sequences in his films. For example, the custard pie finale in *Dr. Strangelove*, the 19 minutes cut from *2001: A Space Odyssey*, the intended closing scene of *The Shining*, and so on (Ciment 2001, 211).

131. Herr 2000, 91.

132. Cited in Kagan 2000, 236.

133. Kolker 2000, 169–170.

134. Chion 2002, 28.

135. The idea that Kubrick needed big stars in order to secure the required budget for the film is a point worth considering. The film cost $65 million, of which a reported $22 million went to Cruise; however, it went on to gross over $50 million in the United States and over $100 million overseas; by November 1999 it had earned a worldwide gross of over $155 million, thus making it, by one way of reckoning at least, Kubrick's most successfully commercial film.

136. Richard Alleva, "Final Curtain: Kubrick's *Eyes Wide Shut*," *Commonwealth*, September 10, 1999.

137. J. Hoberman, "I Wake Up Dreaming," *Village Voice*, July 21–27, 1999.

138. Cited in Phillips and Hill 2002, 69.

139. As Jonathan Rosenbaum commented: "One difficulty I had with *Eyes Wide Shut* the first time I saw it was accepting the caricatural side of Kubrick— his handling of Cruise's 'normality' in the lead role as Dr. William Harford and the mincing mannerisms of the gay hotel desk-clerk — as something other than malicious" (Rosenbaum in Cocks, Diedrick and Perusek 2006, 248).

140. Abrams 2007, 232 and 3.

141. Kreider in Cocks, Diedrick and Perusek 2006, 280.

142. Walker 1999, 344.

143. Chion 2002, 37.

144. Lee Siegel *Harper's Magazine*, October 1999.

145. Cited in Clarkson 2003, 260.

146. Cited in Castle 2005, 492.

147. Thomson 2002, 480.

148. See Karen D. Hoffman in Abrams 2007, 76.

149. See Chion 2002, 9.

150. Nelson 2000, 1.

151. Cited in Lewis 2004, 1051.

152. Of course, the idea of giving New York and New Yorkers a happy ending in 1999, by necessity neglected the then-unknown future reality of what was to come. The events on September 11, 2001, a year linked to Stanley Kubrick's own personal universe, but a year that would prove very different in reality. One might even imagine, albeit within the narrative space of the film's fictional discourse, how Bill and Alice, in their Central Park West apartment, may have heard the planes fly by, felt the impact, seen the flames, and witnessed the towers falling.

153. Ciment 2001, 266.

154. Herr 2000, 85.

155. *Seattle Post,* July 16, 1999.

156. Cited in Kagan 2000, 241.

157. Following on from this, one might assume that Kubrick was suggesting a fantasy life was one potential solution to the *ennui* of married life. In this light, one notes that all of Bill's potential sexual encounters were, to some extent, "illicit," at least in comparison to those experiences found within his marriage: the threesome with the two models, underage sex with Millich's daughter, sex for payment with Domino and Sally, "gay" sex with the clerk at the Hotel Jason and the opportunities for multiple sexual partners at the orgy — thus offering the corollary that the fantasy of illicit sex was the only "safe" alternative to sex within marriage.

Afterword

1. These lines, quoted in the film, derive from Yeats's famous poem "The Stolen Child." As with so much of *A.I.* it is difficult to ascertain whether the Yeats poem was a Spielbergian or Kubrickian allusion. However, given Kubrick's affectation for the only child, one may speculate it may have derived from Kubrick. If so, the poem's fundamental point — that some of us are mere impersonations of a real entity — would seem to have some relevance towards the film's fundamental point of what is real and what is not.

2. For example, Katharina Kubrick's comment: "He was looking forward to doing *A.I.* There was a lot of stuff already finished and ready to go" (Nick James, "At Home with the Kubricks," *Sight and Sound*, September 1999).

3. Steven Spielberg: "He didn't want to make

A.I.; he developed it for himself and then he said, 'This is more you than me'" (*The Culture Show* BBC Television, November 4, 2006). Spielberg suggests it was planned, while Kubrick was alive, that he should direct and Kubrick produce *A.I.* Spielberg went onto suggest much of the so-called sentimental elements of the film derived from the Kubrick/Watson script/treatment: "All the blame I get for destroying Stanley's vision are scenes that Stanley actually came up with. The scenes that people can't believe Stanley conceived and wouldn't have directed himself, are the scenes that I am most credited with spoiling. You know, the whole ending after David and Teddy are rescued underwater and brought into their own future of super-mecha. This was Stanley and Ian's treatment, this was their ninety-seven page treatment that I adapted into my screenplay ... I think one of the things that scared Stanley away from *A.I.* was that it was too much a film for me and too little of the kind of film he was known for, as a great cineaste" (ibid).

4. Alison Castle, in *The Stanley Kubrick Archives*, appears to write with more authority than most on the film, having presumably had direct access to archival materials (see Castle 2005, 504–508). From Castle's discussion of the 87-page treatment, she would appear to back Spielberg's claim that his film did follow, at least relatively closely, the Kubrick/Watson treatment.

5. It seems Ian Watson had the most input into the screenplay, insomuch as his was the only name that survived onto the credits of Spielberg's film.

6. For details of Fanghorn's work, see Reichmann and Flagge 2007, 250–253, Castle 2005, 506–507 and Christiane Kubrick 2002, 173.

7. In a contrary argument, James Naremore has suggested that the use of CGI undermines documentary authority in feature films, bringing "movies closer to the spirit of comic books and animation" (Naremore 2007, 254). Hence, it is possible to argue that Kubrick, who died as CGI was becoming redolent in filmmaking, may not, in the end, have been satisfied with these limitations.

8. A number of critics noted this scene. Lloyd Kaufman saw the film, in this context, as being "emotional pornography" (cited in Sperb 2006, 154). James Naremore commented: "Despite all the fairy-tale sweetness, David is experiencing a kind of Freudian wet dream" (Naremore 2007, 249). Scott Loren read the scene as David bedding "his blurry-eyed mother" (cited in Rhodes 2008, 225). Other critics were more generous: James Clarke considered *A.I.* to be: "undeniably

a celebration of the great, almost unfathomable love, between mothers and their sons" (Clarke 2004, 134). Andrew Sarris saw the "gaze of David toward Monica, and of Monica toward David" as constituting "one of the great love images in all cinema," claiming that it transcended "the romantic and the erotic with the devotionally religious" (Sarris in the *New York Observer*, June 25, 2001). Note also that the Freudian element in the film was self-consciously and satirically acknowledged, perhaps most pertinently in the scene in which David discovered his mother, sitting on the toilet, reading a book on Freud. As Nigel Morris commented, "Psychoanalysis appears perversely redundant in a movie in which the boy opens the toilet door on Monica as she sits, underwear around her ankles, reading, *Freud on Women*" (Morris 2007, 303). This, in turn, may also have been a Spielbergian joke on Kubrick's predilection for bathroom scenes in nearly all of his films.

9. "My Year with Stanley" Sara Maitland *The Independent*, March 12, 1999.

10. See Phillips and Hill 2002 5, for an authoritative discussion of the intertextual allusions to Carlos Collodi's story: "A casual glance at *A.I.* reveals Professor Hobby to be Geppetto, Lord Johnson-Johnson to be Stromboli, Gigolo Joe to be Lampwick, Rouge City to be the Land of Toys/Pleasure Island, the submerged helicopter to be the shark/Monstro the Whale, etc."

11. See James Clarke: "The veneration is made absolute in the images of, and connection made, between the Virgin Mary, the Blue Fairy and Monica" (Clarke 2004, 130). See also Nigel Morris, who argued the Blue Fairy explicitly equated to the Virgin Mary, this being "appropriate enough for a boy born of no woman born" (Morris 2007, 307).

12. Walker 1988, 296.

13. Note, however, the deliberate references to Kubrick's work. Spielberg, in what one might describe as a reverential manner, carefully constructed a number of intertextual references. For example, the framing of the automobile as Monica and David drive through woodland roads referenced *The Shining*, as did the look and design of the caption: "20 Months Later." This is in addition to the aforementioned gestures towards *2001: A Space Odyssey.*

14. Sperb 2006, 142.

15. Christiane Kubrick 2002, 173.

16. Castle 2005, 504.

Conclusion

1. The conspiracy theory that Kubrick may thus have taken his own life seems absurd. Although Kubrick had had the "flu" a couple of weeks before his death and was "pale and tired" (Cocks 2004, 289), he appears to have been in a positive frame of mind. For example, Warner Bros. executive, Terry Semel, talked of speaking to Kubrick on the Saturday morning before he died, and reported that Kubrick was in high spirits: "The good news is he definitely went to sleep that night with a smile on his face" (Bernard Weinraub, "All Eyes for a Peek at Kubrick's Final Film," *New York Times,* March 10, 1999).

2. Another cliché is that Kubrick had an irrational fear of flying; again this was more likely based on a rational understanding of the risks involved. Jon Ronson: "[Kubrick] wasn't afraid of planes; he was scared of air traffic controllers" (Jon Ronson, "Citizen Kubrick," *The Guardian,* March 27, 2004).

3. Herr 2000, 12.

4. Cited in Howard 1999, 181.

5. Op. cit. 21. (Landis has fulfilled this premise by manufacturing a means of inserting the phrase "See you next Wednesday" into several of his films. The line in question is a seemingly insignificant piece of dialogue from *2001: A Space Odyssey.*)

6. Op. cit. 181.

7. Cited in Phillips and Hill 2002, xv.

8. Cited in Phillips 2001, viii. Kubrick has often been compared to Orson Welles (see Cocks 2006, 251; Howard 1999, 18; Ciment 2001, 36; Naremore 2007, 25 and 35). The comparisons are interesting: both Welles and Kubrick began making films in their twenties (both at 25, to be precise); both died at 70; both made (or at least completed) 13 feature films; both made the majority of their films outside of Hollywood. However, note that Welles entered film with all the resources of Hollywood at his command and finished his career making films almost without resources of any viable kind; Kubrick followed precisely the reverse route.

9. Cited in Nelson 2000, 316.

10. Cocks 2004, 173.

11. Falsetto 1996, 192.

12. It is of interest to note that several of Kubrick's other unrealized projects also featured the only child as a significant narrative element; for example: *The Burning Secret, The Queen's Gambit, Perfume,* and so on.

13. Rhodes 2008, 218.

14. Abrahams 2007, 22.

15. Such an argument has not been explored often; however, note Susan White's comment: "Some of the most obscene revelations [in Kubrick's work], as well as some of the most human ones, take place in bathrooms" (in Kolker 2006, 135).

16. Even in those rare Kubrick films that do not include a bathroom setting there is generally some kind of inference; for example, in *Killer's Kiss* when the character of Albert (Jerry Jarret) is cornered in an alleyway he is framed beside a notice on the wall, which clearly states: "No Toilet." See still illustration of this in Ciment 2001, 102.

17. The term is Michael Herr's; see Herr 2000, 50.

18. See Cocks 2004, 199.

19. As Krin Gabbard and Shailja Sharma noted: "One of Kubrick's obsessions, and one of his great achievements as a filmmaker, is his creation of magnificent interiors that become horrifying once we realize that they support what are essentially killing machines" (Cited in McDougal 2003, 94).

20. See Baxter's chapter, "In Castle Kubrick," Baxter 1998, 354–365. The general sense that Kubrick, after his move to the United Kingdom, developed an apparent withdrawal from public life once again comes into play. However, although Kubrick did choose to live in a "citadel" to work from home, this can be misleading. Alexander Walker: "It's crucial to understand that what other people view as a 'hermitage,' he saw only as a severely functional work base" (Walker 1999, 368).

21. Jonathan Culler: "Stories, the argument goes, are the main ways we make sense of things" (Culler 1997, 83).

22. Cited in Nelson 2000, 229.

23. Cited in Castle, 2005, 360.

24. Op. cit. 365.

25. Ciment 2001, 243 and Walker 1999, 18.

26. Kolker 2006, 5.

27. Walker 1999, 17. Note also other comments from Kubrick: "I've always approached every picture I've done just from the standpoint of telling a story" (cited in Hughes 2000, 73). "The purpose of a movie is to tell a story ... I would say that the story has got to be supreme no matter how interesting the form" (cited in Castle 2005, 312).

28. Cited in Cocks 2006, 31.

29. Notes on Film," *The Observer,* December 4, 1960.

30. The number usually specified being six, see, for example, Baxter 1998, 356.

31. For a full reproduction of this photographic assignment see Crone 2005, 162–167.

32. Op. cit. 163.

33. Ibid.

34. Crone perceives, in this last series of shots, that the open and blank window serves to signify the open and blank talent of the subject: "a delicate subversion of her own vain *mise-en-scène* by presenting an empty centre space" (ibid).

35. Note that there was nothing pre-ordained that cinema would be a narrative medium; photography was not and is not narrative based. However, audiences have grown to expect the standard three-act structure in film: wherein character and setting are established, wherein a struggle generally ensues between protagonist and antagonist, wherein there is usually a final struggle in which the protagonist/hero triumphs.

36. Alexander Walker has noted this very point: "Kubrick, it is worth remembering, belongs to a pre-television generation whose sense of drama was still shaped to some degree by the aural impact of radio" (Walker 1999, 54). Jason Sperb also makes a similar point: "The influence of radio ... would encourage Kubrick to use words early on as a form of authoritative narration, at least until he had begun to develop a more cinematic voice" (Sperb 2006, 44).

37. Note how, even in films without the use of voice-over, Kubrick's early draft screenplays originally included such a feature; this is apparent in both *2001: A Space Odyssey* and *Eyes Wide Shut.*

38. Cited in Ciment 2001, 157.

39. See: http://www.brainyquote.com/quotes/keywords/rumor.html.

40. Graf 2002, 2.

41. See Crone 2005, 7.

42. Castle 2005, 460. Similarly, Vincent LoBrutto noted: "Kubrick attempted to see every film released to satisfy his deep affection for the cinema" (LoBrutto 1997, 496).

43. Michael Herr makes just this point: "You could always tell it was a Stanley Kubrick movie the moment it started" (Herr 2000, 95).

44. In terms of the precision of editing, Michel Chion has spoken of "the sensory shock inherent in each cut between shots; each cut feels like a decision, a choice, a chess move" (Chion 2001, 45).

45. Steven Spielberg in the documentary, *Stanley Kubrick: A Life in Pictures* (2001).

46. Transcribed from the CD interview, conducted by Bernstein, included in *The Stanley Kubrick Archives.* Unlike most filmmakers, Kubrick tended to shoot in sequence, this may have

been less efficient in certain ways but it also meant that, in Iain Johnstone's words, "He was free to let a finished scene have an influence on the one that followed it, causing alterations where they arose organically" (Johnstone 2006, 251).

47. Peter Bogdanovich, "What They Say About Stanley Kubrick," *New York Times,* July 4, 1999.

48. Reichmann and Flagge 2007, 29.

49. Rhodes 2008, 96. Edward Quinn: "This principle [the Uncertainty Principle] has been adapted in literary theory, particularly by deconstructionists, to argue that the act of interpretation alters the work it seeks to interpret" (Quinn 2004, 169).

50. In her book, *Against Interpretation,* Susan Sontag argued: "Interpretation is the revenge of the intellect upon art. Even more. It is the revenge of the intellect upon the world." Thus in Sontag's view, to interpret is to impoverish, to deplete the world — in order to set up a shadow world of "meaning" (see Sontag, 1966, *passim*). Whether such a view neglects the dichotomy of the epistemological and ontological argument is questionable, but the corollary of Sontag's view would, ultimately at least, suggest an end to hermeneutics, leaving us merely with what Sontag famously described as, "An erotics of art."

51. See Selden 1993, 51.

52. Baxter 1998, 9.

53. Kagan 2000, 248.

54. Kolker 2000, 174.

Appendix 1

1. Cited in Falsetto 1996, 97.

2. Cited in Crone 2005, 245.

3. See Crone 2005, 178. Kubrick's camera had followed Rocky Graziano into the shower, showing the boxer nude, under cascading water, staring provocatively at the camera. (In a similar light, John Baxter commented on an obvious homoeroticism in Kubrick's low-angle shots of Walter Cartier in *Day of the Fight*; see Baxter 1998, 36.)

4. See Baxter 1998, 107.

5. It is present in satiric form in the "black mass" in *Eyes Wide Shut;* in the blasphemous comments surrounding "Chaplain Charlie" in *Full Metal Jacket;* in the figure of the Reverend Runt in *Barry Lyndon;* in the prison chaplain swearing "Damn you" on the altar in *A Clockwork Orange;* in General Turgidson's hypocritical prayer of thanks in *Dr. Strangelove,* and so on.

6. It is known that the film resurfaced at the Telluride Film Festival in 1991, but apart from such rare opportunities Kubrick's withdrawal of the film would appear total; even several years after his death it is still not available in any officially accessible form. A number of quasi-pirated versions of the film have become available on DVD (for example, a version of the film was released in 2007 by Elusive DVD.com); however, this poses ethical issues for a critic: should she or he attend to an ambiguously legal copy of a film when it is known the maker categorically withdrew it from public consumption?

7. For example, in 1970 Kubrick told Joseph Gelmis: "It's not a film I remember with any pride, except for the fact it was finished" (cited in Phillips 2001, 101).

8. Sperb 2006, 31. Sperb's book went on: "*Fear and Desire* was not a practice piece, but rather the *quintessential* Kubrick film.... It was, in a sense, too explicitly "Kubrick" for even Kubrick's own liking" (ibid).

9. Walker 1988, 285.

10. Walker 1999, 16.

11. Cited in Phillips and Hill 2002, 181.

12. Alexander Walker has perceived of "the feeling of fable" within the film, a tale of "a beautiful girl abducted by an ogreish dance hall owner ... rescued by a valorous young boxer with antecedents in knight-errantry" (Walker 1988, 286).

13. *Killer's Kiss* is usually interpreted as having a stereotypically happy ending, with the two lovers living happily ever after. However, the film's ending may have been more ambiguous; for example, can we be sure Gloria is actually going to go to Seattle with Davy? When she arrives at Penn Street station she has no baggage, although she has had plenty of time to pack, one could speculate that it is possible she had caught the cab to the station simply to say goodbye to Davy. The film purposefully came to an end before this ambiguity could be resolved.

14. Nelson 2000, 8.

15. LoBrutto 1997, 122.

16. Robson 2005, 222.

17. In the instance of the racetrack footage, one might perceive of a potentially specific allusion to Kubrick himself. It is possible that the scene was in some way influenced by Kubrick's March 1947 photographic essay for *Look:* "Aqueduct Racetrack: Hope, Despair, and Habit"; see Crone 2005, 132–145.

18. Cobb's novel had not previously been filmed, but it had been adapted for the stage, running briefly on Broadway in 1935 (see Baxter 1998, 85).

19. The precise origin of this quotation is difficult to ascertain; it is quoted in numerous sources; for example, John Baxter's biography of Kubrick noted: "Winston Churchill would later observe that it [*Paths of Glory*] came closer than any other film to catching the mood .of World War I" (Baxter 1998, 101). However, like other writers, Baxter did not source the quotation, hence, Churchill's remark remains a relevant, if seemingly apocryphal, comment.

20. Cited in Phillips and Hill 2002, 282.

21. Geoffrey Cocks compares the chateau in *Paths of Glory* to other of Kubrick's "high spaces," the Overlook Hotel in *The Shining*, Somerton in *Eyes Wide Shut*, etc. (Cocks 2004, 95).

22. Op. cit. 26.

23. *Spartacus* cost $12 million and grossed some $60 million at the box office, figures Kubrick rarely again matched.

24. Kubrick in 1970, cited in Phillips 2001, 102.

25. Hughes 2000, 66. There was a somewhat facile metaphor here, in the refusal to name names at the end of the film: the insistence of numerous slaves, each one claiming: "I am Spartacus!" This was a clear parallel to both Fast's and Trumbo's refusal to name names in the infamous HUAA hearings, The scene would later be parodied (perhaps deservedly) in various places; most pertinently in *Monty Python's Life of Brian* (1979) with its satiric cries of: "I am Brian!"

26. See Hughes 2000, 67.

27. Fulwood 2003, 16. To facilitate the inclusion of this scene, the dialogue had to be re-recorded, as the original sound recording could not be located. Tony Curtis was available, but Anthony Hopkins replaced the deceased Laurence Olivier in overdubbing the original lines. Hopkins made a convincing mimic, there being no discernible difference in Olivier's voice.

28. Phillips and Hill 2002, 199. One might note how the history of Kubrick's career may have been very different; it has been suggested that had Dore Schary not been fired by MGM, in 1956, then Kubrick's career may have followed a wholly variant route: "Had Kubrick made that first film with Schary, he might well have had a long and productive term in Hollywood" (op. cit. 304). In other words, instead of becoming the independent *auteur*, Kubrick may, in an alternate world, have become a director within the mainstream Hollywood studio system.

Appendix 2

1. Note that in addition to Lyne's remake, a

musical version of the novel had been staged in 1971, written by John Barry and Alan J. Lerner; also, a stage adaptation, by Edward Albee, would be attempted in 1981. However, no matter the pedigree of the adaptors, in both cases the productions were unsuccessful.

2. Note how Kubrick generally updates such things as the hula hoop, rock 'n' roll at the school dance, the Hammer horror film, along with the general *mise-en-scène*: the cars, the motels, the clothing, etc.

3. As James Howard comments: "[Dominique] Swain's Lolita failed to convince as anything other than a 1990s American teenage brat" (Howard 1999, 84). Or as Mark Crispin Miller put it: "While its look is ultra–1947, the movie's sexual theatrics are pure nineties, its lithe little Lo a perfect postmodern hot pants, eager to hump Hum, chew fiercely on his tongue and give him head" (Cocks, 2006, 144).

Appendix 3

1. Sikov 2002, 196–197.
2. Phillips and Hill 2002, 341.
3. Kolker 2000, 123.
4. Robson 2005, 215.

Appendix 4

1. Note that on *Spartacus*, even though Alex North wrote the entire score, Kubrick was considering other music, one being none other than "The Blue Danube." Kubrick's lack of overall artistic control prevented him following through on such a plan; however, by *2001* the situation was different.

2. North apparently used elements of his unused *2001* score for his Third Symphony; he also used parts for later film scores, including *Dragonslayer* (1981). Wendy Carlos: "He [Alex North] cobbled together some of his material later on when he did *Dragonslayer*, and some of it is very effective there. If you played the two CDs side by side you can hear the theme is the same" (Jeff Bond, "Working with Stanley," *Film Score Monthly*, March 1999).

3. Robert Towson, "The Odyssey of Alex North's 2001," *Alex North's 2001: The Legendary Original Score World Premiere Recording*, 1993, Varese Sarabande VSD 5400.
4. Ibid.
5. Ibid.
6. Kolker 2006, 72.
7. This is Kubrick's own description, cited in Agel 1970, 189.

8. Ciment 2001, 177.
9. Phillips 2001, 133.
10. It still seems illogical that front-projected images should not have been projected onto the actors as well as the background; apparently, this was visible on the set but was too faint to be visible within the camera and onscreen.
11. McAleer 1992, 201.
12. Clarke 1972, 32.
13. Cited in McAleer 1992, 199.
14. Agel 1970, 304.
15. Frewin, quoted in "*2001*: The Secrets of Kubrick's Classic," Anthony Barnes, *The Independent*, October 23, 2005.
16. Frewin 2005, 7 and 10.

Appendix 5

1. Kubrick made this claim in a memo dated October 20, 1971 — see Reichmann and Flagge 2007, 157.

2. As critic Maurice Chittenden put it: "Kubrick hoped the film would enable him to eclipse Orson Welles's film *Citizen Kane*" (Maurice Chittenden, "Kubrick's Lost Napoleonic Work: Family Reveals Script for Un-made Epic on Bonaparte," *Sunday Times*, August 28, 2005).

3. One might argue that the economy and discipline of making *A Clockwork Orange*, coupled with its commercial success, went some way to anchoring Kubrick's subsequent creative and artistic independence with Warner Bros.

4. For example, see Ken Adam: "*Barry Lyndon* always seemed to me to have been the dress-rehearsal for *Napoleon*" (Reichmann and Flagge 2007, 95). Also, James Naremore argued that Barry's rise and fall, in microcosm, reflected Napoleon's "historically momentous adventures" (Naremore 2007, 186).

5. Kubrick offers a number of explicit clues: for example, one might note the "in-joke" at the end of *Barry Lyndon;* the film ended on a date — December 1789 — an obvious reference to the French Revolution and the subsequent rise of Napoleon. In a similar way, the scene in *Barry Lyndon*, of Barry's son, Bryan, being pulled along in a carriage by two lambs (See Castle 2005, 181) was a direct "visual rhyme" from the *Napoleon* screenplay: "EXT. TUILERIES GARDEN-DAY King of Rome, now one and a half years old, riding in a magnificently decorated cart, pulled by two lambs" (see Phillips and Hill 2002, 263).

6. The year 1969 was the 200th anniversary of Napoleon's birth; Kubrick's completion of the screenplay on this date may not have been a total coincidence.

7. See Phillips and Hill 2002, 262.

8. See Castle 2005, 497–498.

9. See the commentary, by Adam Baldwin, Vincent D'Onofrio, R. Lee Ermey and Jay Cocks, in *Full Metal Jacket* Deluxe Edition (2008).

10. In another comparison to *Barry Lyndon,* it seems Kubrick had planned to shoot night scenes in *Napoleon* by candlelight; he had had the specialist lenses prepared and had already accomplished the technical research. Apparently, Kubrick believed candlelight would further eroticize the sexually explicit scenes in the film.

11. David Hemmings was also cited as a potential Napoleon; as was Oscar Werner; Werner would be cast in *Barry Lyndon,* in the role of Captain Potzdorf, but then replaced, the role eventually being played by Hardy Kruger.

12. Maurice Chittenden, *Sunday Times,* August 28, 2005.

13. There are a number of public comments that support this; for example, in 1980, remarking, in passing, to Michel Ciment, Kubrick stated: "Napoleon, about whom I still intend to make a film" (Ciment 1983, 197). While In 1987, talking to *Le Monde* journalist Danièle Heymann, Kubrick claimed: "I haven't given up on it [*Napoleon*] yet" (Danièle Heymann, "Stanley Kubrick's Vietnam," *Le Monde,* October 20, 1987, reprinted in Castle 2005, 476–479).

14. Sean Hagen, *The Observer,* April 17, 2005.

15. Duncan 1999, 61.

Appendix 6

1. As an uncredited critic in *The Encyclopedia of Stanley Kubrick* noted: "[Si] Litvinoff initially joined forces with Terry Southern to develop a screen version of *Clockwork.* They planned to shoot the film [from Southern's script] independently in England in February 1968. That version was to star David Hemmings as Alex and John Boorman had agreed to direct" (Phillips and Hill 2002, 208).

2. Biswell 2005, 338.

3. Ibid.

Appendix 7

1. This was John Calley, Warner Bros. executive, speaking shortly before the release of *Barry Lyndon* (cited in Phillips 2001, 167). At that time, only one film — Steven Spielberg's *Jaws*— had managed this, making in excess of $100 million, and *Barry Lyndon* was not destined to make this amount of money. The film found success in Europe, grossing $3 million in France alone, but earned only $9.5 million in America, "much less than the $30 million needed for Warners to see a profit" (Baxter 1997, 295).

2. Kolker, 1988, 70.

3. Kolker 2000, 98. One likely possibility is that Kubrick came across *Barry Lyndon* via his reading of *Vanity Fair,* which he probably read in the light of its Napoleonic content.

4. In this sense Vincent LoBrutto spoke of "Kubrick's time machine visit to the eighteenth century" (LoBrutto 1997, 381). The use of a freeze frame at the end of the film provided one of the few jarring notes, insomuch as Kubrick's camera had otherwise consistently suggested we were actually back in the late eighteenth century.

5. See, for example, Vincent Canby: "Paying scrupulous attention to historical and social detail ... constructing a world of the past in as much vivid detail as Kubrick lavished on the future in *2001*" (Vincent Canby, *Barry Lyndon:* Kubrick's Latest has Brains and Beauty," *New York Times,* December 21, 1975).

6. Kubrick's own specific and definitive opinion of the film is not on record; hence, we have no way of knowing if he considered it his best picture. However, one might perceive of a potential self-reverential gesture in a comment made by Lord Hallam (Bernard Hepton), who says, of a painting by Lodovico Cordway: "This is one of my best pictures." Whether this was also a reference to Kubrick's own opinion of *Barry Lyndon* remains open to question.

7. Naremore 2007, 177.

8. Kolker 2000, 99.

9. Cited in Cocks 2006, 166.

10. Kolker 2000, 157.

11. In a similar way, note how the narrator's voice, reading a report of Sir Charles Lyndon's death, is faded out at the intermission.

12. See Naremore 2007, 180.

13. Julian Rice offers the specific intertextual connection to *Hamlet,* comparing

Lady Lyndon: Lord Bullingdon, you have insulted your father.

Bullingdon: Mother, *you* have insulted my father.

To:

Gertrude: Hamlet, thou hast they [*sic*] father much offended.

Hamlet: Mother, *you* have my father much offended. (*Hamlet* III.iv.8–9; see Rice 2008, 95).

14. Issues of class, always apparent in Kubrick's work, were more exactly positioned in *Barry Lyndon.* Barry, being Irish, of a lower class and with little money, attempts to better himself, but the dominant societal power of the En-

glish (British) state eventually punishes him, leaving him maimed, metaphorically unmanned, and destitute. In this sense, Kubrick's film raised historicist issues. Kubrick's decision, in the early 1970s (at the height of the troubles in Northern Ireland) to make a film about an Irish man, battling and ultimately losing against the might of the English (British) class system, was not without a certain irony and a certain satiric quality. The film might thus be said to represent Kubrick's most cogent meditation on the issue of social class.

15. In a sense, the film was the story of how Barry attempted to forge his own family, but such a venture ending in tragedy, found himself forced back into the Oedipal embrace of his mother.

16. Vincent Canby, "*Barry Lyndon:* Kubrick's Latest has Brains and Beauty," *New York Times,* December 21, 1975.

17. Ibid.

18. In *Time,* December 15, 1975, reprinted in Phillips 2001, 163.

19. Howard 1999, 134.

20. Cited in Castle 2005, 437.

21. Cited in Castle 2005, 430.

22. Naremore 2007, 170.

23. Raphael 1999, 131.

Appendix 8

1. Propp's work was originally published in Russian in 1928 and was first published in English in 1968; see Vladimir Propp, *Morphology of the Folk Tale* (Austin: University of Texas Press, 1968). Propp's main thesis has been regularly cited in other, more accessible forums; see, for example, Michael J. Toolan, *Narrative: A Critical Linguistic Introduction* (London: Routledge, 1988) 14–20.

2. Howard, 1999, 155. Howard went on: "Such a sentimental ending is sadly all too familiar in several of King's other stories put on television, in which God, Love, the Family and the All-American Way are seen to conquer all the evils in the world" (op. cit. 156).

3. Magistrale 2003, 206.

4. Op. cit. 13.

5. Op. cit. 216.

6. Op. cit. 217. Magistrale also detailed the negotiations that took place to enable King to film his own version of the novel; this apparently consisted of a "substantial payment" to Kubrick and a pledge by King that he would "not discuss further Kubrick's film in any public forum" (op. cit. 198). What entails a "public forum" is open

to speculation; however, evidence from King's appearances on *YouTube,* for example, would suggest he did not wholly abide by such an agreement.

7. Cited in Grünberg, 2006, 74.

8. See Nelson 2000, 325–326.

9. See Cocks 2004, 213–214, 231–232 and *passim.*

10. Cocks 1987, 129.

11. On January 20, 1942, Reinhard Heydrich hosted a conference of Nazi party and government officials at the SS headquarters in Wannsee, a suburb of Berlin. The conference lasted only a few hours, but herein laid the plan for the "Final Solution," the attempted destruction of European Jews.

12. Walker 1999, 304.

13. Cited in Ciment 1983, 185.

14. Cited in Falsetto 1996, 245–246.

15. Janet Maslin, "Flaws Don't Dim *The Shining,*" *New York Times,* June 8, 1980.

16. Ciment 2001, 301.

17. As to whether actual footage of the deleted ending survives, this remains uncertain. One presumes if it had been available it would have been included, as a special feature, on the recent DVD versions of *The Shining.*

18. Aljean Harmetz, "Kubrick Films *The Shining* in Secrecy in English Studio, *New York Times,* November 6, 1978.

19. Note: Vivian Kubrick herself appeared in at least four of Kubrick's films: *2001: A Space Odyssey, Barry Lyndon, The Shining,* and *Full Metal Jacket.*

20. Some footage of Kubrick at work can also be seen in *2001: A Space Odyssey — A Look Behind the Future* (1967). Also, Vivian Kubrick shot footage of the making of *Full Metal Jacket,* while this did not result in a dedicated film, parts of it were used in *Stanley Kubrick: A Life in Pictures* (2001).

21. Kubrick himself was not interviewed on camera; in fact, as far as can be ascertained, there are no extensive on-camera interviews with Kubrick preserved on film.

22. Robertson 2001, 160.

23. LoBrutto 1997, 430. This would appear somewhat unlikely given the fact that Danny Lloyd's time on the set was restricted because of his age; one presumes the high-take ratio referred to actor Scatman Crowthers's input into the scene.

24. Falsetto 1996, 282.

25. Ciment 1983, 188.

26. Modine 2005, 268.

27. Frederic Raphael, "Dr. Strangelove, C'est Moi," *The Guardian,* November 26, 2006.

28. Walker 1999, 371.

29. *Kubrick Questions Finally Answered An In Depth Talk with Leon Vitali*, http://www.dvdtalk.com/leonvitaliinterview.html, accessed August 27, 2006.

30. For example, it is clear that, in the early 1980s, Kubrick still possessed many hours of outtake footage of the helicopter shots from the opening of *The Shining*. This is well known as Ridley Scott requested and received "cans and cans," some 30,000 feet of this material to use in the re-edit of the ending of *Blade Runner*" (see Sammon 1996, 303 and 389).

Appendix 9

1. www.visual-memory.co.uk/amk/doc/0065.html, accessed June 14, 2005.

2. Note: Captain January is mentioned in the film by Lieutenant Lockhart: "Joker, I want you to get straight up to Phu Bai. Captain January will need all his people" (Kubrick, Herr, Hasford, 1987, 64).

3. Note that Animal Mother's machete is visible on his back throughout the whole of the film's second half, as if he had been carrying it for a specific purpose.

4. Herr 1978, 13.

5. Op. cit. 17.

6. Op. cit. 53.

7. Op. cit. 161.

8. Op. cit. 184.

9. Op. cit. 35.

10. Op. cit. 100.

11. Op. cit. 182.

12. Op. cit. 78 and 99.

13. Op. cit. 109.

14. Op. cit. 17.

15. Ibid.

16. Op. cit. 20.

17. Op. cit. 67.

18. Op. cit. 195. (Note: this final quotation was used by Hasford as one of the opening epigraphs in his novel.)

19. Op. cit. 150.

Appendix 10

1. www.visual-memory.co.uk/amk/doc/0085.html.

2. Ibid., there is no pagination to the online screenplay.

3. Schnitzler 1999, 116.

4. The comparative section in Schnitzler's novel occurs on page 123.

5. The comparative section in Schnitzler's novel occurs on page 127.

6. The comparative section in Schnitzler's novel occurs on page 129.

7. The comparative section in Schnitzler's novel occurs on page 133.

8. The comparative section in Schnitzler's novel occurs on page 170.

9. The comparative section in Schnitzler's novel occurs on page 171.

10. See Schnitzler 1999, 115.

11. See Deleyto 2006, 32–33, for a further discussion of the use of these specific colors in the film.

12. Nelson 2000, 295.

13. *The Independent*, June 19, 1998.

14. This was the third time Kubrick had used Ligeti's music: the specific selection chosen here, "Musica Ricercata II," was a piece Ligeti had described by stating it was meant as a "knife in Stalin's heart" (cited in Cocks 2004, 146).

15. Dickerson 2003, 109.

16. Op. cit. 110.

17. Op. cit. 112.

18. Op. cit. 113.

19. Ibid.

20. Op. cit. 126.

21. Johnstone 2006, 258.

22. Nick James: "Which of the books is most unreliable?" Christiane Kubrick: "The Baxter and the Raphael." (Nick James, "At Home with the Kubricks," *Sight and Sound*, September, 1999, 15.)

23. See Raphael 1999, 153.

24. Whole pages of dialogue throughout Raphael's book were presented in script format, with quotations from "F.R." and "S.K." offered in precise detail. What critic Robert J.E. Simpson described as "a peculiar blend of recalled conversation" (cited in Rhodes 2008, 236).

25. Johnstone 2006, 250. Note: Raphael's novel of 1971: *Who Were You with Last Night?* may have been distantly related to *Dream Story*, this perhaps being part of Kubrick's motive in approaching Raphael in the first place. The first-person narrator, Charles Hanson, spends a significant part of the novel musing upon monogamy, bourgeoisie values, and the precarious composure between his love for his wife and his attraction to his mistress.

26. Raphael's other screenplays were generally less memorable: *Nothing but the Best* (1964), *Daisy Miller* (1974), and *Coast to Coast* (2003).

27. At one point, as if to further elevate his superior standing, Raphael wonders: "Does he care that the best director has never been Best

Director?" (Raphael 1999, 149). See Appendix 15 for a fuller discussion of Kubrick and Academy Awards.

28. Op. cit. 156. Kubrick had found time, in the late 1940s, to sit in at classes at Columbia University by, amongst others, Lionel Trilling. Raphael noted: "Stanley had pressed his nose to the windows of the academy as Fridolin/Bill did/does to the world of unbridled sensuality.... Part of my hold, such as it was, on Stanley was that he knew and probably exaggerated, my academic credentials." (Op. Cit. 71)

29. Op. cit. 46.

30. Raphael in Cocks 2006, 67.

31. To be fair to Raphael, none of these memoirs, with the exception of Herr's, were of book-length form.

32. Chion 2002, 17.

33. *Pitch Weekly*, July 22–28, 1999.

34. Raphael's book was based on a long article — of about 6,000 words — published in *The New Yorker*, on June 14, 1999.

35. Ibid.

36. Roger Clarke, "Putting the Knife into Stanley," *The Independent*, August 2, 1999.

37. Raphael 1999, 171.

38. One notes that Alexander Walker "likened Raphael's book to a love story, but one of unrequited love" (cited in Rhodes 2008, 236).

39. Raphael 1999, 35.

40. Op. cit. 59.

41. Op. cit. 61.

42. Op. cit. 70.

43. Op. cit. 112.

44. Op. cit. 62.

45. Op. cit. 79.

46. Op. cit. 70.

47. Op. cit. 110–111.

48. Op. cit. 47. (My italics.)

49. Op. cit. 74–75.

50. Op. cit. 90.

51. Op. cit. 91.

52. Op. cit. 107.

53. Op. cit. 109.

54. Op. cit. 111.

55. Op. cit. 157.

56. Ibid.

57. Op. cit. 151.

58. See Raphael's comment: "S.K. is unique in his talent and in his capacity to retain the respect of men who, normally, respect nothing and no one" (op. cit. 111).

59. www.cinemonkey.com/reviews/kubrick-raphael.html.

60. Herr 2000, 73 and 76.

61. Raphael 1999, 115.

62. Shortly after the publication of Raphael's book, the satirical magazine *Private Eye* ran a parody of *Eyes Wide Open*. This can be found at www.visual-memory.co.uk/faq/html/ktemp.html#slot3.2. It is worth reading in the light of the discussion herein.

Appendix 11

1. A diverse range of critics and theorists have questioned *auteurism*; but see, for example, John Hill and Pamela Church Gibson: "Auteur — especially as applied to American film — has been based more on desire than fact" (Hill and Gibson 2000, 12). Also, *auteur* theory, as a pre-theoretical model, would no doubt have been supported by the Leavisite espousal for the close reading of texts; as it also obviously fitted into the Romantic discourse of eulogizing "great men."

2. Available in Lodge 1992, 166–172.

3. Kolker 2006, 4.

4. Falsetto 1996, 288.

5. Nelson 2000, 5.

6. Phillips 2001, viii.

7. Garcia-Mainar 1999, 4.

8. Kolker 1988, 69.

9. Kagan 2000, xiii.

10. Reichmann and Flagge 2007, 30.

11. Cited in Castle 2005, 313.

12. Eugene Archer, "*Spartacus*: Hailed in Farewell," *New York Times*, October 2, 1960.

13. Cited in Castle 2005, 343.

14. In this light, note how the current Hollywood practice of pre-fixing a film with the name of the director would appear to be more a marketing device than any attempt at true *auteur* status.

15. Note that some of the most iconic moments in Kubrick's work appear to have derived from collaboration with actors. For example: Malcolm McDowell's singing during the attack on Mr. and Mrs. Alexander; Jack Nicholson's gleeful shout of "Here's Johnny!"; Gary Lockwood's idea for HAL to lip-read Bowman and Poole's lips in the space-pod; Lee Ermey's improvised dialogue in *Full Metal Jacket*, and so on.

16. The opening helicopter shots were filmed by MacGillivray in Glacier National Park in Montana, without Kubrick's presence.

17. In this contest it is interesting to note that Kubrick routinely operated most of the hand-held camerawork in his films; for example: in *Paths of Glory*, *The Killing*, *2001: A Space Odyssey*, *A Clockwork Orange* and *Barry Lyndon* — this being the most efficient way of attaining the effects and results he required.

18. Howard 1999, 152.
19. Raphael 1999, 66.
20. Falsetto 2001, 169.
21. Cited in Lodge 1992, 171
22. Op. cit. 170.
23. This phrase derives from another post-structuralist critic: Julia Kristeva.
24. Cited in Lodge 1992, 172.

Appendix 12

1. See Cocks 2004, 148, for further details.
2. Cited by Dimitri Rotov, as part of his weblog October 2007: http://cwbn.blogspot.com.
3. In an interview with Raymond Heine, published in *Cahiers du Cinéma*, in July 1957, Kubrick had stated that his "favorite young American writers" were Calder Willingham and Shelby Foote, the latter being mistakenly transcribed as Shelley Foot. The interview is reprinted in Castle 2005, 308–310.
4. Naremore 2007, 15.
5. See Cocks 2004, 149, for further details.
6. See Baxter 1998, 275–276 and Walker 1999, 363, for further details of this project.
7. Castle 2005, 517.
8. Ciment 2001, 253.
9. It has often been said that the novel was unfilmable, given the cinema's lack of an olfactory sense. Therefore, it was perhaps not surprising that *Perfume* lacked the artistic elevation — the same sense of cinematic innovation — found elsewhere in Twyker's work. However, the film was still of interest, Kubrick's remote influence being discernible at a number of points; for example, the maze scene was reminiscent of *The Shining,* while a variation on Handel's "Sarabande," on the soundtrack, drew obvious references to *Barry Lyndon.*
10. It is known that Kubrick drafted the screenplay himself, a number of versions, all relatively faithful to the novel, being extant.
11. Johanna ter Steege and Joseph Mazzello were to head what appeared to be an astutely drawn cast.
12. Reichmann and Flagge 2007, 227.

Appendix 13

1. See Pym 2007, 1023.
2. Bernard 1995, 179.

Appendix 15

1. The single nomination was *Full Metal Jacket's* "Best Screenplay Based on Material from

Another Medium." Neither *The Shining* nor *Eyes Wide Shut* received any nominations at all.
2. Cited in Agel 1970, 325. Mahar was writing in 1968, but his argument is perhaps more pertinent today.
3. Ciment 2001, 43.
4. Ibid.
5. Raphael 1999, 149.

Appendix 16

1. See Robson 2005, 214.
2. Christiane Kubrick cited in LoBrutto 1998, 147.
3. See Silveira 2005, 105: "[The statue] cracks and falls apart, with only one eye left staring at the audience, suggesting the instability of film as a medium of truth."
4. Cited in Watson 2000, 504.
5. See Nabokov 1991, 289, wherein he makes an explicit reference to the La Salle case.
6. See Naremore 2007, 102–3 for a transcription of the lyric.
7. Note: there were other errors in the opening credits, in the standard disclaimer about events and characters being fictitious, the latter word was misspelled as "ficticious," while the later use of the word "occurrence" was misspelled "occurence."
8. Cited in Cocks 2004, 115.
9. Grant B. Stillman, "Last Secrets of Strangelove Revealed," The Kubrick Site, www.visualmemory.co.uk.
10. See Reichmann and Flagge 2007, 90.
11. Op. cit. 100
12. This "joke" would be repeated in *A Clockwork Orange* and (perhaps) in *Eyes Wide Shut*; references also occur in other films as diverse as *Back to the Future* (1985) and *Fight Club* (1999).
13. LoBrutto 1997, 347.
14. Walker 1999, 216.
15. Reichmann and Flagge 2007, 89.
16. Cited in Nelson 2000, 317.
17. See Stork 1997, 79.
18. Cited in LoBrutto 1997, 304.
19. See Clarke 1973, 7.
20. See Cocks 2004, 116.
21. See Rice 2008, 68.
22. In *Barry Lyndon*, Berkoff was first considered for a more substantial part: "I was first up for a larger role but it went to Hardy Kruger and I ended up with the cameo part of Lord Ludd" (Berkoff 2003, 26).
23. "Stanley was making a film about the Warsaw ghetto. I was sure that this would truly be his masterpiece and was relieved and excited

he had made contact again. Shortly afterward, I heard that the project had been shelved in view of *Schindler's List"* (Berkoff 2003, 33).

24. See Baxter 1998, 279.

25. Mark Crispin Miller, *"Barry Lyndon* Reconsidered," *The Georgia Review*, Vol. 30, No. 4, 1976.

26. Cited in LoBrutto 1997, 404–405

27. Reichmann and Flagge 2007, 193.

28. Nelson 2000, 201.

29. See Parker 2007, 189

30. In *The Shining*, it is said Kubrick played the voice of Charlie, the radio weather announcer. As already intimated, Kubrick also reportedly supplied some of the breathing on the soundtrack in *2001: A Space Odyssey*, during Bowman and Poole's excursions in the space pods.

31. Raphael 1999, 140.

32. Johnstone 2006, 250.

33. Castle 2005, 488. This is confirmed by a source none other than *The Guinness Book of World Records. Eyes Wide Shut* being listed as "The Longest Constant Movie Shoot," production on the film lasting for 400 days.

34. See Chris Hastings, "The Stanley Kubrick Files," *The Daily Telegraph*, July 7, 2008.

35. For example, see Hughes 2000, 242, who lists (almost certainly erroneously) Kubrick as "Elderly Man at Sonata Cafe Table."

36. Herr 2000, 7.

37. See Castle 2005, 482.

38. Phillips and Hill 2002, 263

39. See *The Daily Telegraph*, September 23, 1999.

40. Reichmann and Flagge 2007, 137.

41. In fact, the Reichmann and Flagge contained a diverse range of pertinent research material, the issue here being one of translation from German to English.

Bibliography

Books on Stanley Kubrick

Abrams, Jerold J., ed. 2007. *The Philosophy of Stanley Kubrick*. Lexington: University Press of Kentucky.

Agel, Jerome, ed. 1970. *The Making of Kubrick's 2001*. New York: New American Library.

Baxter, John. 1998. *Stanley Kubrick: A Biography*. London: HarperCollins.

Bizony, Piers. 1994. *2001: Filming the Future*. London: Aurum.

Bullard, Galen. 2003. *Kubrick's Prophecy: A Guide to the Insights of 2001: A Space Odyssey*. np: Starling Wavefront.

Castle, Alison, ed. 2005. *The Stanley Kubrick Archives*. Cologne: Taschen.

Chion, Michel. 2001. *Kubrick's Cinema Odyssey*. London: BFI.

_____. 2002. *Eyes Wide Shut*. London: BFI.

Ciment, Michel. 1983. *Kubrick*. London: Collins.

_____. 2001. *Kubrick: The Definitive Edition*. New York: Faber and Faber.

Cocks, Geoffrey. 2004. *The Wolf at the Door: Stanley Kubrick, History and the Holocaust*. New York: Peter Lang.

_____, James Diedrick, and Glenn Perusek. 2006. *Depth of Field: Stanley Kubrick, Film, and the Uses of History*. Madison: University of Wisconsin Press.

Corliss, Richard. 1994. *Lolita*. London: BFI.

Coyle, Wallace. 1980. *Stanley Kubrick: A Guide to References and Resources*. Boston: G.K. Hall.

Crone, Rainer. 2005. *Stanley Kubrick: Dreams and Shadows: 1945–1950*. London: Phaidon.

DeVries, Daniel. 1973. *The Films of Stanley Kubrick*. Grand Rapids, MI: William B. Eerdmans.

Duncan, Paul. 1999. *The Pocket Essential Kubrick*. Harpenden, England: Pocket Essentials.

_____. 2003. *Stanley Kubrick: The Complete Films*. Cologne: Taschen.

Falsetto, Mario, ed. 1996. *Perspectives on Stanley Kubrick*. New York: G.K. Hall.

_____. 2001. *Stanley Kubrick: A Narrative and Stylistic Analysis*. Westport, CT: Greenwood.

Frewin, Anthony. 2005. *Are We Alone? The Stanley Kubrick Extraterrestrial Interviews*. London: Elliot and Thompson.

Garcia-Mainar, Luis M. 2000. *Narrative and Stylistic Patterns in the Films of Stanley Kubrick*. Rochester, NY: Camden House.

Geduld, Carolyn. 1973. *Filmguide to 2001: A Space Odyssey*. Bloomington: Indiana University Press.

Herr, Michael. 2000. *Kubrick*. London: Picador.

Howard, James. 1999. *Stanley Kubrick Companion*. London: B.T. Batsford.

Hughes, David. 2000. *The Complete Kubrick*. London: Virgin.

Jenkins, Greg. 1997. *Stanley Kubrick and the Art of Adaptation: Three Novels, Three Films*. Jefferson, NC: McFarland.

Kagan, Norman. 2000. *The Cinema of Stanley Kubrick*. Northam, Devon: Roundhouse.

Kolker, Robert, ed. 2006. *Stanley Kubrick's 2001: A Space Odyssey: New Essays*. New York: Oxford University Press.

Kubrick, Christiane. 2002. *Stanley Kubrick: A Life in Pictures*. London: Little Brown.

LoBrutto, Vincent. 1998. *Stanley Kubrick: A Biography.* London: Faber and Faber.

McDougal, Stuart Y., ed. 2003. *Stanley Kubrick's A Clockwork Orange.* Cambridge: Cambridge University Press.

Modine, Matthew. 2005. *Full Metal Diary.* New York: Rugged Land.

Naremore, James. 2007. *On Kubrick.* London: BFI.

Nelson, Thomas. 2000. *Kubrick: Inside a Film Artist's Maze.* Bloomington: Indiana University Press.

Phillips, Gene D. 1977. *Stanley Kubrick: A Film Odyssey.* New York: Popular Library.

_____, ed. 2001. *Stanley Kubrick: Interviews.* Jackson: University Press of Mississippi.

_____, and Rodney Hill, eds. 2002. *The Encyclopedia of Stanley Kubrick.* New York: Checkmark.

Raphael, Frederic. 2000. *Eyes Wide Open.* London: Phoenix.

Rasmussen, Randy. 2001. *Stanley Kubrick: Seven Films Analyzed.* Jefferson, NC: McFarland.

Reichmann, Hans-Peter, ed. 2007. *Stanley Kubrick: Kinematograph Nr. 20/2004.* Frankfurt am Main: Deutsches Filmmuseum.

Rhodes, Gary D., ed. 2008. *Stanley Kubrick: Essays on his Films and Legacy.* Jefferson, NC: McFarland.

Rice, Julian. 2008. *Kubrick's Hope: Discovering Optimism from 2001 to Eyes Wide Shut.* Lanham, MD: Scarecrow.

Richter, Dan. 2002. *Moonwatcher's Memoir: A Diary of 2001: A Space Odyssey.* New York: Carroll and Graf.

Schwam, Stephanie, ed. 2000. *The Making of 2001: A Space Odyssey.* New York: Modern Library.

Stork, David, ed. 1997. *HAL's Legacy: 2001's Computer as Dream and Reality.* Cambridge: MIT Press.

Sperb, Jason. 2006. *The Kubrick Façade.* Lanham, MD: Scarecrow.

Walker, Alexander. 1973. *Stanley Kubrick: Directs.* London: Abacus.

_____, Sybil Taylor, and Ulrich Ruchti. 1999. *Stanley Kubrick, Director: A Visual Analysis.* London: Weidenfeld and Nicolson.

Wheat, Leonard F. 2000. *Kubrick's 2001: A Triple Allegory.* Lanham, MD: Scarecrow.

Journal Articles

Full bibliographical details of the articles and essays published on the life and works of Stanley Kubrick would require a book-length listing in their own right. For practical reasons, the articles and essays cited below are restricted to those consulted in the background reading and research for this book.

Acevedo-Munoz, Ernesto R. April–June 2002. "Don't Look Now: Kubrick, Schnitzler, and the Unbearable Agony of Desire." *Literature Interpretation Theory* 13(2).

Alleva, Richard. September 1999. "Final Curtain: Kubrick's *Eyes Wide Shut.*" *Commonweal* 10.

Anger, Cedric. April 1999 "Le Dernier Expressionniste." *Cahiers du Cinéma* no. 534.

Balmain, Colette. Fall 2000. "Temporal Reconfigurations in Kubrick's *2001.*" *Enculturation: Cultural Theories & Rhetorics* 3(1).

Bick, Ilsa J., and Krin Gabbard. Summer 1994. "That Hurts! Humor and Sadomasochism in *Lolita.*" *Journal of Film and Video* XLVI/2.

Bier, Jesse. Summer 1985. "Cobb and Kubrick: Author and Auteur." *Virginia Quarterly Review* vol. 61 no. 3.

Bond, Jeff. March 1999. "Working with Stanley." *Film Score Monthly.*

Boyd, D. 1978. "Mode and Meaning in *2001.*" *Journal of Popular Film and Television* VI/3.

Boylan, Jay H. Spring 1985. "HAL in *2001: A Space Odyssey*: The Lover Sings His Song." *Journal of Popular Culture* vol. 18 no. 4.

Branch, Jana, and Izod, John. Fall 2003. "*Barry Lyndon* and the Limits of Understanding." *Kinema.*

Burgoyne, Robert. Fall–Spring 1981–1982. "Narrative Overture and Closure in *2001: A Space Odyssey.*" *Enclitic* V/2.

Burns, Dan E. 1984. "Pistols and Cherry Pies: *Lolita* from Page to Screen." *Literature/Film Quarterly* vol. 12, no. 4.

Caldwell, Larry W. 1986. "Come and Play with Us: The Play Metaphor in Kubrick's *The Shining.*" *Literature/Film Quarterly* vol. 14, no. 2.

Castle, Robert, and Donatelli, Stephen. September-October 1998. "Kubrick's Ulterior War." *Film Comment* vol. 34, no. 5.

Clancy, Richard. 2002. "A Kubrick Encyclopedia." *Literature/Film Quarterly* vol. 30, no. 1.

Cocks, Geoffrey. Autumn 1987. "The Hinting: Holocaust Imagery in Kubrick's *The Shining.*" *Psychohistory Review.*

_____. Spring 1991. "Bringing the Holocaust Home: Freudian Dynamics of Kubrick's *The Shining.*" *Psychoanalytic Review.*

_____. 2003. "Stanley Kubrick's Dream Machine: Psychoanalysis, Film and History." *Journal of Psychoanalysis* no. 31.

Collins, Floyd. Fall 1989. "Implied Metaphor in the Films of Stanley Kubrick." *New Orleans Review* vol. 16, no. 3.

Combs, Richard. August 1978. "Vivian Darkbloom in the Cinema." *Monthly Film Bulletin* XLV/535.

_____. November 1980. *"The Shining." Monthly Film Bulletin*, XLVII/562.

Cook, David A. 1984. "American Horror: *The Shining.*" *Literature/Film Quarterly* vol. 12, no. 1.

Coppedge, Walter. 2001. *"Barry Lyndon*: Kubrick's Elegy for an Age." *Literature/Film Quarterly* vol. 29, no. 3.

Corliss, Richard. September-October 1998. *"Lolita*: From Lyon to Lyne." *Film Comment* vol. 34, no. 5.

Cossa, Frank. May 1995. "Images of Perfection: Life Imitates Art in Kubrick's *Barry Lyndon.*" *Eighteenth-Century Life* vol. 19, no. 2.

Daniels, Don. Winter 1970/1971. "A Skeleton Key to *2001.*" *Sight and Sound.*

Davis, Natalie Zemon. Summer 2002. "Trumbo and Kubrick Argue History." *Raritan — A Quarterly Review* 22(1).

Dean, J.F. 1978. "Between *2001* and *Star Wars.*" *Journal of Popular Film and Television* VII/1.

DeBellis, Jack. July 1993. "The Awful Power: John Updike's Use of Kubrick's *2001: A Space Odyssey* in *Rabbit Redux.*" *Literature/Film Quarterly* vol. 21, no. 3.

Deleyto, Celestino. June 2006. "1999: A Closet Odyssey: Sexual Discourses in *Eyes Wide Shut.*" *Atlantis* 28.1.

Doherty, Thomas. Winter 1988. "Full Metal Genre: Stanley Kubrick's Vietnam Combat Movie." *Film Quarterly* vol. 42, no. 2.

Dumont, J.P., and J. Monod. Summer 1978. "Beyond the Infinite: A Structural Analysis of *2001: A Space Odyssey.*" *Quarterly Review of Film Studies* III/3.

Enckell, Mikael. 2001. "Eyes Open and Shut." *Scandinavian Psychoanalytic Review* no. 24.

Engell, John. May 1995. *"Barry Lyndon*: A Picture of Irony." *Eighteenth-Century Life* vol. 19, no. 2.

Erlich, Richard D. Winter 1999. "From Shakespeare to Le Guin: Authors as Auteurs." *Extrapolation* vol. 40, no. 4.

Feldman, Hans. Fall 1976. "Kubrick and his Discontents." *Film Quarterly* vol. 30, no. 1.

Fisher, J. September 1972. "Too Bad, Lois Lane: The End of Sex in *2001.*" *Film Journal* II/1, p. 65.

Frey, Mattias. 2006. "Fidelio: Love, Adaptation of *Eyes Wide Shut.*" *Literature/Film Quarterly* vol. 34, no. 1.

Fry, Carrol L. Fall 2003. "From Technology to Transcendence: Humanity's Evolutionary Journey in *2001: A Space Odyssey.*" *Extrapolation* 44(3).

Gabbard, Krin. August 1997. "The Circulation of Sado-Masochistic Desire in the *Lolita* Texts." *Journal for the Psychological Study of the Arts.*

Gans, Herbert J. Fall 1999. "Kubrick's Marxist Finale." *Social Policy* vol. 30, no. 1.

Gehrke, Pat J. September 2001. "Deviant Subjects in Foucault and *A Clockwork Orange.*" *Critical Studies in Media Communication* vol. 18, no. 3.

Gross, Larry. September 1999. "Too Late the Hero" *Sight and Sound.*

Gruben, Patricia. 2005. "Practical Joker: The Invention of a Protagonist in *Full Metal Jacket.*" *Literature/Film Quarterly* vol. 33, no. 4.

Hanson, Ellis. Summer 1993. "Technology, Paranoia and the Queer Voice." *Screen* 34.

Hesling, Willem. 2001. "Kubrick, Thackeray and the Memoirs of Barry Lyndon, Esq." *Literature/Film Quarterly* vol. 29, no. 4.

Hill, Rodney. 2004. "Christiane's Pictures of Stanley." *Literature/Film Quarterly* vol. 32, no. 1.

Hock, David G. Spring 1991. "Mythic Patterns in *2001: A Space Odyssey.*" *Journal of Popular Culture.*

Hoile, Christopher. 1984. "The Uncanny and the Fairy Tale in Kubrick's *The Shining.*" *Literature/Film Quarterly* vol. 12, no. 1.

Hughes, Philip. April 1982. "The Alienated and Demonic in the Films of Stanley Kubrick." *Journal of Evolutionary Psychology* vol. 3 no. 1–2.

Jackson, Kevin. September 1999. "A Short Lexicon of Nadsat." *Sight and Sound.*

James, Nick. September 1999. "At Home with the Kubricks." *Sight and Sound.*

Jameson, Richard T. September/October 1999. "Ghost Sonata." *Film Comment.*

Keeler, Greg. Winter 1981. *"The Shining*: Ted Kramer Has a Nightmare." *Journal of Popular Film and Television* vol. 8, no. 4.

Kelly, Andrew. June 1993. "The Brutality of Military Incompetence: *Paths of Glory.*" *Historical Journal of Film, Radio and Television* vol. 13, no. 2.

Kennedy, Harlan. June 1980. "Kubrick Goes Gothic." *American Film* V/8.

Kilker, Robert. 2006. "All Roads Lead to the Abject: The Monstrous Feminine and Gender Boundaries in Stanley Kubrick's *The Shining*." *Literature/Film Quarterly* vol. 34, no. 1.

Klawans, Stuart. August 1999. "Old Masters: *Eyes Wide Shut* and *Autumn Tale*." *Nation*, vol. 269, no. 5.

Knapp, Elise F. May 1995. "Music in Kubrick's *Barry Lyndon*: A Catalyst to Manipulate." *Eighteenth-Century Life,* vol. 19, no. 2.

Kreider, Tim. 2000. "Introducing Sociology: A Review of *Eyes Wide Shut*." *Film Quarterly* vol. 53, no. 3.

Leibowitz, Flo, and Lynn Jeffres. Spring 1981. "*The Shining*." *Film Quarterly* no. *34*.

LoBrutto, Vincent. October 1999. "The Old Ultra-Violence." *American Cinematographer* vol. 80, no. 10.

Lombardi, Riccardo. 2004. "Stanley Kubrick's Swan Song: *Eyes Wide Shut*." *International Journal of Psychoanalysis* no. 85.

Macklin, T. Summer 1981. "Understanding Kubrick: *The Shining*." *Journal of Popular Film and Television* IX/2.

Magid, Ron. September 1987. "*Full Metal Jacket*: Cynic's Choice." *American Cinematographer* vol. 68.

Maland, Charles. 1979. "*Dr. Strangelove*: Nightmare Comedy and the Ideology of Liberal Consensus." *American Quarterly* 31(5).

Mamber, Stephen. May 1990. "Parody, Intertextuality, Signature: Kubrick, DePalma, and Scorsese." *Quarterly Review of Film and Video* vol. 12, no. 1–2.

Manchel, Frank. 1995. "What About Jack? Another Perspective on Family Relationships in Stanley Kubrick's *The Shining*." *Literature/Film Quarterly* vol. 23, no. 1.

Mattessich, Stefan. 2001. "Grotesque Caricature: Stanley Kubrick's *Eyes Wide Shut* as the Allegory of its Own Reception." *Postmodern Culture* vol. 10, no. 2.

Mayersberg, Paul. Winter 1980. "The Overlook Hotel." *Sight and Sound*.

Metz, Walter. Fall 1997. "Toward a Post-Structural Influence in Film Genre Studies: Intertextuality and *The Shining*." *Film Criticism* vol. 22, no. 1.

Miers, Paul. December 1980. "The Black Maria Rides Again: Being a Reflection on the Present State of American Film with Special Respect to Stanley Kubrick's *The Shining*." *MLN* vol. 95 no. 5.

Miller, Mark Crispin. 1976. "*Barry Lyndon* Reconsidered." *The Georgia Review* vol. 30, no. 4.

_____. January 1994. "*2001*: A Cold Descent." *Sight and Sound*.

Moore, Janet C. Spring 1993. "For Fighting and for Fun: Kubrick's Complicitous Critique in *Full Metal Jacket*." *The Velvet Light Trap* vol. 31.

Naremore, James. Spring 2005. "Love and Death in *AI: Artificial Intelligence*." *Michigan Quarterly Review* vol. 94, no. 2.

Nicholson, Mervyn. 2001. "My Dinner with Stanley: Kubrick, Food, and the Logic of Images." *Literature/Film Quarterly* vol. 29, no. 4.

Noland, Richard W. August 1994. "Individuation in *2001: A Space Odyssey*." *Journal of Evolutionary Psychology* vol. 15, no. 3–4.

Peucker, Brigitte. November 2001. "Kubrick and Kafka: the Corporeal Uncanny." *Modernism/ Modernity* vol. 8, no. 4.

Phillips, Gene, D. 2000. "Re-viewing Stanley Kubrick." *Literature/Film Quarterly* vol. 28, no. 1.

Pipolo, Tony. Spring 2002. "The Modernist and the Misanthrope: the Cinema of Stanley Kubrick." *Cineaste*, vol. 27, no. 2.

Pizzello, Stephen. October 1999. "A Sword in a Bed." *American Cinematographer*, vol. 80, no. 10.

Pocock, Judy. 2000. "Collaborative Dreaming: Schnitzler's *Traumnovelle*, Kubrick's *Eyes Wide Shut*, and the Paradox of the Ordinary." *Arachne* 7(1–2).

Preussner, Arnold W. 2001. "Kubrick's *Eyes Wide Shut* as Shakespearean Tragicomedy." *Literature/Film Quarterly* vol. 29, no. 4.

Pursell, Michael. 1988. "*Full Metal Jacket*: The Unraveling of Patriarchy." *Literature/Film Quarterly* vol. 16, no. 4.

Rambuss, Richard. September 1999. "Machinehead: the Technology of Killing in Stanley Kubrick's *Full Metal Jacket*." *Camera Obscura* vol. 14, no. 42.

Reaves, Gerri. 1988. "From Hasford's *The Short-Timers* to Kubrick's *Full Metal Jacket*." *Literature/Film Quarterly* vol. 16, no. 4.

Robinson, W.R., and Mary McDermott. "*2001* and the Literary Sensibility." *Georgia Review* 26, Spring 1972.

Rollo, Charles. September 1958. "*Lolita* by Vladimir Nabokov." *The Atlantic Monthly* vol. 202, no. 3.

Romney, Jonathan. September 1999. "Resident Phantoms." *Sight and Sound*.

Ross, Benjamin. October 1995. "Eternal Yearning: Stanley Kubrick's *Barry Lyndon*." *Sight and Sound.*

Scheurer, Timothy E. Winter 1998. "The Score for *2001: A Space Odyssey*." *Journal of Popular Film and Television* vol. 25, no. 4.

Schweitzer, Rich. 1990. "Bornt Kill: Kubrick's *Full Metal Jacket* As Historical Representation of America's Experience in Vietnam." *Film & History* 20(3).

Sheehan, Henry. March/April 1991. "The Fall and Rise of *Spartacus*." *Film Comment* XXVII/2.

Smith, Claude J. Jr. 1988. "*Full Metal Jacket*: The Beast Within." *Literature/Film Quarterly* vol. 16, no. 4.

Smith, Greg. October 1997. "Real Horrorshow: The Juxtaposition of Subtext, Satire, and Audience Implication in Stanley Kubrick's *The Shining*." *Literature/Film Quarterly* vol. 25, no. 4.

Snyder, S. Fall 1982. "Family Life and Leisure Culture in *The Shining*." *Film Criticism* VII/1.

Sobchack, Vivian C. 1981. "Decor as Theme: *A Clockwork Orange*." *Literature/Film Quarterly* vol. 9, no. 2.

Southern, Terry. Summer 1994. "Strangelove Outtakes: Notes from the War Room." *Grand Street* vol. 13, no. 1.

Stephenson, W. 1981. "The Perception of "History" in Kubrick's *Barry Lyndon*." *Literature/Film Quarterly* vol. 9 no. 4.

Stevenson, James A. 1988. "Beyond Stephen Crane: *Full Metal Jacket*." *Literature/Film Quarterly* vol. 16, no. 4.

Strick, Philip. Winter 1971–1972. "Kubrick's Horrorshow." *Sight and Sound.*

_____. March 1985. "Ring Round the Moons." *Monthly Film Bulletin* LII/614.

_____. September 2002. "*2001: A Space Odyssey*." *Sight and Sound.*

_____, and Penelope Houston. Spring 1972. "Modern Times: An Interview with Stanley Kubrick." *Sight and Sound.*

Taubin, Amy. September/October 1999. "*Eyes Wide Shut*." *Film Comment* vol. 35, no. 5.

Thompson, Frank. May 1991. "*Spartacus*: A Spectacle Revisited." *American Cinematographer* LXXII/5.

Tibbetts, John C. 2001. "Stanley Kubrick: A Life in Pictures." *Literature/Film Quarterly* vol. 29, no. 4.

_____. 2001. "Robots Redux: *A.I.* Artificial Intelligence." *Literature/Film Quarterly* vol. 29, no. 4.

Titterington, P.L. Spring 1981. "Kubrick and *The Shining*." *Sight and Sound.*

Usai, Paolo Cherchi. Spring/Summer 1995. "Checkmating the General: Stanley Kubrick's *Fear and Desire*." *Image* 38, no. 1/2.

Vaughan, Hunter. n.d. "*Eyes Wide Shut*: Kino-Eyes Wide Open." *The Film Journal,* http://thefilmjournal.com/issue8/eyeswideshut.html.

Watts, Sarah Miles. 2001. "*Lolita*: Fiction into Films without Fantasy." *Literature/Film Quarterly* vol. 29, no. 4.

Welsh, James M. 2001. "A Kubrick Tribute: Adapting to Cinema." *Literature/Film Quarterly* vol. 29, no. 4.

White, Susan. Autumn 1988. "Male Bonding, Hollywood Orientalism, and the Repression of the Feminine in Kubrick's *Full Metal Jacket*." *Arizona Quarterly* vol. 44, no. 3.

Whitehouse, Charles. September 1999. "Eyes Without a Face." *Sight and Sound.*

Whitinger, Raleigh, and Susan Ingram. September 2003. "Schnitzler, Kubrick and *Fidelio*." *Mosaics: A Journal for the Interdisciplinary Study of Literature* vol. 36, no. 3.

Williamson, Patricia. August 2001. "La Petite Mort: Sex Equated to Death — Stanley Kubrick's *Eyes Wide Shut*." *Journal of Evolutionary Psychology.*

Willoquet-Maricondi, Paula. Winter 1992. "Full-Metal-Jacketing: Or, Masculinity in the Making." *Cinema Journal* vol. 33, no. 2.

Wolfe, Gary K. 1976. "*Dr. Strangelove, Red Alert* and Patterns of Paranoia in the 1950s." *Journal of Popular Film* 5(1).

Newspaper and Magazine Articles

As in the case of a listing of journal articles and essays, a bibliography of Kubrick sources in the press, in newspapers and magazines, would be excessively large and perhaps ultimately reductive. The sources below represent a mere fraction of references available and are only those directly quoted or used as background within the text.

Alpert, Hollis. 1966, January 16. "*2001*— Offbeat Director in Outer Space." *New York Times.*

Archer, Eugene. 1960, October 2. "*Spartacus*: Hailed in Farewell." *New York Times.*

Arnold, William. 1999, July 16. "Like it or Loathe it, *Eyes Wide Shut* is a Classic." *Seattle Post.*

Bailey, Andrew. 1972, January 20. "A Clockwork Utopia: Semi-Scrutable Stanley Kubrick Discusses his New Film." *Rolling Stone.*

Barnes, Anthony. 2005, October 23. "*2001*: The Secrets of Kubrick's Classic." *The Independent.*

Blakemore, Bill. 1987, July 29. "The Family of Man." *San Francisco Chronicle.*

Bogdanovich, Peter. 1999, July 4. "What They Say About Stanley Kubrick." *New York Times.*

Canby, Vincent. 1975, December 21. "*Barry Lyndon*: Kubrick's Latest has Brains and Beauty." *New York Times.*

Carty, Peter. 1999, August 6. "Giggling with Kubrick." *The Independent.*

Chittenden, Maurice. 2005, August 28. "Kubrick's Lost Napoleonic Work: Family Reveals Script for Un-Made Epic on Bonaparte." *Sunday Times.*

Clarke, Roger. 1999, August 2. "Putting the Knife into Stanley." *The Independent.*

Crowther, Bosley. 1962, June 14. "*Lolita*, Vladimir Nabokov's Adaptation of his Novel." *New York Times.*

_____. 1964, January 30. "Kubrick Film Presents Sellers in Three Roles." *New York Times.*

Dargis, Manohla. 1999, July 14. "Peep Show: Stanley Kubrick's *Eyes Wide Shut*." *L.A. Weekly.*

Dowell, Ben. 2005, September 11. "1940s Kidnap Case Inspired *Lolita*." *Sunday Times.*

Dreher, Rod. 1999, June 16. "Stanley Kubrick, Self-Hating Jew." *New York Post.*

DuPont, Joan. 2001, September 15. "Kubrick Speaks, Through Family's Documentary." *International Herald Tribune.*

Gilliat, Penelope. 1987, September 6. "Mankind on the Late, Late Show." *The Observer.*

Hagen, Sean. 2005, April 17. "I Flinch at those Stories about Crazy Stanley." *The Observer.*

Harmetz, Aljean. 1978, November 6. "Kubrick Films *The Shining* in Secrecy in English Studio." *New York Times.*

Hastings, Chris. 2008, July 7. "The Stanley Kubrick Files." *The Daily Telegraph.*

Hechinger, Fred M. 1972, February 13. "A Liberal Fights Back." *New York Times.*

Hoberman, J. 1999, July 21–27. "I Wake Up Dreaming." *Village Voice.*

Hofsess, John. 1976, January 11. "How I Learned to Stop Worrying and Love *Barry Lyndon*." *New York Times.*

Howe, Desson. 1999, July 16. "In Kubrick's 'Eyes': Mesmerizing Revelations." *Washington Post.*

Hughes, Robert. 1971, December 27. "The Décor of Tomorrow's Hell." *Time.*

Hunter, Stephen. 1999, July 16. "Kubrick's Sleepy *Eyes Wide Shut*." *Washington Post.*

Johnson, Phil. 1998, June 19. "Classical Music: She's Making Plans for Stanley." *The Independent.*

Kael, Pauline. 1972, January 1. "*A Clockwork Orange*: Stanley Strangelove." *The New Yorker.*

_____. 1980, June 9. "*The Shining*." *The New Yorker.*

Kroll, Jack. 1980, June 2. "Stanley Kubrick's Horror Show." *Newsweek.*

Kubrick, Stanley. 1960, December 4. "Notes on Film." *The Observer.*

Lybarger, Dan. 1999, July 22–28. "*Eyes Wide Shut*." *Pitch Weekly.*

Maitland, Sara. 1999, March 12. "My Year With Stanley." *The Independent.*

Maslin, Janet. 1980, May 23. "Nicholson and Shelley Duvall in Kubrick's *The Shining*." *New York Times.*

_____. 1980, June 8. "Flaws Don't Dim *The Shining*." *New York Times.*

_____. 1987, July 5. "Inside the Jacket: All Kubrick." *New York Times.*

_____. 1999, July 16. "*Eyes Wide Shut*: Danger and Desire in a Haunting Bedroom Odyssey." *New York Times.*

McGregor, Craig. 1972, January 30. "Nice Boy from the Bronx?" *New York Times.*

McWilliam, Candia. 1999, March 13. "There Was an Atmosphere Nicely Posed between a Séance and a Game of Chess." *The Guardian.*

O'Sullivan, Charlotte. 1999, August 27. "Body of Evidence." *The Independent.*

Raphael, Frederic. 2006, November 26. "Dr. Strangelove, C'est Moi." *The Guardian.*

Ronson, Jon. 2004, March 27. "Citizen Kubrick." *The Guardian.*

Rose, Steve. 2000, May 5. "Stanley told Steven: 'You'd Be the Best Guy to Direct this Film.' Kubrick, Spielberg and the *A.I.* Project." *The Guardian.*

Sarris, Andrew. 2001, June 25. (Untitled). *New York Observer.*

Siegel, Lee. 1999, October. "*Eyes Wide Shut*." *Harper's Magazine.*

Siskel, Gene. 1972, February 13. "Kubrick's Creative Concern." *Chicago Tribune.*

Skidelsky, Edward. 2000, January 17. "*Eyes Wide Shut*— Sigmund Freud and Stanley Kubrick." *New Statesman.*

Watson, Ian. 2000, May. "Plumbing Stanley Kubrick." *New York Review of Science Fiction*.

Weintraub, Bernard. 1972, January 4. "Kubrick Tells What Makes *Clockwork Orange* Tick." *New York Times*.

_____. 1999, March 10. "All Eyes for a Peek at Kubrick's Final Film." *New York Times*.

Related Texts

Ailsby, Christopher. 2005. *The Third Reich Day by Day*. Staplehurst, Kent: Spellmount.

Andrews, Robert, ed. 1996. *The Cassell Dictionary of Contemporary Quotations*. London: Cassell.

Appel, Alfred, Jr. 1974. *Nabokov's Dark Cinema*. New York: Oxford University Press.

Barry, Peter. 2002. *Beginning Theory*. Manchester: Manchester University Press.

Beahm, George. 1993. *The Stephen King Story*. London: Little Brown.

Berkoff, Steven. 2003. *Tough Acts*. London: Robson.

Bernard, Jami. 1995. *Quentin Tarantino: The Man and his Movies*. London: HarperCollins.

Bettelheim, Bruno. 1976. *The Uses of Enchantment*. New York: Knopf.

Biswell, Andrew. 2005. *The Real Life of Anthony Burgess*. London: Picador.

Bordo, Susan. 1999. *The Male Body: A New Look at Men in Public and Private*. New York: Farrar, Strauss and Giroux.

Bristow, Joseph. 1997. *Sexuality*. London: Routledge.

Brownmiller, Susan. 1977. *Against Our Will: Men, Women and Rape*. Harmondsworth: Penguin.

Burgess, Anthony. 1998. *A Clockwork Orange: A Play with Music*. London: Methuen.

_____. 2002. *You've Had Your Time: Being the Second Part of the Confessions of Anthony Burgess*. London: Vintage.

Butler, Andrew. 2002. *The Pocket Essential Film Studies*. Harpenden, England: Pocket Essentials.

Butler, Judith. 1990. *Gender Trouble: Feminism and the Subversion of Identity*. London: Routledge.

Catterall, Ali, and Simon Welles. 2001. *British Cult Movies Since the Sixties*. London: Fourth Estate.

Cawthorne, Nigel. 2003. *Vietnam: A War Lost and Won*. Leicester: Arcturus.

Clarke, Arthur C. 1972a. *The Lost Worlds of 2001*. London: Sidwick and Jackson.

_____. 1972b. *Report on Planet Three and Other Speculations*. London: Gollancz.

_____. 1973. *Rendezvous with Rama*. London: Gollancz.

_____. 1975. *Imperial Earth*. London: Gollancz.

_____. 1999. *Greetings Carbon-Based Bipeds!* London: HarperCollins.

Clarke, James. 2004. *The Pocket Essential Steven Spielberg*. Harpenden, England: Pocket Essentials.

Clarkson, Wesley. 2003. *Cruise Control*. London: Blake.

Clegg, Christine, ed. 2000. *Lolita: A Reader's Guide to Essential Criticism*. Duxford: Icon.

Clover, Carol J. 1992. *Men, Women and Chainsaws*. Princeton, NJ: Princeton University Press.

Coffey, Frank. 1997. *The Complete Idiot's Guide to Elvis*. New York: Alpha.

Conrad, Joseph. 1988. *Heart of Darkness*. New York: W.W. Norton.

Costello, John. 2004. *The Pocket Essential Science Fiction Film*. Harpenden, England: Pocket Essentials.

Crary, Jonathan, and Sanford Kwinter, eds. 1992. *Zone 6: Incorporations*. New York: Urzone.

Cuddon, J.A. 1992. *The Penguin Dictionary of Literary Terms and Literary Theory*. Harmondsworth: Penguin.

Culler, Jonathan. 1997. *Literary Theory: A Very Short Introduction*. Oxford: Oxford University Press.

Cyrino, Monica Silveira. 2005. *Big Screen Rome*. Malden, MA: Blackwell.

de Chardin, Pierre Teilhard. 1964. *The Future of Man*. London: Collins.

Deleuze, Gilles. 2003. *Cinema 2: The Time Image*. Minneapolis: University of Minnesota Press.

Dickerson, James L. 2003. *Nicole Kidman*. New York: Kensington.

Docherty, Brian, ed. 1990. *American Horror Fiction: From Brockden Brown to Stephen King*. New York: Macmillan.

Eagleton, Terry. 1983. *Literary Theory: An Introduction*. Oxford: Blackwell.

_____. 1996. *Literary Theory: An Introduction* (Second Edition). Oxford: Blackwell.

_____. 2003. *After Theory*. London: Penguin.

Easthope, Anthony. 1986. *What a Man's Gotta Do: The Masculine Myth in Popular Culture*. Boston: Unwin Hyman.

Fiedler, Leslie. 1997. *Love and Death in the American Novel*. Normal: Dalkey Archive.

Finstad, Suzanne. 2005. *Warren Beatty: A Private Man.* London: Aurum.

Freeland, Cynthia A., and Thomas E. Wartenberg. 1995. *Philosophy and Film.* New York: Routledge.

Freud, Sigmund. 1997. *The Interpretation of Dreams.* Ware, Hertfordshire: Wordsworth Classics.

Fulwood, Neil. 2003. *One Hundred Sex Scenes That Changed Hollywood.* London: B.T. Batsford.

Fujiwara, Chris, ed. 2007. *The Little Black Book: Movies.* London: Cassell.

Garber, Marjorie. 1995. *Vice-Versa: Bisexuality and the Eroticism of Everyday Life.* Harmondsworth: Penguin.

Genette, Gérard. 1980. *Narrative Discourse.* Oxford: Blackwell.

Goldwag, Arthur. 2007. *Isms and Ologies: 453 Difficult Doctrines You've Always Pretended to Understand.* London: Quercus.

Graf, Alexander. 2002. *The Cinema of Wim Wenders: The Celluloid Highway.* London: Wallflower.

Grünberg, Serge. 2006. *David Cronenberg: Interviews with Serge Grünberg.* London: Plexus.

Haskell, Molly. 1987. *From Reverence to Rape: The Treatment of Women in the Movies.* Chicago: University of Chicago Press.

Herdt, Gilbert H. 1982. *Rituals of Manhood.* Berkeley: University of California.

Herr, Michael. 1979. *Dispatches.* London: Picador.

Hill, John, and Pamela Church, eds. 2000. *Film Studies: Critical Approaches.* Oxford: Oxford University Press.

Hill, Lee. 2000. *A Grand Guy: The Art and Life of Terry Southern.* London: Bloomsbury.

Hocquenghem, Guy. 1993. *Homosexual Desire.* Durham, NC: Duke University Press.

Horrocks, Roger. 1994. *Masculinity in Crisis.* London: Macmillan.

_____. 1995. *Male Myths and Icons: Masculinity in Popular Culture.* London: Macmillan.

_____. 1997. *An Introduction to the Study of Sexuality.* London: Macmillan.

Jameson, Frederic. 1990. *Signatures of the Visible.* London: Routledge.

_____. 1990. *Postmodernism, or, the Cultural Logic of Late Capitalism.* Durham, NC: Duke University Press.

Joyce, James. 1993. *Ulysses.* Oxford: Oxford University Press.

Johnstone, Iain. 2006. *Tom Cruise: All the World's a Stage.* London: Hodder and Stoughton.

Katz, Jonathan Ned. 1995. *The Invention of Heterosexuality.* New York: Dutton.

King, Geoff. 2002. *Spectacular Narratives: Hollywood in the Age of the Blockbuster.* London: Tauris.

King, Stephen. 2000. *On Writing: A Memoir of the Craft.* London: Hodder and Stoughton.

Kolker, Robert. 1988. *A Cinema of Loneliness: Penn, Kubrick, Scorsese, Spielberg, Altman.* New York: Oxford University Press.

_____. 2000. *A Cinema of Loneliness: Penn, Kubrick, Scorsese, Spielberg, Altman* (Third Edition). New York: Oxford University Press.

Lacy, Nick. 2005. *Introduction to Film.* Basingstoke: Palgrave Macmillan.

Lehman, David. 1991. *Sign of the Times: Deconstruction and the Fall of Paul de Man.* London: André Deutsch.

Lewis, Roger. 2004. *The Life and Death of Peter Sellers.* London: Arrow.

_____. 2002. *Anthony Burgess.* London: Faber and Faber.

Lodge, David. 1992. *Modern Criticism and Theory: A Reader.* Harlow: Longman.

Lyon, David. 1995. *Postmodernity.* Buckingham: Open University Press.

Lyotard, Jean-François. 1984. *The Postmodern Condition: A Report on Knowledge.* Manchester: Manchester University Press.

Magistrale, Tony, ed. 1991. *The Shining Reader.* Mercer Island: Star Mont House.

_____, ed. 1998. *Discovering Stephen King's The Shining.* San Bernardino, CA: Borgo.

_____. 2003. *Hollywood's Stephen King.* New York: Palgrave Macmillan.

McAleer, Neil. 1992. *Odyssey: The Authorized Biography of Arthur C. Clarke.* London: Victor Gollancz.

McGowan, Todd. 2007. *The Real Gaze: Film Theory after Lacan.* New York: State University of New York Press.

_____, and Shelia Kunkle, eds. 2004. *Lacan and Contemporary Film.* New York: Other.

Middleton, Peter. 1992. *The Inward Gaze: Masculinity and Subjectivity in Modern Culture.* London: Routledge.

Miles, Rosalind. 1991. *The Rites of Man: Life and Death in the Making of the Male.* London: Grafton.

Mitchell, Juliet. 1975. *Psychoanalysis and Feminism.* Harmondsworth: Penguin.

Moi, Toril, ed. 1987. *French Feminist Thought — A Reader.* Oxford: Blackwell.

Morris, Nigel. 2007. *Empire of Light: the Cinema of Steven Spielberg.* London: Wallflower.

Morrison, Toni. 1992. *Playing in the Dark: Whiteness and the Literary Imagination.* London: Picador.

Nelson, James B., ed. 1994. *Sexuality and the Sacred: Sources for Theological Reflection.* London: Mowbray.

Paglia, Camille. 1990. *Sexual Personae.* New Haven: Yale University Press.

Parker, John. 2007. *Jack: The Biography of Jack Nicholson.* London: John Blake.

Parrinder, Patrick. 1987. *The Failure of Theory: Essays on Criticism and Contemporary Fiction.* Brighton: Harvester.

Parsons, Tony. 1994. *Dispatches from the Front Line of Popular Culture.* London: Virgin.

Poe, Edgar Allan. 1962. *Selected Stories and Poems.* New York: Airmont.

Proffer, Carl. 1968. *Keys to Lolita.* Bloomington: Indiana University Press.

Propp, Vladimir. 1968. *Morphology of the Folk Tale.* Austin: University of Texas Press.

Pym, John, ed. 1998. *Time Out Film Guide.* London: Penguin.

_____, ed. 2007. *Time Out Film Guide.* London: Random House.

Quart, Leonard, and Albert Auster. 2002. *American Film and Society since 1945.* Westport, CT: Praeger.

Quinn, Edward. 2004. *Collins Dictionary of Literary Terms.* Glasgow: HarperCollins.

Rainbow, Paul, ed. 1991. *The Foucauldian Reader.* Harmondsworth: Penguin.

Roberts, Graham, and Heather Wallis. 2002. *Key Film Texts.* London: Arnold.

Robertson, Patrick. 2001. *Film Facts.* London: Aurum.

Ruthven, K.K. 1984. *Feminist Literary Studies.* Cambridge: Cambridge University Press.

Sammon, Paul M. 1996. *Future Noir: The Making of* Blade Runner. London: Orion.

Schwenger, Peter. 1984. *Phallic Critiques: Masculinity and Twentieth Century Literature.* London: Routledge.

Screen (no editor). 1992. *The Sexual Subject: A Screen Reader in Sexuality.* London: Routledge.

Sedgwick, Eve Kosofsky. 1985. *Between Men: English Literature and Male Homosocial Desire.* New York: Columbia University Press.

_____. 1994. *Epistemology of the Closet.* Harmondsworth: Penguin.

Segal, Lynn. 1994. *Straight Sex.* London: Virago.

Selden, Raman. 1993. *A Reader's Guide to Contemporary Literary Theory.* Hemel Hempstead: Harvester Wheatsheaf.

Showalter, Elaine. 1990. *Sexual Anarchy: Gender and Culture at the Fin de Siècle.* New York: Viking.

Siann, Gerda. 1994. *Gender Sex and Sexuality: Contemporary Psychological Perspectives.* London: Taylor and Francis.

Sikov, Ed. 2002. *Mr. Strangelove: A Biography of Peter Sellers.* London: Sidgwick and Jackson.

Simpson, Mark. 1994. *Male Impersonators.* London: Cassell.

_____. 1996. *It's a Queer World.* London: Vintage.

Slocum, David J., ed. 2001. *Violence and American Cinema.* New York: Routledge.

Sontag, Susan. 2001. *Against Interpretation and Other Essays.* New York: Picador.

Spargo, Tamsin. 1999. *Foucault and Queer Theory.* Cambridge: Icon.

Stokes, Philip. 2003. *Philosophy: 100 Essential Thinkers.* London: Arcturus.

Storey, John. 2001. *Cultural Theory and Popular Culture: An Introduction.* Harlow: Pearson.

Tambling, Jeremy. 1988. *What is Literary Language?* Buckingham: Open University Press.

Tatar, Maria. 2003. *The Hard Facts of the Grimm's Fairy Tales.* Princeton, NJ: Princeton University Press.

Theweleit, Klaus. 1987. *Male Fantasies.* Minneapolis: University of Minnesota Press.

Thomson, David. 2002. *The New Biographical Dictionary of Film.* London: Little Brown.

Tompkins, Jane. 1992. *West of Everything: The Inner Life of Westerns.* New York: Oxford University Press.

Toolan, Michael J. 1988. *Narrative: A Critical Linguistic Introduction.* London: Routledge.

Underwood, Tim, and Chuck Miller, eds. 1990. *Fear Itself: The Horror Fiction of Stephen King 1976–1982.* London: Pan.

Walker, Alexander. 1988. *It's Only a Movie, Ingrid: Encounters On and Off Screen.* London: Headline.

Warhol, Robyn R., and Price Herndl, Diane, eds. 1991. *Feminisms: An Anthology of Literary Theory and Criticism.* New Brunswick, NJ: Rutgers University Press.

Watson, Peter. 2000. *A Terrible Beauty: A History of the Ideas that Shaped the Modern Mind.* London: Weidenfeld and Nicholson.

Weedon, Chris. 1991. *Feminist Practice and Poststructuralist Theory.* Oxford: Blackwell.

Wolff, Janet. 1995. *Resident Alien: Feminist Cultural Criticism.* Cambridge: Polity.

Wood, Michael. 1975. *America in the Movies:*

or "Santa Maria, It Had Slipped My Mind."
London: Secker and Warburg.

Yeats, W.B. 1974. *Selected Poetry.* London: Pan.

Žižek, Slavoj. 2001. *The Fright of Real Tears: Krzysztof Kieslowski Between Theory and Post Theory.* London: BFI.

Source Novels

Aldiss, Brian. 2001. *Supertoys Last All Summer Long.* London: Orbit.

Begley, Louis. 1992. *Wartime Lies.* London: Picador.

Bryant, Peter. 1958. *Two Hours to Doom.* London: T.V. Boardman.

Burgess, Anthony. 1974. *A Clockwork Orange.* Harmondsworth: Penguin.

_____. 2000. *A Clockwork Orange.* Harmondsworth: Penguin.

Clarke, Arthur C. 2001. *2001: A Space Odyssey.* London: Orbit.

Cobb, Humphrey. 1966. *Paths of Glory.* London: Corgi.

Fast, Howard. 1974. *Spartacus.* London: Mayflower.

George, Peter. 2000. *Dr. Strangelove, or: How I Learned to Stop Worrying and Love the Bomb.* London: Prion.

Hasford, Gustav. 1985. *The Short Timers.* New York: Bantam.

King, Stephen. 1977. *The Shining.* London: New English Library.

Markham, Felix. 1975. *Napoleon and the Awakening of Europe.* Harmondsworth: Penguin.

Nabokov, Vladimir. 1991. *The Annotated* Lolita. New York: Random House.

Schnitzler, Arthur. 1999. *Dream Story.* Harmondsworth: Penguin.

Thackeray, William M. 1975. *Barry Lyndon.* Harmondsworth: Penguin.

White, Lionel. 1988. *The Killing.* Berkeley: Black Lizard.

Published Screenplays

Kubrick, Stanley. 2000. *Stanley Kubrick's* A Clockwork Orange. Southwold: Screenpress.

Kubrick, Stanley, Michael Herr, and Gustav Hasford. 1987. *Full Metal Jacket: The Screenplay.* New York: Knopf.

Kubrick, Stanley, and Frederic Raphael. 1999. *Eyes Wide Shut: A Screenplay.* Harmondsworth: Penguin.

Nabokov, Vladimir. 1974. Lolita: *A Screenplay.* New York: McGraw-Hill.

UK Television Documentaries

The Making of The Shining (first broadcast October 4, 1980): Vivian Kubrick.

Stanley Kubrick: The Invisible Man (first broadcast June 20, 1996): Paul Joyce.

The Last Movie: Kubrick and Eyes Wide Shut (first broadcast September 5, 1999): Paul Joyce.

The Return of A Clockwork Orange (first broadcast March 18, 2000): Paul Joyce.

2001: The Making of a Myth (first broadcast January 13, 2001): Paul Joyce.

Stanley Kubrick: A Life in Pictures (first broadcast September 3, 4, 5, 2001): Jan Harlan.

Stanley Kubrick's Boxes (first broadcast July 15, 2008): Jon Ronson.

Soundtrack Recordings

Spartacus (1960). Decca DL-79092.

Lolita (1962). MGM SE 4050.

Dr. Strangelove ... (1964). Colpix 464 S.

2001: A Space Odyssey (1968). MGM CS-8078.

A Clockwork Orange (1971). Warner Bros. K46127.

Barry Lyndon (1975). Warner Bros. K56189.

The Shining (1980). Warner Bros. HS 3499.

Full Metal Jacket (1987). Warner Bros. 7599-256132.

Alex North's 2001, The Legendary Original Score (1993). Varese Sarabande VSD 5400.

Eyes Wide Shut (1999). Warner Bros. 9362-47450-2.

Eyes Wide Shut: Music from Stanley Kubrick Movies (1999). Golden Stars GSS 5179.

Selected Websites

Bright Lights, www.brightlightsfilms.com

Film Philosophy, www.film-philosophy.com

Image, www.imagesjournal.com

The Internet Movie Database, www.imdb.com

Kubrick Multimedia Film Guide, www.indeli bleinc.com/kubrick

The Kubrick Site, www.visual-memory.co.uk

Reverse Shot, www.reverseshot.com

Rouge, www.rouge.com.au

Warner Bros., www.kubrickfilms.com

Index